P9-CDW-120

WHISTLESTOP

WHISTLESTOP

My Favorite Stories from Presidential Campaign History

John Dickerson

New York Boston

Cover design by Jarrod Taylor
Cover photography: John Dickerson © CBS Photo Archive/Contributor; White House © Tetra Images

Twelve
Hachette Book Group
1290 Avenue of the Americas, New York, NY 10104
twelvebooks.com
twitter.com/twelvebooks

First Edition: August 2016

Twelve is an imprint of Grand Central Publishing. The Twelve name and logo are trademarks of Hachette Book Group, Inc.

Library of Congress Control Number: 2016941542

ISBNs:
978-1-4555-4048-8 (hardcover)
978-1-4555-4046-4 (ebook)

Printed in the United States of America

RRD-C

10 9 8 7 6 5 4 3

To Anne, Brice, and Nan

Contents

PART IV
Gambits and Gambles

PART V
Too Close to Call

PART VI
Tar and Feather

PART VII
Crashing the Party

Timeline of U.S. Presidential Elections

Election Year	Winner	Other Major Candidates
1788–1789	George Washington (*no party*)—69 electoral votes	John Adams** (*no party*)—34 electoral votes John Jay (*no party*)—9 Robert H. Harrison (*no party*)—6 John Rutledge (*no party*)—6
1792	George Washington (*no party*)—132	John Adams** (Federalist)—77 George Clinton (Democratic-Republican)—50
1796	John Adams (Federalist)—71	Thomas Jefferson** (Democratic-Republican)—68 Thomas Pinckney (Federalist)—59 Aaron Burr (Democratic-Republican)—30 Samuel Adams (Democratic-Republican)—15 Oliver Ellsworth (Federalist)—11 George Clinton (Democratic-Republican)—7
1800	Thomas Jefferson (Democratic-Republican)—73 [32]	Aaron Burr** (Democratic-Republican)—73[32] John Adams (Federalist)—65 Charles Cotesworth Pinckney (Federalist)—64

Election Year	Winner	Other Major Candidates
1804	Thomas Jefferson (Democratic-Republican)—162	Charles Cotesworth Pinckney (Federalist)—14
1808	James Madison (Democratic-Republican)—122	Charles Cotesworth Pinckney (Federalist)—47 George Clinton (Democratic-Republican)—6 James Monroe (Democratic-Republican)—0
1812	James Madison (Democratic-Republican)—128	DeWitt Clinton (Federalist)—89
1816	James Monroe (Democratic-Republican)—183	Rufus King (Federalist)—34
1820	James Monroe (Democratic-Republican)—228/231 [33]	John Quincy Adams (Democratic-Republican)—1
1824*†	John Quincy Adams* (Democratic-Republican)—84[34]	Andrew Jackson† (Democratic-Republican)—99[34] William H. Crawford (Democratic-Republican)—41 Henry Clay (Democratic-Republican)—37
1828	Andrew Jackson (Democrat)—178	John Quincy Adams (National Republican)—83

Election Year	Winner	Other Major Candidates
1832	Andrew Jackson (Democrat)—219	Henry Clay (National Republican)—49 John Floyd (Nullifier)—11 William Wirt (Anti-Masonic)—7
1836	Martin Van Buren (Democrat)—170	William Henry Harrison (Whig)—73 Hugh Lawson White (Whig)—26 Daniel Webster (Whig)—14 Willie Person Mangum (Whig)—11
1840	William Henry Harrison (Whig)—234	Martin Van Buren (Democrat)—60
1844*	James K. Polk* (Democrat)—170	Henry Clay (Whig)—105 James G. Birney (Liberty)—0
1848*	Zachary Taylor (Whig)—163	Lewis Cass (Democrat)—127 Martin Van Buren (Free-Soil)—0
1852	Franklin Pierce (Democrat)—254	Winfield Scott (Whig)—42 John P. Hale (Free-Soil)—0
1856*	James Buchanan* (Democrat)—174	John C. Frémont (Republican)—114 Millard Fillmore (American Party/Whig)—8

Election Year	Winner	Other Major Candidates
1860*	Abraham Lincoln* (Republican)—180	John C. Breckinridge (Southern Democrat)—72 John Bell (Constitutional Union)—39 Stephen A. Douglas (Northern Democrat)—12
1864[35]	Abraham Lincoln (National Union)—212	George B. McClellan (Democrat)—21
1868	Ulysses S. Grant (Republican)—214	Horatio Seymour (Democrat)—80
1872	Ulysses S. Grant (Republican)—286	Horace Greeley (Democrat/ Liberal Republican)—0[36] Thomas A. Hendricks (Democrat)—42 B. Gratz Brown (Democrat/ Liberal Republican)—18 Charles J. Jenkins (Democrat)—2
1876*‡	Rutherford B. Hayes* (Republican)—185	Samuel J. Tilden‡ (Democrat)—184
1880*	James A. Garfield* (Republican)—214	Winfield Scott Hancock (Democrat)—155 James Weaver (Greenback)—0
1884*	Grover Cleveland* (Democrat)—219	James G. Blaine (Republican)—182 John St. John (Prohibition)—0 Benjamin Franklin Butler (Greenback)—0

Election Year	Winner	Other Major Candidates
1888*†	Benjamin Harrison* (Republican)—233	Grover Cleveland† (Democrat)—168 Clinton B. Fisk (Prohibition)—0 Alson Streeter (Union Labor)—0
1892*	Grover Cleveland* (Democrat)—277	Benjamin Harrison (Republican)—145 James Weaver (Populist)—22 John Bidwell (Prohibition)—0
1896	William McKinley (Republican)—271	William Jennings Bryan (Democrat/Populist)—176
1900	William McKinley (Republican)—292	William Jennings Bryan (Democrat)—155 John Woolley (Prohibition)—0
1904	Theodore Roosevelt (Republican)—336	Alton B. Parker (Democrat)—140 Eugene V. Debs (Socialist)—0 Silas C. Swallow (Prohibition)—0
1908	William Howard Taft (Republican)—321	William Jennings Bryan (Democrat)—162 Eugene V. Debs (Socialist)—0 Eugene W. Chafin (Prohibition)—0

Election Year	Winner	Other Major Candidates
1912*	Woodrow Wilson* (Democrat)—435	Theodore Roosevelt (Progressive)—88 William Howard Taft (Republican)—8 Eugene V. Debs (Socialist)—0 Eugene W. Chafin (Prohibition)—0
1916*	Woodrow Wilson* (Democrat)—277	Charles Evans Hughes (Republican)—254 Allan L. Benson (Socialist)—0 James Hanly (Prohibition)—0
1920	Warren G. Harding (Republican)—404	James M. Cox (Democrat)—127 Eugene V. Debs (Socialist)—0
1924	Calvin Coolidge (Republican)—382	John W. Davis (Democrat)—136 Robert M. La Follette Sr. (Progressive)—13
1928	Herbert Hoover (Republican)—444	Al Smith (Democrat)—87
1932	Franklin D. Roosevelt (Democrat)—472	Herbert Hoover (Republican)—59 Norman Thomas (Socialist)—0
1936	Franklin D. Roosevelt (Democrat)—523	Alf Landon (Republican)—8 William Lemke (Union)—0
1940	Franklin D. Roosevelt (Democrat)—449	Wendell Willkie (Republican)—82
1944	Franklin D. Roosevelt (Democrat)—432	Thomas E. Dewey (Republican)—99

Election Year	Winner	Other Major Candidates
1948*	Harry S. Truman* (Democrat)—303	Thomas E. Dewey (Republican)—189 Strom Thurmond (States' Rights Democrat)—39 Henry A. Wallace (Progressive/ Labor)—0
1952	Dwight D. Eisenhower (Republican)—442	Adlai Stevenson (Democrat)—89
1956	Dwight D. Eisenhower (Republican)—457	Adlai Stevenson (Democrat)—73
1960*	John F. Kennedy* (Democrat)—303	Richard Nixon (Republican)—219 Harry F. Byrd (Democrat)—15[37]
1964	Lyndon B. Johnson (Democrat)—486	Barry Goldwater (Republican)—52
1968*	Richard Nixon* (Republican)—301	Hubert Humphrey (Democrat)—191 George Wallace (American Independent)—46
1972	Richard Nixon (Republican)—520	George McGovern (Democrat)—17 John G. Schmitz (American)—0 John Hospers (Libertarian)—1
1976	Jimmy Carter (Democrat)—297	Gerald Ford (Republican)—240

Election Year	Winner	Other Major Candidates
1980	Ronald Reagan (Republican)—489	Jimmy Carter (Democrat)—49 John B. Anderson (*no party*)—0 Ed Clark (Libertarian)—0
1984	Ronald Reagan (Republican)—525	Walter Mondale (Democrat)—13
1988	George H. W. Bush (Republican)—426	Michael Dukakis (Democrat)—111
1992*	Bill Clinton* (Democrat)—370	George H. W. Bush (Republican)—168 Ross Perot (*no party*)—0
1996*	Bill Clinton* (Democrat)—379	Bob Dole (Republican)—159 Ross Perot (Reform)—0
2000*†	George W. Bush* (Republican)—271	Al Gore† (Democrat)—266 Ralph Nader (Green)—0
2004	George W. Bush (Republican)—286	John Kerry (Democrat)—251
2008	Barack Obama (Democrat)—365	John McCain (Republican)—173
2012	Barack Obama (Democrat)—332	Mitt Romney (Republican)—206

* Winner received less than an absolute majority of the popular vote.

† Losing candidate received a plurality of the popular vote.

‡ Losing candidate received an absolute majority of the popular vote.

** The second-place winner was elected vice president as per the law in effect prior to the ratification of the Twelfth Amendment.

Introduction

Across from the mayor's office in Manchester, New Hampshire, is a little exhibit celebrating the first-in-the-nation primary. I interviewed Senator Rand Paul there as I covered his unofficial kickoff to his 2016 presidential campaign.

In the Primary Room is a replica of a newspaper about another Senate candidate, Edmund Muskie of Maine. The headline of the 1972 *New Hampshire Sunday News* reads, "Muskie Calls Loeb a Liar." The deck adds "Senator Rants Emotionally at Publisher." It was a turning point for Muskie. In a speech on a flatbed truck in the snow, he attacked William Loeb of the *Manchester Union Leader* and appeared to cry. Supporters said they weren't tears, but melted snow. Popular lore held that the fallout from the crying doomed Muskie's candidacy.

It's a familiar tale to campaign junkies. It's one of the stories reporters might rehash after a long day following candidates. One person recounts a little piece of the story, is topped by the next one, and a third reporter embellishes. Since I wasn't at the bar yet, I posted a picture of the newspaper on Instagram, with the caption "It made me weep." Jonathan Martin of the *New York Times* posted not long after, "It was the snow!!!!" Peter Hamby of CNN quoted from Muskie: "This man Loeb doesn't walk, he *crawls*."

This book grew out of exchanges like that one. Over the last six presidential cycles I've covered, I've collected a lot of stories like this about previous campaigns. While you're watching one race, there's usually an echo from the past that gives you a guide about what might happen. I've put some of those stories down here, retaining the thematic structure of reporter conversations where we hopscotch across time—talking about 1948 one moment and 1976 the next.

Watching Edmund Muskie's New Hampshire crucible on film in order to write chapter six, it was even more colorful than I had known, but reading the oral history of the campaign, I realized it's a story about something more than just a candidate crack-up. It's really a story about how expectations for a campaign can sink a candidate. That tale of expectations is one story we see again and again in presidential campaigns, even the 2016 race. Chapter four, the story of Bill Clinton's 1992 comeback in the Granite State twenty years later, is about how expectations worked in an entirely different fashion.

When I first told some of these stories on the *Slate* podcast *Whistlestop*, I took my cues from what was happening in the political conversation in 2015 and 2016. Donald Trump's surprise success was historic. So was Bernie Sanders's unexpected string of victories. But there were also historical antecedents. Reading old newspapers on my iPad while flying back from an interview with a 2016 candidate, the stories felt very familiar. The broken links to the past tell us something too about how we've changed our standards and about the values and thinking behind the way we look at presidential campaigns today.

The 1840 presidential campaign circus that helped sell William Henry Harrison to the public seemed a lot like the Trump circus seems today. The candidates couldn't be more different—Harrison was packaged as a humble farmer, and Trump was running on his wealth—but the daylong parade the Whigs devoted to their candidate was as raucous and issue-free and pitched to the appetites of the masses as a Trump rally kicked off by the candidate buzzing a stadium in his 757 or the helicopter rides he was giving at the Iowa State Fair. At the same time, John Quincy Adams, who fretted about candidates who made gaudy appeals to the people, would look at the rise of the reality-show candidate and say, "This is what we worried about."

Andrew Jackson is losing his place on the twenty dollar bill, but his argument for the wisdom of the people over the elites sounds a lot like what Bernie Sanders and Donald Trump are saying today. To understand Bernie Sanders requires understanding the frustration people have about an economy they think is rigged, but it can also be explained in the historical liberal yearning for a process where the people have a chance to overthrow the powerful and the privileged. That story starts in chapter thirteen in 1824 and moves through Truman in 1948, McGovern in 1972, and Dean in 2004.

These are stories about personalities—Jefferson, Truman, Kennedy, Reagan—but campaigns are also a reflection of the country that elevates or destroys those personalities. Real dreams are at stake. When the McGovern campaign crumpled over his choice of Thomas Eagleton as his running mate, it may very well have doomed the liberal experiment for a generation, as historian Bruce Miroff suggests. If Edward Kennedy and Howard Dean had managed their campaigns better, perhaps their ideas would have prevailed. Gerald Ford and Ronald Reagan had a dramatic fight during the 1976 campaign that might have looked like just a battle over delegates in a chess match for power, but at the heart of that campaign was an ideological battle about what was possible in government and what it meant to be a conservative. The capitulation Ronald Reagan saw in Gerald Ford is the same one Republican candidates identified in their GOP leaders in 2016.

The elements of passion, authenticity, and ideas wind through all of these moments. On the Republican side, the echoes of 1952 and 1976 are everywhere as the GOP wrestles for its identity in 2016 and as the establishment and grassroots tussle for supremacy. The #NeverTrump movement shares so many parallels with the 1964 Stop Goldwater movement that it even includes Governor Mitt Romney playing a very similar role to the one his father, Governor George Romney, played a generation before. In George Wallace's 1968 campaign we hear such close echoes of Donald Trump that it's as if the transcripts have been transposed.

When I first started as a secretary at Time Inc. in New York, I lived in the Strand bookstore on weekends, where a little nook contained lots of the books that I've relied on here. The prices written in pencil in the corners under the covers were just right for my budget. I had read them over the years as I covered campaigns. Going through them as I wrote *Whistlestop*, I found plane tickets from the Dole campaign in 1996, old business cards, napkins, and hasty marginalia that seemed vital at the time, judging from the check marks, asterisks, and exclamation points. I'd carried some of those books to my first two conventions in 1992. In the days before cell phones, one of my jobs was to care for the phones reporters used on the convention floor. I'd set them out at the start of the day and collect them for safekeeping overnight.

I came across old friends like John Stacks, the author of *Watershed*, a book about the 1980 campaign. He promoted me to be a reporter at *Time*, and my copy of his book has a fringe of Post-it notes all curled and brittle from age.

I also spent a little time with my mother. She was a political reporter who covered some of these races. She'd had a stroke and was hospitalized during the first campaign I covered, so we never got to talk about this life much, but when she died I became the keeper of her books. There she was in the margins of Theodore White's books on the presidency. Senator Hugh Scott, who helped draft Eisenhower in 1952 and was run over by Goldwater in 1964, signed his book to her with "To Nancy Dickerson: Peripatetic, percipient—and pretty too!" (You could get away with that kind of fanny pat back then.) When William White signed his book about Senator Robert Taft to her, she was six years from being married to my father.

Elections are a way voters search for a sense of control over their lives. They are also a national conversation about what we believe, our national purpose, and how to keep ourselves on track. Because the American experience is so grounded in its founders and the system they created, history gives us the outline for our present narrative. We look back at it when we're writing about the present to remind ourselves of where we fall short, but also of the promise and glory in the four-year competition to make things better.

I hope you enjoy these moments of campaign history. They are just a few stops along the way. There are many great Whistlestops to come, from the past and in the future.

PART I

Inflection Points

1980—"I Am Paying for This Microphone, Mr. Green"

When writing, it's better to show than to tell. This is true with campaigning, too. It's better if you can demonstrate your presidential qualities than if you simply talk about them. The problem is, candidates are stuck giving speeches all the time. Their days are full of telling. If a candidate has shown leadership in the past, all they can do is talk about it. It's a marvel that some strategist hasn't contrived to roll a baby stroller down the street just so a long-shot candidate can leap to the rescue in order to display their mettle to the voters.

In Nashua, New Hampshire, on February 23, 1980, Ronald Reagan came as close as you can to showing what it looks like to be a leader, in a confrontation over a debate. It was the Saturday night before the state's primary, and two thousand people were packed into the Nashua High School gymnasium, creaking on their folding chairs and holding their thick overcoats on their laps. They had come to see a debate between Ronald Reagan and George Bush, the two Republican front-runners, but standing on the debate stage with Bush and Reagan were four of the other Republican candidates.

That was a problem. But what Ronald Reagan did next would give him his moment, which some people think turned the Republican nomination his way, and we all know where that led. Whether it did start things off for the fortieth president or not, the moment became a symbol for the instant Reagan rescued his campaign and hastened the rise of showmanship in the evaluation of the modern presidency.

Bush: Thunder out of Iowa

George Bush, the former Director of the CIA and U.S. Ambassador to China, arrived in New Hampshire as the winner of the Iowa caucus. He boasted of the "Big Mo," his idiosyncratic description of political momentum, a dubious quality that candidates claim but which the voters delight in denying them—particularly in New Hampshire, where primary voters seem to be raised from birth to dash political hopes.

Bush promised he was going to unite the party and take on the vulnerable Democratic incumbent, Jimmy Carter, whose approval rating had dipped to 30 percent.

Reagan was in a spot. The candidate who had missed the GOP nomination by a whisker in 1976 was supposed to be the front-runner. Bush had beaten him by only two points in Iowa, but that was enough to strip Reagan of his sheen of inevitability. "Reagan does not look like he'll be on the presidential stage much longer," wrote *Boston Globe* columnist Robert Healy. Jack Germond and Jules Witcover wrote, "A rough consensus is taking shape . . . that George Bush may achieve a commanding position."

Reagan had to find a way to battle back. Polls showed that he was nine points behind Bush in New Hampshire.[1] Fortunately, he had the support of the publisher of the *Manchester Union Leader*, William Loeb. The paper was the largest in the state, but more important, its publisher woke up every morning with the look of a man who had just taken a surprise teaspoon of vinegar. That sparked in him an urge to demolish George Bush. Loeb called him a "phony candidate." He said he was merely the tool of the "entire Eastern Establishment, the Rockefellers and all the other power interests in the East."

Let's Settle this Man to Man

There were five other candidates besides Reagan and Bush: Rep. John Anderson, Senators Bob Dole and Howard Baker, Rep. Phil Crane, and former treasury secretary John Connally. But after a forgettable debate in Manchester, Bush and Reagan agreed that it might be best for the two of them to have their own debate—to settle things like men without the others there trying to do their own pushing and shoving.

Both candidates wanted to portray the nominating fight as a two-man contest. Bush thought he could put away Reagan once and for all, and Reagan thought he could use his actor's skill onstage to claw back the stature he'd lost in Iowa. The *Nashua Telegraph* was happy to host the face-off.

Senator Dole didn't like being pushed out of the picture a second time. The first time he'd been shoved aside was when the voters of Iowa gave him less than 2 percent of the vote—less than voted "No Preference." ("I've just been campaigning in Iowa," Dole would tell New Hampshire voters, with a comedian's pause. "For no apparent reason.") Dole—a former chairman of the Republican National Committee—and Baker, complained to the Federal Election Commission that the *Nashua Telegraph* was violating campaign laws: the exclusion of the other candidates amounted to an in-kind contribution to the Bush and Reagan campaigns.

The FEC advised the *Nashua Telegraph* editor, John Breen, that he might be violating the law. Reagan had a ready work-around. He agreed to pay for the debate himself. He stroked a check for $3,500, and the mano a mano was back on.

On the day of the debate, however, Reagan changed his mind. The other candidates had sent him telegrams arguing it was fair to include them. He agreed, saying they should all be there. Bush said no. He wanted to have the one-on-one debate to sharpen the differences. He also knew that as the front-runner, if he agreed to the full Thanksgiving dinner guest list, each candidate would come after him.

Bush made it a matter of principle. He announced he wasn't going to go back on his word. He would abide by the original agreement with the *Nashua Telegraph*. Bush stood on shaky ground in advocating for a two man debate. He and Reagan had already struck a blow against fairness by colluding with the local paper to do their own dinner theater production. Having changed the rules in the first place, they could just agree to change them right back. A full debate was objectively fairer if Bush wanted to have a conversation about playing things fair and square. So sticking to his word was an obvious dodge.

Reagan called the other candidates and asked them to show up at the debate. None of the outcasts asked what Bush thought, because they were happy to be invited to the party and weren't going to check to make sure both parents approved.

Was it Reagan's sense of fair play that caused him to change his mind, or did he have cold feet? Did he not want to face George Bush alone? Or was he hatching an elaborate theatrical trap?

The way Reagan aide Craig Shirley tells it, the whole thing was cooked up by Reagan's campaign manager, John Sears, who saw an opportunity to make Reagan look commanding and make Bush look small. Expanding the field was also a way to limit the chances of a Reagan gaffe and lower the possibility that the five other candidates would be "bad mouthing us the last three days," as one Reagan confidante put it.[2]

The confrontation to come was so premeditated, says Shirley, that the Reagan team made sure that they had an ally working the public address system at the Nashua high school so that Reagan would have control of the microphone.

Talk Loudly and Carry a Big Microphone

The Reagan and Bush camps met at the high school and decamped in separate classrooms, and four of the five also-rans huddled together in the music room. They would later refer to themselves as the Nashua Four, because when you're stuck in the room with the trombones and glockenspiels, it's useful to pass the time giving yourself a name.

The debate hour arrived and nobody took the stage. The Bush and Reagan teams were fighting each other over whether to include the others; each was sending emissaries over to the other's classroom to have expletive-laden debates about who was trying to hornswoggle whom. Bush was adamant. If he backed down it would look like Reagan had made him do so.

In one particularly testy exchange, Reagan sent Sen. Gordon Humphrey to try to convince Bush to participate with the larger group. The two men were not friends. Humphrey suggested Bush was harming the party. Bush roared back, "No fu——ing way! I've worked all my life for this and I'm not giving it up... I've done more for party unity than you'll ever know!" (Did the patrician Bush really use that expletive? Perhaps, but this story has grown to such proportions that it's possible this is an embellishment. It's a loose rule that once a story gets passed around on the campaign trail it gains a new expletive in every third retelling.)

Before the row over the rules became the story, Bush had told reporters that he wasn't going to attack Reagan during the debate. There was going to be no "hemoglobin count," he said. That was a metaphor for political confrontation. What was happening in those tile hallways, however, was actual confrontation.

Reagan and Bush encountered each other in the hallway. "I'm not going on unless this goes as planned," said Bush. Reagan walked out onto the stage anyway.

When Bush and Reagan finally emerged into the packed hall the crowd was fussy and acting out. They'd been waiting for over an hour. General election debates are held in near-laboratory environments. If there is an audience, they are threatened with home foreclosure if they make too much noise. Primary audiences are far more rowdy, however, particularly if they're at a relatively low-cost event in a high school gymnasium. What are you to do in a gymnasium but cheer and stomp your feet? In one account, a campaign staffer said the room was "like the bar scene from *Star Wars*," which in 1980 might not yet have been the cliché it is today.

Everyone was riled up as Reagan and Bush took their seats. But wait, there were four others on stage. Baker, Dole, Anderson, and Crane stood behind, with no chairs, looking like the sad members of some lost tribe. (John Connally declined to be a part of the charade.)

The audience started pleading for the forlorn four. "Give 'em a chair," yelled one person.[3] Another fellow suggested that Sen. Howard Baker (who was short) could stand on the table instead of taking a seat.

Dole tried to lean over and speak into one of the microphones, but editor John Breen of the *Nashua Telegraph*, who was moderating the debate, blocked him from doing so.

The publisher of the paper said it was starting to feel like a boxing match. Perhaps embracing this spirit, the chair-deprived candidates raised their hands in unison like they were triumphant fighters.

Bush stared ahead, stone-faced, trying not to participate in the madness. He looked like a child who adopts a middle-distance stare while being chastised.

Reagan's aide Jim Lake took a piece of paper from NBC anchorman John Chancellor's notebook and wrote a note to Reagan: "Everybody's with you."

Reagan looked over at him and winked. (Again, this is what Reagan boosters say happened. Given the frosting that comes with each retelling, it's a wonder someone hasn't claimed that Reagan paused to wrestle a bear to the ground before resuscitating an elderly widow who had fainted.)

But then again, maybe Reagan did wink. He was a man who knew how to play his moment.

Editor John Breen, who did not know how to play his moment, tried to start the actual debate, even while the four discarded candidates were loitering there in the crosswalk. He offered some introductory remarks into his microphone.

As he did, Reagan tried to interrupt the editor. He could because his microphone was on, and they had the sound man on the payroll.

"I am the sponsor and I suppose I should have some right," said Reagan. Breen ordered Reagan's microphone turned off, but the technician ignored him. Breen tried to cut Reagan off a second time. That was when Reagan, now seated, let him have it. Red in the face like he'd just sprinted up a few flights of stairs, he turned and thundered while jabbing the table in front of him, "I am paying for this microphone, Mr. Green!"

The crowd roared with approval.

We don't often get to see candidates when they're angry. And that was particularly true of the sunny Ronald Reagan. But boy, did he look angry. When Breen first asked that his mic be cut off, Reagan stood up and moved toward him like he was going to use the microphone to brain him. When he finally did pop, he called Breen "Mr. Green," which was of course not his correct name, but no one really cared. This was not a time for fact-checking.

While this cowboy action was taking place, George Bush looked like he was in another film, and in that film he was not the hero and wasn't going to get the girl. There was "no solution in sight," wrote Francis Clines of the *New York Times*, for Bush, who had been campaigning on the slogan "There's no problem Americans can't solve."[4] He looked so much like the East Coast prep school vision of entitlement, it was almost as if he'd been asked to audition for that part in the school's winter play. The moment, wrote reporter Jules Witcover, contributed to the perception that Bush "had the backbone of a jellyfish."

Reagan looked like the leader who had taken charge. He was seizing the moment the way he said he would with the Soviets. Since his 1976 campaign he had been boasting that he would be tougher in negotiations than either the Ford or the Carter administrations. He would know how to act in the moment. And here he was, acting in the moment.

Editor Loeb of the *Manchester Union Leader* must have been attending church regularly in the previous weeks, because the exchange appeared to answer his prayers for opportunities to make a series of small-minded attacks. He editorialized that Bush "looked like the little boy who thinks his mother might've dropped him off at the wrong birthday party."[5]

A Bush staffer told *Newsweek*, "It was a crisis, and our man failed to respond."[6] Later Bush would tell Jon Meacham, "I looked like a fool. Not my finest hour, to say the least."[7]

After the confrontation, the four candidates (remember them?) left the stage. With no seats and no one to bring them seats, there was not likely to be a role for them in the second act of the drama.

Instead, they went into the band room, where they held a press conference for an hour. The press was covering them and not the actual debate. Reagan appeared the champion of free speech, while the candidates castigated Bush for excluding them from the democratic process. The coverage was full of quotes like this one from Sen. Howard Baker, who said, "If George Bush is the nominee I'll support him. But I do not plan on George Bush being the nominee. He is not wearing that crown very well, and I'm going to do what I can to make sure that doesn't happen. Because I think too much of the Republican Party to see it go down the tube."

"We want a president, not a king," Bob Dole told the *Chicago Tribune*. He also said, "I'll never understand George Bush's attitude as long as I live. They stiffed us. That's what they did. They stiffed us. They said, 'You can't come,' and they had the help of the paper. No doubt in my mind, Bush and the *Nashua Telegraph* are in this together." In one account, Dole whispered to Bush, "I'll get you someday, you f——ing Nazi." (Nixon had pushed Dole out of his post at the RNC in 1972 in favor of Bush, so there was some history between the two men.)

Reagan had all of the candidates and the audience aligned with him against Bush. To control the damage, Bush cut a radio spot in the days after the debate that protested, "At no point did George Bush object to a full candidate forum." That, of course, only put more gas on the fire. Anyone who might have forgotten the whole thing had a radio ad to remind them of how Bush had acted.

Though the debate had not been televised live, the radio ad plus the controversy meant that the clip of Reagan seizing the microphone and saying, "I am paying for this microphone, Mr. Green," was shown over and over again on the evening and morning television. It became a national story.

Green with Envy

Reagan went on to wallop Bush in New Hampshire, 50 percent to 23 percent, a shock that was compounded by the fact that the *Boston Globe* had polled just days before the primary and said the two men were dead even. Reagan then went on to win all but five of the remaining thirty-three Republican contests.

Was the moment orchestrated, or did Reagan simply improvise like all good actors? It was probably a bit of both. John Sears, the campaign chief who had managed the showdown, was reported in newspaper accounts to have been seen at the end of the melee grinning broadly as he leaned against one of the gym lockers. He smiled at a reporter and said it was just "another day on the campaign trail."[8] The great irony is that if Sears was the puppeteer of this great moment, he was not given credit for it by the candidate. Sears was fired the day New Hampshire voters went to the polls.

Sears was the leftover victim of the Iowa caucus defeat. The New Hampshire campaign had also convinced Reagan that Sears's insistence on substance and proving Reagan had an in-depth knowledge of the issues—which Reagan found annoying—was getting in the way of campaigning.[9]

Did this turn around the Reagan campaign? We should be skeptical that single moments can do that, but it probably helped. It made Reagan look good, made Bush look bad; it reinforced that it was a two-person race, which both men wanted; and it narrowed the conversation to a note that was good for Reagan just before people went into the voting booth. If New Hampshire voters were late deciders that year, as they have been every other year, then they went into their local polling places with the image of Ronald Reagan in the middle of Main Street taking on the invading desperadoes.

We just don't know how *much* it helped. There's a fallacy of the "key moment" in presidential races, where campaigns are turning in a particular direction and then a cinematic moment like this takes place and people invest that moment with the significance as if it were the beginning of a trend, rather than an event that took place while a trend powered by different forces was already well under way.

In the view of Reagan's pollster, Richard Wirthlin, which was supported by exit polling interviews, Reagan had already surged over Bush with his performance in the Manchester debate three days before the Nashua debate. What the high school showdown had done was drive home that point. According to Wirthlin, the repeated television coverage of Reagan bellowing "I am paying for this microphone, Mr. Green!" reaffirmed the image of Reagan as a "dynamic, commanding and appealingly human candidate," while making Bush look like "a stiff, formal and uncommunicative one."[10]

Word of the moment spread because reporters were there to cover the debate. There were a lot of celebrities from the press corps there—including CBS's Walter Cronkite and NBC's John Chancellor—which helps give a moment lift. When events happen in front of famous news anchors and columnists, they can boast about it, and in doing so, boast about their on-the-scene reporting. So they have every incentive to tell the story and give it tremendous weight.

For Reagan, the Nashua moment became an impediment to improving relations with Bush after the nominating race was over. He thought his adversary had shown unpardonable weakness. "I don't understand it," he said. "How would this guy deal with the Russians?" When Reagan was resisting picking Bush as his running mate—going so far as to contemplate naming his old adversary Gerald Ford—he referred back to this moment as one where he had lost faith in Bush.

Leading up to the debate in New Hampshire, Bush's campaign had been focused on making Bush look more substantive, but what they really needed in the age of the personal presidency was a spectacle—a moment that emphasized Bush's leadership abilities. (Bush would face this challenge again in 1988 and orchestrate a fight with CBS News anchor Dan Rather to give himself the spectacle he needed.) It may seem depressing that theater plays such a role in presidential politics, but voters aren't as passionate about substance as they say they are. What they do remember is image. Similarly Reagan's famous speech at the 1976 GOP convention was not about substance, but about a feeling. Reagan and his campaign intrinsically understood this.

When the respective campaigns went into New Hampshire, Bush was focused on avoiding mistakes, giving tight lectures and subdued rhetoric.[11] Reagan was focused on image building that showed a wider range of his emotional makeup and leadership qualities.

Whatever impact the microphone seizure had, the ability to grab the moment and show cinematic leadership in front of all the cameras was seen as such a boost in Reagan's mind, that his wife memorialized it. When Nancy Reagan was looking for artifacts from each of the presidents for an exhibit at the Reagan Library, she chose the microphone from the 1980 debate in Nashua.[12]

1960—The Catholic Candidate

On Monday, April 11, 1960, John Kennedy flew into Charleston, West Virginia, aboard the 1948 Convair CV-240 aircraft his father had bought him from American Airlines. He was tan from a brief Jamaica vacation with his family, from whom he had been absent on the campaign trail. His wife joked that their two-year-old daughter's first words were "'plane,' 'good-bye,' and 'New Hampshire.'"

The Massachusetts senator was a little grumpy as he reclined in his seat. He'd beaten his rival, Sen. Hubert Humphrey, in the Wisconsin primary, but the press judged that he didn't beat him by enough. Now he was having to fight for his life in West Virginia, where Humphrey had already been campaigning for a week. Kennedy had only himself to blame. If you're going to take a new route to the presidency, you have to abide by the new rules you've set for yourself.

It's one thing in politics to run a good campaign the traditional way, to successfully perform the compulsory routines and seize moments, accumulating victories in the march to your nomination. It's another thing, though, to construct a new path to your party's nomination by circumventing the existing power structure. That was what John Kennedy did to win the 1960 Democratic nomination. The West Virginia primary marked the turning point.

Taking the "V" out of "VP"

During the midterm elections of 1958, Kennedy was the featured speaker at the Morgantown, West Virginia, Jefferson-Jackson Day Dinner—the name nearly every local Democratic Party gives to their annual fund-raising event in honor of the party's founders. Kennedy was already so popular—having almost been selected as the party's vice presidential nominee in 1956—local radio stations broadcast his speech live. He'd been on the road all year making speeches, shaking hands, and helping other Democrats get elected. He'd done the same thing two years earlier in 1956, traveling to twenty-six states to campaign for the Stevenson-Kefauver ticket. There was almost no Democrat who had done more. Kennedy was not simply being charitable. He was planting seeds, making contacts, and building a campaign organization for the 1960 presidential race.

If we wonder why politicians start campaigning for president from the crib, we can blame Kennedy. Future candidates emulate the successful campaigns that have come before. In 1958 Kennedy had already hired his presidential pollster. He told his old friend, Charlie Bartlett, a correspondent for the *Chattanooga Times*, "Now, this is the time for me." Bartlett responded, "You have plenty of time. Why not wait?" Kennedy replied, "No, they will forget me. Others will come along."[13] When another friend advised in 1957 that Kennedy stop appearing in so many magazine profiles, the senator said that as a vice presidential contender who had lost to Estes Kefauver in 1956, he hoped the profiles would "help take the 'V' out of 'V.P.' " If you're charting moments when politics switched from being about accumulated experience to accumulated press clippings, put this moment on the timeline. (In 2008, Kennedy's younger brother, Sen. Edward Kennedy, would advise Barack Obama to grab his moment and run for president before his first term in the Senate was even over.)

Kennedy formally announced his campaign on Saturday, January 2, 1960, in the Senate Caucus Room. He picked Saturday because he wanted to make the important Sunday papers, and he picked the Senate Caucus Room because voters valued government service. Today candidates arrange their photo ops to emphasize their outsider credentials. Washington experience is a liability. The only way a candidate would announce from the Caucus Room would be if they could be photographed pushing down on the plunger of a dynamiting device.

Kennedy didn't just announce that he was running; he outlined his path. He declared that the Democratic primary elections were the true testing ground for the candidates, saying those seeking to compete with him should do so in the primaries. If Senators Lyndon Johnson of Texas and Stuart Symington of Missouri couldn't beat him in the primaries, they wouldn't be able to beat Richard Nixon in the fall.

This sounds reasonable to us now, but it was a cheeky gambit in 1960 from the jumpy upstart. Party bosses and power brokers picked the favorite candidates—and there were plenty of men in the race with better résumés in the Senate, like Humphrey, Johnson and Symington, as well as former governor Adlai Stevenson of Illinois. The only way Kennedy could get around this blockage was, like Andrew Jackson before him, to declare a moral superiority to his chosen route to the presidency. It's a time-honored ploy. If you can't compete with your opponents on their turf—experience, longevity in the Senate, and favors traded with party insiders—point to your turf and say that's the true spot where the competition should take place.

Many of the old-school Democrats thought Kennedy was too young, too Catholic, and too inexperienced to win the presidency. At forty-two, he was the youngest presidential candidate in American history. So Kennedy had to use the primaries to prove he had presidential skills. He was improving his résumé while simultaneously applying for the job.

This was a key moment in linking campaigns to governing. In 1916, President Woodrow Wilson called campaigning "a great interruption to the rational consideration of public questions," but now, if you are a successful campaigner it's expected you'll be a successful president. In 1992, when Bill Clinton won, Dan Quayle said, "If he runs the country as well as he ran his campaign, we'll be all right." President Obama used the campaign to elevate himself in a similar way. His strategist David Axelrod wrote in his book about the 2008 campaign, "The campaign itself also is a proving ground for strength . . . How you respond to the inevitable challenges you'll face will reveal much about your strength and preparedness for the job."

Kennedy's attempt to make primaries the key to victory wasn't a new idea in Democratic presidential politics. In 1952 and 1956, Sen. Estes Kefauver tried to play the insurgent candidate, defying the party establishment. Party leaders weren't going to support him for the nomination, so he worked to win the primaries. He won twelve of those fifteen contests in 1952, starting in New Hampshire, but the nomination that year went to Adlai Stevenson, who competed in none of the primaries. The strategy fizzled, because most states still chose their delegates to the Democratic convention through the state conventions, not the primaries, and the state conventions were dominated by the party elites, especially the mayors and governors of large Northern and Midwestern states and cities. Kefauver had targeted just those sort of people in his investigations of organized crime. They were happy to repay the favor by denying him the nomination. Given Kefauver's defeats, in 1959, the conventional view was that the primary route to the nomination was a dead end.

Chain Store Glamour

The stage for West Virginia was set in Wisconsin, where Kennedy had exchanged several rounds of low blows with Humphrey. The primary was a battle for votes, but it was also a battle over expectations—that loose and gooey set of standards that shift and slip, turning wins into losses and turning second-place finishes into victories.

On the one hand Kennedy should have been an underdog in Wisconsin. Humphrey was from Minnesota, a neighboring state, which meant Wisconsin's counties on the border were likely to go for Humphrey. Sage Democrats advised Kennedy to not even compete with him there. Humphrey was also a liberal whose politics were closer to the state's liberal tradition. That meant Humphrey had the local papers on his side. That didn't just mean he had the editorial boards rooting for him; it also meant he got favorable stories and Kennedy got the fuzzy end of the headlines. When Alabama governor John Patterson endorsed Kennedy, one Madison newspaper ran a story with the headline 'BAMA GOVERNOR, NEGRO HATER IN KENNEDY CAMP.[14]

What Kennedy had going for him was that he was a Catholic. Thirty-five percent of Wisconsin was Catholic—including my grandparents, which has nothing to do with this story but I thought you should know. Kennedy also had hustle. He worked the streets, the clubs, the bars, and the department stores. He had money to pay professional volunteers and had a touch for the art of campaigning. When he met someone important, they'd inevitably receive a handwritten note, an innovation every candidate afterward has copied.

Humphrey complained he was being outspent and out-glamoured. He said Jackie and Rose Kennedy, who were campaigning for Jack, were "queen and queen mother among the commoners, extracting obeisance, awe, and respect. They lacked only tiaras, and you knew that if crowns were needed, Joe Kennedy would buy them. I felt like an independent merchant competing against a chain store."[15]

It was an unusually cold winter, too, which exacerbated Humphrey's financial disadvantages in Wisconsin. By the end of March, it had snowed ninety inches in Milwaukee. Kennedy was flying around in that neat plane that his dad had bought him, but Humphrey had to drive in his rented grayhound bus turned campaign coach though the dog logo stayed on the side. To snatch moments of sleep, he stretched out on an army cot in the back while sliding along the highways.

Things went well for Kennedy in Wisconsin until late March. The Lou Harris polls showed him far ahead in nine of the ten districts. There was speculation among the press that he would sweep Wisconsin. Then, Kennedy's religious affiliation became an issue.

A Humphrey supporter placed an ad with the Wisconsin Press Association (an organization of weekly newspapers) calling for a "square deal" for Humphrey. Since Kennedy was going to win the Catholic vote as a bloc, that meant Humphrey wasn't getting a square deal. Anyone could vote in the Democratic primary, which meant Republican Catholics might vote for Kennedy out of papist loyalty. To balance things out, said the ad, Protestants should vote for Humphrey.

Then, anti-Catholic leaflets appeared. There was some evidence pro-Kennedy forces sent them on purpose to Catholic households to make Catholics angry enough to turn out on Election Day.

While it was hard to score a winner in the back and forth, Kennedy was hurt by conversation. He was becoming the Catholic candidate. That undermined his résumé-building exercise. If Kennedy won, it would be seen as a victory for Catholics. Kennedy was trying to use these primary contests as proof of his skills. Whether you're baptized Catholic or not is not a skill.

On election night the Kennedy brothers went to war with CBS News over the network's emphasis on religion. Walter Cronkite cited pollster Elmo Roper, who said that every Republican Catholic had crossed over to vote in the Democratic primary for Kennedy. Cronkite then interviewed Kennedy and asked him about the religious nature of the vote, keeping the focus on the issue. Afterward, Bobby Kennedy screamed at Cronkite. Since CBS had relied on computer projections developed by IBM and the Columbia University Bureau of Applied Social Research, Bobby later called IBM president Thomas

Watson and asked him to suppress the analysis of the religious voting patterns in Wisconsin that had been the basis of Roper's report.

John Kennedy then phoned Frank Stanton, the president of CBS, and reminded him that if he, Kennedy, were elected, he would have the power to name members of the Federal Communications Commission, which oversaw the regulations affecting the broadcast networks. This thuggish behavior showed much the Kennedys didn't want the victory to be seen as a Catholic victory. Humphrey wasn't just running against a chain store, he was running against a chain gang with prosciutto-thin was to perceived threats.

In the end, Kennedy won 56 percent of the vote in Wisconsin. It should have been interpreted as a strong win, but the press read the result exactly as Kennedy feared they would. They attributed the victory to Catholic pride. Given that, it was underwhelming. *How could Kennedy, with his money, organization, and the Catholic support, not have won by more?*

The next day's headline in the tone-setting *New York Times* read, RELIGION BIG FACTOR IN KENNEDY VICTORY. The *Washington Post* headline read, TRIUMPH FOR KENNEDY NOT UP TO EXPECTATIONS.

It became immediate conventional wisdom that since Kennedy had won because of the Catholics, he wouldn't do as well when he competed in states without a large Catholic bloc. If that didn't hurt him in the future primaries, it would certainly hurt him in the general election.

Humphrey was emboldened by the loss. The Kennedy camp tried to start a whispering campaign that he should get out of the race. They said he was just a stalking horse for Johnson, denying Kennedy wins with the purpose of ultimately stepping aside and letting the Texas Senator take the nomination at the convention.

Humphrey scoffed at that charge. "Politics is a serious business, not a boy's game, where you can pick up the ball and run home if things don't go according to your idea of who should win." Kennedy was acting like a spoilsport, which only supported the idea that he had not done well in Wisconsin.

Kennedy's primary strategy was backfiring. The contest he'd chosen to compete in was making him look smaller.

Country Roads to the White House

After the great Wisconsin uncertainty, Kennedy had to do well in West Virginia. Some local Democrats thought it was too big a gamble. The primary wouldn't bind delegates to the victor at the convention, but if Kennedy lost, it would be a death blow.[16] But Kennedy had raised the stakes on the primaries. If he had avoided West Virginia it would have undermined his case. "The West Virginia primary... is of great importance to Sen. John F. Kennedy," wrote Carroll Kilpatrick of the *Washington Post*, "because his campaign is based on his ability to present himself as 'a winner.' If he loses here on May 10, that image will be tarnished."[17] On the other hand, if he won "only by a hair," said Senator Nixon, engaging in cross-party punditry, "it will all be over but the shouting."[18]

When Kennedy's campaign plane landed in West Virginia the polls looked bad. In late 1959, a Harris poll showed him beating Humphrey 54 percent to 23 percent. After Wisconsin, a poll taken of one of West Virginia's most populous counties, showed Kennedy twenty points behind. The campaign asked county chairmen in the state what had happened, and the consensus response was: "No one in West Virginia knew you were a Catholic in December. Now they know."[19]

In West Virginia, Catholics represented less than 4 percent of the population. Kennedy's original strategy entering the state was to avoid the issue. He tried to dispatch with the topic immediately in his campaign speeches: "I want to talk to you about the issues of the campaign—not questions of private religious belief—not where candidates go to church—not whether one denomination or one church is better than another."[20]

The topic couldn't be hidden under a bushel. "We've never had a Catholic president, and I hope we never do," said one West Virginia woman. "Our people built this country. If they had wanted a Catholic to be president, they would have said so in the Constitution."[21]

One woman in Huntington, West Virginia, stuck her tongue out at Kennedy as he passed by, a shocker for a candidate who was habituated to receiving more favorable salutations from the opposite sex.

The *Wall Street Journal* seized the moment to sit everyone down and make a broad point about gender and bias. "There is the strong impression in the course of hundreds of interviews that women, old or young, are far more likely than men of similar age to be voting on the basis of anti-Catholic sentiment. This is perhaps partly because their daily lives are more circumscribed in contacts and travel than those of their menfolk, and partly because they go to church more."[22]

In the April 30 edition of the *West Virginia Hillbilly*, a reputable weekly despite how it may sound to city folk, the front page headline read: PA AIN'T SELLING HIS VOTE TO NO CATHOLIC. A Presbyterian minister explained: "There are many smaller sects that tend to be fanatical and bigoted. They are in the rural areas mainly. Some of these people are just plain scared of Catholics."[23] Roughly half the voters in West Virginia lived in rural areas.

The newspapers and mailboxes were full of monkey business. An ad in the *Charleston Gazette* asked, "Who is the bigot? A candidate for the Presidency believes it is a mortal sin for him to worship with a faith other than his own. A voter votes against him on account of this belief. Who is the bigot?"[24] A postcard was sent from a Brooklyn address to two editors in New Cumberland: "You Protestant rebels better vote for Kennedy May 10 if you know what is good for you. We can burn you at the stake again as we did three hundred years ago if Kennedy doesn't win." The typewritten signature of the obvious attempt to arouse prejudice against Kennedy read, "Irish Catholic."[25]

Under heavy fire, Kennedy switched tactics. If his Catholicism was a live wire thrashing on the ground, instead of running away from it, he was going to grab it until all the energy was drained from the issue, a metaphor that actually makes no sense if you know anything about how electricity works. So don't go grabbing any electrical wires: it will not win you the West Virginia primary.

Walter Lippmann was stumbling around for a metaphor, too. "The religious issue is an ugly and dangerous one," he wrote, "but as with a nettle, the best thing to do is grasp it firmly."[26]

It was a gutsy move, the kind of risk taking a president must engage in constantly. Kennedy talked about the issue at every stop and ran ads about his faith, which showed voters asking him questions like whether he would be controlled by the Catholic Church. One ad started, "Here is Walton Shepherd, Charleston attorney, asking in effect how the senator's religion would affect the discharge of his duties as president." Kennedy responded:

> West Virginia, as you know, has the least members of my faith in any state in the United States, population's about 3 percent or 4 percent. If I felt that there was an inhibition in my ability to fulfill my oath of office, which I've taken on the five times I've been elected to the Congress, and which I took when I entered the service, then, of course, I would not have come to West Virginia. I mean, I'm not wholly without some judgment, and if I felt there was some reason why I could not answer your question, that I am as prepared and able to fulfill my oath of office as any other American, then quite obviously, I would have not run in West Virginia, nor I would have run for the presidency, nor would I take, as I have taken on many occasions, the same oath that the president of the United States takes to defend the constitution...
>
> I have been in the Service to the United States. I spent three years in a hospital afterwards. My brother was killed in the war. My sister's husband was killed in the war. I'd like to know whether there is some opinion that I am unable to fulfill my office of citizenship. There isn't. And I think that I wouldn't have come in West Virginia unless I felt that the people of West Virginia believe in the Constitution, Sec Article 1, which provides for the separation of church and state, and Article VI,

> which says there shall be no religious test for office. That's why Massachusetts was founded, Maryland, a good many of the Southern states were founded on the principle of religious freedom. I believe in that, and we will have a chance to see whether there is going to be an opportunity to discuss the serious issues facing the United States in a very dangerous and trying time. I don't happen to believe that one of those serious issues is where I go to church on Sunday.

As Kennedy gained ground, Humphrey started to get defensive. He pleaded that *he* wasn't making an issue of religion. His campaign blamed Kennedy for raising the topic so Kennedy could take umbrage for attacks on his religion. They were right. That was what Kennedy was doing. He was creating the impression that Humphrey wasn't playing fair, which hurt the liberal senator's reputation and transformed Kennedy into a sympathetic character. A vote for Kennedy was a vote for tolerance, and a vote for Humphrey was not.

Also, while Humphrey may not have been taking direct aim at Kennedy's religion, his aides were talking about it, making sure reporters knew it was central to Kennedy's support. They said the high number of Catholics in Nebraska explained why Humphrey wasn't competing in the state's primary.[27] And Humphrey's surrogates were as subtle as a foghorn. West Virginia senator Robert Byrd, who played the fiddle, campaigned for Humphrey by opening his rallies with a rendition of "Give Me That Old Time Religion."

A Campaign in Pictures

Dwight Eisenhower had run television ads in 1952, but Kennedy's ads in West Virginia in 1960 were arguably the first pivotal TV spots in American electoral history. In one, Kennedy greeted coal miners before they took the elevator five hundred feet down the shaft for their eight-hour shift. Kennedy, in his suit and thin tie, explained to the men with smeared faces wearing dented hard hats that Massachusetts textile workers faced the same displacement the miners did.

Kennedy worked the miners hard, also meeting them after their shifts. Their faces and clothing caked with black dust, they would pause to listen to his pitch before making it to the bathhouse.

Teddy White, in *The Making of the President 1960*, explained why these stops were effective for Kennedy. "Humphrey, who had known hunger in boyhood, was the natural workingman's candidate," he wrote, "but Kennedy's shock at the suffering he saw in West Virginia was so fresh that it communicated itself with the emotion of original discovery."[28]

Kennedy loved to tell a story about these kinds of encounters. In a probably apocryphal exchange, a mine worker confronted Kennedy:

"Is it true, Mr. Kennedy," he asked, "that your father is one of the richest men in America?"

Kennedy said yes.

"Is it also true," the man asked him, "that you never wanted for anything in your whole life?"

Again, Kennedy agreed with the rough outlines of the question.

"Would it be fair to say that you've never worked a day in your life?"

Kennedy agreed, if by work he meant the clock-punching labor the man and his weary colleagues were doing.

"Well, Mr. Kennedy, let me tell you something. You ain't missed a thing."[29]

Kennedy loved this story the way he loved all stories, even the ones that weren't wholly flattering. He was just a more charismatic campaigner than Humphrey. "As the campaign went on, there's no denying that he presented a picture of reality, vim, vigor, health, honesty, and integrity that was difficult for any candidate to match," remembered John E. Amos, a Democratic National Committeeman from West Virginia.[30] It was this picture of vitality—expressed through the reality show of the primary—that would forever change campaigning in the mass-market era.[31] How candidates looked on the stump would become ever more important.

Kennedy's single-spaced schedules are one enormous block of tightly packed text outlining a tour of radio and TV stations, rallies, and private meetings interrupted by stops for how-do-you-do and nice-to-meet-you at the Court House steps, an ox roast, street campaign tours, shopping malls, the General Store and restaurants like the Smoke House and Island Creek Grill.[32]

When Kennedy campaigned like this in Ohio his hands had became so swollen from greeting voters that he had to ice them at the end of the day.

At one stop, Kennedy stood on the hood of a parked station wagon and railed against the weak federal food program.[33] He pointed out "Eisenhower curtains," that appeared on hundreds of miners' homes—boarded-up windows of frame houses in which miners and their families lived before the economic blight.[34] "The entire Republican administration won't listen," Kennedy said, "because I don't think they care." He promised that as president he would throw the force of the government behind an effort to force companies to consider the problems of those over forty-five who were unemployed.[35]

Newspaper accounts of the campaign include countless stops punctuated by heavy rain and cold. To meet shift workers at the plants and mines, candidates often had to do their hand pumping at 2:00 a.m. after one shift had knocked off, or at 5:30 a.m. when the morning shift was starting. It sounds miserable.

The schedule was so grueling that Kennedy lost his voice. He drank glass after glass of milk to soothe it. But he was required to stop talking for several days, communicating with his friend Bartlett on one campaign swing through a series of index cards the two men handed back and forth, scribbling their comments and replies. He drafted his brother Ted to speak for him in Weirton and campaign organizer Matthew Reese to give another speech. In notes scribbled to Reese, Kennedy wrote: "Can we get away without speaking today?" Then, "Matt you can say the Senator has an infected throat."

Kennedy built a ground game in West Virginia, like the one he had in Wisconsin. Citizens for Kennedy had about fifty committed volunteers in the state to Humphrey's eleven. "What distinguishes the new school from the old school is the political approach of exclusion versus inclusion," wrote White. "In a tight, old-fashioned machine, the root idea is to operate with as few people as possible, keeping decision and action in the hands of as few inside men as possible. In the new style, practiced by citizens' groups and new machines, Republicans and Democratic alike, the central idea is to give as many people as possible a sense of participation; participation galvanizes emotions, gives the participant a live stake in the victory of the leader." This wisdom would be handed from campaign to campaign. I feel like I heard this exact quote from Howard Dean's strategists in 2004 and when I first stood in Barack Obama's 2008 headquarters hearing their theory of that campaign.

Unlike the Wisconsin campaign, though, Kennedy did not deploy the Kennedy women. "They were judged too attractive, too well dressed and too rich to parade before the people of this economically depressed state, with its thousands of unemployed coal miners," said the *New York Times*.[36]

The Jack Hammer

Kennedy played old-style hardball in West Virginia. Robert Kennedy approved an attack on Humphrey's war record, or lack of war record. Kennedy's surrogate, Franklin D. Roosevelt Jr., the son of the late president, called Humphrey a draft dodger for not serving in the armed services. Humphrey explained that he had not been in the services because he had a double hernia.

Once the issue was splashed across the papers, Kennedy, who had a distinguished war record as a naval officer, issued a statement declaring, "Any discussion of the war record of Sen. Humphrey was done without my knowledge and consent, and I disapprove of the injection of this issue into the campaign." That statement ensured—and was planned—to keep the story alive for a few more days.

FDR Junior's biggest role was as a character witness for Kennedy. Liberals thought Kennedy wasn't liberal enough and that Humphrey was more in touch with the regular guy. "Jack Kennedy has that same heart, that same understanding and that same ability as my father," said Junior in a Kennedy ad. "He is picking up where my father left off. Remember this when you vote on May 10: vote Kennedy." Franklin D. Roosevelt had been a particular friend to West Virginia after the Depression, and one West Virginia reporter said that the Roosevelt nod was like "God's son coming down and saying it was all right to vote for this Catholic, it was permissible, it wasn't something terrible to do."[37]

Humphrey fought back by bringing up Kennedy's wealth. "I don't have any daddy who can pay the bills for me," he told audiences in towns where half the families were on relief.[38] He warned of politicians with ready money trying to buy the election. "I can't afford to run around this state with a little black bag and a checkbook," said Humphrey. The senator was speaking truth. The Kennedy team made sure the local party bosses were well paid. Humphrey referred to his opponent's campaign as "the most lavish, extravagant, and expensive campaign program West Virginians have ever known." He told voters on the trail in Pineville, "It's up to the voters, if they want this campaign decided by measurement of money that can be expended or the philosophies of the candidates. There are three kinds of politics: the politics of big business, the politics of the big bosses, and the politics of big money, and I'm against all of them. I stand for the politics of the people."

Humphrey lashed out at Bobby Kennedy, too. "I'd suggest that brother Bobby examine his own conscience," said Humphrey, "about innuendos and smears. If he has trouble knowing what I mean, I can refresh his memory very easily. It's a subject he should not want opened." Humphrey was making a reference to disgraced Wisconsin senator Joe McCarthy, Bobby Kennedy's former boss, who had been censured by the Senate for smearing those in the federal government he suspected of being communists. Things got so heated between the two campaigns that one deputy sheriff said, "We haven't had this much excitement since Main St. burned to the ground in 1928."[39]

President Harry Truman even had to weigh in. Interviewed on his morning walk one day, the former president volunteered that he had sent a message to both campaigns: "Now, boys, don't hurt each other."

Stump Speeches in Close Proximity

On May 7, the two candidates participated in something advertised as a debate but which wasn't much more than parallel stumping. Kennedy had refused to debate Humphrey in Wisconsin, arguing that their positions were essentially the same and there was no point in having an event where they would come together to agree with each other in close proximity. that's what the West Virginia debate wound up being like, but Kennedy was able to make his case for the primaries as the best way to pick presidents.

"Because the presidency is the key office, as no other office is, it is my judgment that any candidate for the presidency should be willing to submit their name, their fortunes, their record, and their views to people in primaries all over the United States. West Virginia has a primary, and that is the reason I am here. I did not have to come. I came of my own free will. There are no delegates involved. A setback here in defeat will be a major one. But nevertheless, I came, and I must say I am extremely glad I came. I think this is the best experience and the best education that an American political leader can have, whether he serves in the presidency or serves in the Senate."

Truman had called primaries "eyewash," and party elders had warned that they were dangerous popularity contests. Kennedy was arguing that they were an essential ingredient required for the office.

Unless you've met workers at the shift door before sunrise or shuffled your feet awkwardly before the shaft down into the mine, you couldn't govern the nation. The Democratic politicians hoping to be nominated based on their experience didn't have the right kind of experience.

The tidbits picked up from campaigning started to fill Kennedy's speeches. He learned the difference between Charleston and Charles Town, and spoke with easy specificity about the number of cans of powdered eggs a family would have to live on when the father lost his job mining coal.

The issues in that candidate debate fifty-six years ago touched on the themes of automation in a way that feels very modern. "The problem that West Virginia is facing is the problem that all America is going to face," said Kennedy. "That is the problem of what happens to men when machines take their place. We produced more coal than we did twenty years ago in West Virginia, but there are thousands of men who mined in 1940 who can't find a job. What is happening in the coal industry in the last ten years in West Virginia is going to spread all over the country. When a machine takes the job of ten men, where do those ten men go? What happens to their families?"

Pundits: Kennedy Sure to Lose

Leading up to Election Day, the prognosticators draped black crape over Kennedy. The *New York Times* sought the election forecasts of the editors of twenty-four weeklies from West Virginia's six congressional districts. Eleven forecast a statewide victory for Humphrey. Only four thought Kennedy would win. The others didn't know. "With one or two exceptions, every West Virginia political leader and newspaper writer that this reporter has interviewed has predicted a victory for Sen. Hubert H. Humphrey (D-Minn) in next Tuesday's primary," wrote Carroll Kilpatrick in the *Washington Post*.[40] Kennedy said he'd be lucky to get 40 percent of the vote, which may have been an expert act of setting expectations, a lesson learned after Wisconsin.[41]

The pundits were wrong. Kennedy won the West Virginia primary in a landslide, 61 to 39 percent. His Catholicism had been a nonissue. Kennedy won nearly 90 percent of the counties. He won in the cities and lots of rural areas, too.

Humphrey withdrew from the race that night.

Kennedy arrived at the Democratic convention with only six hundred delegates, not enough to secure the nomination and questions about whether he was up to the job. President Hary Truman put it bluntly: "Senator, you—are you certain that you are quite ready for the country, or the country is ready for you in the role of president in January 1961? I have no doubt about the political heights to which you are destined to rise, but I'm deeply concerned and troubled about the situation we are up against in the world now and in the immediate future. That is why I hope that someone with the greatest possible maturity and experience would be available at this time. May I urge you to be patient?"

Kennedy would not be patient. He had shown in the tough primaries that he could handle the pressure. He won the nomination on the first ballot, defeating old bulls like Lyndon Johnson and Adlai Stevenson, who had not participated in the primary process.

The primary victories had helped him convince newspaper reporters and magazine editors that he was the choice of Democrats outside Washington.[42] The West Virginia primary not only showed a young senator could win votes, it also answered the religious question. "Senator Kennedy, who chose the tough preferential primary road to victory, had demonstrated to the party's big state leaders that he could win votes," said the *New York Times* in its coverage of Kennedy's convention acceptance speech. "He reasoned that only through the primaries could he, as a Roman Catholic, remove the lingering fear of party leaders that he was destined for the same kind of defeat suffered by former Gov. Alfred E. Smith of New York, a Catholic, in 1928."[43]

In the end, the tough fight in West Virginia was the best thing that could have happened to Kennedy. Fortunately for he and his brother had been total failures intimidating the press on the Catholic issue after Wisconsin. Had Humphrey gotten out of the race and denied Kennedy the West Virginia crucible, Kennedy wouldn't have had a proving ground where he could elevate his stature and improve as a candidate.

Early in his administration Kennedy would admit that being a good campaigner wasn't enough. "I spent so much time getting to know people who could help me get elected president," he said, "that I didn't have any time to get to know people who could help me, after I was elected, to be a good president.".

However, the campaign trail West Virginia did influence his presidency. During the West Virginia primary a Kennedy ad in the paper showed votes for Senator Humphrey would land in a garbage can beside a road heading back to Minnesota, while votes for Senator Kennedy would drop from the ballot box through the roof of the White House. As the candidates crisscrossed West Virginia, Kennedy told crowds, "West Virginia has the first chance in a hundred years to nominate a President of the United States." This is a familiar boast to modern ears, but it was a gamble back then on the primary having any lasting meaning in the nominating process.

Kennedy was right in his prediction about the role the state would play. Voters there would see past his faith if they believed he cared about them and their lives. Since West Virginia had fulfilled its end of the bargain, Kennedy upheld his end. On his second day as president, Kennedy issued his first executive order, increasing the amount of food distributed to needy people in economically distressed areas, a response to the hunger he observed in West Virginia during the campaign.[44]

PART II

Comebacks

1948—Truman off the Cuff

Everett Collection Historical / Alamy

On a Monday night in the spring of 1948 a group of President Harry Truman's advisers met for their weekly gathering at the Wardman Park Hotel in Washington, D.C., overlooking Rock Creek Park. Over steak dinner, the men discussed the president's reelection. The situation looked bleak.

The elections two years earlier had been a disaster for Democrats. The Republican Party had been out of office for fifteen years, but in the congressional elections of 1946, Democrats had lost fifty-four seats to the Republican Party in the House and eleven seats in the Senate, allowing the GOP to take control of both chambers.

Americans had experienced a postwar boom, but they worried about another depression as the wartime price controls were adjusted. Columnists warned that no prosperity could last that long. Factories returning to peacetime production couldn't adjust. Inflation was growing—18 percent in 1946 and almost 9 percent in 1947.

The New Deal had codified the idea that presidents could control the economy. Truman didn't seem up to the challenge. In the early days of Truman's administration, columnists asked "What would Roosevelt do if he were alive?" Now Republicans joked, "What would Truman do if he were alive?" When he did act, the president was seen to have botched it. Labor strikes during his term had paralyzed the oil, lumber, textile, and electrical industries. Newspapers began talking about worker "revolts." Truman had seized the railroads and then delivered a national address that depicted labor leaders at traitors. The entire action was panned. To err, they said, is Truman.

Leading up to the 1948 campaign, a number of Democrats wanted Truman to step down to improve the party's chances. The Democratic National Committeeman from New Jersey and Illinois, and FDR's sons Jimmy and Franklin Jr. all opposed his nomination.[45] "At the very center of the Truman administration," wrote Walter Lippmann, "there is a vacuum of responsibility and authority."

Truman's top counselor, Clark Clifford, had been reading and rereading a thirty-one-page memo from Washington lawyer James Roe, which outlined an emergency set of steps required to save the incumbent. "I do not know whether Mr. Truman would be elected if everything done in this memo were done to perfection, "wrote Roe". But I do know that if no attempt is made to do the major suggestions, us Democrats ain't got a chance in hell."

The first suggestion was to send Truman west, where Republicans were making inroads. But how to do it? The Monday Night Group, as the assemblage was called, needed a creative solution—creativity being in short supply, as demonstrated by the bland name they had given themselves. They didn't have the money to fund a political trip, so they had to make any trip look official in order to spend all that taxpayer money.

Undersecretary of the Interior Oscar Chapman said Robert Gordon Sproul, the president of the University of California, Berkeley, had invited the president to speak at the school. That, plus a celebration to christen a new turbine on the Grand Coulee Damn gave Truman's advisers the pretext to launch the president westward.

To get to California, Truman took a seventeen-car train, a long and winding way to touch millions of voters and lay the groundwork for his presidential campaign. It would be the first of three such train trips he would take, traveling thirty-one thousand miles in all. It became the iconic modern example of the American campaign—a candidate moving from town to town, winning over people through determination and contact. Today that kind of mass conversion of voters would be impossible. General election campaigns are largely decided by party affiliation. With a shrinking number of independent and persuadable voters, candidates stump in order to fire up their coalition. Truman succeeded in 1948 by accumulating votes person by person. It was a cinematic victory of the underdog who persevered through grit. It also exemplifies a familiar modern tale in which pundits completely misread the electorate.

Truman Is a Gone Goose

"Truman is a gone goose," conservative former congresswoman Clare Boothe Luce told the Republican convention, his "time is short" and his "situation is hopeless." In March 1948, the president's approval rating had dropped to 36 percent. The accidental president, selected in a hurry in 1944 and then thrust into the job when FDR died, was never served by the comparison to his predecessor. In death FDR seemed twice the size of ordinary mortals. Truman seemed thoroughly average: average height, average weight, and average intellect. "When Franklin Roosevelt died in 1945 and Harry Truman took his place," wrote Robert Allen and William Shannon in *The Truman Merry-go-Round*, "it was as if the star of the show had left and his role had been taken by a spear carrier from the mob scene."[46]

It looked as if Truman was headed back to Missouri after the election. "If Truman is nominated," columnists Joseph and Stewart

Alsop wrote, "he will be forced to wage the loneliest campaign in recent history." A campaign billboard in Tulsa, Oklahoma, summed up the view: "Truman said he wasn't big enough to be president—and he ain't. Vote Republican in '48."[47] A Truman loyalist wrote to the president that there appeared to be "a national stampede, gathering dangerous and revolutionary momentum" to "drive you from the White House."[48]

Truman was so unsure about his election, he let Eisenhower know that if the general wanted to run for president, Truman might be happy to be his running mate.[49] The Americans for Democratic Action, which should have been supporting the Democrat, launched an effort to draft Eisenhower. The final insult to the incumbent arrived by telegram. The Democratic leader in the State of Washington asked the president to consider serving as chairman of the Draft Eisenhower Committee.

The Shakedown Cruise

Clifford dubbed the trip to Berkeley the Shakedown Cruise, because he knew his candidate needed a workout to get in campaign trim. The strategy to improve Truman's standing hinged on improving his connection with voters.

Truman was an awful public speaker. He delivered his remarks as if he were reading a list of new public ordinances. Bright eyed and quick stepping, Truman always seemed to be rushing around—the attentive shopkeeper adjusting window displays. He thought procrastination a sin. His speeches reflected that constant sense of hurry. He put the emphasis on the wrong words. He stuck to his text so faithfully that he kept his head down, focusing through his ordinary spectacles so as not to miss a word on those typewritten pages. This gave audiences a grand view of the top of his head.

Truman's advisers told him to adopt a "prophetic, personal voice." He was told to emphasize his conversational tone to appeal to the "average fellow" who wanted to know what was going to happen to him and his family. The president was told his speaking should be more in the form of a person-to-person talk, not a recitation. He was pushed to speak extemporaneously, or "off the cuff," an expression that was still new enough that it appeared in the papers in quotation marks to denote its peculiarity.

Truman test-drove the new chat in a radio address in April 1948. "It was the best summary of our foreign policy I have ever heard," wrote a *Washington Post* reporter. "If any of his aides were in the hall and failed to make note of his performance, then they have missed the opportunity of a lifetime. If the President were to go to the people and talk to them as he talked to us that night, he would be a very hard man to beat in November."[50]

The *Washington Post* editorial page was not impressed. For its members, "off the cuff" was an occasion to wag the fingers. They piled up a string of backward-running sentences criticizing the new style. "Truman's new technique in addressing the people was illustrated by his extemporaneous speech for the National Conference on Family Life. He spoke with complete lack of formality and undoubtedly succeeded in communicating his ideas to the audience in a personal manner. That sort of address certainly holds his listeners more effectively than the reading of a set speech which has been prepared and combed over carefully by presidential advisers. It is said that the President intends to employ this new technique when he makes his tour of the West … Mr. Truman cannot get away from the fact that his words become those of the President of the United States. When the President speaks, something more than an off the cuff opinion or remark is expected, unless he is talking informally and off the record for a small group. Much as we applaud the President's courage and flexibility in experimenting with a new technique, therefore, we cannot suppress the hope that when he speaks for the whole nation for the whole world to hear, that the advantages of weighing his words will not be overlooked."

Democrats worried, too. "While the President's homely language has a calculated appeal to the man in the street, it is felt that the attending sacrifice of dignity is proving more injurious than helpful," wrote a reporter for the *Chicago Daily Tribune* in a piece with the headline ORATORY LEAVES LEADERS OF BOTH PARTIES COLD.[51]

The *Ferdinand Magellan* Leaves the Station

Truman and his aides didn't listen to the critics. They launched him westward, ready to present the new chatty style. On June 3, the Presidential Special glided out of Washington's Union Station headed toward the first stop in Crestline, Ohio. "If I felt any better, I couldn't stand it," said the President. Roe's memo had outlined seventeen states in the Northeast, Midwest, and West "which went to one party or another by very narrow margins in 1944." (We have at most a dozen battleground states in 2016.) The map for the trip and subsequent ones was orchestrated to hit as many political hot spots as possible, as Truman worked to stitch together a coalition of farmers, labor, liberals, and African-Americans.

The last car on the caravan was the luxurious, 142-ton, armor-plated and air-conditioned *Ferdinand Magellan*. Through a door Truman could access the rear platform from which he spoke to the crowds. The train also included a staff bedroom car, four press bedroom cars, a press workroom, and two dining cars.

The official Truman campaign would not start until Labor Day, but no one was fooled. This was an official campaign trip, hence the bunting, marching bands, and city fathers at each stop. Even Truman joked about his "nonpolitical trip." The *New York Times* editorial page cracked the code: "President Truman... decided that it is time to be aggressive on a grand scale. The trip to the Pacific is the full challenge of battle to all his foes, in or out of the Democratic Party... The national campaign, at any rate, is definitely on."

"A Bunch of Birds"

In his 1948 State of the Union address, Truman battered Republicans with proposals that were authored to create confrontation. Clifford and Truman's other strategists had convinced themselves that the policy goal for 1948 was Truman's reelection, not the actual passage of policy. If they worked for bipartisan agreement they might achieve little victories, but if they reelected the president, they could enact sweeping reforms of Social Security, housing, and veterans support legislation in the next term.

With those fights roiling, Truman pounded his opponents from that rear platform of the train. He told crowds and reporters that the Eightieth Congress was the worst in history. He called Republicans "a bunch of birds" and "mossbacks." He spoke of the "gluttons of privilege" on Wall Street and the crimes of the National Association of Manufacturers. "Give 'em hell, Harry," a leather-lunged fellow yelled from the crowd. "I tell the truth and they just think it's hell," responded the president. The papers noted that "few candidates for the Presidency have ever used such ferocious language from the stump."[52]

Republicans roared. They accused Truman of running like a sheriff, not a president, and of trying to scare the country through class-based appeals like the quasi-communist candidate Henry Wallace, who was running that year on the Populist ticket. House Majority Leader Charles Halleck said Truman was the worst president in history. Rep. Cliff Clevenger of Ohio called him a "Missouri jackass." Sen. Robert Taft rushed to join the pile-on but stumbled. He said Truman was "blackguarding Congress at whistle stops all over the country."

Did you see what he did there? I didn't notice it either. But umbrage needs only the smallest pebble. *Whistlestop* is not a dirty word to us. It's the name of this book pushing you along through a gentle reading euphoria (one hopes). But for Taft to call those towns in which Truman was stopping mere whistlestops was to denigrate their size and importance—a whistlestop being a place you don't stay in for very long because there wasn't much there to give you pause. (As opposed to a *Whistlestop* book, which is something to luxuriate in on the couch while you watch the sun move across the living room.)

Democratic officials telegraphed their colleagues along the president's route and asked them to express "whether you agree with Senator Taft's description of your town as a 'whistle stop.'" In Indiana, a correspondent wrote, "Senator Taft is in very poor taste to refer to Gary 'whistle stop.' 135,000 citizens of America's greatest steel city resent this slur." From Idaho, "If Taft referred to Pocatello as, quote, a 'whistle stop,' it is apparent he has not visited progressive Pocatello." On and on, from across the country, correspondents in the little towns made a big noise.

In a war for the hearts and minds of farmers, you can appeal to them through policy or you can appeal to them through their cultural connections. Truman was paying a once-in-a-lifetime presidential visit to show these voters he cared about them. In contrast, a GOP leader was treating them like they lived in flyover country. Voters who had been blaming Truman for their woes now saw that he was one of them, and they started to look at Washington Republicans as out of touch.

The crowds liked Truman even when he was criticizing them. "If you send another Republican Congress to Washington, you're a bigger bunch of suckers than I think you are, "said the president." Two-thirds of you stayed at home in 1946 and look what a Congress we got! That is your fault. That is your fault." At another stop Truman asked, "How many times do you have to be hit on the head before you find out what's hitting you?" Imagine a candidate saying that now, telling the voters that they were responsible for the country's troubles. They'd be hounded by every cable pundit who has ever graced a green room.

Truman was being so tough because he was trying to "knock the defeatism" out of Democrats and put some fight in them. Democrats worried that FDR's magical coattails had "become a substitute for doorbell ringing" and the hard business of organizing political campaigns.[53]

Trumanisms

Sometimes when Truman spoke off the cuff he went off the rails. Speaking before a big crowd in San Diego he said the West's rising population made more water imperative. "You are going to come to the saturation point of population unless you can get some more water."

At least twice he appeared in front of the blue velvet curtain on the train platform in his pajamas and bathrobe. He said, "I understand that it was announced that I would speak here. I'm sorry. I'd gone to bed, but I thought I would let you see what I look like, even if I didn't have on my clothes." (Upon hearing this, the *Washington Post* editorial board undoubtedly required a stiff drink.)

In southern Idaho, Truman dedicated the new Willa Coates Airport and started his speech by praising the brave boy who had died for his country. He was then informed by Willa's tearful mother that Willa was not a boy. She was a girl, and she had not died in the service of the country. She had died in a civilian plane crash.

Truman had "elevated the wisecrack into a policy," said the *New York Times*. On June 11, 1948, while campaigning in Eugene, Oregon, Truman said, "I got very well acquainted with Joe Stalin, and I like old Joe! He is a decent fellow. But Joe is a prisoner of the Politburo. *He* can't do what he wants to." The president gave fuel to Republicans who said he was too soft on Russia. Officials from the State and Defense Departments sent word to the train. The president must withdraw his remarks. Truman realized he'd been too glib about the Soviet tyrant and leading American adversary. "Well, I guess I goofed," said Truman.

We're Just Mild About Harry

Truman returned from Berkeley with a new fluency on the stump. "We learned a great deal about how to conduct a campaign," Clifford recalled about the shape-up, "and these lessons were to serve us well when the final round began in September. Without the June trip, I doubt the whistle-stops would have succeeded in the fall."[54]

Before Truman could get to the fall, though, he had to make it through his party convention. Democrats were not rallying to the president. One of the signs at the convention read, "We're Just Mild About Harry." One week prior to the convention, Northern liberals and Southern segregationists tried to draft General Eisenhower, who refused.[55]

The Democratic party was split. On the far left, communist-leaning Democrats supported Henry Wallace, the nominee of the Progressive Party who promised universal government health insurance, an end to the cold war, full voting rights for black Americans, and an end to segregation. On the right, segregationists in the South supported Dixiecrat candidate Strom Thurmond, who opposed all of those things.

Truman studiously avoided talking about civil rights on the stump and on his tour. His adviser Clifford was blunt in conversations with reporters. To talk about the issue would split the party. Still, Truman did shake the hand of Mrs. E. L. Harrison in Waco, Texas, a woman described as "a Negro and a rank-and-file member of the Interracial League. She filed through with other voters to a few boos from the crowd."[56] In Ardmore, Oklahoma the papers noted that Truman had spoken to an audience in which "Negroes were mixed in with whites."[57]

The Associated Press wrote about the Democratic convention: "The Democrats act as though they have accepted an invitation to a funeral." William Manchester wrote that "Democratic delegates had a grim and hammered look."

The die-hard Democrats in the audience hadn't really seen this new Truman—the fighting, extemporaneous fellow who had been occasionally caught in his pajamas on that back train platform. So when Truman rose to the sound of the gavel to accept his nomination at 12:42 in the morning, he was a surprise. He woke the audience with his urgent high-pitched tones and arms chopping the air. The crowd was given a lift.

"Senator Barkley and I will win this election and make Republicans like it," Truman roared. "And if voters don't do their duty by the Democratic party, they are the most ungrateful people in the world."

Then Truman delivered the masterstroke of his convention. Truman called Congress to come back into session to finish the work that they had not done. What better way to keep the fights going with Republicans than to order up a whole new round of them? The *New York Times* said that this "set the convention on fire." *Time* magazine said, "There was no doubt that he had lifted the delegates out of the doldrums. He had roused admiration for his political courage."

Truman was trying to drive a wedge between the conservative Republican majority in Congress, which took its energy from the Midwest, and its moderate nominee, Governor Thomas Dewey from the Northeast. Republicans took the bait. They were apoplectic, which Truman very much appreciated. Congressman Hugh Scott of Pennsylvania, who would later help draft Dwight Eisenhower in 1952 said, "It was the act of a desperate man who was willing to destroy the unity and dignity of this country and his government for partisan advantage after he himself has lost the confidence of the people."

Despite the caterwauling, Republicans worried Truman might be successful. Privately, Scott argued that Republicans should cooperate with Truman in order to deny him a campaign message. Taft disagreed: "We're not gonna give that fellow anything." Truman had asked the Republicans to pass legislation that voters cared about—aid to education, a minimum wage increase, housing assistance, and an extension of Social Security. All of that had antecedents in the Republican platform, crafted at moderate Dewey's convention. Truman said Republicans didn't even want to embrace their own platform.

Sticking with the Whistlestops

On September 17, 1948, Truman took the second of his three train trips. It was 21,928 miles, more than twice the 9,504 miles of the first trip, and nearly as far as it would take a person to travel the globe.

Truman was sixty-four. But he wasn't worried about his health. He loved a good fight. When a home-state dentist suggested earlier in the year that it was time for him to back out of the race, Truman said, "I was not brought up to run from a fight." He told his staff, "It's going to be tough on everybody. But that's the way it's got to be. I know I can take it. I'm only afraid that I'll kill some of my staff, and I like you all very much and I don't want to do that." (He was already breaking them financially making them live on a campaign stipend of $6 a day, which meant most would come back from the trip deep in debt.)

Any deaths would have been particularly tragic, because they would have been in the service of what was widely seen as a lost cause. "Democratic leaders here are wearing long faces over the Truman tour," said the *Chicago Daily Tribune*, "frankly expressing concern . . . that Mr. Truman is drawing citizens as President rather than as candidate."[58]

On September 9, a week before the wheels of Truman's train started rolling on the second trip, pollster Elmo Roper wrote, "Political campaigns are largely ritualistic . . . All the evidence we have accumulated since 1936 tends to indicate that the man in the lead at the beginning of the campaign, is the man who is winner at the end of it . . . The winner, it appears, clinches his victory early in the race and before he has uttered a word of campaign oratory." So Roper stopped polling. He figured Dewey was the winner.

Never mind, Truman kept putting John Henry's hammer down on the Republicans, spurred by those in the audience who yelled "Pour it on, Harry!" He preached against "trickle down" policies. He declared that the typical Republican was a shrewd man with a calculating machine where his heart should be. "The Republicans had begun to nail the American consumer to the wall with spikes of greed," he said. In Iowa, he said Republicans had put a "pitchfork in the farmer's back." Congress was thoroughly surrounded by lobbyists, the most in history. He called on voters to deliver a new Congress, one that cared more about "the common people" than "the interests of the men who have all the money."

In Jersey City, a parade of one thousand women carried banners denouncing the Republican Congress and urging Truman's reelection. "The only meat we can buy is horse meat—who is to blame but the Republican Congress?" read one sign. "Big business eats porterhouse steaks—we get horse meat."[59]

Truman kept it up as the leaves turned from green to brown and the days grew shorter. He sometimes stopped sixteen times a day. By October 26, the president had worked himself into such a state that he said Republicans were the tools of fascists and compared them to Hitler and Mussolini. "When a few men get control of the economy of this nation, they find a front man to run the country for them. Before Hitler came to power, control over the German economy passed into the hands of a small group of rich manufacturers bankers and landowners."

Think about that for a moment. Today partisans throw around Hitler analogies because they don't know their history. They are roundly denounced for doing so. In 1948, World War II was a fresh memory. Rubble still littered the streets of some European cities, and the incumbent American president was comparing the entire opposition party to fascists in Italy, Hitler in Germany, and the Japanese who launched the sneak attack on Pearl Harbor. It was an extraordinary thing for a president to say.

Truman's Boiler Room Wasn't on the Train

Truman wasn't just being critical about Republicans in Washington. He was making targeted appeals at every stop too. The whistlestop tour represented an innovation in campaign research. Before arriving in any town, Truman got a short briefing about it from a dossier produced by seven people working in an airless office in DuPont Circle in Washington, D.C. In Philip White's brilliantly titled book *Whistle Stop*, he argues that it was the research team that made these train trips so effective. It wasn't invective that was winning voters; it was the deployment of town-specific information that helped Truman make connections with those unfamiliar faces staring up at him.

Truman gave 352 addresses over three different trips, which spanned thirty-three days. At each stop he showed he understood something about the town he was in, which helped him make his larger values case against Republicans. He was saying, *I'm for the working man, whereas they're surrounded by lobbyists and care only about their jewel-encrusted self-interest.* By knowing a local fact, he demonstrated he was on their side. "He talks and thinks the way they do," said the *Washington Post* of his style, "when he isn't reading Washington gobbledygook speeches."[60]

Truman had been accused of making the office smaller, but that smallness was now paying off. The president was applauded for his "directness and plainness of speech." Papers reported that the audiences "like his folksy off-the-cuff talks far more than his ghost-written, full-dress speeches."[61]

The president talked about flood relief in the Pacific Northwest, labor relations in Detroit, a grain bin shortage in Iowa, and civil rights in Harlem. He was the kind of guy voters could trust to know about them when he was in office.

Truman talked about when he lived as they did, boarding outside of Kansas City for $5 a week.[62] Sometimes the president would augment his regular fellow act with an actual deed that showed he had roots. Upon spying a horse, he'd walk over to its owner, open the horse's mouth, and from the arrangement of teeth know how old the horse was. "Imagine that," one of the shocked horse riders told the Associated Press. "Who'd thought the President of the United States knows about horses?" (Truman was so approachable, a man rushed the stage to get one of his famous two-pump handshakes and was stopped by the Secret Service and fined $50.)[63]

He got so folksy as the trip went on, it was said "the farther west Truman traveled the taller the corn grew—in the field and in rhetoric."[64] He told stories about his grandparents at every stop until it became obvious that he had more stories than the four humans he was attributing them to could possibly accomplish. "There seemed to be hardly a rear stop, sometimes, when Grandfather Young or Grandfather Truman weren't brought up. Generally, they had an adventure in the vicinity."

Well-wishers handed him gifts along the way: a peace pipe, spurs, flowers, chewing gum, jelly beans, and a rod and reel. Each stop would end the same way. "How'd ya' like to meet my family?" The crowd would erupt in cheers and Truman would bring them out his wife and daughter.

The nationally syndicated journalist H. I. Phillips wrote, "I size Harry Truman up as a pretty sound careful prudent, non-acrobatic fairly old-fashioned American whose Missouri background and training will keep him from going haywire. I see him as a horse sense individual, with much of the pioneer love of traditional American ways."

The *Washington Post* saw a man transformed: "He can hardly be recognized for the same Harry S. Truman who, when he started his campaign two months ago, was the candidate the Democratic Party had swallowed with grimaces of distaste after trying to substitute for him almost anybody else."

Dewey Have to Vote for Him?

While Truman was letting it all hang out on the campaign trail, Governor Thomas Dewey was stuffing it all in. Truman was acting like the hungry challenger, calling the GOP nominee to "come down and fight." Dewey ran a cautious challenger's campaign, hoping to make the White House on the strength of antipathy toward the incumbent. FDR had needled him into combat in 1944, and he wasn't going to fall into that trap again. The Dewey campaign was so careful, its strategists removed attacks on FDR from locally produced literature so as not to offend fans of the deceased president.[65]

Dewey offered solid generalities while he waited for the White House lease to run out. He presented himself as high-minded and public spirited. He promised to bring the country together. He called on the audiences "to move forward shoulder to shoulder to an even greater America…to tackle problems with stout purpose and full heart."[66] He polished apples. He praised motherhood. He left no abrasions on the ears of his lulled audience.

It's very hard to say nothing for so long. The body has a natural inclination for novelty and variety and vim. To resist its impulses, the nonthreatening candidate has to keep adding more water to the porridge. This creates the conditions where a man can go too far and suddenly wind up saying, "America's future is ahead of us," which is indeed something Dewey said. He was such a stiff Alice Roosevelt Longworth referred to him as "the little man on the wedding cake."

An editorial in the *Louisville Courier-Journal* summed it up: "No presidential candidate in the future will be so inept that four of his major speeches can be boiled down to these historic four sentences: Agriculture is important. Our rivers are full of fish. You cannot have freedom without liberty. Our future lies ahead."[67]

"He was the only man who could strut sitting down," wrote one wag. "He coasts out like a man who has been mounted on casters and given a tremendous shove from behind," wrote Richard Rovere in the *New Yorker.*

Toward the end of the campaign, Dewey felt enough pressure that he had to try to match the president on the rails. At one point outside of Swanton, Ohio, their two trains passed ten feet from each other,

Truman was on his way to give it to Dewey in Toledo, and Dewey was on his way to catalog Truman's limitations in Chicago. (The headlights flashed each other, but the candidates didn't wave.) [68]

In another case, the two candidates shared the same room at the Statler Hotel in Boston. The hotel suite was notable for having a television in the wall. As soon as Truman checked out, Dewey checked in, an exchange he was hoping to repeat in January.

You could see the differences in the two campaigns in ways big and small. Dewey had a manuscript delivered to his train rostrum. Truman carried his official speech with him in a black case, but when he spoke from the train it was "much more helter-skelter, hit and miss, hot and human," wrote Drew Pearson.

As Dewey was preparing to speak at one stop, the train started to move backward toward the crowd. Peril! The train stopped just a few feet from the crowd. Only brows were furrowed. No injuries. Still, Dewey wanted to have a stern word with someone. "That's the first lunatic I've had for an engineer," said Dewey. "He probably ought to be shot at sunrise, but I guess we can let him off because no one was hurt."

When you push bromides all the time, people focus on the gaffes. When you say something that is the least bit interesting, it so startles people that they make a big deal about it. Newspapermen who had been poking into the typewriter one dull paragraph after another suddenly had a fun little story. Dewey's outburst rocketed around the union halls and railroad houses across the country, acting as a turnout mechanism for Truman.

Dewey Defeats Truman

Despite Dewey's formality and stuffiness, it cannot be overstated how much the press thought he was going to win. *Life* magazine put Dewey over the caption THE NEXT PRESIDENT OF THE UNITED

STATES. The *New York Times* headline predicted THOMAS E. DEWEY'S ELECTION AS PRESIDENT IS A FOREGONE CONCLUSION.

Newsweek published opinions from fifty political reporters, and all fifty predicted that Truman would lose. When they brought the news to Truman—he was somewhere out on his train tour—he said, "Oh well, those damn fellows? They're always wrong. Forget it boys, let's get on with the job." The *Washington Post* said that reporters "know in their bones that only a colossal blunder can cost Dewey the Presidency."[69]

Our heaviest giggling should be reserved for those columnists who had written their stories on Monday to be published on Wednesday after the election. Drew Pearson, one of the most influential commentators of the day, wrote, "I surveyed the close-knit group around Tom Dewey, who will take over the White House eighty-six days from now." He then triumphantly named all of the members of the new president's cabinet. Joseph and Stewart Alsop, brothers who could change administration policy with a well-timed piece, wrote, "The first post-election question is how the government can get through the next ten weeks. Events will not wait patiently until Thomas E. Dewey officially replaces Harry S. Truman."

The press wouldn't let go of this belief. Even at midnight on election night, Truman woke up and heard the radio announcer say that he was ahead by 1,200,000 votes, before continuing to say, it was still the case that Truman was "undoubtedly beat."

In the end, Truman not only won the presidential election, Democrats totally flipped control of Congress. Democrats won nine seats and took control of the Senate. In the House, Republicans lost seventy-five seats and control of the House—the largest gain for either party in any House election since then. Until the rise of Donald Trump, which pundits totally missed, this was the greatest collective mistake in the history of punditry. As a poetic coda, Truman held up the famous *Chicago Daily Tribune* with the headline DEWEY DEFEATS

TRUMAN on the back platform of his whistlestop train, perhaps the most iconic moment in American presidential elections.

The election of 1948 was such a shock that William Manchester lists this in his short catalog of moments that Americans of that generation could remember along with Pearl Harbor, the death of Franklin D. Roosevelt, and the assassination of John Kennedy. The conservative *New York Sun* said, "You just have to take off your hat off to the beaten man who refuses to stay licked. Mr. Truman won because this is still a land which loves a scrapper in which intestinal fortitude is still respected."

At least the pundits had a good sense of humor about themselves. A huge sign hung across the *Washington Post* building and it read, "Mr. President we are ready to eat crow whenever you are ready to serve it." The Alsop brothers, who had been so spectacularly wrong, wrote, "There is only one question on which professional politicians, poll-takes, political reporters and other wiseacres and prognosticators can any longer speak with much authority: That is how they want their crow cooked." (In 2000, the television networks called Florida for Al Gore but then had to retract it, NBC's Tom Brokaw said: "We don't just have egg on our face. We have an omelette.")[70]

The train tour had paid off. The farm vote which had gone to the Republicans in 1944 came back. Voters in small towns, which Senator Taft had called "whistlestops," turned out for Truman, too.

Historians see forces at play in 1948 that were not apparent to Truman and his strategists at the time. Though Truman didn't talk about civil rights much on the campaign trail, he carried the African-American vote in the cities by a large margin which was crucial to winning Ohio, Illinois, and California. Labor turned out in force, too, rather than splitting off to vote for Wallace. Truman won 70 percent of the union vote, which wasn't expected given that the railroad union had once announced that they were going to spend every penny in the brotherhood's treasury to defeat him.[71], [72] Union workers had lined the railroad tracks during his visit to cities—in some wards, party workers were threatened with loss of payroll jobs if they didn't get people to rally. On Election Day, they drove voters to the polls and arranged babysitters.[73]

The Southern Democrats who had defected to the Dixiecrat party did not take as many votes from Truman as his men had feared. But was that because it was always a weak movement, or did the Dixiecrat party become less attractive once Truman charged out on the campaign trail?

The 1948 Truman campaign is a romantic one. It is the greatest comeback in campaign history. Truman was Everyman in 1948. As the *New York Times* noted, "Mr. Truman could be the composite American of 1948." But the trick was choosing a method of campaigning that accentuated that style and fit with his message of sticking up for the little man against the special interests. His form followed function.

Truman offered people what he would have wanted—an opportunity to see him, get a measure of him—and when they did they found he was just like them. "Most of you people are working people, just as I've been all my life. I have had to work for everything I ever received. I never went into a political campaign in my life that I didn't have a fight to obtain what I thought was real and for the benefit of the people."

Truman was fighting just like the average American was fighting. "Truman reintroduced Americans to themselves, and it provided a comforting identification," wrote historian Steven R. Goldzwig.

Could this kind of campaign happen again? Campaign reporters certainly hope so. It validates all the candidate behavior they watch so closely for signs of meaning. Voters should hope so, too. The Truman success offers the hope that maybe through a candidate, voters can be shifted out of the rigid ruts they're in. Maybe a candidate with a new style and blunt talk can shatter the sclerosis of the system. That's what

John McCain tried in 2000. It was what Donald Trump was successful doing in the Republican primaries of 2016.

If a Truman-like comeback is still possible today, it may also be possible that candidates could get onto a train again and go across the country, traveling from town to town and having actual conversations with voters about politics. That would be great, because that would mean more whistlestops. And future editions of this *Whistlestop*.

1992—Till the Last Dog Dies

AP Photo/stf/Ron Frehm

On Sunday, January 19, 1992, five Democratic presidential candidates assembled in the studios of WMUR in Manchester, New Hampshire, for what looked like the most depressing public access telethon in history. They wore boxy blue and gray suits and sat at desks, surrounded by black curtains. They were there for a Democratic debate between former Senator Paul Tsongas, Governors Jerry Brown and Bill Clinton, and Senators Bob Kerrey and Tom Harkin. Each man offered inoffensive thoughts about the economy and the War on Drugs, topics that would seem quaint given what was about to be Topic A. Kerrey suggested using the military to fight the War on Drugs, an idea that could get a candidate arrested in Democratic politics a few election cycles later. Bill Clinton nearly boasted about his use of the death penalty in Arkansas, another idea that would fall out of favor.

At the end of the conversation, moderator Cokie Roberts probed each candidate about the biggest threat to their electability in a general election. She asked Governor Clinton to respond to the: "concern on the part of members of your party that these allegations of womanizing, that the Republicans will find somebody and that she will come forward late, and that you would lose the all-important Democrat women's vote."

The question came at a scary time for the Clinton campaign. He was up in the polls. A survey by the *Boston Globe* and WBZ-TV showed Clinton leading with 29 percent, followed by Paul Tsongas at 17 percent, and Bob Kerrey at 16 percent. But rumors of affairs had appeared in a supermarket tabloid. Then they'd migrated to the *New York Post* under the headline WILD BILL and a *Daily News* story headlined I'M NO GARY HART appeared days before the debate.

At first, the Clinton team tried to laugh off the reports. Clinton had called them "cash for trash" stories, and his strategists shamed the media into not covering them. The press was ambivalent. The old standard was that personal issues were only covered if they affected a candidate's fitness to serve. Thomas Eagleton's treatment for depression was an issue when he was picked as McGovern's vice presidential running mate but were affairs? After the 1988 campaign, where Gary Hart was driven from the race after a rumored extramarital affair, the press was criticized for shallow coverage, so editors were nervous.

Clinton's encyclopedic understanding of policy and mastery on the stump also made him an attractive candidate for reporters to cover, but there were *a lot* of Clinton rumors. He had a sloppy, St. Bernard–like quality—the part of his personality that won him the nickname "Bubba"—and these stories of bounding from one escapade to another didn't seem out of character.

Shortly before the debate, Hillary Clinton weighed in: "Is anything about our marriage as important to the people of New Hampshire as the question of whether they will be able to keep their own families together?"

The candidate himself answered Roberts's debate question this way: "I live in a place like New Hampshire where we know each other by our first names, and even your enemies curse you out by your first name. I think it is highly unlikely, given the competitive environment in which I've been in, that you have anything to worry about on that score."

It wasn't a denial. It was a version of the "Nothing to see here" response. Sometimes that works and reporters go on looking for something else. Other times, it is like a candidate throwing the entire breakfront of china into the air. A pause ensues, and then there is a loud and extensive symphony of breakage. This would be the latter case, initiating what would be perhaps the most topsy-turvy set of events in the modern political era. Clinton's campaign went from soaring high to a screaming descent. It looked like the front-runner was headed for the side of Mt. Winnipesaukee. In the end, the jalopy, with no landing gear and leaking oil, skidded down the runway in an ugly mess of sparks. It was gruesome, but under the circumstances just staying alive was a triumph. Bill Clinton, through perseverance and spin—two qualities that would become hallmarks of his presidency—would turn a second-place finish in New Hampshire into a victory that would take him on to the presidency.

Running to Lose to George Bush

Nineteen ninety-two wasn't supposed to be a good year for Democrats. George Bush's approval rating in March 1991 after the Gulf War was 89 percent.[74] Prominent Democratic leaders like Gov. Mario Cuomo of New York, Sen. Lloyd Bentsen of Texas, and Rep. Richard Gephardt of Missouri all passed on running. They were sure that if they actually got in, they would lose.

The mind-set was captured perfectly by *Saturday Night Live* in a skit called "Campaign '92: The Race to Avoid Being the Guy Who Loses to Bush." It opens with the moderator saying, "Welcome to this, the first of a series of debates among the five leading Democrats who are trying to avoid being forced by their party into a hopeless race against President George Bush. Most of them have already announced that they're not interested in the nomination, but each, of course, is under enormous pressure to be the chump who will take on the futile task of running against this very, very popular incumbent."

For the rest of the skit, the Democrats held a debate in which they each tried to top the other in explaining why they were unfit to run against George Bush, and why the other candidates would lose to Bush by less. The most famous line came at the very end of the skit. Phil Hartman, playing Mario Cuomo, summed up his negative qualities by saying, "I have mob ties."

Cuomo had flirted with entering the race all the way up to the primary filing deadline in New Hampshire, even leaving a plane waiting to take him from New York to fill out the paperwork himself. But at the very last minute the governor never boarded the plane and the engines were turned off. With all the other A-list candidates having benched themselves, Bill Clinton, the Rhodes scholar and five-term governor of Arkansas, was the front-runner.

Newsweek said at the start of 1991 that Clinton was garlanded with four-leaf clovers. Here's the *New York Times*: "If the buzz inside the Capital beltway can be believed, the Democrats may well have a candidate before they even have a real campaign. Governor Bill Clinton of Arkansas, by virtue of his early strength in organizing and fundraising, not to mention message-making and pundit-stroking, has become the hot candidate for the post Cuomo period."

Clinton was doing so well the *Boston Globe* ran this headline: MEDIA'S FRONTRUNNER TAG CUTS BOTH WAYS FOR CLINTON. In other words, he was so far ahead, expectations might now be too high. The *Globe* said, "Clinton's new prominence has helped raise expectations that he will win the New Hampshire primary, suggesting that he might pay a heavy price if he does not, just as Edmund S. Muskie and Walter F. Mondale did." In 1972 Muskie won, but actually lost, when George McGovern did better than everybody expected. Mondale lost to Gary Hart in 1984.

New Hampshire always plays a big role in presidential races, but in the '92 cycle the state was even more important, because Iowa had a favorite son candidate in Senator Tom Harkin. The winnowing that usually took place in Iowa had to take place in New Hampshire.

Clinton was on the rise, but his wandering eye was a problem. After Roberts asked her debate question, *Washington Post* columnist Mary McGrory wrote about the "two debates" taking place in Democratic politics in a piece headlined THE WHISPERING CAMPAIGN TRAIL. One debate had been on the stage with Roberts, the other debate was "occurring all over New Hampshire, indoors and out, early and late, and it could last until Feb. 18, the day voters go to the polls." The two debates were about to collide, McGrory wrote, and it was going to have political consequences. McGrory talked to New Hampshire state senator Jeanne Shaheen, who would become governor of New Hampshire and later senator. Shaheen told McGrory that she had been a Hart supporter in 1988. She was asked to join the Clinton team, but she declined, signing up with Bob Kerrey instead, explaining simply to McGrory, "I've been there," meaning she had dealt with candidates who had been ruined by their action pants.

60 Minutes Gamble

The bombshell arrived on January 23, four days after the debate in which Clinton promised that there would be no bombshell disclosures. The *Star* tabloid printed a story about rumors of several Clinton liaisons, including what the paper claimed was a twelve-year affair with Gennifer Flowers, a former nightclub performer.

The Clinton campaign was under siege. To seize the advantage, media strategist Mandy Grunwald suggested the Clintons go on CBS's *60 Minutes* before the Super Bowl, the most-watched night of television in America.

In the interview, the Clintons were seated on a sofa across a coffee table from CBS correspondent Steve Kroft. Twice, before the interview, producer Don Hewitt, kneeling off camera, urged Clinton to confess to adultery. "It will be great television," Hewitt said, "and I know television." Clinton wouldn't do it. He said he barely had any relationship with Flowers, sexual or otherwise. "There's nothing out of the ordinary there," he said. He talked about one instance in which he was on the phone with Gennifer Flowers while his wife was in the room as an example of how blase the relationship had been. Flowers had been tarred by rumors, and he was giving her assistance on the phone about how to manage these rumors of possible liaisons. No big deal.

Hillary Clinton offered her view of Flowers: "I felt as I've felt about all of these women: that they... had just been minding their own business and they got hit by a meteor... I felt terrible about what was happening to them."

Clinton offered a motive for why Flowers would change her story: "It was only when money came out, when the tabloid went down there offering people money to say that they had been involved with me, that she changed her story. There's a recession on."

What about the other women? He didn't want to get into specific charges, but the candidate did say that there had been a crisis in his marriage at one time. He admitted causing pain in his marriage, but that he and Hillary Clinton still loved each other. During the interview the couple patted each other in various ways.

Kroft kept trying to get the clamshell open and get Clinton to admit he'd had an affair, claiming the public was anxious to hear it. Clinton didn't bite: "I have acknowledged wrongdoing. I have acknowledged causing pain in my marriage. I have said things to you tonight and to the American people from the beginning that no American politician ever has. I think most Americans who are watchin' this tonight, they'll know what we're sayin'. They'll get it."

It was an extraordinary moment in campaign history. A reporter was cross examining a candidate about his most intimate actions and relationships while his wife who he had betrayed sat close enough to feel his pulse. It was like a mix between a therapy session and a visit to the principal's office.

Kroft gave up and suggested that the only reason the Clintons were so relentlessly on message was that they had an "understanding" or "arrangement." That set Clinton off. He wanted to slug Kroft, he later wrote. "Wait a minute, wait a minute. Wait a minute," the governor said. "You're—you're looking at two people who love each other. This is not an arrangement or an understanding. This is a marriage. That's a very different thing."

Hillary Clinton interjected pointedly: "You know, I'm not sittin' here, some little woman standin' by my man like Tammy Wynette. I'm sittin' here because I love him, and I respect him, and I honor what he's been through and what we've been through together. And, you know, if that's not enough for people, then heck, don't vote for him."

It was a moment of real television, which proves something that many candidates forget: only when being asked tough, probing questions does a candidate have a chance to respond with forceful answers that are memorable and make them look commanding. It's like hitting off of a fast pitcher. The ball goes farther when you finally do make contact.

At some point during the session, one of the very bright, very hot overhead lights came loose, nearly hitting Mrs. Clinton. She had to lunge sideways. The narrow escape only seemed to further emphasize the obvious tension in the room that had Americans glued to their seats.

Bill Clinton wrote that he flew home and watched the show before the Super Bowl with his daughter, Chelsea, who said, when it was over, "I think I'm glad you're my parents."

Flowers Delivery

The interview helped put Clinton back on track. In an ABC poll taken soon after, 79 percent of respondents said that the press had no business poking into the private lives of the Clintons. The *60 Minutes* appearance had worked so well for the Clintons that press critics said they snookered the venerable CBS institution into becoming a public relations vehicle. The appearance didn't mark the end of the story, though. The next day Flowers held a press conference at the Waldorf Astoria, in New York where she reiterated her claims: "Yes, I was Bill Clinton's lover for twelve years. And for the past two years I have lied to the press about a relationship to protect him. The truth is I loved him. Now he tells me to deny it. Well, I'm sick of all of the deceit and I'm sick of all of the lies."

Flowers played audiotapes that included some racy talk. Most important was an exchange in which a voice that sounded like Clinton's said, "If they ever hit you with it, just say no and go on. There's nothing they can do. I expected them to look into it and come interview you. But if everybody is on record denying it, you've got no problem." (Clinton's denials on *60 Minutes* flipped from seeming genuine, to seeming frighteningly calculated.)

The tapes were seen as a death blow to the campaign. Flowers may have been paid $100,000 for the story, but the voice on the tapes sounded like the five-term governor of Arkansas running to be president. In the movie *The War Room*, which chronicles the '92 Clinton campaign, Dan Payne, a political consultant in the northeast, says, "The friction in this is going to be too much for Clinton to survive. I think it's only a matter of days before he can get out, if not hours." Watching from the sidelines, Sen. Al Gore bet his chief of staff that Clinton would never get the nomination.

The disclosure was such an issue for Bill Clinton because the lurid details of the affair raised issues about his electability, which had so far been Clinton's great selling point. He was seen as such a great general election candidate because he was a synthesis between the two parties. He was not too liberal—some Democrats in New Hampshire accused him of being more like a Republican than a Democrat. He was going to revive the party after the Carter years by attracting conservative voters. If he had a character issue, though, that no longer seemed possible.

An internal campaign memo showed how much Clinton was bleeding with women voters. Written by pollsters, Celinda Lake and Stan Greenberg, one section was headed, "Trusting the Man." It read: "College women and younger women voters are a difficult problem, particularly as we move out of the south. Since Gennifer Flowers, these women have been more negative about Bill Clinton. They have ranked him significantly lower on being honest, trustworthy, having family values, and being politically expedient... At the most fundamental and personal level, these women voters do not trust Bill Clinton, a politician they have barely heard of. They find it difficult to vote for a candidate that they do not trust at such an elemental level. As one woman concluded, 'It's an integrity issue that is hard to overlook.' "

Women voters had been introduced to Bill Clinton, through Gennifer Flowers, and it produced a screen that blocked out his other messages. It had also provided a powerful framework for interpreting other messages. It was easy for these women to see Clinton's commercials as slick, politically expedient, and see him as a candidate who was "saying all things to all people."

The Comeback Kid

The Governor responded by throwing himself into the campaign and in a way that let every voter see how hard he was working. This would become a signature move of his presidency. In the face of scandal or attacks, he redoubled his efforts. "Everybody said I was dead as a doornail," he remembered. "I was taking a whipping in the press and I was dropping in the polls." So he went back to the gymnasiums, the Rotary clubs, and the diners, arguing that the people of New Hampshire cared about things other than his sex life. They cared about wages, and jobs, and the things he'd been talking about at length and in detail and that would help change their circumstances.

He preached against the "brain-dead politics" of the left and the right that cared more about character assassination and tearing people down than coming up with solutions. "The people of New Hampshire desperately want this election to be about them, their lives, their problems, their future," he said. "They're trying very hard not to be diverted, and I'm gonna do my best to support their efforts." At another stop he said, "I'm asking the voters of New Hampshire to achieve a level of sophistication, no one else has ever asked of them before."

The polls showed just how much people were feeling the economic pain and looking for just the answers he was offering. When people were asked who benefited most from the Reagan-Bush policies, 82 percent said, "The rich." Nearly 60 percent said, "A Democratic president would care more about the needs of the middle class." The question of which candidate cared more was going to be the most important one in the general election. Clinton's personal problems were a challenge to his electability, but he was also showing aptitude for addressing the fall election's key issue.

The polls also showed something else that helped Clinton. Not that many people cared about the Gennifer Flowers story. In several surveys taken after the *60 Minutes* broadcast, he was the front-runner. ABC News found eight of ten Americans felt marital infidelity should not be a presidential campaign issue and the media should move on to other topics.[75] He might be out of the woods.

A New Nightmare

While Clinton was weathering the storms of his private dalliances, he was hit with another bolt from the past. On February 7, eleven days before the New Hampshire primary, the *Wall Street Journal* explored old charges that Clinton had dodged the Vietnam draft.

The allegation was that as a shaggy-haired college student, Clinton had pulled a bait and switch in 1969, avoiding the draft by promising to go into the ROTC, but then never actually following through. The *Journal* had two new sources, but they weren't perfect. Both seemed politically motivated and thus might be easy to dismiss. What added fuel to the fire, though, was Clinton's totally implausible response to the story. He said he hadn't tried to game the system. He said he'd put his name back into the draft after saying he would go into the ROTC when four of his friends were killed in Vietnam. No one believed that anyone would learn of the death of four friends and then take steps to possibly go join them. If the Gennifer Flowers story had raised worries that Clinton could tell easy lies, this response confirmed those worries. The Clinton campaign was in "meltdown," as his pollster Stan Greenberg put it.

Clinton's poll numbers dropped twenty points in about forty-eight hours. The *Journal* produced a letter that the twenty-three-year-old Clinton had written in 1969 thanking an official for "saving me from the draft," saying it was the only way he could avoid it while still maintaining his "political viability." How duplicitous could a fellow be? Clinton was caught in a credibility hairball.

Clinton's opponents pounced. "My problem is not with the evasion of the draft," said Nebraska senator Bob Kerrey, a decorated war veteran who had lost his leg in combat. "My problem is with the veracity of the statements themselves. They do not in several areas have the ring of truth." Later during Clinton's presidency, Kerrey would say he was an "unusually good liar." Iowa senator Tom Harkin said, "The last thing Bill Clinton needs is another story questioning his veracity."

Paul Tsongas tried to stay above the fray, but he didn't try too hard. "I hope the issue of the draft won't crowd out other issues," he said, thus raising the issue of the draft. This is a familiar ploy: *I hope that the issue of the draft won't crowd out our discussion of taxes, and the draft won't crowd out our discussion of welfare, and the draft won't crowd out the word* draft *in sentences like this one that have the word* draft *in it a lot to remind you that the issue of the draft is one you should be paying attention to. Draft.*

Clinton's opponents threw his words back in his face. In 1988, he had opined that Dan Quayle's draft issues were a problem not because of what George Bush's Vice Presidential nominee had done at the time, but because his explanations were not believable. Clinton had said, "What matters is not what you did, what matters is just level with us and tell us exactly what it is that you did." Bubba, censure thyself.

Bob Kerrey started campaigning with his old war buddies to keep the story in the news. At this point Clinton said, "I felt like a turd in the well."

George Stephanopoulos, Clinton's communications director, thought after the draft stories came out, *That's it. We're done.*

The governor responded to this second crisis as he had to the first one, by becoming a tornado of campaign activity. He campaigned eighteen hours a day, appearing on television shows, standing for hours at shopping malls, and shaking every hand he could reach. Clinton showed in his entire body how hard he was working—his face ballooned and reddened. His campaign also shifted resources, moving $350,000 to New Hampshire for advertising and another $150,000 for other expenditures like videos promoting his record and campaign that were handed out to voters at shopping centers.[76]

Then, six days before the election, Clinton uncorked the expression that would become synonymous with his comeback. "They say I'm on the ropes because other people have questioned my life, after years of public service," he told an audience in Dover, New Hampshire. "I'll tell you something. I'm going to give you this election back, and if you'll give it to me, I won't be like George Bush. I'll never forget who gave me a second chance, and I'll be there for you till the last dog dies."

Clinton campaigned until the last dog died and when the votes were tallied, he came in second, losing to Paul Tsongas 33 to 25. It was a loss, but it was a smaller loss than might have been expected when people were shopping for flowers to send to his political funeral. Expectations can make New Hampshire outcomes wobbly. In 1972 Muskie lost by not beating McGovern by enough. In 1968 Johnson won, but "Clean" Gene McCarthy got much closer to an incumbent president than he was supposed to, so it was seen as a big defeat for Johnson.

Clinton had been ahead by twelve points three weeks before the vote. He lost by nine points—a twenty-one-point difference. Still, he spun it as a victory. Late in the evening, the candidate arrived at the microphone, worn out but jubilant. "While the evening is young and we don't know yet what the final tally will be, I think we know enough to say with some certainty that New Hampshire tonight has made Bill Clinton the comeback kid."

PART III

Collapses

1988—Dukakis Tanks

AP Photo/Michael E. Samojeden, File

The presidential campaign of 1988 is not remembered as a competition over weighty issues of the day. Character questions dominated the primaries. The Democratic senator Gary Hart squandered his front-runner status when he was photographed with a comely-blonde-not-his-wife nestled on his lap. Senator Joe Biden was caught plagiarizing another politician's speeches and had to leave the race. The *Wall Street Journal* reported that Pat Robertson, the evangelical preacher who finished second in the GOP Iowa caucuses, had his first child a few months before his marriage.

Just after Memorial Day, 1988, Lee Atwater, the top strategist for Vice President George Bush's presidential campaign, took steps to ensure that the general election wasn't going to be much more high minded. Atwater called in the campaign's top researcher, Jim Pinkerton. He ordered him to find every speck of dirt he could on Democratic nominee Massachusetts governor Michael Dukakis. Atwater, a South Carolina native known for his hardball tactics, held out a three-by-five card and said "You get me the stuff to beat this little bastard. And I want you to put it on this card. You can use both sides."[77] George Bush, the Republican nominee, had fallen behind Dukakis by sixteen points in the polls that spring. Atwater was fixing to change that.

The researcher, Jim Pinkerton, fulfilled the concise request with seven entries. They covered Dukakis's position on national defense, his record on taxes and spending, the pollution of Boston Harbor, his opposition to the death penalty and his opposition to strict sentences for drug posession as well as his veto of legislation requiring teachers to lead their classes in the Pledge of Allegiance. The most damaging item on the card was Dukakis's support of prison furloughs.

Atwater and his men used the card to launch one of the most sustained and successful bombardments of an opponent in the modern media age. The Bush campaign did not promote a vision of the future around which voters could rally; it was a relentless assault on Dukakis's past, intended to characterize him as weak, esoteric, and liberal. Like all successful image-based attacks, the salvos created such a fever in their target that Dukakis blundered into inhabiting the caricature Republicans painted of him.

When Lee Atwater ordered that card to be filled, he could never have imagined that Michael Dukakis would respond to the charges of weakness by lowering himself into a tank and pressing the self-destruct button.

Let Me Fix That For You

In retrospect, it looks like Michael Dukakis was a flawed candidate and that Bush was the inevitable victor, but Bush did not look good at the start of the 1988 campaign. No sitting vice president had been elected to the presidency since Martin Van Buren in 1836. John Adams and Thomas Jefferson are the only other two on that list.

Ronald Reagan had put the country on the path to prosperity, but as Bush prepared for the campaign, Reagan faced a mushrooming scandal. Administration officials had sold arms in an attempt to bring about the release of American hostages—a break from Reagan's stated policy. They had used the proceeds of those sales to support the Nicaraguan Contras, an illegal covert operation. Supercreative, yes, but illegal.

All of this had Bush very antsy. The Vice President was running to continue the "Reagan Revolution," but he also wanted to shake loose of the administration and engage in the campaign as his own man. "The root of all this unease," wrote Richard Ben Cramer in *What It Takes*, "was Bush couldn't make news because Bush had nothing to say. Without an opponent—*me* instead of *him*—the Bush campaign was about . . . nothing."

To move out of Reagan's shadow, Bush took a tour of conservative conventions and stations of the cross, including a dinner celebrating the life of *Manchester Union Leader* publisher William Loeb, who had savaged Bush as a candidate in 1980. The conservative outreach was unconvincing. George Will, the conservative columnist, nearly channeled Loeb with his withering critique: "The unpleasant sound Bush is emitting as he traipses from one conservative gathering to another is the thin tiny 'arf.' The sound of a lap dog." That was not nice at all.

Bush just couldn't wriggle out of that image. This led his campaign strategists to suggest in the spring of 1988, that the vice president break with Reagan in some public way to show that he was independent. Bush wouldn't do it. He was ambitious, but he was loyal, too. He wasn't going to undermine the president.

When a story appeared suggesting Bush had said something negative—privately—about Attorney General Ed Meese, who faced conflict-of-interest charges over a company he was investigating in which he had an investment, Bush issued one of the best denials of all time. "I deny that I have ever given my opinion to anybody on anything."[78]

Atwater suggested leaking that Bush was behind the ouster of

Reagan's chief of staff, Don Regan. Though Bush's political team and Nancy Reagan wanted Regan out the door, the vice president wouldn't betray the president, who wanted to keep his chief of staff. "You help me in Iowa and New Hampshire," Bush told his political aides. "Don't meddle in the White House."

A lot of good it did him. Bush might have been loyal, but that didn't mean Reagan's staff wanted to promote him. Bush felt marginalized. "It's almost as if I don't exist," Bush said to his audio diary.[79]

The Wimp Factor

"*Spin doctor* is a locution we must keep our eyes on for 1988," wrote *New York Times* columnist William Safire.[80] The term was born in the 1984 cycle, but it became famous in the next race. Spin, the act of shaping a story for political gain, became a story in itself as the press started covering the strategies and strategists of the candidates as much as the actual positions and actions of the candidates themselves. One analysis of debate night coverage in 1988, relative to the campaigns that had preceded it, showed a significant increase in the amount of attention paid not to what the campaign was actually doing, but to the spin the campaign was emitting to put the best gloss on what was happening.

Spin doctors shaped the public relations and persona of each candidate, and this became as important as the strategy of where and how he would win votes. Bush's top spin doctors, Lee Atwater and Roger Ailes, represented the state-of-the art talents in packaging a candidate for the twenty-four-hour news cycle.

But Bush's spin doctors had a challenge. His identity crisis went beyond being merely seen as an appendage to Ronald Reagan. He was seen as a wimp, a word that followed him around like a Kick Me sign. Bush's softness had been a mark against him as far back as when President Gerald Ford had considered him as a vice president in 1974. In 1984, *Doonesbury* cartoonist Garry Trudeau ran a week of strips depicting George Bush as having "placed his manhood in a blind trust" in order to be Reagan's running mate and sign on to his more conservative policies.

Wimpiness was a low-grade problem for Bush until October 1987, when *Newsweek* magazine put the idea on doorsteps, newsstands, and waiting room tables in doctors' offices. Bush appeared on the cover of the magazine in a yellow windbreaker, piloting his boat, a sturdy gaze on his face as he fixed his jaw against the wind and adversity. (It looked like an ad for a local fish restaurant known for its scrod.) The headline: FIGHTING THE WIMP FACTOR. Ouch. The story was brutal. "Bush suffers from a potentially crippling handicap—a perception that he isn't strong enough or tough enough for the challenges of the Oval Office."

In the popular imagination, the office of the presidency requires masculinity and toughness. Republican voters in particular, care about this attribute. In polls, the GOP is associated more with power than Democrats, who are associated with warmth. The discussion of masculinity and the presidency is so elemental it often drives right to the trousers. When James Carville wanted to cut down candidate Barack Obama, he said that Hillary Clinton had a more complete set of male gonads than he did. When Kennedy described Adlai Stevenson, he chose an unflattering description of him as he emerged from the shower. When Sen. Marco Rubio tried to undermine Donald Trump, he questioned the size of his hands, hoping to conjure unflattering correlations with the size of Trump's penis. In related news, at Donald Trump rallies it was possible to see a man wearing a shirt that read, Donald Trump: Finally Someone with BALLS.

It was a little crazy to call Bush a wimp. He'd been a fighter pilot in World War II. When his plane was hit, he finished the bombing run and then parachuted out of his plane. You cannot do that if you are a wimp. Your chute won't open. Bush had a far more macho and heroic résumé than Reagan, but Reagan's rugged Western looks and his actor's sense of command made Bush seemed slight by comparison.

Bush had also run the CIA. He was U.S. envoy to China during the thaw. These are not jobs for a veteran of the fainting couch.

Nevertheless, Bush's prudent nature, and his difficulty marshaling declarative sentences, put it in the air that he didn't have the mettle for the job. In ways big and little, Bush's team tried to fashion a new image. For example, they would tell the Secret Service to let the press know when Bush was jogging so that reporters could witness him doing so—vigorous outdoor activity Reagan didn't do.

The most elaborate attempt at toughening Bush's image came in January 1988, just two weeks before the Iowa caucuses, in a preplanned fight with Dan Rather. The CBS anchor was scheduled to interview Bush on the *CBS Evening News*, a rare event. It was live because Ailes didn't want the network editing the exchange ahead of time to make Bush look bad. In the days leading up to it, the campaign worried that Bush was being set up. The interview was going to be a tough prosecution about his role in the Iran-Contra affair. In Ailes's account, he was even being told by people inside CBS that the interview was an attempt to end Bush's campaign, an unfounded conspiracy theory that put them in battle mode.[81]

By the time Ailes sat with Bush at the vice president's ceremonial office in the Capitol on the night of the interview, he was preparing the candidate for the highest stakes confrontation possible. "You've either got to go in there and go toe to toe with this guy," said Ailes to Bush, "or you're going back to Kennebunkport." In 1980, Reagan had grabbed the microphone in Nashua and energized his campaign while Bush sat passively looking on. This was Bush's chance to use a press confrontation to do the same.

When viewers watched the curtain go up on the *Evening News*, they saw Bush seated behind a vast desk supporting a gavel the size of Thor's hammer, signifying the vice president's ceremonial role as president of the Senate. A dark oil painting with an ornate frame hung on the wall behind him, and to his left on the desk sat another frame with a headshot of President Reagan, facing outward toward the camera, just as someone might display a picture of their spouse. To Bush's right, a television showed the broadcast as it was playing. Bush looked like the head of a junta that had just come to power in some country you're not sure you've heard of.

The key issue was whether Bush knew that the administration was trading arms for hostages. Bush would deny that he did in the Rather interview, but we know now from Bush's diaries and Jon Meacham's book, *Destiny and Power*, that the truth is different. Here's what Meacham wrote: "The record is clear that Bush was aware that the United States, in contravention of its own stated policy, was trading arms for hostages as part of an initiative to reach out to moderate elements in Iran."

Rather and Bush started bickering almost immediately as the candidate took issue with the piece that ran before the interview, which suggested Bush had been in a meeting where the swap was discussed. "You've impugned my integrity by suggesting with one of your little boards here, that I didn't tell the truth about what—what—Felix Rodriguez. You didn't accuse me of it, but you made that suggestion. And other people were in the meeting, including Mr. Nick Brady. And he has said that my version is correct. And so I find this to be a rehash and a little bit, if you'll excuse me, a misrepresentation on the part of CBS, who said you're doing political profiles on all the candidates. And then you come up with something that has been exhaustively looked into."

This gives you some flavor of Bush's staccato speech and how loaded he was for argument. He objected to the content and the way the content was framed, rebutted the content, but did all of it only partially. The two men went a few more rounds back and forth. They interrupted each other repeatedly. It was a live, ragged exchange.

Secretary of State George Shultz and Secretary of Defense Caspar Weinberger had been in meetings with Bush where they had argued against the weapons for hostages swap. He had not only been in the meetings, he'd not embraced their opposition. When the vice president insisted that he was out of the loop, both men (who didn't agree on much) were flabbergasted. "VP was part of it," Shultz said, according to notes in a meeting with Treasury Secretary Nick Brady. "Getting drawn into a web of lies. Blows his integrity. He's finished, then. Should be very careful about how he plays the loyal lieutenant role now."[82]

So, Rather was actually onto something in this interview, but Bush wouldn't relent. He was going toe to toe with Rather, as his media coach (and campaign podiatrist) Ailes had suggested.

As the fight raged on live television, Ailes motioned to Bush and held up a piece of paper that had written on it, in all caps, "Walked off the air." It was a signal for Bush to unleash a stinger he had in his back pocket: "It's not fair to judge my whole career by a rehash on Iran. How would you like it if I judge your career by those seven minutes when you walked off the set in New York?" (Rather, angered because CBS decided to shorten the news broadcast one night to air a tennis match, walked off the set and caused the network to go black for six minutes). Rather responded, "Well..." Bush kept on: "Would you like that?" Tough! The sea captain comes alive!

Afterward, the vice president was not sure how it had come across. He called his son, George W., who told him, "Man, you knocked it out of the park." Ted Koppel of *Nightline* said that Rather had allowed himself to be maneuvered into serving, quote, as "high priest in the ceremonial de-wimping of George Bush." Democratic strategist Robert Squier said "I think George Bush has decided that press bashing—is a blood sport. And since he needs to, sort of, pick up the manliness in his profile—he picked out—Dan Rather last night, and had a shot at him."

Bush Finds His Macho Against Dole

In the '88 nominating race, Bush came in third in Iowa. He had won the state in '80, so it was a particular blow for his campaign. He had to revive things in New Hampshire, the way Reagan had been forced to in 1980. It meant he'd have to go negative on Senate Republican leader Bob Dole.

Bush's advisers, Ailes and Atwater created an ad called "Senator Straddle." Every time Dole showed up on the screen there were two Dole faces pointed toward one another, with the word *Straddled* on the screen. The narrator cycled through a series of issues on which Dole had two positions, from an intermediate-range missile treaty to import oil fees. The hit on taxes was the most potent: "Bob Dole straddles, and he just won't promise not to raise taxes. And you know what that means."

When Bush was shown the ad, he said, "God. That's awful."[83] It was awful because the ad distorted Dole's positions. Still, the ad was a way to distinguish him from Dole in the tax-sensitive Granite State. Even the hint of a tax increase had hurt Reagan during his fight with Ford in 1976.

Bush didn't want to run the ad at first. He thought it was too hard. (Wimp!) His aides felt the ad was crucial, not just to winning the state but the entire nomination.[84] A New Hampshire victory was required to set the stage for the March 5 South Carolina primary as well as Super Tuesday on March 8.

Bush and his aides met Saturday before the primary. The candidate was informed that internal polls showed him two points down. After one last attempt at resisting, Bush caved. His wife, Barbara, and New Hampshire's Republican governor John Sununu had argued for running the ad.

But was it too late? Ordinarily it would have been too late to change plans for weekend commercials. Sununu had a relationship with one of the operators of Channel 9, though, and they agreed to substitute the straddle ad for the others scheduled Sunday through Tuesday.[85] Ailes had connections that helped get the ad on Boston networks. In the end, the buy was large enough so that the theoretical viewer in New Hampshire would have seen it eighteen times over the final three days.

Bush won New Hampshire 38 percent to 29 percent. After Dole grumbled over his loss, he took a famous shot at Bush in a postgame interview. NBC's Tom Brokaw asked Bush if he had any message for Dole. The vice president wished him well, especially since Dole was on the program with him at the time. Dole was asked the same question: did he have a message for Bush, with whom he shared the broadcast? Dole was not constrained by politeness. "Tell him to stop lying about my record," he said. (This is why candidates don't usually appear on programs together.)

If the Rather confrontation was public proof that Bush wasn't a wimp, the use of his ad against Dole in New Hampshire was internal proof that he could play hardball when it was required. The ad probably didn't turn the tide. A postelection analysis by Bush's pollster Richard Wirthlin showed that only two percent of voters mentioned the tax issue as important in their vote.[86] But the ad did serve as a shape-up exercise for Bush and his team. The candidate was now just fine with going negative. This would help in the battle to come.

Bush also got more comfortable using empty symbolism in New Hampshire. Shedding his elite image, he climed into the cab of an 18-wheeler and took it for a tentative ride. He put on a blue ski jacket and cap and threw snowballs. He also humbled himself. "Here I stand, warts and all," Bush said. "Maybe in some ways I'm a little more taciturn than I could be... Let me tell you, don't take the private side of me for a lack of passion and a lack of conviction about the United States of America... I don't always articulate, but I always do feel, and I care too much to leave now. Our work isn't done, so I'm working my heart out up here. I'm asking for your help."[87]

Where's George?

If you believe that successful presidential candidates are an answer to the deficiencies of the incumbent, Dukakis looked like a good model. Reagan was seen as a disengaged ideologue. Dukakis, by contrast, was pragmatic, detail oriented, and a manager at ease with technology and with a vision for the future. He was a so-called Atari Democrat, named after the popular Atari computer gaming console. The son of Greek immigrants, he was a devoted public servant. Dukakis also had an approachable side. He cut his own grass, took public transportation to work, and loved to talk about his outdated snow blower.

At the Democratic convention in Atlanta, in the summer of 1988, Dukakis and the Democratic crowd portrayed Bush as weak and ineffectual—a subordinate to Ronald Reagan. In his speech, Ted Kennedy listed what he saw as a series of shortcomings of the Reagan years, and then after each one asked: "Where's George?" Soon the crowd was chanting, "Where's George?"

James Baker, the Bush strategist, wrote in his memoirs, "They ridiculed him, both as a public figure and a human being. If that's how they wanted to play their hand, more power to them. The irony, however, is that many of the same people who jumped from their seats to cheer these mean-spirited attacks, would later whine about George's campaign being too negative."[88]

Baker is revising history. It's helpful to portray Bush's tough campaign as a mere counterpunch to a Democratic effort. But the Bush team had not been pushed into being tough on Dukakis because the Democrats had been tough on the vice president at their convention. From the start they'd planned to run a campaign to define Dukakis, because they were having such a hard time defining George Bush.

As early as May 1988, many months before the Democratic convention, Ailes had won Bush's approval for a plan to define Dukakis. Bush had been a little nervous about attacking so early. "It looks like we're desperate." Ailes said back to him, "We are desperate."[89]

Ailes wrote a memo outlining how they would define Dukakis. "On Election Day, the voter must know three things about Michael Dukakis. He will raise taxes. He is opposed to the death penalty, even for drug kingpins and murderers. And he is an extreme liberal. Even a pacifist on the subject of national defense."[90]

When Dukakis became the nominee, the Bush campaign dispatched a team of six young operatives to Massachusetts in a motor home. In a two-week blitz, they scoured twenty-five years of the daily

Boston Herald and the weekly *Phoenix*, and then twenty-five years of the *Boston Globe*, culling 135,000 quotes.

No morsel was too small, including the Brookline city council minutes of 1949, where they found a letter written by Dukakis protesting the U.S. intervention in Korean.[91] They also discovered that Kitty Dukakis, his wife, had written a statement in her yearbook about stopping male oppression. The opposition team assembled a 312-page textbook called—wait for it—*The Hazards of Duke*, the title a parody of the popular television show. This was the larger version of the material on that three-by-five card that Pinkerton had given Atwater.

Willie Horton for Vice President

The Dukakis opposition file included one case in which an African-American murderer named Willie Horton got a furlough from a Massachusetts penitentiary. On his weekend of liberty, he attacked a couple in Maryland, raping the woman and stabbing her fiancé. "If I can make Willie Horton a household name, we'll win the election," said Atwater.

This would become the most potent attack against Dukakis. The name first surfaced in a Democratic debate. Sen. Al Gore asked Dukakis about the furlough program. Eleven furloughed murderers bolted and decided not to go back to prison. Two of them had committed other murders while out on passes.

When Bush's research maven Pinkerton looked into the story further, he found a mountain of coverage in the Massachusetts papers. The Bush campaign raised the issue in an ad.

Was it a racially motivated attack to make so much of the prison furlough issue because its most violent abuser was black? After the election, the campaign managers met at Harvard to talk to journalists and academics about the presidential race. Atwater almost came to blows with Susan Estrich, the manager of the Dukakis campaign, over the use of racially charged stereotypes in the Horton ad, not just because Horton was an African-American but because he'd raped a white woman. Estrich pointed out that she herself had been a victim of rape and charged that the Bush team was playing on Southern fears about predatory black men.[92]

The Bush men wanted to make Horton an issue, but they never used his image. The mug shot image of Horton was used by an outside committee supporting Bush. The Bush team said they didn't know about its usage, but several people involved in the PAC had worked for Ailes. It is standard operating procedure for campaigns to let their surrogates know about or use information too hot for the campaign to use directly, though there is no evidence of that in this case.

Ailes loved the attack in general, but he made the case that the campaign would never have wanted to use Horton's image. The Bush ad just showed prisoners going through a revolving door. The campaign wanted people to be afraid that crime would increase. If they used the picture, it would have started a controversy over race.

Democrats tried to fight back. They pointed out that the furlough program had been instituted in Massachusetts by Dukakis's Republican predecessor. Ronald Reagan had also presided over such a program in California. Nearly forty states had similar programs.

As a congressman, Bush had helped found a chain of halfway houses and spoke warmly as vice president of the work they did. One inhabitant in these halfway houses committed murder. The Democrats ran their own ad: "In 1968, George Bush helped an ex-convict fund a halfway house for early release felons in Houston, Texas. In 1982, one of those prisoners raped and murdered a minister's wife."

It sounds like a tit-for-tat attack. If voters cared about Horton, they'd care about Bush's equivalent problem. But there's a built-in imbalance. In political battle the advantage often goes to whichever campaign controls the issue, not necessarily who is winning or losing on a given debate point. When you're playing on the other guy's turf, your response, as good as it may be, only keeps the issue in the conversation. When it's a conversation that is bad for your party, you're losing. In a face-off over which candidate was weak on crime, it was easier for voters to imagine that a Democrat was weak on crime, because that was what people already thought about Democrats. With the ad, Democrats were extending the debate on crime, which was good for Bush.

Going After Dukakis' Brain

In early August, Michael Dukakis would not release his medical records. Rumors had surfaced that he had been treated by a psychiatrist—that was why he wouldn't release the records. This wasn't on the 3×5 card, but it fell nicely into the strategy of raising questions about Dukakis. John Sununu, who would become Bush's chief of staff, earned his Nixon Dirty Tricks merit badge by suggesting reporters look into the reports, though he had no evidence there was any merit to them. Newspapers helped by making reference to Sen. Thomas Eagleton's mental health history and how it had disqualified him as McGovern's running mate in 1972.

When President Reagan was asked at a press conference about the issue, he said he "was not going to pick on an invalid." Reagan quickly apologized and said he was just joking, but Democrats thought the joke was a calculated effort to ignite the false rumor and spread it around Washington. There's no faster way to spread a rumor than to joke about it. People repeat the charge but don't have to worry about being right about it because they're only joking, after all.

Politically, the smear worked. It forced Dukakis to hold a press conference with his doctor to deny that he'd been treated for depression.

As the Bush team kept clicking through its list of attacks, they commissioned focus groups to see if they were working. The furlough attack was; voters were turning away from Dukakis and turning toward Bush. The campaign told the group that Dukakis had vetoed a bill requiring public school teachers to lead students in the Pledge of

Allegiance, and the reaction was strong. It was more evidence, as the Bush people had been saying, that Dukakis was out of touch with the mainstream. Bush also referred to Dukakis on the stump as a card-carrying member of the American Civil Liberties Union, a phrase that cleverly re-evoked the Joe McCarthy–era charges of subversion when traitors were labeled as card-carrying members of the Communist Party.

At rallies, Bush treated the flag question as the most vital one in America. Campaigning with President Reagan in Los Angeles, Bush said he would have signed the bill requiring teachers to say the Pledge of Allegiance, which Dukakis had vetoed in 1977.

"What is it about the Pledge of Allegiance that upsets him so much?" Bush asked to the approval of the crowd. "It is very hard for me to imagine that the Founding Fathers—Samuel Adams and John Hancock and John Adams—would have objected to teachers leading students in the Pledge of Allegiance to the flag of the United States."[93]

While Bush painted Dukakis as "the other," he wrapped himself in flags and apple pie, which is very gooey. He visited Findlay, Ohio, known as Flag City, and he visited a flag factory in New Jersey. "What would make Dukakis even easier to beat," wrote James Baker, "was that his campaign apparently didn't understand the importance of symbolism in American life and American politics."

Duke Tanks

Dukakis first responded to the attacks on his patriotism with seriousness. "Don't you think it's about time you came out from behind the flag," he said, "and tell us what you intend to do to provide basic health insurance for 37 million Americans?"[94] The response was in keeping with his vision of the campaign. Dukakis repeatedly said he would campaign on the issue of competency. He wouldn't engage in the gimmicky exchange of symbols. He would keep the conversation focused on what people cared about: issues.

Good notion. Bad idea. Bush was able to paint Dukakis as weak on every issue without eliciting a strong symbolic response. In the blunt exchange of a campaign, you can't talk your way into showing strength. You have to offer some kind of symbolism. Changing the subject wasn't working. Dukakis faced his own version of the wimp charge. The Bush team had argued that his overall weakness meant that he was not going to be able to keep America safe as commander in chief.

Dukakis didn't respond by getting in a fight with a broadcaster. Instead, his team finally put together a display for the press that was meant to burnish his credentials as a commander in chief by using symbols to demonstrate that he would keep America safe as president. Ninety reporters were hauled out to the General Dynamics facility in Sterling Heights, Michigan, on a clear September day. They pointed their bright faces and cameras towards a hangar-like building, from which emerged a sixty-eight-ton M1A1 Abrams Main Battle Tank.

In the tank stood the Democratic candidate. The the way the campaign hoped to stage the moment was to have Dukakis first appear in a stationary tank, without any headgear. That would be the photo opportunity. The advance team was mindful that you never want your candidate to be caught wearing a funny hat not of his own choosing. Then, after the press had gotten their shot, the candidate would move across the field in the tank wearing a tank commander's helmet, which was a mandatory safety requirement. As a nice perk, General Dynamics had written the candidate's name across the brow.

There was a problem with this strategy. Just because the campaign wanted the photo of the day to be the helmet-free image of the candidate that didn't mean that photographers and television cameramen wouldn't find the picture of the candidate peeking out of the turret wearing a mushroom cap on his head more fetching and send that one to their editors.

As the tank rumbled, Dukakis stood through the hatch, shot smiles, and pointed forward with his index finger. It was not a commanding image. He either looked like someone trying to be something he wasn't, or he looked like just exactly who he was: a man who enjoyed pushing around his lawn mower but who had no business being jostled about in a tank like a bobble-head toy. It looked desperate and grasping, like what a person who had no idea what being commander in chief would think was required of a commander in chief.

The reporters brought to witness the event doubled over in laughter, according to Josh King, a former presidential advance man who made a study of the debacle in his book *Off Script*. "Nice event," one staffer said to the advance man in charge. "It may have cost us the election, but besides that it was great."[95]

The next day there wasn't much coverage of the candidate's morning speech on foreign policy which demonstrated his knowledge and vision. The lead in the *New York Times* read, "Forget John Wayne and Clint Eastwood. Forget Rambo. Meet Macho Mike Dukakis."[96] The helmet was later referred to as a "Snoopy dog hat."[97] Bush's advisers saw the video of Dukakis in the tank and immediately turned it into an ad. In the spot, the narrator describes all the weapons systems Dukakis did not support, while the footage of him riding in the tank plays.

The ad was so good, the Bush team sat on it like an egg. They let it hatch during the third game of the World Series.

Do Not Tank Your Candidate

A "Dukakis in the tank" moment, that's how it has come to be known. It's the expression used in politics to describe a self-inflicted wound in the art of campaign stagecraft. The lesson is supposed to be: don't put your candidate in an implausible situation that doesn't fit with his character, or step on his carefully thought-through policy speech. But the lesson is larger than that. Don't let your opponent define you so that you have to make up the deficit with emergency pantomimes. Respond and respond quickly.

The Dukakis campaign had been forewarned. In *Bad Boy*, the story of Lee Atwater's life, John Brady relates that Pug Ravenel, a

Democrat who lost to Atwater in South Carolina campaigns, wrote to the Dukakis campaign early on. His letter advised, "My very strong belief is that Lee Atwater is the premier negative strategist in American politics. I have the deep suspicion that Atwater will begin hitting Dukakis very early. Perhaps even before the convention. If Mike does not respond right away, he could risk having the negatives well set in the minds of Americans before he could begin to change them."[98]

So why hadn't Dukakis taken the advice? He wanted to run a positive campaign, at least in public. The Reagan years were divisive, and he wanted to give the American people an uplifting message.

That's a noble goal, but being uplifting was not all that was required in that nasty stub end of an election. "Anyone who felt good about American politics after the 1988 presidential campaign probably also enjoys train wrecks," said *Newsweek*. "Or maybe a day at the beach watching an oil slick wash ashore."[99]

The campaign was driven by defining Dukakis negatively, not by building up George Bush. As Baker wrote, "I make no apologies for going after Dukakis on prison furloughs, the Pledge, or anything else. He led with his chin on a lot of these issues, and we used them to take him out."

The successful effort to define Dukakis was precise and devastating, and it proved that George Bush was no wimp. Though Bush did worry to his diary about the charge that he had taken the low road. "I don't know what we could do differently," he said to his diary. "We had to define the guy."

1972—Vote for Muskie or He'll Cry

AP Photo, File

On February 26, 1972, dozens of reporters gathered in the snow around a flatbed truck in downtown Manchester, New Hampshire. Locals were accustomed to sudden gatherings of reporters. They return every four years like cicadas. But even by historical standards this was a strange happening. The night before, the Democratic front-runner, Sen. Edmund Muskie, had called the group to meet at 9:30 the next morning in front of the offices of the *Manchester Union Leader* newspaper. He'd rented the truck and the public address system and warned that news would be forthcoming.

When the candidate arrived, it was still snowing, wilting notebooks and causing reporters to curse their ballpoint pens, which had stalled in the weather. The senator mounted the truck in overcoat and scarf with a doily of snow in his bushy hair from the six-block walk he had just completed. A radio reporter lifted her microphone, wrapped in white plastic to protect it from the snow. In the footage of the moment, it looks like someone is trying to feed Muskie a Tootsie Pop.

The senator launched. He denounced the *Union Leader*'s publisher, William Loeb, as a "gutless coward" and threatened him with violence. "It's fortunate for him he's not on this platform beside me," he said.

The *Union Leader* was the largest paper in New Hampshire, reportedly reaching 60 percent of the state. Loeb, a staunch conservative with a bald head shaped like an angry egg, had been attacking Muskie for months, calling him "Moscow Muskie" and layering on ad hominem personal attacks of the kind Rush Limbaugh has used to accumulate such a tidy fortune. As one humorist put it, the *Manchester Union Leader* "opposes Muskie, his wife and any great-grandchildren the Muskies may some day have."[100]

Muskie hadn't been in New Hampshire much. As a senator from Maine, he hoped his neighbor status would give him a cushion in the state. Plus he was the front-runner, which meant he had to compete everywhere, and he'd been pumping hands in Florida and Illinois. In his absence, the attacks sunk in.

Recently Loeb had escalated. He had published an editorial on the front page of the paper charging Muskie with using an ethnic slur, and he'd printed a story about Muskie's wife. "He has lied about me and my wife," said Muskie, calling Loeb "a mudslinging, vicious and gutless liar."

The small band of Muskie boosters who gathered with the reporters applauded, but their gloves muffled the the clapping, making it sound like someone was beating a rug. "Give 'em hell, Ed," yelled one. Another amplified, "Give 'em holy hell."

When Muskie moved to the topic of his wife, he broke up. He talked and then he paused. Was he crying? It was hard to tell in the snow. "This man doesn't walk," he said of Loeb. "He crawls." The word *crawls* becomes onomatopoetic as it crawls out of Muskie's mouth.

In popular campaign lore, this is the moment where the wheels shot off of Ed Muskie's campaign wagon of inevitability and went rolling down the lane. It is treated as a gaffe from which he never recovered. That's true, but there's more to it than a momentary fracture. The big lesson of the Muskie Cry is about how tough it is to be a front-runner. Expectations force you to spread yourself too thin and raise the bar on how well you have to do to meet them. When you're the front-runner, winning sometimes isn't enough.

More Democratic Candidates Than Voters

Nineteen seventy-two looked like a good year for Democrats. Domestic economic woes and President Nixon's vacillation on issues from busing to affirmative action had led to big GOP losses in the 1970 midterms. Nixon had been elected in 1968 promising to end the war in Vietnam, and instead he had escalated the conflict by invading Cambodia in 1970, leading to riots on college campuses. The election of 1972 was the first election in which the "Twenty-Six-ers" could vote; these were the eighteen- to twenty-one-year-olds who had been let into the process by the Twenty-Sixth Amendment.

With so much opportunity, a lot of Democrats wanted to run for president. The field included Senators Henry "Scoop" Jackson of Washington, Edmund Muskie, George McGovern of South Dakota, and Hubert Humphrey and Eugene McCarthy of Minnesota. John Lindsay, the Republican mayor of New York who had switched parties, was running, as was Los Angeles mayor Sam Yorty. George Wallace, governor of Alabama, was also in the mix. House Ways and Means chairman Wilbur Mills had launched a campaign, as had Rep. Shirley Chisholm, the first African-American woman elected to Congress and the first African-American major-party candidate to run for president.

"There are more candidates than voters," Russell Baker joked.[101] Humorist Art Buchwald quoted an imaginary New Hampshire voter:

"I've got an appointment with John Lindsay to shake hands tomorrow. He already shook hands with me last week in Concord for CBS, but his people say he wants to shake hands again in Waterville Valley for NBC."

Muskie led the pack. In January, he topped Ted Kennedy 32–27 in the Gallup Poll. McGovern languished at 3 percent; he was regularly referred to as having "only the dimmest chance of being the Democratic presidential nominee."[102] Kennedy had declined to run; he was still reeling from the political fallout after the 1969 car accident on Chappaquiddick Island in which his passenger, Mary Jo Kopechne, drowned. Pollsters asked about him anyway, though, because they couldn't help themselves. Every race has a Titan Not Running, whether it's Gerald Ford in 1980, Mario Cuomo in 1988 and 1992, Colin Powell in 1996, Al Gore in 2008, Sarah Palin in 2012, or Joe Biden in 2016. Editors in New York ask themselves about these candidates over lunch with each other. Columnists sitting at the next table who overhear this chatter are moved to speculate. Pollsters really don't want to be left behind, so they ask about these candidates, and their findings are then cause for another round of speculation. This usually culminates in emergency reports that the White Knight candidate is absolutely running, which only momentarily precede official announcement from the candidate that he or she is never running ever again even to catch a bus.

In 1968 Muskie had been Hubert Humphrey's vice presidential running mate. In the intervening years he'd served as kind of the Leader in Waiting. That status meant that on Election Eve in 1970 he delivered what was effectively the Democratic response—a high-profile speech dissecting Nixon. The other candidates envied Muskie and the national stature that response conferred on him.

But being a front-runner is a pain. It obligates you to a lot of compulsory exercises. If you're the likely nominee you can't camp out in one state. You have to campaign everywhere, opening up vulnerability in the states where your opponents *can* camp out. This would bite George W. Bush in New Hampshire in 2000. He had to campaign everywhere, while John McCain could just focus on the Granite State.

A front-runner also has to be cautious and appeal to everyone. Muskie was against the war, but he was not such a radical antiwar candidate that he would be associated with the agitators voters were blaming for unrest in the cities where riots, marches, and crime they thought resulted from permissive liberalism was rampant. Candidates with an eye on the general election—when you're a front-runner, that's the kind of candidate you are—didn't want to be associated with the big-city Democratic machines that were getting blamed for all that lawlessness.

When the front-runner is careful it creates appetites. The electorate wants candidates who seem authentic. This is a problem with which Hillary Clinton is chronically familiar. John Gilligan, the governor of Ohio, described the timidity of Muskie's appeal, or lack of it: "Another poultice and another nostrum, only with a little nutmeg stirred in." (Bad for politics but a delicious nightcap during the holidays).

Sen. George McGovern, on the other hand, was saying things that attracted the energy in the party—the black vote, the antiwar vote. He was pointed. He was talking about a political movement that would restore democracy and the American promise.

The Canuck Letter

The first sign that things weren't going well for Muskie came in Iowa, where he beat McGovern by only thirteen points in the precinct caucuses. Muskie should have done better, the pundits concluded. (Some people mark this as the first time the Iowa caucuses made an impact. They were a tiny little thing then, but with each race the results have grown in stature. By the 2016 race, the caucuses had grown to the point that Microsoft sponsored a media center where correspondents from Japan talked over Dutch television anchors.)

Two weeks before the vote in New Hampshire, with McGovern rising, Muskie was hit with a major scandal. The *Union Leader* published a letter that purported to be from a man in Florida who had been with Muskie while he visited a drug rehabilitation center. The letter was printed in childlike handwriting and it read as follows:

> Dear Mr Loeb—
>
> I saw you on TV the other night and my friends [*sic*] father gets your newspaper. We went to Ft Lauderdale to meet Sen Muskie—we were right beside him at Seed House when one of the men asked him what did he know about blacks and the problems with them—he didn't have any in Maine—a man with the senator said No, not blacks but we have CANNOCKS
>
> What did he mean? We asked—Mr Muskie laughed, and said come to New England and see.

Some French-Canadians consider the term *Canuck* to be offensive. It's like calling a Polish person a Polack. Forever after, the letter would be known as the Canuck Letter, and it suggested that Muskie was in on the joke, making fun of Canucks.

Manchester had a considerable French-Canadian population—somewhere between 30 and 40 percent of the vote, according to the papers at the time. Loeb editorialized next to the letter: "We have always known that Senator Muskie was a hypocrite, but we never expected to have it so clearly revealed as in this letter sent to us from Florida."[103]

The Muskie campaign freaked out. They commissioned an informal poll, calling voters to see what they thought. They learned the candidate was bleeding. Muskie's internal polling showed that he had lost ten points. The *Boston Globe* did a poll, and it found Muskie dropping by double digits. It was such a swerve in the numbers that the *Globe* commissioned another poll to double-check the finding. The second poll ratified the first.

This was the emergency that put Muskie in a mood to ankle his way down the snowy Manchester street and climb up on the flatbed that he had ordered to be parked in front of the *Union Leader* offices. He brought with him three Franco-American supporters and the director of the drug treatment center in Florida to vouch for his character and to say that the account contained in the letter never happened.

"I remember as a boy being called a Polack," Muskie said. "It was a term of derision. I hated it. I would never use a term like that with respect to another ethnic group."[104]

They Should Have Known: Nixon!

The reason that Muskie didn't remember using that term is that the episode was entirely made up. The letter sent to the publisher had been penned by one of Nixon's henchmen.

One of the favorite techniques of the Nixon gang was to write anonymous letters from various people. It was just one of the many ways they monkeyed with other campaigns. Sometimes they would order pizzas to the opposition's campaign offices, or a campaign manager for a rival would get a phone call in the middle of the night informing him that his driver had arrived and was waiting in the lobby. He had ordered no such driver. When they were really in a mood they put on ski masks and broke into the headquarters of the Democratic Party at the Watergate.

Parents, when you read *Whistlestop* to your children as all right-thinking parents should please skip this next sentence. This was known to those in the business as Dirty Tricks and more colloquially as something more coarse that Sen. Ted Cruz referred to in the 2016 race as "copulating with a rodent."

Famed Watergate reporters Carl Bernstein and Bob Woodward of the *Washington Post* published a story about the Canuck Letter in October 1972, long after Muskie had bowed out. They reported that law enforcement officials said that the Canuck Letter was a fabrication and probably the best example of political spying and sabotage conducted on behalf of President Nixon's reelection. It was directed by officials of the White House and the Committee for the Re-Election of the President.

The main author of the sneakiness was a Nixon press aide named Ken Clawson, who'd bragged to a female colleague of Woodward and Bernstein's that he had been behind the letter. The editor in chief of Loeb's newspaper conceded that Clawson had been useful to the paper in connection with the Canuck Letter.

Clawson later denied it, but that may have had more to do with his personal life than with having written the letter. Clawson had bragged about the dirty trick while having drinks with an unmarried woman in her apartment. When he heard that fact was going to be included in the newspaper, Clawson famously pleaded to be kept out of the story by saying, "I have a wife and a family and a dog and a cat."

An important aside: Woodward and Bernstein's *Washington Post* article was published on October 10, 1972, long after the New Hampshire primary was over, but less than a month before the general election. Woodward and Bernstein revealed the president's reelection campaign was behind a phony letter that destroyed the Democratic Party front-runner, and yet Nixon went on to win that election. If that happened today, a new cable news network would be formed simply for the purpose of completely melting down while covering the scandal.

Jane and Big Daddy

The Canuck Letter wasn't what made Muskie cry, though. "I've been in politics all my life," he said on that platform. "I'm not a child.

I know the sorts of things that happen. I've got to be prepared to take them. What really got me was this editorial attacking my wife." Muskie read the editorial's headline, which was BIG DADDY'S JANE.

Loeb had not written the editorial. It was a piece from the December 27 issue of *Newsweek*, run several weeks later in the *Union Leader*. In the *Newsweek* piece, Jane Muskie was traveling with reporters, many of them from the society columns, and she was letting her hair down in the company of this chatty group.

She said, at the beginning of one conversation, "Let's all tell dirty jokes." She then asked for her purse so she could have a cigarette. She confessed to liking a few drinks before dinner and then a drink after dinner. She said, "Because the next day, everything seems to work just right." Who among us can't agree with that?

Muskie's wife referred to drinking with a certain expertise unfamiliar to the amateur. "I can't mix booze and wine or I get a headache and have little dreams." And she called her husband, jokingly, Big Daddy. He was many years her senior.

Magazine writers of the time were not kind. "Mrs. Muskie is plumpish despite daily drills in Yoga, which find her balancing on her shoulders in hotel rooms along the campaign trail. On her feet and speech-making, Mrs. Muskie is no spellbinder."[105] That's not very nice, and that's a shame because Jane Muskie sounds like a lot of fun. In any stable country, all of this behavior would only accrue to the benefit of the weary candidate. It has long been the stable foundation of democracies that the spouse of the president should be fun at parties.

Muskie thought so, too, and he thought reprinting a two-month-old editorial on the front page of the *Union Leader* was an attempt to call his wife's character into question as a way to hurt him.

It was when he came to this section of his public reading in the snow that he got wobbly. "He's talking about my wife," he said, pausing and then trailing off. "But it's fortunate for him he's not on this platform beside me...A good woman." He fought to regain composure, and while he did, it took so long, a supporter of Muskie's shouted out, "Who's with Muskie?" And the crowd cheered while he gathered himself together.

Tracks of His Tears

Loeb didn't let too many more snowflakes fall before seizing the opportunity. "Boy! That's not the man I want to have with his finger on the nuclear button." Bob Dole, the Chairman of the National Republican Committee, said the display indicated once again that Senator Muskie lacked stability.[106]

Muskie had been running a kind of reasoned, cool-headed campaign. He was frequently referred to as Lincolnesque. This shattered that image. "Muskie must have known that it is doubtful that most television viewers seeing a grown man standing in a snowstorm and unable to speak, would automatically say to themselves, 'That's my kind of president,' " wrote David Broder of the *Washington Post*.[107]

It also didn't play well against the images of the incumbent. While Muskie was breaking down, Nixon was over in China looking like a strong chief executive. On the evening news, Nixon was astride the world and Muskie was melting in the snow.

Teddy White interviewed Muskie about the incident for *The Making of the President 1972*. "I'd been down to Florida, then I flew to Idaho," explained Muskie. "Then I flew to California, then I flew back to Washington to vote in the Senate, and I flew back to California, and then I flew into Manchester and I was hit with this 'Canuck' story. I'm tough physically, but no one could do that—it was a bitch of a day. The staff thought I should go down to the *Union Leader* to reply to that story. If I was going to do it again, I'd look for a campaign manager, a genius, a schedule-maker who has veto power over a candidate's own decisions. You got to have a czar. For Christ's sake, you got to pace yourself. I was just goddamned mad and choked up over my anger."[108]

In the oral history of the campaign, the staffers tell a different story. Tony Podesta, who ran the show in New Hampshire, said the whole assault on Loeb was Muskie's idea. The candidate rang him up and barked orders. "I want a flatbed truck. I want a sound system. I want to go stand out in front of that newspaper and I want to tell that guy what I think of him."[109]

"I'm probably not the first person to say he had a bit of a temper," remembers Podesta. "And he was—sort of pounding on the table and raising his voice and was really furious with Loeb and furious with what he had said about Jane, and furious with the fact that he'd attacked, you know, brought his family into it. It was sort of really a low blow."

There was also a strategic reason for the outburst. Muskie was being criticized for being too calm and collected and reasonable. He was too aloof. "Muskie is not getting to the guts of the voter," Governor John Gilligan said.[110] This was a chance for him to show passion. "My stomach told me that it was time to say publicly what I thought of him," Muskie later said. So much of the coverage was about what the candidates' gut told them and what the voters felt in their guts, Muskie was making a gastrointestinal pitch.

Troublesome moments like this present a candidate with a presidential challenge. Take the lumps and let it go, or do something to address the new situation. Overreact and you make the problem worse. Do nothing and you look insulated and clueless. This is what being president is like every day.

Muskie's team reacted by cocooning. "I shouldn't have broken down like that," Muskie said to Podesta, who responded, "Oh, you know, it's a human. You're being a human being. It's a human situation." He tried to convince the candidate that he looked authentic and real. "This was not a canned political speech," Podesta said. "This was not something your speech writer wrote for you, you know. You're speaking from the gut; that's what people wanna hear from you. So I said, 'Don't worry about it. It's a good thing.' "

Muskie's wife, Jane, tried to defend him. "The question is, do you want a man in charge of this country who's a human being or one who never allows emotion to come in?"[111]

Did Muskie Really Cry?

Is this one of those situations where the first reports were wrong and the candidate got a raw deal as a result? George Herbert Walker Bush was reported to have not recognized a supermarket scanner when confronted with one. He knew what the scanner was, but the story lived on anyway.

I watched the Muskie video, and it's clear he is very emotional. His voice cracks when he talks about his wife. He has to stop for ten seconds or more, and he appears to wipe his eyes and nose. Had he not reacted to the cheap shot at his wife, who was collateral damage to his ambition, we might have reason to wonder about his emotional relationships and the coldness of his heart. Alas, that wasn't the way they thought about things back then. The charge from his opponents was that an emotional candidate was disqualified from being president.

Muskie was clearly emotional, but his supporters, trying to cover for their man, wisely focused on the narrow fact of whether he shed actual tears. They said he shed no tears. It was the snow. They hoped that if they could refute the specific fact, it would dispel fears his opponents were trying to raise about his underlying emotionalism.

The *Washington Post*'s David Broder is credited with putting the idea in play. In his dispatch, he makes Muskie sound like a bubbling mess. "With tears streaming down his face and voice choked with emotion, Sen. Edmund S. Muskie (D-Maine) stood in the snow outside the *Manchester Union Leader* this morning and accused its publisher of making vicious attacks on him and his wife." "Streaming down his face" suggests something altogether different than what appears visible on the video. Other reporters had written about the crying, but they had put it further down in the piece, and some didn't mention it at all.

No one else had the impact that David Broder did. He was the leading political reporter of the day. His stature inserted this idea into papers across the country in which his column was syndicated.

With a little historical perspective, the Muskie team is less defensive. "I've always felt that, although he denied that he cried, I think it was clear that tears did come to his eyes," said George Mitchell, a top Muskie aide at the time. Mitchell was appointed to the Senate in 1980, after Muskie resigned to become secretary of state.[112]

Muskie's Real Problem

What was probably even more powerful was the piece Broder wrote two days later that had nothing to do with the waterworks. The headline read, SUPPORT FOR MUSKIE WAVERS IN NEW HAMPSHIRE. He'd interviewed seventy-five people. This was the first piece to say that Muskie was in trouble. Jack Germond of the *Baltimore Sun*, another legendary campaign reporter, penned a similar piece, and then Johnny Apple produced a story along the same lines for the *New York Times*, talking to more than one hundred people around the state. Apple described Muskie's support this way: "Those who support him do so grudgingly, without passion, like children forced to choose between broccoli and cabbage." (Broccoli, obviously.)

It was not fun to be a voter interviewed by the *New York Times* for this race. The *Times* described one of these voters talking about the candidates as "a dumpy woman behind the counter of a North Conway luncheonette." Another one is described as "an Irish-American housewife who lived in a tacky Dover apartment."

None of the pieces said voters weren't supporting Muskie because he cried. Some voters were turned off, but other voters thought it humanized him. The most troubling voter emotion recorded was a lack of enthusiasm. Muskie was lighting no one's hair on fire, McGovern, on the other hand, was working the state hard. He was the one for whom voters seemed to be showing enthusiasm.

New Hampshire Result

In the end, Muskie won New Hampshire with 46 percent of the vote. McGovern got only 37 percent. A win, right? The problem is that when you're the front-runner, and you're from a neighboring state, 46 percent of the vote is underwhelming. Also, at the beginning of the race, McGovern only had 3 percent of the vote. So while Muskie was falling short, McGovern was climbing to great heights. "Senator George McGovern may have won more in losing than Sen. Edmund S. Muskie gained in winning," said the *Portland Press Herald*.[113]

At this point, campaigns complain that it's the press setting expectations for the front-runner that are arbitrary. The problem in this case is that it was Muskie's own New Hampshire in-state campaign manager, Maria Carrier, who had predicted that he would at least get 50 percent. Muskie had essentially backed her assessment. This is now known as the Maria Carrier rule, which is that you just never predict how you're going to do unless it's well short of how you actually expect to do.

Carrier compounded things when the results came in and she told reporters that the result was "heartbreaking." Muskie did not sound like a winner in the aftermath: "We didn't have the time or the resources to make a maximum showing in New Hampshire. We deliberately sacrificed the possibility of a maximum showing in order to have some resources left for other primaries."[114]

The *Wall Street Journal* said, "The New Hampshire results, instead of providing hoped-for Muskie momentum for these battles ahead [the upcoming primaries in Florida, Illinois and Wisconsin] have raised psychological and political hurdles he must fight to overcome." The *Journal* also had this great piece of punditry: "Yet Mister McGovern still stands only the slimmest of chances of winning the nomination, he's almost surely too liberal for the bulk of the party."[115]

The fall comes hard to a former front-runner because all the hype is used against him. "The American voter's quite a guy, isn't he?" asked Scoop Jackson after the New Hampshire primary. "Only last week a national magazine said that Senator Muskie had all the states except a couple lined up. Last night, the crystal ball just broke. Despite the polls, the American voter spoke and made it a wide open contest."[116]

As the candidates headed for the other primaries, Muskie struggled to fight back, and the crying episode dogged him. Groucho Marx said, "He's seriously thinking of running for President? That would make a great comedy sketch. The politicians are providing the comedy that the comedians used to provide." When the senator made it to Florida he was reportedly greeted by bumper stickers that read, Vote for Muskie, or He'll Cry.

Bob Dole, who enjoyed a laugh at his opponent's expense, said "I don't blame Muskie for crying. If I had to run against Mr. Nixon, I'd do a lot of crying, too."[117]

How did McGovern respond? Well, since he was a soft man of the left, you might have expected him to offer his opponent a hug. But since he was a B-24 Liberator pilot who flew missions over Germany during World War II and won the Distinguished Flying Cross, he was a little tougher than that. When Muskie charged that the voters who had propelled George Wallace to a victory in Florida were bigots, and called Wallace "a demagogue of the worst kind," McGovern responded by pushing him into the street: "People got the impression Muskie was crying again instead of responding to a problem we've got to do something about."

The reason McGovern thought Muskie might cry again was that he came in fourth in Florida, the state he'd been working on while neglecting New Hampshire. The *Bridgeport Post* said that coming out of Florida, Muskie had "reverse momentum,"[118] which is so bad I don't think it's even a concept in physics.

At a press corps dinner at the time, a song about Muskie put it this way: "When the voters see Abe Lincoln start to cry / It's no wonder that they wonder why I try. / I won up in New Hampshire by a margin not too great / And tear-dropped into Florida and blew the whole damn state."

He Came Across as Fuzzy

The primaries continued and Muskie even won in Illinois, but his campaign was out of gas. He tried to show more energy on the stump and no more Lincolnesque nice guy, but that just led to altercations with voters. "Play the other side of the record," one student shouted at his speech. "What's your position on busing?" another student called out. "I just gave it to you," said Muskie. "Give it again," the student said. "I still don't understand it."[119] (At this point, Muskie might have come out for the repeal of the Twenty-Sixth Amendment.)

So why did Muskie lose? The main reason seems to be that he spread himself too thin, didn't stir enthusiasm, and took New Hampshire for granted. Here's what *Time* magazine said: "He'd come across as fuzzy, an establishment kind of politician in a year when voters want revolt. And he's been unable to put his brand on any issue that can attract the fed-up, turned-off voter." In this election year, younger voters who had been agitating on campus turned out for the first time. They wanted to hear somebody talking about getting out of Vietnam, and Muskie was just out of sync with that. He wasn't the most liberal candidate on the Vietnam question.

Here's how George Mitchell explained Muskie's problems: "Muskie's appeal was to reason, to legislative accomplishment, to sort of general policies in the best interest of the country. The primary electorate was interested in emotion, passion, strong views on every issue. And the general election candidate who tries to navigate a nomination process by not being clear on very hot-button issues finds it difficult in that nominating process." The *Dallas Times Herald* noted Muskie's "seeming lack of commitment to anything in particular. 'Trust Muskie,' he begged. 'Why?' " the majority of New Hampshire voters replied.

There's a bit of a contradiction at work here. Muskie wasn't emotional enough for liberal voters, but crying was seen as an emotional display too soupy for a man who sought the presidency.

Hunter S. Thompson characterized the end of the Muskie campaign this way: "Midway in the final week of the campaign, Muskie himself began dropping hints that he knew he was doomed... When the sense of depression began spreading like a piss-puddle on concrete, he invited the campaign-press regulars to help him celebrate his fifty-eighth birthday at a small hotel on a snowy night in Green Bay. But the party turned sour when his wife mashed a piece of the birthday cake in the face of *Newsweek* reporter Dick Stout, saying, 'One good turn deserves another, eh Dick?' "[120]

Fifteen years after the campaign was over, David Broder wrote about what happened in New Hampshire. "It is now clear that the incident should have been placed in a different context: Muskie was victimized by the classic dirty trick that had been engineered by agents of the distant and detached President Nixon. The Loeb editorial that had brought Muskie out in the snowstorm had been based on a letter forged by a White House staff member intent on destroying Muskie's credibility. But we didn't know that, and we didn't work hard enough to find out... Had those facts been known, I might have described Muskie in different terms, not as a victim of his over-ambitious campaign strategy and his too-human temperament, but as the victim of a fraud, managed by operatives of a frightened and unscrupulous President. That story surely would have had a different impact... Unwittingly, I did my part in the work of the Nixon operatives in helping destroy the credibility of the Muskie candidacy."[121]

Would things have been different if the Muskie cry hadn't been a media obsession? Perhaps, but Muskie had a lackadaisical campaign: He tried to be all things to all people, he didn't organize the state (at the last minute he had to bus supporters in from Rhode Island), and McGovern outhustled him. He showed his passion in his work ethic. In forty-seven days of campaigning, Muskie spent thirteen in New Hampshire and McGovern spent twenty-four.

Long after the campaign was over, Mrs. Muskie reflected on the moment: "I'm not happy driving through Manchester, New Hampshire, even today."

1972—Eighteen-Day Nightmare

Time, inc.

On July 13, 1972, twenty-one members of the McGovern for President staff collapsed around the table in the conference room at the Doral Hotel in Miami Beach, Florida. The night before had been exciting and late. Delegates to the Democratic convention had put their candidate over the top. It was the culmination of an underdog campaign against the party establishment and a more recent convention fight challenging the winner-take-all rules that had given McGovern the California delegates.

Their bleary task was to help the South Dakota senator pick a running mate—his first presidential-level decision. The floor was thrown open to suggestions. There were a lot of jokes. "The mood was light, relaxed to the point of frivolity," wrote Gary Hart, McGovern's campaign manager and future Colorado senator. "Victory was being savored for the first time in the light of day. It was like a group of fraternity boys who had spent most of the night successfully stealing the rival school's mascot."

Finally, Frank Mankiewicz, a veteran of Bobby Kennedy's campaign and the adult in the room, called everyone to order by ringing a glass with a spoon. "We have three hours to choose the deputy commander of the free world," he said. They had to hurry, because fighting for those California delegates had eaten up a lot of the campaign's time and attention. McGovern would have to reveal his sidekick to the world that night at the convention. He could not announce a player to be named later.

There was something hollow about the vice presidential culling process, Names were discussed, but they all had the same defining quality: they were all not Ted Kennedy. Mankiewicz described just how much the candidate and his team wanted the Massachusetts senator. "The only question on the staff about Teddy was how many fingers they'd be willing to lose to have him."

Kennedy had said no, but after McGovern won, the nominee thought he could help his Senate colleague reconsider. Kennedy said no again. McGovern called a number of his other colleagues, and they weren't game, either: Humphrey, Mondale, Muskie all said no. It might have been that Nixon seemed unbeatable in the general election. It might also have seemed that McGovern was just too liberal to get elected.

Whatever the reason, McGovern had just a few hours and needed a running mate. This was not the way you were supposed to pick the understudy for the leader of the free world.

Hart was particularly undone. He had promised himself the process would not be rushed. Vice presidents mattered. President Nixon had been Eisenhower's vice president, and two out of the last four presidents had come to power through the vice presidency. Hart remembered how chaotic Kennedy's selection of Johnson had been in 1960. Vice Presidential selections in the past had always been a little chaotic because the running-mate was often chosen at the convention to heal party fractures after tough convention fights. McGovern's team had more time than nominees in the past, they just didn't use it. Now Hart was presiding over an even more chaotic process. "What had started as a happy day putting frosting on the cake, was disintegrating into a nightmare."[122]

I'll Go with Tom

Finally McGovern emerged from his bootless phone calls getting turned down by his Senate colleagues. "I think I'll go with Tom," he said. He meant Tom Eagleton, the forty-two-year-old senator from Missouri. McGovern, who had also pledged to avoid the messy way vice presidents had been picked in the past, chose Eagleton after considering him for less than an hour. When he called to offer his running mate the job, the conversation lasted sixty-seven seconds, which is only a little longer than it takes to order and pay for a roast beef sandwich with cheese and no mayo. "You must be kidding," Eagleton said when McGovern called. "Before you change your mind, I accept." When McGovern rang off the phone, the clock started on the timer of a bomb that would detonate in eighteen days and destroy the McGovern campaign.

Today campaigns sift through a candidate's every Facebook posting and video rental record from the '80s to make sure they returned all the videocassettes fully rewound. Campaigns are so careful because of what happened to Tom Eagleton—or what became known as the Eagleton Affair, after *Time* magazine had called it that on the cover.

It is a perfect example of how not to pick a nominee and of how not to do damage control once you've made a campaign blunder.

The McGovern Insurgency

McGovern had run a successful insurgent campaign, coming from nowhere to beat a strong field. He'd done it by building a coalition of minorities and first-time younger voters. The Twenty-Sixth

Amendment had opened up the vote to the twenty-five million voters between ages eighteen and twenty-one. He was proving that there was a silent majority on the liberal side, too, waiting to break the lock of big money and replace the self-dealing insiders. "If people could be made to feel there was still hope through working in the system, they might draw encouragement and inspiration," wrote Gary Hart in his campaign history *Right From the Start*.

The challenge for McGovern was that conservatives were opposed to the silent liberal majority. Even in the Democratic Party, some complained the South Dakota senator was too far to the left on issues like abortion and marijuana and Vietnam. It was said that he wanted to legalize pot. He didn't. He just wanted to decriminalize it. It was said that he favored abortion on demand. He didn't. He just believed that it should be up to the states to decide that issue.

The tensions within the Democratic Party were on full display when McGovern campaigned in the Nebraska primary. He asked former governor Frank Morrison to help him set the record straight on these two issues. Introducing McGovern, Morrison said, "We have in our state tonight one of the finest young men in America. He is a great patriot. A highly decorated war hero who loves his country and wants to serve us as president. But he has been subjected to a vicious campaign of smears and innuendo. They say George McGovern is for the legalization of marijuana, but I say—"

At this point, younger voters in the audience cheered for the legalization of marijuana. That interrupted Morrison. And then he continued on: "George McGovern does not advocate the legalization of marijuana." This then excited boos in the audience. The gov. then tried again. "They say George McGovern is for abortion on demand, but I tell you—" Again, huge applause for abortion on demand. When he pointed out that was not McGovern's position the crowd voiced its disapproval.

This tension soon found its way into a pithy phrase that would tattoo the campaign for all time. Columnist Robert Novak wrote a piece based on a number of phone calls he'd placed to Democratic senators. He quoted one of them as saying, "The people don't know McGovern is for amnesty, abortion, and legalization of pot. Once middle America—Catholic middle America in particular—finds this out, he's dead." Because of the column, McGovern became known as the candidate of "amnesty, abortion, and acid." (Yes, he said "pot" and not "acid," but for the sake of alliteration, pot is a gateway drug.) It would be almost impossible for McGovern to shake that pithy label. (For those of you who have the commemorative *Whistlestop* workbook, please write down that alliterative phrase. We're going to come back to it later at the end of our story.)

This problem with conservatives meant McGovern needed a candidate to help him balance the Democratic ticket ideologically. He had the hippies and the women's libbers, but he needed the Catholics and the union workers. That was where Tom Eagleton came in. He was a Catholic. He had movie-star good looks, and he was also tight with the unions.

Eagleton was also pro-life. That was not the issue in Democratic politics that it would be today. A pro-life candidate would never be picked to run on a Democratic ticket now but at the time Eagleton's cultural conservatism actually was a positive, because it gave balance to McGovern.

Vetting Eagleton

After McGovern announced that he had picked Eagleton, Gary Hart and Frank Mankiewicz asked the Missouri Senator's political handlers if there were any problems in his background that would disqualify him. Mankiewicz also quizzed Eagleton personally, asking about illegitimate children, trouble with women, or anything at all that might embarrass the candidate. Eagleton gave an emphatic no on each specific count but also in broad general terms. There were rumors that Eagleton drank a little too much and that he might have had a mental issue somewhere in his past. Eagleton's administrative assistant said, he checked himself into the hospital once for exhaustion, but that was it. No big deal. Just the kinda rumors, you know, that go around in the press.

Mankiewicz and Hart and the rest of the whole McGovern campaign were just totally exhausted from the fight, and they were ready to hear easy answers. There was no one person specifically assigned to check the backgrounds of vice presidential choices, so the task fell to everyone which meant it was really handled by no one. They were already overworked. As Mankiewicz said, "It was a very hectic time, I must have had not two things on my mind, but maybe eighty."

Mankiewicz gave the OK to McGovern. The candidate checked out some rumors himself with his Senate colleagues about Eagleton's drinking and was told, according to McGovern, "that's a lot of baloney."[123] On that day, July 13, he called the vetting to a halt and felt reassured about the pick.

Everyone went off on vacation after the convention to relax after the long slog and recharge for the big coming fight against Richard Nixon. "The campaign had begun," wrote Mankiewicz of that moment in his memoir, "and Senator McGovern's doom had been sealed."

Reporters Start Digging

Not long after Eagleton joined the ticket, Clark Hoyt, a twenty-nine-year-old reporter for the Knight Ridder newspapers, was assigned to write a profile about him. He flew to St. Louis and did what journalists did in the predigital age. He asked the *St. Louis Post-Dispatch* if he could have access to their newspaper clip files on Eagleton.

"They brought in these massive files full of old clippings," Hoyt remembers. As he read through them, he noticed there were gaps in the Eagleton coverage. He'd been in the news a lot as attorney general, and as lieutenant governor. But there were dark periods.

Simultaneously, a colleague of Hoyt's at the *Detroit Free Press*—which was also part of the same newspaper chain—received an anonymous call from someone claiming to be a McGovern supporter who said Eagleton had a history of mental illness. He was sure that Nixon was going to bring it up during the campaign. The person gave the name of a doctor who would have firsthand knowledge of the treatments Eagleton had received, in which seizures were electrically induced in patients to provide relief from psychiatric illness. It was called electroshock therapy.

Hoyt found the doctor and knocked on her door. She answered.

"I am Clark Hoyt of the Knight newspapers. And did you treat Senator Eagleton at a psychiatric hospital where he was admitted with electroshock therapy for depression?" Hoyt asked.

The doctor's face drained of all its color. "I can't talk to you about that," she said and slammed the door shut.

Story confirmed. But Hoyt couldn't exactly publish that exchange. He returned to his research, including hunting down the nurse who had been there for the therapy.

Simultaneously, the McGovern campaign started hearing rumors and getting nervous. While they were on vacation, they heard stories about reporters who were nosing around in Eagleton's past. What they didn't know was how far the noses had gotten. Were they just getting little whiffs of these rumors they'd already shot down? Or were reporters getting a full snootful?

Then the campaign got its own anonymous call. The unidentified caller described Eagleton's visits to psychiatric institutions and described the electroshock therapy.

Mankiewicz and Hart immediately thought Nixon was behind the call. They had no evidence, but it turned out they had every reason to be suspicious. Nixon had talked about Eagleton's mental health with his advisers Pat Buchanan and Chuck Colson. He advised the line of attack for Republicans shouldn't be the senator's health but the fact that he had lied to McGovern. That way you'd surface the mental health charge, which would do the real damage, without being accused of overtly doing so.

McGovern's staffers called Eagleton and asked for a meeting on Thursday, July 20, in the Senate dining room, seven days after his pick had been announced. The senator admitted that he'd been to the hospital three times. Mankiewicz asked him about the diagnosis and Eagleton said "Melancholia," to which Mankiewicz responded, "There's no such disease. Maybe there was a hundred years ago."

Finally, Eagleton admitted that he'd undergone electroshock therapy, but he insisted he was fine. It was all in the past and he didn't have any lingering psychiatric issues. They asked that he hand over his complete medical records. (What would later come out was that in the late '70s, after this episode was long in the past, Eagleton would be diagnosed with bipolar II disorder.)

At this point, Clark Hoyt and the McGovern campaign knew the same thing. But neither the campaign, nor the reporters knew what the other knew.

July 21: Meeting in South Dakota

McGovern's aides flew to South Dakota the next day, the twenty-first, to put the problem before their boss. Mankiewicz had dialed around to psychiatrists. Each of them had the same opinion: Senator Eagleton could adequately perform any job to which he'd be assigned, except president of the United States.[124] What to do? On the one hand, no candidate had been cut from a ticket so fast, so McGovern had to keep Eagleton. On the other hand, Nixon, who was running on his mastery of world affairs, would charge that the Democratic ticket had an unstable vice president one heartbeat away from being leader of the free world.

McGovern aides were irritated that Eagleton had not been straight with them. He'd been coy each time they'd asked him a question. He had an apparatus that seemed to be a part of an ongoing deception.

His brother, a doctor, and his staff operated as a kind of moat around him, telling diverting stories every time someone asked about Eagleton's disappearances. When he was asked about the medication he took, the senator explained that no one needed to worry about that, because he had the prescription in his wife's name.

Rumors started showing up in the press. Investigative journalist Jack Anderson published a story—later debunked—that Eagleton had been arrested for drunk driving. McGovern felt overwhelmed. A friend called him during this time to offer support. The senator was about to go canoeing. "Do you know how to paddle a canoe?" the senator joked, suggesting that he felt he was in the middle of a creek without one.

Later that day, McGovern went to see *The Candidate*, a film about a politician who challenges the establishment and succeeds doing it his own way, but once his prospects improve against an unassailable incumbent, the deal starts to change. The insurgent McGovern must have found it a little too realistic—and not just because he had a small role in the film playing himself.

Meanwhile, Clark Hoyt and his colleague Robert Boyd kept reporting. They'd found the nurse and she'd confirmed the treatments. They flew to South Dakota to talk to the McGovern campaign.

In today's press environment, a lot of people probably would just go with the story. Or, the first rumor would have been on Twitter and then it would be out there and everyone would cover it. But Hoyt and Boyd wanted to take their reporting and get official comment. They'd get the answers from Eagleton and not simply publish a sensationalist account.

On July 23, Mankiewicz looked at all the reporters' material and promised he'd get back to them, according to Hoyt. Mankiewicz said the campaign would provide the medical records and Eagleton to give the full story.

Two days later, Eagleton and his wife also arrived in South Dakota to talk to McGovern. The entire team met in a log cabin at Sylvan Lake. Reporters Hoyt and Boyd stood outside waiting. Every once in a while, the staffers from the McGovern campaign pulled back the curtain to see if the two reporters were still out there.

Finally the curtain parted, and it was bad news for the reporters. They'd done all the work and done the right thing by bringing the story to the campaign, but the campaign was going to deny them their scoop. A press conference was announced for July 25, in which the campaign would put their own spin on things.

Gary Hart was a part of this decision team. Scooping the reporters would come back to haunt him during his 1988 presidential campaign. When reporters from the *Miami Herald* confronted him about his alleged affair with Donna Rice, he promised to get back to them. Fearful that he would pull an end run of the kind he pulled with Eagleton, they went ahead and published the story.

July 25: Not a Routine Press Conference

At 11:30 in the morning on Tuesday, July 25, reporters assembled in the small, pine-paneled auditorium at the Black Hills resort for what they expected to be a routine press conference. McGovern introduced Eagleton by saying, "There is one matter…on which I prefer that Senator Eagleton address you." As Eagleton rose, Eleanor McGovern slipped into the chair next to Mrs. Eagleton and squeezed her arm in solidarity.[125]

The senator announced he'd been treated in psychiatric institutions, but he was still pretty coy about it. "Part of the manifestation of my fatigue and exhaustion relates to the stomach," he said. "I'm like the fellow in the Alka Seltzer ad who says 'I can't believe I ate the whole thing.' But I do get, when I do overwork and tire myself, kind of a nervous stomach situation."[126] Reporters had to pull the electroshock therapy piece from him in questioning. You didn't do that for a nervous stomach.

McGovern stood by his man. "As far as I'm concerned, there is no member of that Senate who is any sounder in mind, body and spirit than Tom Eagleton. I am fully satisfied and if I had known every detail that he discussed with me this morning, which is exactly what he has just told you here now, he would still be my choice for the vice presidency of the United States."

What only McGovern's closest aides knew at the time was that McGovern's daughter was also suffering from depression. If he had abandoned his running mate, it would've been like abandoning his daughter.

McGovern also decided to stick it out because he believed that he knew best. Like many candidates, he thought he was the smartest campaign manager. It was an ongoing problem. His strategist, Fred Dutton, had written McGovern a memo in which he outlined the problem. "No major presidential candidate in modern history has successfully pulled off being both the jockey and the horse—both the candidate and the man who is also really running the campaign."

The press conference was another instance of McGovern thinking he knew how things would play out. He'd declare his support for Eagleton and that would be it. If he was standing by his running mate, there was no other issue. In an interview with ABC, McGovern said he viewed his choice of Eagleton as irrevocable.[127]

Eagleton Tries to Gut It Out

After the press conference, Hoyt and his colleague Boyd were given a bit of a booby prize. They'd lost their exclusive, but they got the first interview with Eagleton on his way to the airport.

Immediately Eagleton wanted to get back on the campaign trail to show that he was fit and he was fighting. If he could be a vigorous campaigner, he'd be just fine as a vice president. On the way to the airport, Hoyt and Boyd interviewed him. Hoyt remembers that the senator answered every question, which suggested ease with the issue, but he chain-smoked Pall Malls with desperation. He'd smoke half a cigarette and light a new one off the old one. "He was sweating so profusely," remembers Hoyt, "that he soaked through his sports jacket.

And I realized when I got to the airport, I was soaking through also because of him. I folded up my notebook and said, 'That's all I have.' Eagleton slumped over in his seat and said, 'Thank God.' " (The story Clark Hoyt and Robert Boyd would write about the affair would win the Pulitzer Prize.)

July 26–28: The Fallout

The story didn't go away after the press conference, and the accounts appearing in papers weren't good for the campaign. Eagleton, had emerged at the convention like a jack-in-the-box. He was so unknown, Nixon's vice president Spiro Agnew, called him "Tom Who?" Suddenly he had turned into a household name.

He confronted the topic of his mental health at every campaign stop. Stories in the press mentioned that he had been McGovern's fifth pick, undermining him.[128] "It's cost us two weeks productive effort, which is the least it has cost us," said one of McGovern's California officials.

On July 27, fifteen days after he'd made the selection, McGovern talked to Dr. Karl Menninger, a psychiatrist who advised him to ask Eagleton to step down. While McGovern was getting that counsel in one ear, he was doing things to box himself in. An Associated Press story suggested McGovern was thinking about dropping Eagleton. To knock that down, McGovern put out the word that he had "no intention of dropping [Eagleton] from the ticket."and was "1000 percent for Tom Eagleton"—a phrase that would come back again and again and again.

The story was out of control. On July 28, the *New York Times* called for Eagleton to step down, as did the *Washington Post* and *Baltimore Sun*. The *New York Post* said, "In this year of a great national decision . . . he has disqualified himself by his apparent act of concealment."[129] A Herblock cartoon showed a couple talking, with the caption, "Well, McGovern May Not Mind That Eagleton Didn't Level with Him, But *I* Mind."

The campaign money dried up. Howard Metzenbaum, a wealthy McGovern backer who would later serve in the Senate, said he expected Eagleton to withdraw.

The newspapers were full of tallies showing support for keeping or dropping the candidate. One said fifty-five people had called the campaign expressing support for keeping Eagleton on the ticket. A woman from Wyalusing, Pennsylvania, wrote: "Don't forget you're now certified as sane, which is more than the rest of them can say." One McGovern supporter from Michigan wrote about Eagleton's recent appearance on *Face the Nation*: "Thomas Eagleton's TV appearance was a magnificent display of honesty, character and courage. As one of your potential one million small contributors, you will lose my support if you drop him."[130] Said another: "If you dump Eagleton, we dump you. Don't let the old politics destroy great hopes."[131]

A twenty-two-year-old McGovern volunteer from New York wired in with a different view: "We did not work for your candidacy for four years to see it thrown down the drain by Eagleton's incomprehensible actions. I sympathize with his problem but I do not want him ever as my president."[132] Letters and telegrams piled up on every flat surface. "I am not going to be stampeded by a handful of telegrams," McGovern insisted.

The news papers also included armchair diagnoses from doctors who didn't really know anything about Eagleton's condition. "Eagleton's illnesses are no more commendable or shameful than if it were appendicitis or gall bladder," Horace Rubenstein, a Chicago psychiatrist, said. "I can think of a few presidents who could have benefited from such treatment." Forty-one people attending the Institute in Crisis Intervention said letting go of Eagleton would perpetrate an unfair stigma against the mentally ill.[133]

Republicans weighed in. "The people simply aren't going to want to put a mental patient in charge of the nuclear trigger button," said one Republican spokesman. "The best thing that can happen for us is for them to keep Eagleton on the ticket."

Overwhelmed, McGovern felt he couldn't shove out his number two, but he hoped that he could create the conditions that would encourage Eagleton to take the leap himself. After all, Eagleton had said when he was selected that if he ever become a problem for the ticket, he'd pull himself off. So McGovern tried to send him the memo with the subject line, "You are a problem for the ticket. Please go away."

Eagleton responded by hunkering down. He thought it was good for the ticket to fight the story. He told reporters in San Francisco, "The way this issue has turned around, I'm a distinct plus to the ticket. I'm gonna stay on the ticket. That's my firm, irrevocable intent." Eagleton told McGovern: "Sure I'll cost you some votes amongst the worrywarts, but, George, I'll get you more votes amongst people who respect a fighter."[134]

At other times Eagleton compared himself to John Kennedy, who broke the barrier for Catholics. He would break the mental health barrier. "In San Francisco this morning," said one paper, "Thomas Eagleton seemed like the only remaining true believer in his own cause."[135]

Eagleton's problems extended beyond health; he had been dishonest. He admitted he'd lied to the press when he'd disappeared to check himself into electroshock therapy. "When you need rest, one of the things you need rest about most is rest from the press," he said.

This meant every new wrinkle in the story as he parceled it out highlighted his dishonesty. For example, he admitted he took an occasional, "very sporadic" tranquilizer after saying that his condition had been dormant for six years. Asked if he would consider taking a psychiatric test, he said he would do so only if the other candidates did, which was a very sassy thing to say given the circumstances.

Eagleton piled explanation upon explanation, saying at one point he was fighting for his son. "You have to understand about Terry. I am his hero, just as my dad was my hero. I've got to win. I've got to do it for Terry. I've got to make it for Terry."[136]

On July 28, McGovern dropped a series of extremely unsubtle hints to reporters. The first was in a story by Jules Witcover of the *Los Angeles Times*. He interviewed the candidate in McGovern's Sylvan Lake cabin. The story suggested that Eagleton should remove himself from the ticket.

That evening McGovern table-hopped in the Lakota Room of the Sylvan Lake Lodge, talking to reporters about his woes. Financial contributors and party leaders were telling him something had to be done about Eagleton. On orders from his chief fund-raiser he had put the brakes on a direct-mail money appeal to one million Democratic voters. The revelations might doom the cash request.

The candidate sounded a lot less sure than he had been. "The question is to evaluate at a time when the country's uptight and anxious, uncertain, how much more strain you can put in the system," he mused. "I don't know."[137]

To those who were there, McGovern's "tone of voice implied that Eagleton was dead."[138] The next morning, after reading the story, Eagleton called McGovern for reassurances. McGovern mumbled and suggested they meet in Washington following his return.[139]

Did he have to chat with reporters that way? Eagleton wondered. "Why... didn't he pick up the phone, call me collect if need be, and say, 'Tom, it's over. There are too many imponderables in your candidacy. Your presence on the ticket jeopardizes my candidacy for the Presidency of the United States.' "[140]

Sunday July 30, Eagleton took his case to *Face the Nation*. While he was defending himself, the Democratic National Chairman and vice chairman went on *Meet the Press* and urged Eagleton to quit.

It was open chaos in the party. Everyone seemed to have an opinion. Senator Eagleton should resign, said Jesse Jackson, "because he is medically a statistical risk."[141] In the papers, McGovern aides were quoted evaluating what qualities they'd look for in Eagleton's replacement.

Cloakroom Check-up

On July 31, McGovern and Eagleton met in the Senate Marble Room. It was their last meeting as running mates, but Eagleton hadn't given up. "I'm about as determined as one human being can be determined that I'm going to stay in the race," he said. For fifteen minutes the doomed vice president pitched why he should stay on the ticket. He tried again to convince McGovern that if he were allowed to campaign, the issues would run out of steam.

Eagleton dialed his doctors who had treated him and let McGovern talk to them while he left the room.[142] It didn't convince the candidate. McGovern told Eagleton he had to withdraw from the ticket.

Eagleton ultimately agreed, but he wanted a managed departure. He would get off the ticket, but it would be agreed by the both men that it was not his mental capacity that made him unfit for the job. They would say the kerfuffle that had exploded around his treatment made it too politically difficult for him to stay on the ticket.

Eagleton threatened McGovern. If he or any of his aides said he was kicked of the ticket because of his mental issues, he would fight him all the way to November.[143]

That night Eagleton formally announced that he was leaving the ticket. "I will not divide the Democratic Party, which already has too many divisions," he said. He was white-faced and perspiring heavily. It was the first time in Democratic Party history a vice president had been dropped from the ticket. McGovern-Eagleton buttons skyrocketed in price. "Nobody is going to get these buttons from me," said one woman. "They'll be worth a fortune."[144]

McGovern At Sea

Senator Eagleton had acted in bad faith with McGovern and his aides. He didn't tell the truth and when he did, he told it slowly so that it became a several-day story. In the public eye, though, he looked like the wronged victim. He wrote a three-page essay in *Newsweek*. He wrote a page in *Time* magazine. He appeared on CBS News the day after he left the ticket to say he shouldn't have been dropped.

According to McGovern's pollster, Eagleton became the most popular politician in America. People thought he had gotten a raw deal. McGovern couldn't defend himself by explaining everything that had happened behind the scenes.

Before all of this happened, McGovern was a political ace who had run an amazing insurgent candidacy. After the Eagleton affair, he was seen as a bungler who had blown his first big presidential choice. "Tom will be hurt, but the frightful negative is that in his first appointment, George blew it," wrote syndicated columnist Warren Rogers. "People will ask: if he can't pick a vice president, can we trust his judgment on selecting the chairman of the joint chiefs? A negotiator with the Russians? Cabinet officers?"[145]

Before Eagleton, McGovern was seen as clean and highly moral. Suddenly he was being described as a Nixon-like fellow who dropped his running mate for politically opportune reasons. As historian Bruce Miroff writes "This produced a disastrous new image for McGovern. Both cold-blooded opportunist and hapless bungler."[146]

In the fallout, McGovern lost the Missouri State Democratic Party chairman Delton Houchins, who was annoyed that Eagleton had not been given time to prove himself. "Senator McGovern was not strong in Missouri to begin with," said Houchins. "And I think this quick brush-off of Senator Eagleton will prevent him from carrying this state definitely in the fall. I've been a lifelong Democrat and I'm going to continue to be. But this fall election will find me and my friends spending our money and working to elect our state, congressional, and local tickets."

Debbie Barber, who had seconded Eagleton's nomination at the convention, said she was disappointed. "I am concerned with—with the youth—particularly so because a lot of young people felt that McGovern was so idealistic. What he did. What he decided to do shows him as a practical politician. And I hope that doesn't discourage a lot of young people who we really need to count on to push McGovern through."

McGovern replaced Eagleton with Sargent Shriver, a former ambassador to France and a former director of the Peace Corps, but the campaign never recovered. The ripples were enormous. While McGovern might not have beaten Nixon, he wouldn't have lost as badly as he did. That might have set up a possible bid for him in 1976.

There was also fallout for the liberal approach McGovern championed. By losing so badly, Bruce Miroff argues in *The Liberals' Moment*, McGovern became the left's Goldwater—the candidate who most embodied the views of the ideological purists but who could never win in a general election. Those ideas had appeared to fail the electoral test so thoroughly, but if Eagleton had doomed the ticket, those ideas never had a chance to get a fair hearing.

In 2007, after Tom Eagleton's death, Robert Novak revealed that Eagleton had been the source of the infamous quote during the Democratic primary that spawned the "abortion, amnesty, and acid" line that damaged McGovern. Now just to keep the time line straight, Eagleton had said it during the primaries, when he had no idea in the world that he would ever become McGovern's running mate. He became McGovern's running mate, in part, to mitigate the acid, abortion, and amnesty rap that had dogged McGovern since Novak first published that quote.

Bob Shrum, the Democratic strategist who worked for McGovern, upon hearing Novak disclose the Eagleton news, said, "Boy do I wish Eagleton would have let you publish his name. Then he never would have been picked as vice president... We had a messy convention, but [McGovern] could have, I think in the end, carried eight or ten states, remained politically viable. And Eagleton was one of the great train wrecks of all time."

2004—The Dean Scream

AP Photo/Paul Sancya

Three Exclamation Points

The indispensable three-volume *History of American Presidential Elections* has a section on key quotations from every race. In the chapter on 2004, the first quote is from Sen. John Kerry trying to explain his vote on Iraq war funding. "I actually did vote for the $87 billion before I voted against it." There's also a partial transcript of President George W. Bush's long response to a question about what he thought his biggest mistake had been since 9/11.

Then there's a quotation from Howard Dean on January 19, 2004. It's labeled as an Iowa caucus concession speech. "Not only are we going to New Hampshire, [Sen.] Tom Harkin, we're going to South Carolina, and Oklahoma, and Arizona, and North Dakota, and New Mexico. And we're going to California and Texas and New York, and we're going to South Dakota and Oregon and Washington and Michigan, and then we are going to Washington, D.C., to take back the White House. Yeah!!!"

These three exclamation points are the best simple writers can do to capture what is known as the Dean Scream, the prolonged howl from the third-place finisher in that year's Iowa caucus that became a national sensation. There is no grammatical term for using three exclamation points, but in musical notation it's known as fortississimo.

Sheldon Alberts of the *Boston Globe* wrote, "His neck bulged, his face reddened and he bounded about with arms flailing, jabbing a wireless microphone toward his supporters. It is impossible to capture in print the rabid nature of his speech, but on several occasions he actually bared his teeth in a lupine snarl that made one wonder when and where he had been bitten."

The television networks matched Dean's exuberance and exceeded it. They aired the scream hundreds of times in the following days as Dean's campaign fell apart. It cemented the idea that the scream killed the campaign. But while the greater-than-usual exhalation of air over the vocal folds was something to marvel at, it didn't doom the campaign. Dean had to give a concession speech for a reason; he came in third. In the end, Dean was an undisciplined candidate whose innovative insurgent campaign couldn't overcome a few of the remaining rules of politics. What sundered Dean was the voter's reaction to negative campaigning, the revolt from a party apparatus he had challenged, and voters' flight to security in uncertain times of terrorism.

The scream was more like a supernova, the manifestation of the last burst of energy from a dying star. It was a symetric end to a campaign that burst into the political world with a similar kind of unpredictable force. Dean's campaign manager, Joe Trippi, said, looking back: "For the first time in my life, maybe the first time in history, a candidate lost but his campaign won."

Elections in the Age of Terror

Elected Democratic officials were in a pinch during the election year of 2004. Two-thirds of their base opposed the war in Iraq, but many of their presidential candidates had supported it. Sen. John Edwards voted in favor of granting President Bush the authority to attack Iraq. Sen. John Kerry had voted for the war, too. So had former House Democratic Leader Dick Gephardt.

This was a sad bunch of prospects for Democrats who wanted a clean break. The grass roots already thought George W. Bush had been given the presidency illegally by the Supreme Court after Al Gore won the popular vote in 2000. They thought it was crazy for establishment Democrats to argue that a candidate like John Kerry was a good candidate because his military record would allow him to blunt Republican attacks that Democrats were weak on national security. They wanted to offer voters a real choice. They wanted somebody who spoke the old-time religion, who gave them something to stomp their feet about.

From Message to Messenger

Vermont governor Howard Dean didn't start his campaign angling to be a liberal hero. In Vermont, he'd been a pragmatic, get-the-job-done governor. He wasn't a Democratic Party hero of the base. He wanted to promote universal health care and policies to encourage early childhood development. "Pre–Iraq war, that's all he ever talked about," Joe Trippi said of the two issues. "He's a smart guy, but he was under no illusions that he was going to be the nominee of the party." He didn't have the money or a nationally compelling message. The former internist whose shirts were too tight in the collar and whose socks were too lose around the ankles couldn't compete for dollars with those senators and a House Democratic leader who had been in the game so long.

As of January 31, 2003, the Dean campaign had a staff of seven people, $157,000 in the bank, and 432 supporters. He was referred to as the invisible man. At that point in January he was at 1 percent in Iowa. Eighty-two percent of voters couldn't tell you who Howard Dean was. Iowa senator Tom Harkin, who would later endorse Dean, introduced him in those early days at a rally as John Dean, who you may remember was the counsel to the White House under the Nixon administration.

One year later, things were different. After months of ignominy and toiling in obscurity, Dean's staff had grown to four hundred, and the campaign raised $50 million from 600,000 registered supporters.

How did that boom happen? Dean gave Democrats something to cheer for.

While George Bush prepared for war, liberals on MoveOn.org seethed about the weakness of Washington Democrats. George Soros spent $15 million trying to give voice to that anger. "When I hear President Bush say, 'You're either with us or against us,' it reminds me of the Germans. My experiences under Nazi and Soviet rule have sensitized me," said Soros. The problem: there was no candidate for the wing of the party that compared the sitting president to famous fascists.

Dean broke with the Washington Democrats. "What I wanna know is what in the world are so many Democrats doing supporting the president's unilateral intervention in Iraq?" he asked at the California state convention in March 2003.

Dean quoted the late Minnesota senator Paul Wellstone, who had recently died in a plane crash, saying that he represented "the democratic wing of the Democratic Party." That meant more than simply that Dean had the right policy positions. It meant he was offering a campaign that would make Democrats *feel it*.

Dean's success was grounded in creating a campaign experience through the use of the Internet and decentralization, and it enlivened Democrats. It was what they had been missing. You can tell somebody about heartache, or you can write *Love Story* and make them cry. That was what Howard Dean did. He made voters feel the movement by getting them involved.

There's a tradition of this in the Democratic Party. The outsider insurgents' route to success gets people involved not simply to advocate for a man or certain policies, but to redeem the system in which they want to believe. Gary Hart wrote about it in his memoir of the 1972 McGovern campaign, *Right from the Start*. "If people could be made to feel there was still hope through working in the system, they might draw encouragement and inspiration." Like McGovern, Dean argued that the status quo had been broken, that the two parties were too similar and that breaking that lock could take place only through citizen participation.

Jerry Brown, the governor of California, made this pitch in 1992 through use of a 1-800 phone number to let people donate directly to campaigns and in small amounts. "It is my conviction," said Brown, "as the basis of my candidacy, that by limiting contributions to what the average person can actually give, that we're building a movement, a cause to take back power. And give a shift in direction so that our nation can live up to its premise that all of us are created equal and we have an inalienable right to life, to liberty, and to the pursuit of happiness." Bernie Sanders did this in the Democratic primary in 2016.

Draining big money was crucial to reforming politics because money was becoming more important than ideas in the Democratic party. The candidate with the most money bought the most ads, and strategists, and pollsters and that made them almost impossible to defeat. An insurgent with innovative ideas could never find an audience for those ideas without money, because they needed funds to compete—to buy ads and travel. Liberals also believed the money chase narrowed the field of acceptable ideas. Politicians in both parties were soliciting the same types of people who had roughly the same ideas about issues like trade and national defense.

The reliance on money meant candidates had to line up high-dollar donors and endorsements early in the preprimary competition. If they didn't, they lacked the ability to go on. It's a circular system that makes it hard for insurgents like Jimmy Carter, who came out of nowhere to win the nomination in 1976. "An average person like I was, just a peanut farmer back in 1976, would be absolutely impossible," said Carter in 2003. "There's a criterion for success in

American politics now—the Democratic or Republican Party—and that is extreme wealth, or access to major wealth."

A New Sugar Daddy: The People

Dean had to find a way around the traditional system that was so reliant on money, or find a way to raise money through some new route. Trippi had worked with high-tech start-ups and thought it might be possible to run a campaign like an entrepreneurial venture.

The experiment started small. On his first day, Trippi suggested putting a link to the website Meetup.com on the Dean campaign website. The service allowed people with similar interests to get together. Voters who liked Dean's message and who felt the Democratic Party had abandoned them started meeting. Little by little, the size of the meetings grew. The campaign wasn't organizing this. Voters were doing it themselves. "It was as if the world were shifting right before our eyes," says Trippi. "The ground was rumbling beneath our feet. As techies, we'd been hearing for decades that the Internet would radically transform American life. Well, the future is happening right now, to us."

Under the usual Democratic Party empowerment scenario, the candidate exhorts voters to come together. Dean's followers were coming together on their own. They were enacting a level of participation that previous Democrats could only dream of.

When you listen to Trippi talk about the Dean campaign, his tale sounds different. It's not obsessed with the candidate. Trippi tells the story about a movement. "Howard Dean didn't create the movement," he wrote. "In many ways, the movement created the Dean for America campaign."

Even members of the movement felt this way. "He seemed like a good, honest man with a fine sense of history, imaginative ideas, a strong set of values, and lots of hands-on, community-based experience," said Lisa Null, a dedicated volunteer to the campaign, "but the campaign was more in love with itself than with him."

Soon those who met up started to send in money. When the list of Meetup Dean supporters reached about twenty-two thousand people, one of them e-mailed another suggesting that when they donated, they should add a penny so the campaign would know the donation was coming from Meetup. This was how decentralized the organization was. Usually the campaign wouldn't need to be notified that people were donating money, because they would have hunted them down and squeezed them repeatedly for a donation. Because the Meetup participants were organizing themselves, the campaign wasn't even sure who they all were. Soon, $400,000 came in, in small donations, each one with a penny attached.

The stories of self-motivation grew. A woman sold her bike for seventy-five bucks and donated the money to the Dean campaign. Suddenly donations started coming in with notes that said, "I sold my bike for democracy."

When the number of supporters grew to thirty thousand, the campaign sent out an e-mail to the list asking to help close a $83,000 shortfall in their quarterly deadline. Dean received $400,000 over the Internet in just five days.[147]

During a $2,000-a-plate fund-raiser hosted by Vice President Dick Cheney, the campaign posted a picture of Dean eating a turkey sandwich on DeanforAmerica.com. Small donations poured in. Dean outraised Cheney by $200,000 taking in over $400,000.

Raising money gave Dean the fuel to run, but also it validated his strategy with the insider class. Whatever they were cooking up in the back office at Dean headquarters in Burlington, Vermont, it was producing the most important thing a campaign needs, which meant he couldn't be dismissed. They were doing something right. That in turn gave sustenance to the people turning their lives upside down to support Dean. His message that everybody counts in politics was succeeding and getting noticed by more than true believers.

The money and spontaneous support allowed Dean to perform feats of strength. In August 2003, he launched a Sleepless Summer

Tour, a 6,147-mile, ten-city rampage. The name was based on the idea that unemployment and the lack of jobs and health care, had Americans sleepless, while President Bush slept soundly at his Texas ranch during his traditional August vacation.[148] Dean flew a 737 campaign plane referred to as "Grassroots Express" and decorated with plastic tufts of grass. At the last rally in Bryant Park in New York, he carried with him a red baseball bat, a reference to the graphic on his campaign website that showed donors the progress toward reaching fund-raising goals.

Dean saved an enormous amount of time and mind-share that is usually lost to raising money. Normally, candidates have to make regular trips into the suburbs to a country club or some vast house with an indoor track or a vintage car collection. They commune with a small group of check-writers who insist on pressing their ideas on the candidate which they are sure will win him the election. Or the candidate has to devote several hours a day begging for money on phone, an act of supplication that can wither the stoutest souls. Dean was largely freed from that.[149]

In the end, eight hundred thousand people from half of the counties in the United States gave Dean an average of $77 each. Fifty million dollars was the total raised, a record-breaking $15 million in one quarter alone. One quarter of these contributions were from people under thirty years old. Many of them wrote in asking to volunteer. The movement grew to the point where the campaign had to send out e-mail solicitations in stages so as not to overwhelm the servers and capacity of the Dean computers.[150]

The question the Dean campaign then faced was: Could they do everything right? Just because they'd found a new way to rake in dollars didn't mean they had the solution to transform every other part of the modern campaign or that their innovations in press management, candidate discipline, and advertising would pay off.

Iowa or Bust

In the early days of the campaign, Joe Trippi outlined a path to the nomination with the Iowa precinct caucuses at the center. Dean needed to finish in first or second place. Because Dean had been a governor in a state that neighbored New Hampshire, he'd probably do well in the first-in-the nation primary. With a one-two Iowa–New Hampshire punch, that would slingshot him into contention in South Carolina and Super Tuesday states in the South. He really needed momentum for South Carolina, because Senator John Edwards, had been born there and represented neighboring North Carolina.

Dean learned to talk about the system that had been created around him and make it a part of his pitch. "The biggest lie people like me tell people like you," he would tell his audiences, "from stages like this at election time is that if you vote for me, I'm gonna solve all your problems. The truth is, the power to change this country is in your hands, not mine."

Dean described a new political feedback mechanism with his supporters. "The Internet community is wondering what its place in the world of politics is. Along comes this campaign to take back the country for ordinary human beings, and the best way you can do that is through the Net. We listened. We pay attention. If I give a speech and the blog people don't like it, next time, I change the speech."

Dean also had his own blog people—which sounds like something the kids say they are afraid might be under the bed—who wrote for his campaign blog keeping the organization in touch with its constituency.

Dean was creating a new extension of the Jeffersonian and Jacksonian connection between the people and their politicians. He wasn't just a candidate supported by the people. He was a candidate whose campaign was partially being built by the people.

Even though Dean was running outside the traditional structures of campaigns, he still had to engage with the compulsory exercises of politics. One of those was an appearance on *Meet the Press* with Tim Russert.

It was a disaster. One newspaper declared, "It was perhaps the worst performance by a presidential candidate in the history of television. Full of vagueness, meandering, no clarity, a little bit of irritation, snippiness."

Within minutes of the interview, the Dean blog started filling up with messages of support from the Deaniacs. "Our supporters weren't running for cover," wrote Trippi, "they were running to help." The Dean following wasn't just lifting him up, it wasn't allowing him to fall.

Dean vs. Gephardt

Dean's closest competitor in Iowa in the summer of 2003 was House Democratic Majority Leader Richard Gephardt. In 1988, Dean, then a lieutenant governor in Vermont, had gone to Iowa to campaign for Gephardt. He didn't support Michael Dukakis from the neighboring state of Massachusetts. Gephardt went on to win in Iowa. Heading into the election of 2004, he was the front-runner who looked as if he was going to win again.

By the fall of 2003, Dean was close enough to Gephardt that the front-runner took a shot at him. He said Dean was going to cut with Medicare and Social Security. Dean responded in November with an ad showing Gephardt in the White House rose garden with the president, announcing details of the congressional resolution authorizing Bush to go to war against Iraq. The papers covered Dean's ad as the first negative ad of the cycle. All he'd done was show that Gephardt had supported Bush's, position that had become so toxic it *seemed* negative.

The back-and-forth would go on until January 2004. It was the start of Dean's downfall. It pulled him into an old-fashioned fight making him look like every other politician. The press coverage became less about his insurgent campaign and about issues. The conversation focused on politics and tactics, turf where it was harder to lift people.

In the cut and thrust, Dean also started to gaffe. In an interview with the *Des Moines Register*, he said, "I still want to be the candidate for guys with Confederate flags in their pickup trucks. We can't beat George Bush unless we appeal to a broad cross-section of Democrats."

When Dean had articulated this idea more eloquently, it was an appealing sign of toughness. He wasn't going to let Republicans claim a monopoly on patriotism and national pride. But his opponents pounced. "I would rather be the candidate of the NAACP than the NRA," John Kerry said in a statement. Protesters interrupted Dean rallies waving the Confederate flag.

In 2015, just nine years later, the Republican governor of South Carolina would take the Confederate flag down from outside the South Carolina state house after a racially-motivated mass shooting. In just nine years, association with the Confederate flag would be toxic in both parties.

That wasn't the only issue on which Dean, a liberal hero, was out of sync with orthodoxy. In Walter Shapiro's book, *One-Car Caravan*, about the run-up to the 2004 campaign, Dean takes a state's rights approach to gun control. "My position on guns for the presidential race is that states can do whatever they want. And if California wants to have gun control, let them have as much gun control as they want. Just don't pass it nationally." Now Democratic candidates mostly compete to show who can offer tougher national gun control measures.

Getting Too Popular

Joe Trippi pinpoints the decline of the Dean campaign in Iowa to the precise date, December 9, 2003, the day that Dean was endorsed by Al Gore. It was huge news for the campaign and for a candidate who had been at 1 percent in the polls. Bill Bradley, Gore's rival in 2000, also endorsed Dean. He was starting to look like a lock for the nomination. That's why Trippi said it signaled the end, Expectations were now out of control and Dean's opponents were spurred to unlock their opposition research files.

In one ad run to raise fears about Dean's ability to be a tough commander-in-chief, Osama bin Laden's face appears on screen while the narrator talks about Dean. Push polls were conducted where voters were called at home and asked what sounded like poll questions, but which were really intended to convey dark, unfounded smears about Dean.

There's a theory in politics that the closer the election gets, the more pragmatic voters get. They start to imagine the person in the Oval Office. Can they handle it? Do they have the experience? Have they been tested? The voters also start to think more about electability. This is the theory that Hillary Clinton tried to play on in 2008 when she said, "It's time to pick a president." She was trying to force voters to end their dalliance with the inexperienced Barack Obama and get them to concentrate on the skills and qualities and attributes used in the actual job.

It didn't work for Clinton, but in 2004 Democrats started hitting Dean on two issues of pragmatism—he was unelectable and he didn't have the skills. He couldn't get the job, and if he did he'd be a bad president.

Opponents pushed stories that Dean didn't have the temperament to be president. He couldn't handle the pressure in difficult times. Was he too angry? Columnist Joe Klein wrote that "there is a recklessness about the man, an adolescent screw-you defiance that runs much deeper than the steady stream of gaffes produced by his projectile candor." Dean started to be referred to as "the angry man."

When a campaign is under siege, everyone has to be disciplined, including the candidate. Dean was moving in the other direction, according to his pollster. "Our candidate's erratic judgment, loose tongue, and overall stubbornness wore our spirits down," wrote Paul Maslin, Dean's pollster. "He refused to be scripted, to be disciplined, or to discipline himself, in his remarks about everything from the Red Sox and the Yankees to Middle Eastern diplomacy. I later likened it all to repeatedly tapping an egg against the edge of a kitchen counter: eventually the egg would break."[151]

Dean played into Maslin's fears about his recklessness when, in December, he said that capturing Saddam Hussein hadn't made America safer.[152] He might have been right; it's certainly what Donald Trump says in 2016. But it was the kind of thing that one couldn't get away with that election. In January, 2004, after Hussein's capture, 60 percent of Americans approved of the Iraq War.[153] This made Democrats nervous, especially when the candidate running wasn't a foreign policy heavyweight. He was giving Republicans ammunition to hit him on a party weak spot.

Looking back, Dean said he knew he had to tone down his speeches to answer this concern but he couldn't help himself. "I could feel it slipping away," Dean told the documentary filmmakers for the FiveThirtyEight website. "I needed to make some changes in the campaign. I needed to rein myself in and become less alarming to the establishment, and I was unable to do that because I'd get out there and I would talk about policy and there was no adrenaline rush and people kind of went 'uh-huh, uh-huh,' and I really wanted that huge charge of being able to crank them all up and to believe in themselves again and get enthusiastic and I would succumb to that."[154]

Trippi also perceived a coordinated effort by the Democratic establishment to squash a candidate who was a threat to their power. "You are, by definition, the classic outsider," he wrote Dean in a memo. "But think about the fear and anger you have engendered from the [Democratic Leadership Council]." The Democratic Leadership Council was an organization allied with Bill Clinton that pushed the Democratic Party to adopt policies closer to the center of the political spectrum in order to win elections.

The fight over whether Dean had the temperament to lead was really a proxy fight for the battle between the Democratic Party's centrist wing and its liberal wing. "The other candidates, and many of the Washington establishment, they are not afraid you are George McGovern or Jerry Brown," wrote Trippi about those defeated candidates. "No, what they are afraid of is that you're Jimmy Carter." In other words, they worried he was going to win and become president.

Sen. Evan Bayh, a conservative Democrat, put the threat from Dean this way: "It is our belief that the Democratic Party has an important choice to make. Do we want to vent, or do we want to govern? The administration is being run by the far right. The Democratic Party is in danger of being taken over by the far left."

Late-Breaking Video

A week out from the Iowa caucuses, General Wesley Clark's campaign assisted its competitors in Iowa. The former NATO commander was running a New Hampshire–centered campaign, but he didn't want to face a rising Dean in New Hampshire, so his operatives put out a video of Dean criticizing the Iowa caucuses. It was a recording of an appearance on a Canadian political talk show from several years earlier. The interviewer asked Dean what he thought of the Iowa caucus system. Dean responded that the revered institution was classist and a bad way to select a president.

He did not insult cows and corn, but he might as well have done so. When you're campaigning in Iowa, you are not supposed to challenge the greatness of the Iowa caucuses. This is particularly true if your campaign manager has staked your entire strategy on coming in second or first in Iowa.

Local news stations did big, long stories on the video discussing whether Iowa was significant or not. Dean's numbers started to plummet.

To distract from the video, Dean aired an Iraq war ad, hitting all his Democratic rivals for supporting the war. In response, Gephardt put up an ad saying that Dean would cut Social Security and Medicare.

In a multicandidate race, a candidate who engages a single opponent in combat can inadvertently commit murder-suicide. They tear down their opponent but also irritate voters who don't like the negative campaigning. In the 2016 GOP race New Jersey governor Chris Christie attacked Florida senator Marco Rubio, and they were both diminished. This also happened with Dean and Gephardt. They went after each other in that final week, and both men went down.

The Orange Hat Rescue

Sinking, the Dean campaign turned again to its base—the 3,500 committed volunteers. They came from all over the country to knock on 200,000 doors to spread the Dean message. They wore orange stocking caps and called themselves the Perfect Storm, based on a posting that Joe Trippi had made on the campaign blog back in May. It was one last populist push by this campaign that had been defined by the grassroots lift beneath it. One hundred and eighty volunteers came from Texas, 50 from Pennsylvania, and 25 from California. Some even came from Japan. They made that one last, symbolic lunge for the people's campaign that Dean had run.

Although it looked as if Dean was losing altitude and his campaign's internal polls were grim, nobody really knew for sure how he was doing. It's hard to measure the impact of a movement. He had certainly made the conventional wisdom peddlers and pundits wrong before. No one had believed in the beginning that this governor from Vermont who was at 1 percent in the polls would ever go anywhere anyway. The campaign that had been created by all these Meetup meetings, that had been built on the Internet, that had broken these fund-raising records through word of mouth and small donations—it might just very well be able to pull it out in the end.

Days before the vote, rumors spread that Dean aides had commitments from fifty thousand caucus goers, more than enough to win, and Dean seemed happy to play up expectations. "We expect to do well," he said. "I believe we can win, and I believe we will win, based on the efforts that are going on to get people out. We're working as hard as we possibly can to win the whole thing."[155]

It didn't happen. The old rules kicked in. On caucus night, the damage that Dean insiders had worried about—the negative fight with Gephardt and the fatigue with Dean's insistent volunteers—had in fact hurt him. After Democratic voters gathered in 1,993 schools, libraries and living rooms to state their preference, he came in third, a massive plummet from a month earlier when people were talking about Dean as the eventual party nominee. John Kerry won 37.6 percent of the vote, John Edwards won 31 percent of the vote, and Howard Dean came in with just 18 percent of the vote.

Dean peaked at 29 percent in Iowa twelve days before the voting.

His polling average was down to 22 percent the night of the caucuses. Between his high and his ultimate vote, he dropped 11 percentage points.[156]

It wasn't just that Dean lost. He lost with the groups that were supposed to be a part of his unique movement. Kerry beat him among young adults, liberals, heavy Internet users, those who strongly disapproved of the war with Iraq, and first-time caucus goers.[157] "Thank you, Iowa," Kerry said trying to conjure the echo of Bill Clinton's 1992 New Hampshire win, "for making me the Comeback Kerry."[158]

Release the Kraken

On Dean's campaign bus they heard Ted Koppel on ABC set the challenge for him: "Howard Dean came in a disappointing third tonight and now has to act as though it doesn't really matter."[159]

Before Dean took the stage at the Val Air Ballroom, he asked Tom Harkin what he should do. The senior senator from Iowa said he should take off his jacket and "let 'er rip." Dean's communications director informed the press corps at the back of the ballroom that the candidate was going to be feisty and fiery. She predicted Dean would walk onstage, take off his jacket, hand it to Sen. Tom Harkin, and roll up his sleeves as a way to show everyone that he was getting right back to work after Iowa. She said Dean was fired up! That was definitely the direction of his fire: up.

Dean's big goal was to rally the room of 3,500 people. They were depressed. They had sold their bikes and donated their pennies and trekked across the country to wear orange hats and knock on the doors of people they didn't know. Dean felt an obligation to them and to the idea behind the campaign. It was a campaign about empowerment and how you couldn't let the conventional disappointments keep you from working your heart out for ideas you cared about. Dean wasn't just battling for his candidacy; he was trying to save the starter yeast that needed to survive whether he did or not. "There were 3,500 kids waving American flags who'd worked their hearts out for me for three weeks. I thought I owed it to them to really try to pep them up again," said Dean.[160]

The television cameras did not capture this dynamic. The picture that was beamed to the world was a tight shot focused on Dean as he spoke. Viewers at home couldn't see how the audience was screaming like mad before he ever handed his coat to Tom Harkin. The audio setup also exacerbated the problem. Television cameras plug into the central audio feed that comes out of the microphone, so they picked up every little peep from Dean but not the roar of the crowd that he was having to shout over. "Not only are we going to New Hampshire, Tom Harkin, we're going to South Carolina and Oklahoma and Arizona. And North Dakota and New Mexico! We're going to California and Texas and New York! And we're going to South Dakota and Oregon and Washington and Michigan! And then we're going to Washington D.C. to take back the White House! Yeah!!!" For the audience at home it sounded like a primal and unhinged rumble of words moving towards a precipice, capped by the whoop the deranged man makes as he leaps to his doom.

There was also a thematic disconnect. Dean was trying to sell the claim that he was excited by the outcome—look how far he had come!—but the fact was he'd had his pants handed to him that night.

Never mind. To the room it was a tonic. Like the moment on *Meet the Press*, the pundits thought it was terrible, but the faithful thought it was great. They were fired up. They were waving flags. They were shouting out states as he went through them. They loved his defiant tone and that he was a fighter. He'd been told he couldn't do it all along, and look at this organization he'd been able to build. This was the spirit that had gotten Dean's supporters into the process in the first place.

Unfortunately no cable news producers were die-hard Dean fans. The cable networks played the scream close to seven hundred times in four days. Another estimate had the number at close to nine hundred. The repetition was devastating. It made Dean look bonkers. He was a laughingstock. (The impression left by this kind of coverage is lasting.

Twelve years later, a Google search of Dean pictures finds four from the "Scream" speech in the first seven results.)

The late-night comedians rejoiced in the bounty. "Did you see Dean's speech last night?" asked Jay Leno. "Oh my God, now I hear the cows in Iowa are afraid of getting Mad Dean disease. It's always a bad sign when, at the end of your speech, your aide is shooting you with a tranquilizer gun." Jon Stewart portrayed Dean as the over-the-top announcer at a monster truck rally.

David Letterman said, "Here's what happened: The people of Iowa realized they don't want a president with the personality of a hockey dad." It all made Dean, who was stiil a pretty disciplined and straight-laced New Yorker, look more than a little kooky. Stories about his temperament had a fresh example. And every time a late night comedian made a joke, cable channels replayed it, asking pundits to weigh in on whether it was hurting Dean. After a while, Dean tried to join in. He appeared on Letterman to read a Top Ten list. The topic: "Ways I, Howard Dean, Can Turn Things Around." The number ten way was "Switch to decaf." The number one way, Dean said in the bit, was, "Oh, I don't know—maybe fewer crazy red-faced rants."[161]

The Scream led to wide-ranging analysis. "We all know it's this almost novelistic moment where he had this what must be incredibly painful downfall in Iowa, and you see this thing coming out of his id. I mean it's so real it's almost scary to watch it," said media critic William Powers on NPR.[162]

The Internet also responded unfavorably. A Kansas City entrepreneur started selling "I Have a Scream" buttons on the web. Howard Stern put the speech to some music by AC/DC. *Right Magazine*, an online political journal for students at Wheaton College, outside Chicago, posted a two-minute clip called the "Dean Goes Nuts Remix," which was downloaded more than seven thousand times between Tuesday morning and early evening. "It took me two hours in the middle of the night, until two or three in the morning," Jonathan Strong, the creator told *Newsweek* http://www.newsweek.com/yeagh-remix-125495.

"I came back from class Tuesday afternoon and it was all over the Internet. I purchased seven more gigs of bandwidth, took a nap, and, when I woke up, my site was down again." The entrepreneurial spirit was now working against Dean. His scream had become the first political meme. Or, as Maureen Dowd put it, Dean had transformed himself "from Internet deity to World Wide Wacko."[163]

Did the scream kill the Dean campaign? No. The candidate had spent 110 days campaigning in the state, almost forty more days than his closest competitor, John Kerry.[164] He had outspent all his opponents in advertising. His campaign was predicated on a first- or second-place finish in Iowa, and when that didn't happen it took the energy out of his movement. The old rules of politics seemed to have kicked in, which made his rise seem like a fling before voters settled down to the hard business of picking someone for the job. John Kerry felt like the candidate required to take on an incumbent in dangerous times. "In a very basic way, we lost that primary a few months before the scream ever happened," said Dave Kochbeck, the former information technology director for Dean's campaign.[165] Dean looks at the scream the same way. "I came in third. That had already happened."

This doesn't excuse the television news networks. There was no journalistic reason to show the scream hundreds of times. The overkill may have been a bit of schadenfreude. Dean had said he was going to go around the traditional kingmakers in the press and the party. He had been successful for a time, diminishing their influence. So when he fell, they delighted in replaying his collapse. It reaffirmed the power of the gatekeepers.

Could the Dean campaign have been more disciplined in the home stretch? Dean could have responded more crisply to the assaults from other candidates. He could have been more disciplined in what he said. "I just wasn't ready for prime time," Dean told *Esquire*. "I came from a state of six hundred thousand people. I had an intensely passionate following. I wasn't anticipating how rough it would be, and we didn't really have much discipline on the campaign. I was an undisciplined candidate."

The orange-hatted door knockers could also have been put to better use. Many were Deaniacs from New York and California who lacked the local connections Iowans appreciate. They were also swarming the streets of Iowa without coordination by field organization strategists, which meant they weren't converting voters or mobilizing the voters as effectively as possible. Like a start-up that gets too much money too fast and doesn't have the infrastructure to handle it, the energy of the Dean effort was spilling out over the ground.

"We had all these crazy Dean fans calling people, but the system wouldn't update the lists," Adam Mordecai, a staffer on the Dean Internet team, told *Esquire*. "So Iowans would get twelve, fifteen calls a day from rabid Dean supporters. We probably chased off half our support that way."[166]

But if Dean had traditional discipline would he have gotten as far as he did? It's the organic and nontraditional approach that made Dean so attractive, and that has made Sanders and Trump so attractive in 2016. "I lead with my heart and not my head," Dean would say. "That's the only chance we have against George Bush."

The campaign turned listless after Iowa as Dean tried to tone down his campaign rhetoric. "I'm not perfect," he repeatedly told crowds, apologizing for the outburst. The papers noted his new calmer style everywhere he went. "He looked a bit sheepish and hangdog at his drop from larger-than-life-to-smaller-than-life. He seemed lost without his eyebrow-arching anger and devilish smile and not sure how to proceed," wrote Maureen Dowd. Dean told audiences things like, "Those of you who came here intending to be lifted to your feet by a lot of red-meat rhetoric will be a little disappointed."

Whatever happened to those ideas about health care and early childhood development? The second topic isn't much discussed, but Barack Obama expanded health care access in his signature legislative achievement as president. He couldn't have been in a position to do that if he hadn't won Iowa in 2008. He did so by building on the strategy in Iowa that Howard Dean and Joe Trippi and all of Meetup's attendees helped launch four years earlier. The scream had an echo.

PART IV

Gambits and Gambles

1964—Stop Goldwater

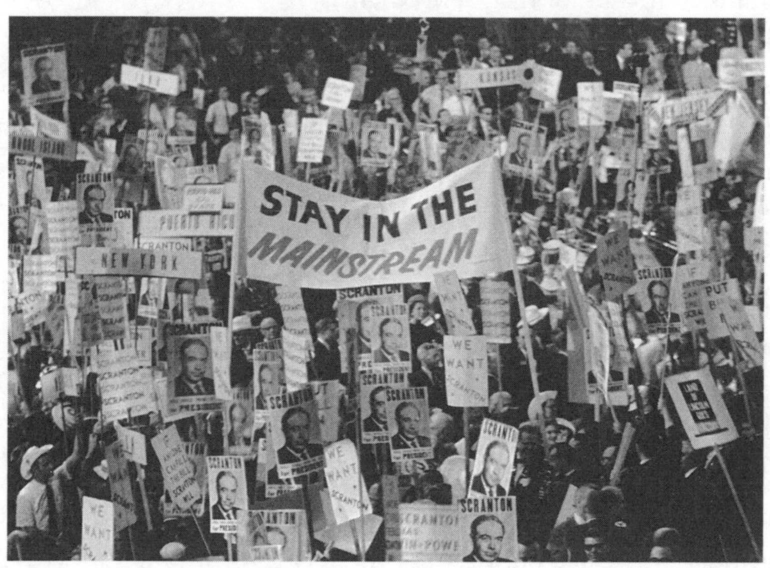

Rocky Go Home

On July 14, 1964, Nelson Rockefeller stepped to the podium at the Republican National Convention to get abused. It was nearly 10:00 p.m. Convention managers made sure to delay the proceedings as long as they could to deprive him of a satisfyingly large television audience. But if only a modest number of people were watching him at home, all eyes were on him in the hall.

Rockefeller, who would famously give a protester his middle finger as Gerald Ford's vice president in 1976, might as well have been doing the same to this audience. His jaw was clenched as the jeers echoed off the walls of the Cow Palace, an aging concrete Quonset-like structure outside San Francisco. The audience supported conservative Arizona senator Barry Goldwater, the all-but-certain nominee, and viewed Rockefeller, with his fondness for glossy art magazines, as the sneering embodiment of the Eastern establishment, which looked down at conservatives like Goldwater and his followers as unwashed ignoramuses. Rockefeller had competed against Goldwater in the primaries and ravaged their hero, labeling his followers kooks and declining to mask his contempt for their movement.

The clash had played out most severely in the California primary. Rockefeller campaigned against Goldwater's "reckless belligerence" on foreign policy. Two weeks before the vote, Rockefeller, up thirteen points in the polls, had sent a mailer to California voters asking, "Who do you want in the room with the H Bomb button?"

Just days before the primary, however, Rockefeller's new wife gave birth to their first child. This reminded everyone that he once had an incumbent wife whom he divorced in order to marry the challenger. She was fifteen years his junior and competed with him for scandal, in that she was married with four children at the time of their affair. William Loeb, the publisher of the influential Manchester, New Hampshire, *Union Leader* had called Rockefeller a "wife swapper." Goldwater fans asked during the primary: "Do you want a Leader or a Lover in the White House?[167]

Rockefeller had lost in California, and now that he was back in the state months later, he was getting it from both sides.

The day before, as the GOP convention was starting, Rockefeller had been heckled while addressing twenty-five thousand civil rights marchers (including baseball great Jackie Robinson) who had gathered on Market Street in San Francisco to protest Goldwater. When he promised a strong civil rights plank in the GOP platform, they responded,[168] "Too late, too late."

"We want Johnson!" they yelled. It was the classic fate of the middle-of-the-road candidate not just to be reviled, but to be associated with the extremists in his own party he opposed.

Convention organizers had given the vanquished Rockefeller only five minutes to speak to the convention, but his remarks were a concentrated blast against the extremism and racism he said was ruining the party. "These are people who have nothing in common with

Americanism," said Rockefeller, "The Republican Party must repudiate these people."

The crowd booed. "We want Barry!" they chanted. Then the noisemakers picked up. Like the Whos in Whoville on Christmas Day, the Rockefeller haters blew squeeze-horns and toy trumpets and hooters. Someone pounded a giant bass drum. Those with cowbells got busy.[169]

Rockefeller couldn't be heard and stopped talking. Goldwaterites seated in the rafters shouted themselves hoarse. Organizers, who were all in the Goldwater camp, reminded the speaker that he had a time limit. "You control the audience, and I'll make mine five minutes," he snapped. He was exhausted having been kept up the night before by prank phone calls to his hotel room.

His remarks were interrupted twenty-two times in five minutes. "This is still a free country, ladies and gentlemen," Rockefeller said, condemning "infiltration and takeover of established political parties by communist and Nazi methods."

"It was as if Rockefeller were poking with a long lance and prodding a den of hungry lions," wrote Theodore White in *The Making of the President 1964*.[170] "They roared back at him."

It was a contentious moment that marked the last noisy shot fired in a months-long losing battle to stop Goldwater from winning the Republican nomination. The immediate stakes were not high for Rockefeller's speech. By the time he gave it, Rockefeller and his allies had already been defeated, but the ferocity of the exchange highlighted how passionate both sides still felt. The bitterness would last for years.

The audience was angered afresh because Rockefeller sounded like a Democrat, casting them as the villains in the national morality play. If you held a different view from his—particularly on civil rights—you were a racist or an extremist. Or, at the very least, you were giving comfort to people with those views.

Two nights later, Goldwater answered Rockefeller's charge in his acceptance speech. "Extremism in the defense of liberty is no vice," he said to roars of approval so loud they overwhelmed the capacity of the microphone, making it crackle. "And let me remind you also, that moderation in the pursuit of justice is no virtue."

This is what a real party fight looks like: when people stand up at a candidate's nominating convention and denounce the forces that allowed the candidate to win the nomination, and the candidate fires right back with a defense tied to the ideas rooted in the country's foundational ideals.

The Republican Party conventions of 1952 and 1976 were cliff-hangers, but they can't match the 1964 GOP convention for the melting heat of ideological combat. The fight to stop Barry Goldwater was a fight about first principles and values, not just tactical disputes about how to use a party's power. In the 2016 campaign, Republicans unhappy with Donald Trump started a #NeverTrump movement, and it failed just as spectacularly. The fights of 1964 proved that blunt exchanges over deeply held views about the size of government, the threats to liberty, the protection of rights and the security of a nation sharpen what parties and their leaders believe in. Elections are a time for choosing more than just candidates.

Tale of Two Cow Palaces

The last time the Republican Party visited the Cow Palace, an unlovely, oversized barn originally built to host a livestock convention, was in 1956, for Eisenhower's second nomination. Before Eisenhower Ulysses S. Grant was the last Republican president to go on to a second term. The '56 convention was, at the time, the high point for the modern GOP—and a high water mark of comity—but at the Cow Palace in 1964, the crowd was in a raucous mood and rushing in an entirely different direction.

The Republican Party of 1964 had clear left and right wings in a form that would be unrecognizable today. Previous nominees had quickly worked to sew up the divisions and preached unity. In 1960 Goldwater himself had been a part of that unity effort, telling his allies on the right to "grow up" and work for the nominee, Nixon.[171] "If we want to take this party back—and I think we can someday—let's go to work," he said. In 1964, though, Goldwater was sounding a call to arms. It was fine with him if the moderates jumped in a lake.

Twice since the New Deal, moderates had nominated New York governor Thomas Dewey and twice he had lost, once to FDR and once to Truman. Conservatives were fed up with "me too" candidates who didn't give voters a clear break with New Deal Democratic rule. In 1952 conservatives fell in love with Robert Taft, but Eisenhower interrupted their dreams and gave moderates eight years in the White House.

For conservatives, Eisenhower's victories had come at the cost of principle, and in defeat they sharpened their thinking. The *National Review*, the organ of the movement, opposed Eisenhower and his move toward centrism. Its publisher, William Rusher, said that "modern American conservatism largely organized itself during, and in opposition to, the Eisenhower Administration." Goldwater called the Eisenhower administration a "dime-store New Deal."

As if to punctuate the point, when Eisenhower stopped in Amarillo, Texas, on the way to the '64 convention, two young men hurled a Goldwater sign in a fit of enthusiasm. They were not aiming at the ex-president but hit him nevertheless, causing him to double over.[172]

Moderate Republicans like Rockefeller supported the national consensus toward advancing civil rights by promoting national legislation to protect the vote, employment, housing and other elements of the American promise denied to blacks. They sought to contain Communism, not eradicate it, and they had faith that the government could be a force for good if it were circumscribed and run efficiently. They believed in experts and belittled the Goldwater approach, which held that complex problems could be solved merely by the application of common sense. It was not a plus to the Rockefeller camp that

Goldwater had publicly admitted, "You know, I haven't got a really first-class brain."[173] Politically, moderates believed that these positions would also preserve the Republican Party in a changing America.

Conservatives wanted to restrict government from meddling in private enterprise and the free exercise of liberty. They thought bipartisanship and compromise were leading to collectivism and fiscal irresponsibility. On national security, Goldwater and his allies felt Eisenhower had been barely fighting the communists, and that the Soviets were gobbling up territory across the globe. At one point, Goldwater appeared to muse about dropping a low-yield nuclear bomb on the Chinese supply lines in Vietnam, though it may have been more a press misunderstanding than his actual view.[174]

Conservatives believed that by promoting these ideas, they were not just saving a party, they were rescuing the American experiment. Politically, they saw in Goldwater a chance to break the stranglehold of the Eastern moneyed interests. If a candidate could raise money and build an organization without being beholden to the Eastern power brokers, then such a candidate could finally represent the interests of authentic Americans, the silent majority that made the country an exceptional one.

Goldwater looked like the leader of a party that was moving west. His head seemed fashioned from sandstone. An Air Force pilot, his skin was taut, as though he'd always left the window open on his plane. He would not be mistaken for an East Coast banker.

The likely nominee disagreed most violently with moderates over the issue of federal protections for the rights of black Americans. In June, a month before the convention, the Senate had voted on the Civil Rights Act. Twenty-seven of thirty-three Republicans voted for the legislation. Goldwater was one of the six who did not, arguing that the law was unconstitutional. "The structure of the federal system, with its fifty separate state units, has long permitted this nation to nourish local differences, even local cultures," said Goldwater.

Though Goldwater had voted for previous civil rights legislation and had founded the Arizona Air National Guard as a racially integrated unit, moderates rejected his reasoning. They said it was a disguise to cover his political appeal to anxious white voters whom he needed to win the primaries. He was courting not just Southern whites but whites in the North and the Midwest who were worried about the speed of change in America and competition from newly empowered blacks.

Here Come the Governors

The Stop Goldwater movement took shape not long after he won the California primary on June 2. Goldwater's opponents weren't just worried that Goldwater's hawkishness and scattershot positions—which seemed to shift from interview to interview—would lose him the presidency. They worried he would irreparably stain the party and hex Republicans also running for election that year.

Sen. Ken Keating of New York said he would not run as a Republican against Bobby Kennedy, but as an independent. Sen. Hugh Scott of Pennsylvania, who had been chairman of the Republican Party and had been a part of the successful Draft Eisenhower movement, said that if Goldwater were nominated, he'd bring thirty Republican members of Congress down with him that November.[175] New York senator Jacob Javits, a moderate Republican, said that Goldwater's victory would wrench the social order out of its sockets.

"The Republican establishment is desperate to defeat me," Goldwater said. "They can't stand having someone they can't control."

On June 7, a month before the GOP convention, fifteen Republican governors sat at breakfast at the Cleveland Sheraton before a meeting of the National Governors Association. If anyone was going to stop Goldwater it would be the governors.

Historian Rick Perlstein explains why: "Republican governors were moderates because governing a state was a moderating job. It was they who were responsible for mass transit and hospitals and housing and job training...It was they who would have to clean up the mess if a conservative White House were able to turn off their federal funding spigot. And it was they who would have to call out the National Guard should the civil rights revolution come to blows."[176]

Goldwater had the most delegates heading into the convention, but not enough to clinch the nomination, so a challenger could overtake him in San Francisco at the convention. The problem for the Republican governors was that no one would step forward and challenge Goldwater. Rockefeller was out. He'd tried during the primaries, but his loss in California and the bitterness from conservatives meant he could not make an appeal to the convention as a consensus candidate. The other problem was that he was already used up by the process, familiar from overexposure. "The harder the candidates ran," noted *Time* that year, "the weaker they looked. The less the non-candidates ran, the better they looked."[177]

George Romney, the governor of Michigan, was an obvious next choice. He fit in the noncandidate category, but that was his problem. He'd promised his constituents long ago that he would stay a noncandidate. Still, he crafted a strong statement denouncing Goldwater at the meeting. He said that Goldwater's nomination meant the party's alternatives were between "providing responsible leadership or the suicide of the Republican Party."[178]

Next in line was William Scranton of Pennsylvania, the imperturbable former congressman who had been in the governor's chair for only a little over a year. Senator Scott had formed a presidential committee for him, just as he had for Eisenhower.

Scranton's colleagues had expected him to announce that Sunday on CBS's *Face the Nation*. He had been preparing to. He'd even had a conversation with Eisenhower about taking on Goldwater and gotten the clear signal that Ike wanted him to run. Eisenhower called Scranton's candidacy "good for the health and vigor" of the party."

Eisenhower had written an article for the *New York Herald Tribune* describing his ideal candidate, and though he didn't name any names, the candidate he described had qualities which were all the opposite of the ones Goldwater had. The former president said the candidate must support the United Nations and civil rights, praising the GOP leadership for working with Johnson to pass the Civil Rights Act. After the article, Goldwater appeared at a rally with an arrow under his arm, making it look as though he had been shot in the back, to show "some of the problems I've had in the last few days."[179]

With Eisenhower's implicit support, Scranton started making lists and crafting battle plans. Others took the same hint. Based on the ex-president's signals, supporters of Ambassador Henry Cabot Lodge Jr., another moderate, who had actually won the New Hampshire primary when his name was submitted while he was still overseas as ambassador to Vietnam, pledged their support for Scranton. Everyone was ready to go, but then on the Sunday before Scranton was to appear on *Face the Nation*, Eisenhower called him and said he didn't want to be part of a Stop Goldwater movement.[180]

The rug yanked from beneath his feat, Scranton managed to avoid falling flat on his face until he was in front of the cameras and could do it properly. He put his announcement statement in his pocket and pretended he wasn't running. Under simple questioning Scranton behaved as if he'd carried off a bank heist and still had wads of cash stuffed in his pants. He kept calling the questioner "sir" and denied he was thinking about challenging Goldwater at all.

Known for having "an analytical mind that travels fast to the major points," he had come to say sharp things, but wound up saying nothing at all. It seemed *Time* magazine had been prescient when in 1962 it wrote of his gubernatorial race that Scranton had been "tugged reluctantly into every public job he has ever held."[181]

While the governors rushed between their hotel suites asking each other what to do, Richard Nixon arrived in Cleveland with his own plan to stop Goldwater. His loss in 1960 and subsequent exile had actually allowed the conservative movement to grow. Because Nixon wasn't the heir apparent to the nomination, Goldwater could rise. Nixon's plan was to draft Romney, about which Romney was rightfully suspicious. The Michigan governor thought Nixon might be setting him up for a fall as a way to remove competition for a later run Nixon might want to make. After a flurry of activity, which included a covert men's room meeting between Romney and Nixon to discuss the draft offer, the idea went nowhere.[182] Without a candidate to take on Goldwater, Nixon nevertheless made a pitch for one at a press conference: "Looking to the future of the party, it would be a tragedy if Senator Goldwater's views, as previously stated, were not challenged and repudiated."

By the end of the national governors' meeting, no new hats were in the ring. Goldwater's supporters saw their man acting with strength. The opposition, on the other hand, looked weak. "They didn't unite," wrote Roscoe Drummond in the *Washington Post*, who then turned to his metaphor basket. "They folded—like a crushed matchbox—under the Goldwater bandwagon." Teddy White called the meeting at which there had been much activity but no progress "the Dance of the Elephants."[183]

Richard Norton Smith, in his book about Nelson Rockefeller *On His Own Terms*, tells a story that captures the hollowness of the establishment movement. During the California primary, Rockefeller's aide Stu Spencer turned to the candidate and said, "Governor, I think it's time to call in the Eastern Establishment." To which Rockefeller responded, "You're looking at it, buddy. I'm all that's left."

Scranton Comes Alive!

A week after the uneventful governors' meeting and a month before the convention was to start, Governor Scranton decided to jump in after all, finally telling a small group of aides after a long meeting at his home, "I am going to run." It was a fairly bland statement, but a former Eisenhower aide now working with Scranton was swept up in the moment. Grabbing a blank paper from the coffee table, he wrote down the governor's words and said: "I'm keeping this for my scrapbook." It would ultimately be a thin volume.

Scranton had changed his mind, said aides, for three reasons: Goldwater's vote to oppose the civil rights bill, which was cast days after the Cleveland governors' meeting, the "rebellion" by Pennsylvania lawmakers in Harrisburg at the idea of a Goldwater nomination, which would bring them all early retirement, and his fear that Goldwater would doom the entire party.[184]

"The nation, and indeed the world, waits to see if another proud political banner, which is our own, will falter, grow limp and collapse in the dust," said Scranton to a frenzied audience at his announcement rally. "Has the Republican Party, a great many of our fellow citizens are asking, outlived its usefulness? Of course, the answer is no... Lincoln would cry out in pain if we sold out our principles. But he would laugh out with scorn if we threw away an election."

Scranton set out to woo delegates across the country. He carried a poll, commissioned by his campaign, that showed 62 percent of Republicans would vote for Johnson against Goldwater.[185] He argued that Goldwater was talking nonsense off the top of his head and misunderstood how the American economy worked. Said Scranton, "The Republican Party wonders how it will make clear to the American people that it does not oppose Social Security, the United Nations, Human Rights and sane nuclear policy."[186] It was no time, he said, "to go off half-cocked in the field of foreign policy."[187]

Rockefeller threw his weight behind his colleague, but picking up delegates was not easy. Those supporting Goldwater were not budging. "I will vote for you if my vote alone is the only vote you obtain," read one telegram sent to Goldwater. Another admirer said, "I give Barry my blood and the marrow from my bones."[188]

Eugene Patterson of the *Atlanta Constitution* described the Goldwater legions as "[a] Federation of the fed-up dismayed by moral laxity, greed, the tax collector and the erosion of yesterday's individualistic aspirational culture by social engineers and legislators masquerading as judges."

This made it very difficult for Scranton to court delegates. The *Chicago Tribune* reported that in Cleveland he had "run into a cold front on the shores of Lake Erie. Ohio's Republican leaders, who will control 58 votes in the party's national convention, icily absented themselves from the Scranton day activities in Cleveland, pleading prior engagements."[189]

In Illinois, Scranton's attempted to win the support of Everett Dirksen, the Senate majority leader, who had pushed the Republican senators to support the Civil Rights Act, went nowhere. Scranton asked Dirksen to run as a favorite son candidate to lock up the state's delegates but he refused.[190] The Senate leader predicted to the press the next day that Goldwater would be elected on the first ballot. When Scranton and Goldwater went to the Illinois caucus, Goldwater won fifty-eight delegates while Scranton won none.

Cow Palace Guard

When Scranton arrived at the Cow Palace, his pickaxe broken from such fruitless prospecting, he was still fighting to keep the GOP from turning into "another name for some ultra-rightist society."[191] The Stop Goldwater movement focused on making the case the Arizona senator would be a disaster for the party in the fall. Perhaps that would shake some delegates loose.

Delegates had to run a gauntlet of two hundred billboards for Scranton and Goldwater on the drive from the airport. In their hotel rooms they found an envelope with three buttons, labeled "For Liberals," "For Moderates," and "For Conservatives." A note encouraged them, "Wear the button you like best and if you really want to win in November, wear a big smile and vote for Bill Scranton."[192]

The competition was stiffer than perhaps it seemed. On the

outside, the Goldwater operation had all the frantic boosterism that makes conventions so gaudy. Goldwater girls, dressed in sombreros and tasseled boots, flounced around while California delegates holding helium-filled, gold-colored balloons waved a large Bear Flag. The candidate had been furnished with a gold Cadillac for use during the week. In the Goldwater hospitality suite in the "Room of the Dons" at the Mark Hopkins hotel, two thousand cases of an effervescent soft drink, gold in color and labeled "Goldwater," was available thanks to a North Carolina soft drink manufacturer who had whipped it up for the occasion. "The right drink for the conservative taste," it read on the green-and-gold can.

All this fun masked a stern Goldwater backroom operation. If you were traveling through the Mark Hopkins hotel you didn't dare try to stop on Goldwater's floor. If you did by mistake a thick-necked set of fellows would narrow their eyes at you, and you'd know it was time to move on. Security was tight because both campaigns were at the same hotel, staying just a floor apart in a setup that had their offices and private quarters interlaced like layers on a cake. Security guards manned the elevators and the stairways. When Governor Scranton's wife tried to take the stairs to her husband's office, she was stopped and not allowed to pass. The security men didn't care who she said she was.

Goldwater delegates were paired off in a buddy system, whereby they were constantly in touch with somebody from the campaign to make sure that they stayed on the team. If someone from the Scranton or Rockefeller operations tried to get them to cast their ballot for Scranton, the Goldwater forces would get in touch, have a conversation, and make sure they were still thinking the right way. They may also have been prohibited from swimming a half hour after eating.

Delegates were instructed to look out for the attentions of young ladies who might be trying to sway them off their opinion or put them in a compromising position that would make them susceptible to blackmail. Delegates were monitored everywhere they went, to and from their hotels. Everything was tracked in the headquarters. "It was like the combat information center on a warship," wrote William Middendorf, an operative on the campaign who would later become secretary of the navy, "complete with edge-lighted plastic panels upon which we scribbled data with grease pencils.[193]

The Goldwater team also set up its own independent communications system. They not only ran telephone wires from the headquarters to each of the thirty-six hotels where Goldwater delegates were staying, but also had two kinds of walkie-talkie systems to keep communications flowing, all with jam-proof antennas.[194] If any delegate got wobbly or the state total fell below what was expected, Goldwater troops could pounce. Lawyers were armed with tape recorders and Polaroid cameras as well as the rules of delegate selection in all states, ready to file suits if there was any funny business. The Goldwater supporters in the rafters may have been kooks, but the fellows in narrow ties in the windowless trailers outside the hall were highly competent kooks.

"What in God's Name Has Happened to the Republican Party?"

The tension between Goldwater supporters and moderates led to confrontation at unexpected times. "You're nigger lovers—communists!" someone yelled at James Brophy and family when they left the Georgia delegation for Goldwater and switched to support Scranton.[195]

Henry Cabot Lodge Jr., the winner of the New Hampshire primary that year, was accosted by a man who said, "I voted for you in 1960, but never again, you're terrible." Lodge was seen as the quarterback behind the Taft defeat in 1952 and chief archetype of moderate Republicanism. Lodge shot back, "You're terrible, too."

Ambassador Lodge had come back on a mission to save his party after a young captain in Vietnam asked him if he was going to return to "help Scranton." In his suite visiting with *Newsweek* editor Osborn Elliott, Lodge asked, "What in God's name has happened to the Republican Party? I hardly know any of these people."

Whoever those new people were, they were attracting more converts faster than Scranton was. Governor Jim Rhodes of Ohio, who had been one of the coordinators of the Stop Goldwater efforts at the Cleveland governors' conference, threw his support to Goldwater. He told Scranton that he thought the backlash in Ohio cities against race riots might be replicated in other places. It was beginning to appear as if Goldwater had a bigger movement behind him than any of his detractors had supposed. He predicted that he would surprise everyone just as Truman had done against Dewey in 1948.[196]

Outside the convention hall, the anti-Goldwater demonstrations in the streets continued. Protesters from the Congress of Racial Equality were trying to block the delegates from getting into the Cow Palace. "Barry Goldwater must go," read one placard. There was a forest of creative expression: "Defoliate Goldwater," "Vote for Goldwater—Courage, Integrity, Bigotry."[197]

The forty-thousand-person demonstration in San Francisco was the largest protest since the March on Washington in August of the previous year. Signs read, "Goldwater for Fuhrer, Freedom Is Dead, Hitler Was Sincere, Too"; "Goldwater in '64: Bread and water in '65; hot water in '66"; "Vote for Barry, stamp out peace"; "I'd rather have scurvy than Barry-Barry."[198] At another Goldwater rally a sign read "Barry go home," with a swastika in the *O*.

Lyndon Johnson's strategists worried about the backlash. They called the marches and riots "Goldwater rallies," because they feared the violence would push white voters to Goldwater.

On the last day of the convention, a continent away in New York, a fifteen-year-old, James Powell, was shot by a police lieutenant after making a lunge at him with a knife. It led to clashes in Harlem with rioters using garbage cans, glass bottles, and anything else close at hand. Gunfire was the official response. Looting followed. "If they just keep on rioting in Harlem you are going to have unshirted Hell," Lyndon Johnson said in a conversation with Texas governor John Connally, "and you're going to have it in New York, you're going to have the same type of rebellion there, and in Chicago and Iowa . . . this thing runs deep. You're going to see more cross-voting this year."[199]

Playing to the Cameras

Having failed to win over delegates, Scranton's last desperate gambit, was to draw Goldwater out, in the hopes the Arizonan's famous loose tongue would embarrass him and send scared delegates running to Scranton. "Will the convention choose the candidate overwhelmingly favored by the Republican voters, or will it choose you?" Scranton asked Goldwater in a letter. (He was relying on his own polls to make that assertion about the Republican voters favoring Scranton over Goldwater.) "With open contempt for the dignity, integrity, and common sense of the convention, your managers say in effect the delegates are little more than a flock of chickens whose necks will be wrung at will." The letter continued, excoriating Goldwater for his casual approach to the use of nuclear weapons and charging that he had allowed himself to be used by radical extremists. Finally it threw down a challenge to debate before the voting: "You must decide whether the Goldwater philosophy can stand public examination—before the convention and before the nation."

Goldwater erupted. He and Scranton had been friends. They'd served in the same Air National Guard unit together while in Washington. Their wives were friends (and stories during the convention attested to the women promising to maintain their friendship). Scranton had said before running that he had no intention of attacking Goldwater. But this was a full-throated assault. Even Rockefeller hadn't gone this far.

Goldwater responded with a terse statement: "Governor Scranton's letter has been read here with amazement. It has been returned to him." The Goldwater campaign sent out thousands of copies of the two letters to delegates. Scranton had written the letter—or more accurately, an overheated aide had written the letter—in the thrall of their own spin. The Scranton camp assumed the delegates were looking for a way to get away from Goldwater. Nope, they loved Goldwater. When those delegates saw how they had been characterized in the letter and how Goldwater, their pick, had been described, they became even more supportive of him. To other delegates, Scranton just looked reckless. There were reports that the letter had caused Scranton to even lose the support of some of his own people.

Other gambits, like an effort to get the platform committee to attest to the constitutionality of the Civil Rights Act, also failed. The final attempt to change the dynamic would involve embarrassing Goldwater in front of the television cameras, to either shake loose delegates or at least gain leverage for changes in the party platform.

The television networks had put a lot of effort into covering the 1964 convention. There were 5,423 credentials issued for the press, of which 3,963 badges were issued to representatives of radio and television stations.[200] They built power substations and constructed skyboxes high above the seats so that wise commentators could survey the groupings of delegates like armies on the battlefield. ABC pulled in a general for the task. Eisenhower was hired as an official commentator for the network.

Rockefeller's speech on extremism was intended to take full advantage of the television spotlight. Its official purpose was to plead for an amendment to the platform, proposed by Pennsylvania senator Hugh Scott, denouncing "extremist" groups. But the Goldwater forces knew it was a veiled attack on their candidate. The third-term senator had the support of the virulent anticommunist John Birch Society, which he refused to distance himself from, even though its leader had accused Eisenhower of treason and of being a communist agent. '

Melvin Laird, a congressman from Wisconsin and future secretary of defense who was running the show for Goldwater, thwarted Rockefeller by asking that the platform be read into the record before the governor spoke. The platform was 8,500 words. It took ninety minutes. Rockefeller was pushed out of prime time.

Rockefeller should have known he'd get a stout reception. Quiet Dwight Eisenhower had been taken aback when his ad-libbed line earlier in the evening about "sensation-seeking columnists and commentators" provoked a primal howl from the approving audience.

Journalist Murray Kempton's description of the response to Rockefeller captures the party tension so well, Richard Norton Smith made it the epigraph of his Rockefeller biography: "There came down upon Rockefeller from those galleries a howl of hatred which was not of an opinion but of a human being who embodied everything these people had hated for 20 years....He just stood there and began his prose in the armor of a magnificent contempt. Who cares what he said; it was what he was that night."[201]

When the convention finally voted, Goldwater swamped Scranton. He got 883 delegates and Scranton just 214. As a show of unity, Scranton walked to the podium to urge a unanimous vote for Goldwater. He was greeted by "We Want Barry."[202]

"In the campaign of 1964, Bill Scranton was a loser," wrote his biographer George D. Wolf. "He lost the nomination because he never really sought the presidency. The 'Scranton Boomlet' is an object lesson in how not to win a presidential nomination."[203]

Put Your Money on X

For Barry Goldwater and conservatives, the victory was a turning point in the growth of the cause. They had won, but also the establishment had lost. Those who had fought the Arizona Senator left the convention shaken. "The deliberately exclusionary acts and precepts of these newly-crowned Republican leaders posed serious problems for hundreds of Republican candidates," wrote Senator Hugh Scott of his thoughts leaving the convention. "The on-coming right-wing crusade confronted them—and me—with a dilemma that was moral as well as political."[204] Richard Nixon shared the lesson he'd taken away from the shift in party politics in a conversation with aide Pat Buchanan, saying, "Buchanan, if you ever hear of a group getting together to stop X, be sure to put your money on X." Nixon's argument was that anybody who has enough power from the people to require a movement to stop them has the power of the people, and that's all you need in politics.

But Barry Goldwater didn't have all the people. He went on to lose to Lyndon Johnson in one of the most lopsided defeats in history. In a campaign ad, Johnson returned to the Cow Palace convention and the ideological splits in the Republican Party. In the spot, a jittery Republican voter, dressed in a dark suit with standard-issue glasses, engages in a therapy session with the viewing audience about his fears about Goldwater. He's a little undone and one gets the impression that he (or the actor playing him) will conclude his remarks and rush to the first bar he finds on Broadway for a double:

> I don't know why they just wanted to call this a confession. I... I simply don't feel guilty about being a Republican. I've always been a Republican. My father is, his father was. The whole family is a Republican family. I voted for Dwight Eisenhower, the first time I ever voted. Goldwater, now it seems to me we're up against... a very difficult kind of a man. This man scares me... A reporter will go to Senator Goldwater and he'll say, "Senator, on such and such a day, you said, and I quote, 'blah, blah, blah.'" Whatever it is, end quote. And then Goldwater says, "Well, I wouldn't put it that way." I... I can't follow that.
>
> Was he serious when he did put it that way? Is he serious when he says he wouldn't put it that way? I... I... I just don't get it... I... I... I wish... I wish I was as sure that Goldwater's against war, as I am that he's against some of these other things. I tell you, those people who got control of that convention, who are they? I mean, when the head of the Ku Klux Klan, when all these weird groups come out in favor of the candidate of my party, either they're not Republicans or I'm not. I've thought about just not voting in this election, just staying home. But

you can't do that because that's . . . that's saying you . . . you don't care who wins. And . . . and I do care. I think my party made a bad mistake in San Francisco. But I'm gonna have to vote against that mistake on the third of November."

Vote for President Johnson on November third. The stakes are too high for you to stay home.

Even in defeat, the movement behind Goldwater would define the Republican Party for the second half of the twentieth century and afterward. The party's center moved west geographically and right ideologically. Though Republican nominees would never be crowned again at the Cow Palace, the next pair of two-term Republican presidents, Richard Nixon and Ronald Reagan would both come from California. In 1956, the party had emerged from the Cow Palace unified behind a moderate candidate. In 1964, it emerged a party in turmoil, having selected an unelectable nominee. But the fractious, more conservative party of '64 was the future of the GOP.

2000—The Straight Talk Express

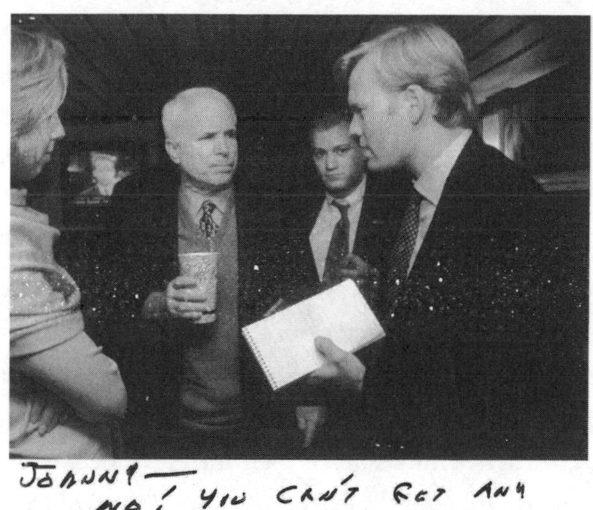

In the winter of 2000, a bus called the Straight Talk Express dominated the New Hampshire highways from Manchester to Nashua to Keene to Dixville Notch and every town in between. The final stop on the itinerary was to be the presidency.

Three-term Arizona senator John McCain sat at the back of the coach, on the other side of the galley kitchen, at the center of a horseshoe banquette. A dozen or so reporters encircled him, including a *Time* magazine correspondent who thought it was a good idea to grow sideburns that year and who hadn't been able to get off the trail long enough to get a haircut. Some of us sat on the top of the banquette to make more room, denting the bones on our backsides as the bus rocked. It was maximum occupancy at a rolling campaign conversation that was part policy debate, part Catskills revue, and part sermon about the big-money corruption that had made Washington ineffective and scraped the virtue out of public service.

The senator looked around for his coffee. "This is what happens when you hire people on work-release programs," he joked as a staffer hurried to get it to him. Throughout the New Hampshire campaign his hand was rarely not warmed by a large plastic cup of Dunkin' Donuts coffee. The only thing that separated Senator McCain's hands from his coffee were voters anxious to greet him and the hand sanitizer he asked for upon returning to the bus afterward.

"Give me a squirt of that stuff," he would say before sitting down. An aide would hand him a small plastic bottle or squirt a flat bottomed teardrop of clear liquid on his palm. He'd rub them like he was trying to kindle fire, but awkwardly, as if someone were behind him trying to stop him. The fighter pilot's arms are restricted, broken in the plane crash that made the young naval aviator a prisoner of war in 1967. The enemy doctors didn't care too much how those broken arms were set, and he carries the result of their indifference all over his body.

"Okay, what do you got?" he asked, before we could even settle in.

"If I can go at this one more time, Senator," asked one reporter about a charge McCain's rival, Governor George W. Bush, had made about his Senate record.

"Once more into the breach, my friends!" he exclaimed, quoting from *Henry V.* "Until we fill up the gaps with our English dead!"

The conversation ricocheted. He talked about taxes, Social Security, the failure of the Comprehensive Nuclear-Test-Ban Treaty in the Senate. "We really have not responded either structurally or psychologically to the end of the cold war, even after nine years," he said. He recounted scenes from *Viva Zapata!,* his favorite film. He explained why *For Whom the Bell Tolls* was his favorite book. He seemed ready to answer anything.

If McCain ever veered into trouble, his top strategist, Mike Murphy, would employ an emergency comedy diversion. He would unspool a campaign story and you could feel it being embellished as he told it, like the one about time the police mistook him for an Alan Keyes staffer during the 1996 GOP presidential campaign. The irascible, voluble never plausible Keyes staged a hunger strike when he was shut out of a primary debate and then showed up to make his case in person before candidates took the stage.

The topic of campaign finance dominated the conversation. "The trial lawyers control the Democrats," McCain said, "and the drug companies and HMOs control the Republicans." The push for cash had distorted public policy, he argued, and it led to a larger rot. It made people cynical and blasé about their country's future, leaving the government in the hands of the self-interested, who would only invite more cynicism.

Asked to assess how his project to get big money out of politics was going, McCain said: "As Chairman Mao used to say: It's always darkest before it's totally black."

The Straight Talk Express rolled out in the predawn and stopped well after the sun went down, often crawling through New England snowstorms. It carried the sixty-three-year-old McCain's insurgent campaign to 114 New Hampshire town halls that election season. John McCain's 2000 campaign was historic not just for the rags-to-riches political story of a long-shot insurgent taking on the establishment. It was the last gasp of a pre-Internet age, without tweeting, blogging, and streaming, which has turned campaigning into something approaching a continuous live event.

McCain offered as much of a window into a candidate's authentic self as was possible in the artificial, authenticity-shielding campaign circus. It was a last stutter before campaigns became a constantly turning cycle of controversy, kept spinning by the need for fresh hot takes to keep page views growing and permanent ideological warfare that makes it easier to raise campaign and special interest dollars.

2000: No GOP Front-Runner

There was no Republican front-runner in 2000. In 1996, Bob Dole had started the campaign in the top slot. In 1988, it had been George

H. W. Bush. In 1980 it was Reagan. But in 1998 there was no candidate who everyone agreed started at the top of the heap.

Texas governor George W. Bush would soon move into pole position with one of the most masterful sustained campaigns to win the invisible primary of party elites in recent memory. His strategist Karl Rove set about systematically wooing the donors and elites in the GOP and built an inevitability campaign out of thin air.

GOP losses in 1998 set the foundation for the Bush campaign. The Republican Party, in control of Congress, had pushed to impeach President Bill Clinton. It was widely seen to have been a huge political mistake. Republican pollster Frank Luntz called the campaign against the president "the stupidest single political decision that I know of." Nineteen ninety-eight was a "six-year itch" election; in such a year the party in the White House usually loses an average of twenty-nine seats in the House and six seats in the Senate. Impeachment was so unpopular that Democrats picked up seats in that 1998 election.

House Speaker Newt Gingrich had been the impeachment campaign general, and the 1998 election was his Waterloo. He stepped down shortly after the election losses. The GOP revolution that Gingrich led in 1994 seemed to have petered out, leaving the party looking for a new stable from which to pick its next horse. They looked to the governors, and Bush was a worthy political pick. While the GOP was creating history with its losses in Washington, Bush was making history with his victory in Texas. He picked up seven of every ten votes; two-thirds were women. Almost fifty percent of Hispanics voted for him. He won a third of Democrats.

Bush was a crossover success who'd worked with a Democratic legislative leader. He talked about education, an issue that would matter in the fight for suburban women voters. Bush also talked about compassion, using government to help the least among us. Even when he talked about GOP policy standards like tax cuts, he framed the discussion around the image of the waitress mom who had to struggle through several jobs. He acted and spoke like a general election winner.

That was a good start, but what made Bush inevitable was the alliance building and fund-raising that the public doesn't see but which shapes the forces that make candidates very hard to beat. Bush's top strategist, Karl Rove—his office lined with historic memorabilia from the eras of Abraham Lincoln, Teddy Roosevelt, and William McKinley—created a careful, Austin-based, front-porch campaign. While in public Bush resisted speculation about his presidential campaign, Rove worked behind the scenes to bring the money raisers, lobbyists, and party brains into town to meet with Bush. The governor announced the formation of an exploratory committee on March 7, 1999, by which point he was endorsed by 80 GOP House members, vastly more than anyone else.

By June 1999 Bush had raised $37 million, and by September, $50 million. The establishment opened up their cash-filled suitcases and showered him with bundles of hundreds. In the end, Bush would raise almost $100 million, from nearly three hundred and fifty thousand individual donors from all fifty states, setting new records.

The Bush campaign's innovation was in its empowerment of 246 "Pioneers," who had all pledged to raise $100,000 by bundling contributions from their friends, who'd donated the maximum amount possible. (In the Bush administration, a little more than forty percent of the Pioneers would end up getting jobs.) Bush became the consensus favorite with every lobbyist, longtime GOP fund-raiser, and inside Republican. He was a lock. He was in the books before they were opened and long before voters ever got out their rubber mallets to pound in the first yard sign.

I'll Tell You the Truth

John McCain, meanwhile, was a long shot. Bush had the family name and was friendly with insiders. McCain had a reputation for irritating his colleagues. He didn't play nice, and even when he did, it was often with Democrats on issues like campaign financing reform and anti-tobacco legislation. He also had no special connection with the social conservatives in his party. Bush, on the other hand, had a well-known and compelling conversion story. He wasn't just appealing to evangelical Christians. He was one of them.

In January 1999 McCain was polling at 8 percent. Bush was at 42 percent followed by Elizabeth Dole, who would soon fade. At McCain's first town hall event in Peterborough, New Hampshire, in July 1999, at just about the time I was assigned to the campaign, forty people showed, mostly, McCain joked, because he was serving free ice cream.

McCain's strategy was candor and constant campaigning. At almost every stop, the senator would close his remarks by saying, "I'm going to tell you something. I may have said some things here today that maybe you don't agree with. And I might have said some things that you hopefully agree with. But I will always tell you the truth." This always got a standing ovation. It was a simple promise not to lie.

How could people buy it? Because they always want to. It's the electoral triumph of hope over experience. No matter how much people hate lying politicians, they still wait in the cold and wear themselves out on hard bleachers to hear the promise of something approximating truth, and if they couldn't get that, they still found it attractive to be around someone who knew that they cared about being lied to. It meant he showed them respect.

McCain was playing on the same piano Jimmy Carter had rolled across Iowa in 1976 after the Nixon years. It shouldn't have been such a crowd-pleaser for McCain to say he wouldn't lie, but after the Clinton years, where the president was filmed arguing over the meaning of the word "is," this was thrilling for audiences.

McCain did more than promise though. His entire campaign was founded around candor. There was the bus's name, of course, but he also conveyed it in the way he talked to voters, disagreeing with them and then giving them a chance to respond. He called out his party for its sins. He called himself out for his sins. McCain could tell juvenile jokes or say something that was not politically correct, but when he did, he knew he was out of bounds and admitted he was a jerk. If he didn't at first admit it, he could be appealed to by pointing out that he'd fallen short of his own sense of character.

Other politicians fogged up the stage with bilious clouds of safe phrases, bromides, and pleasing pieties mouthed for the moment but synthetic at heart. McCain seemed to actually believe things. His biggest passion was limiting the role of money in politics, which had candor at its heart, because McCain was telling a truth about a system he could benefit from if he just kept his mouth shut.

The constant need to raise big money to stay in office warped legislation, but McCain was additionally worried about how that system bred cynicism. "When the people come to believe that government is so corrupt that it no longer serves [the Constitution's goals] our culture could fragment beyond recognition as people seek substitutes for the unifying values of patriotism."

Politicians can say they want to make America great again. McCain had a theory about how to do it based on promoting old truths. That couldn't work if people were cynical. "My job," McCain said, thinking of the presidency, "will be to inspire people to commit themselves to causes greater than their self-interest...People say there are no great causes, but everywhere a senior citizen has no shelter, there is a great cause, and everywhere there is a hungry child, there is a great cause, and everywhere people are killing themselves for ethnic or sectarian reasons, there is a great cause."

McCain had some experience with the unifying values of patriotism. The hitchy way he walked was proof that he knew in his bones—particularly the broken ones—what words like *character*, *value*, *patriotism*, *honor*, and *duty* meant. He had kept his word as a POW, staying true to a code and refusing to jump the line to get early release.

But John McCain wasn't running a holier-than-thou campaign—at least not all the time. McCain talked about his flaws more in one day than most politicians do in a lifetime. He talked about cheating on his first wife and about his hot temper. He said, "Spinning is lying," and then when he caught himself spinning to reporters on the bus, he called himself out on it.

He also knew that what he was selling was an act at some level. Authenticity in politics is necessarily artificial. Even if you are letting people see you as authentic, you're doing it for political, not authentic reasons. McCain was encased in a plan to not act like a politician. But he knew that plan was itself artifice. So he tried to prove that he was on the level, only to be pulled back into the pursuit of his ambition, which required having to behave like a politician. During the South Carolina primary he hid his belief that the state should take down the Confederate flag from flying over the statehouse. It was the struggle of the imperfect, and while he failed—sometimes in big ways—his authenticity surpassed his rivals' by leagues. (After the primaries he returned to South Carolina to publicly apologize for not calling for the removal of the Confederate battle flag. He said he had compromised his principles out of political self-interest.)

Where a traditional candidate might be inclined to go into a crouch during a controversy, McCain would douse campaign brushfires with admissions. Asked once about his communications director Dan Schnur, who had talked about an internal campaign disagreement in the press, McCain didn't clam up. He added to the story with more tales of campaign misbehavior by top aides Mike Murphy and John Weaver. "One of the fun things about our campaign is that we do have people disagree and sometimes publicly," he said, starting what would be a sleight of hand to make a bad story look good. "I try to beat the living daylights out of them for doing it, but people say [the campaign is] seat-of-the-pants, unstructured, undisciplined and that's all true. But we wouldn't be having fun if we weren't like that. Dan Schnur had a disagreement on that issue and I appreciate that. How many times has [Mike] Murphy been leaking crapola in a way that builds his prestige and diminishes this great American? How many times has that happened? And look at [John] Weaver, who is the incarnate of evil."

McCain was running as an antidote to the first baby boomer president. "After seven years of Bill Clinton ... the inchoate grown-up factor has taken shape in the electoral mind," wrote *Time* essayist Lance Morrow. "There is a hunger. Call it an unarticulated disgust to see a mature adult in the White House the next time around."[205]

Faith Based Initiative

McCain's campaign was built around his new book *Faith of My Fathers*, a moving account of his Naval officer father and grand-father which also told the story of McCain's Vietnam experience. The Senator demurred when people called him a hero—it's not that heroic to get shot down, he'd say. He deflected praise by praising others he'd served with. Yet his campaign events featured posters with the rugged picture of McCain standing in his flight suit in front of his plane during the war.

Whether voters liked McCain or not as a candidate, they flocked to his book signings, where he looped the Sharpie pen awkwardly to sign their names as best as his injuries would allow. Voters held up copies of the book at his rallies. Under a president who had dodged the draft, the campaign seemed like a redemption of the Vietnam War for a new generation.

It was as if McCain was building a bridge between his book and Tom Brokaw's book *The Greatest Generation*, which had returned the ideas of selflessness and sacrifice to the national conversation. While other politicians were telling stories about legislation, and voters were trying to follow rabbit-hole debates about ideological purities, McCain was telling stories about heroism and death and codes of honor.

McCain's other secret ingredient was that he was entertaining. He played a Borscht Belt comedian whose patter became so familiar, many of us covering him could recite it word for word.

"Thank you to all of you for being here," he would say while audience members settled in. "Anyone who wants to take a nap, go right ahead while we're waiting. Okay?" He'd usually start with the story about his first town hall in Peterborough. "They had a poll that showed that I was at three percent approval. And that poll had a five percent margin of error. So I could've conceivably started this campaign at minus two... I seek your sympathy—because I'm from the state of Arizona. We have so little water there the trees chase the dogs." He would be the first president to have Hail to the Chief include a rim shot.

"Here's our problem in Arizona," McCain continued. "Barry Goldwater, from Arizona, ran for president of the United States. Morris Udall, from Arizona, ran for president of the United States. Bruce Babbitt, from Arizona, ran for president of the United States. Arizona may be the only state in America where mothers don't tell their children that someday they can grow up and be president of the United States. I wanna fix that. I think it's a terrible thing for mothers in Arizona."

Morris Udall jokes are a favorite of all candidates, but McCain had known the former congressman when they served in the House together, and visited him in his last years at a veterans' hospital where he was suffering from Parkinson's. "When he was running for president in 1976, Mo Udall walked into a barbershop in Manchester, New Hampshire. And he said, 'Hi. I'm Morris Udall from Arizona. And I'm runnin' for president of the United States.' And the barber said, 'Yeah. We were just laughin' about that this morning.' "

McCain would end the funny stuff, make some remarks about taxes or defense, always explain why campaign finance reform was important, and then he'd take question after question. Sometimes he would get into fights with people in the crowd. They'd leave saying they had respect for him even though they didn't agree.

Almost always, McCain would wrap up the event with the story of Mike Christian, one of his fellow prisoners of war. Even after a hundred hearings, it was hard to work on whatever you were doing at the back of the room while he told it. While in captivity, Christian, who had been captured a year before McCain, fashioned a bamboo needle and knit an American flag inside his blue prison uniform, using the shreds of a handkerchief. "Every evening before we would have our bowl of soup, we would put Mike Christian's shirt on the wall of our cell," McCain described, "and say the Pledge of Allegiance. Now, I will freely admit to you saying the Pledge of Allegiance to our flag and our country is not usually the most important part of our day. I want to tell you, in that prison cell, a couple of guys that have already been there for seven years, pledging our allegiance to our flag and our country was indeed the most important part of our day."

One day the Vietnamese searched the cell, found Mike Christian's shirt with the flag sewn inside of it, and took him away for a beating. After a time, they threw him back in the group cell, bleeding and swollen. "We cleaned up Mike as well as we could," said McCain. "You could imagine, he was not in great shape. And I went over to lay down on the slab to go to sleep. And as I did, I happened to look over. And in the corner of the cell, beneath the dim lightbulb with a piece of white cloth and piece of red cloth and his bamboo needle and another shirt, with his eyes almost shut from the beating that he had received, was, of course, my friend, Mike Christian, sewing another American flag. Mike wasn't sewing that flag because it made him feel better. He was sewing that flag because he knew how important it was to us. To pledge our allegiance to our flag and country."

The story drained the room of noise. People cried. Everything was still until McCain talked again, sometimes with a little difficulty, kick-starting himself because even after telling the story so many times, the story still surprised him. "I think of Mike all the time. But I also know that there are young men and women who are serving today who are every bit as good or better than Mike and I were. And I'm so proud that we are associated with the best of America. Who are serving in our nation's armed forces. Who are carrying on the noble tradition of a young man from a small town near Selma, Alabama, named Mike Christian."

Audiences erupted not just because of the story, but because McCain was giving them the freedom and inspiration to cheer and applaud for ideas that had seemed dusty and out-of-date. The idea of heroism and doing the right thing when no one is looking. It literally felt good for McCain's audiences to cheer for him.

After a long, draining town hall most politicians would need to recharge. They'd relegate the press to the overflow bus with the bathroom door that doesn't close and swings open and shut, fanning the odor. Not McCain, he was back on the bus, coffee in hand, asking: "What else?" If you covered him, you had to bring extra notebooks. Sometimes we quietly wished the candidate would stop talking.

Why did he keep talking on the bus after all that talking with voters? Friends and former POWs who'd suffered with him said that McCain was making up for the time that he'd been in solitary confinement. When he came back from Vietnam after his release he'd done a version of this, reading everything that he could get his hands on that had been written while he was away. He went to school about the war that he had missed while he was in prison. He kept going at that same pace.

Bush on Lockdown

McCain's act was entertaining, but it was a seemingly fruitless joyride. George W. Bush had the race well in hand. He was the establishment favorite. The polls showed it for much of 1999 and into the start of 2000. That's why the Bush campaign didn't let their man do anything risky. They kept him from sharp objects and only let him cut with the scissors with the rounded edges. "We have a message a day and we want to stick to it," said a Bush aide when asked why Bush wasn't interacting with the press the way McCain was. "We are not going to have one big, fat news conference on our schedule where everyone can come ask questions about what you think is the news of the day."

Bush had too much to lose. And he also had too many adventures with the English language to talk all the time. The governor improved on his father's strange locution by minting entirely new ways of speaking. "I know how hard it is to put food on your family," he said once while describing the plight of single mothers. "I know the human being and fish can coexist peacefully," he said during another stop. "Families is where our nation finds hope, where wings take dream," he mused. "Rarely," said the candidate who spoke with passion about education reform, "is the question asked: Is our children learning?"

While McCain was running a New Hampshire campaign of freewheeling town halls, Bush was running a national campaign in all the states, giving set-piece speeches, shaking hands quickly and moving on to the next arid event. His boosters scoffed at McCain's puny one-state gambit. This is the problem with being the front-runner. You have to campaign everywhere. In New Hampshire, Bush's strategy gave support to the impression that he was aloof and trying to coast to the nomination on his money, his name, and all his establishment support. Emily Mead, who worked in the Bush White House of the candidate's father before returning to New Hampshire to run a small policy think tank, saw it coming. According to *Time* magazine, she even sent a warning out to Barbara Bush who wrote back saying she would pass on the warning to the campaign. "Three months went by and he was hardly here at all," said Mead. "You can't run a campaign like that and expect to win."

Trying to Put the Straight Talk Express in a Ditch

As McCain started to rise at the end of 1999, the Bush campaign and the establishment slowly turned their heads toward the pesky challenger. The main target? His temper. The largest newspaper in McCain's home state, the *Arizona Republic*, published a highly unusual editorial in which it declared, "There's also reason to seriously question whether McCain has the temperament and the political approach and skills we want in the next president of the United

States." Arizona governor Jane Hull went public with her experiences of holding the phone away from her ear while McCain yelled at her.

McCain had enemies in the Senate, too, because whenever he argued for campaign finance reform he would say, essentially, that it was corrupting all the Republican senators. His colleagues were disgusted by his self-aggrandizing morality act, which came at their expense. It was a critique not unlike the one they would make about Sen. Ted Cruz in 2016.

Stories started to leak about McCain's behavior in the Senate. When McCain fought for legislation he did it the way he boxed at the U.S. Naval Academy, where he would charge into the center of the ring and throw punches until somebody went down. He lashed out at Alabama senator Richard Shelby, who voted against former Texas senator John Tower for secretary of defense in 1989. McCain, who had worked for Tower and revered him, told Shelby after his vote, "You'll pay for that." (McCain later wrote how, after the vote, he approached Shelby "to bring my nose within an inch of his as I screamed out my intense displeasure over his deceit.)[206] McCain also fought with navy secretary John Dalton, calling him up to report: "You're finished." During disagreements with New Mexico senator Pete Domenici and Texas Senator John Cornyn, McCain used words more appropriate for a drunken bar brawl than the euphemism wrapped Senate cloakroom.

McCain's temper became so much a part of the conversation that I asked him if he'd ever sought counseling or medication for his anger. He said no, after looking at me like I was crazy, but added that his staff, which had been with him a long time, frequently talked him down from his passions.

Underlying the temperament question was a more insidious one: Had his time as a prisoner of war loosened the bolts on his self-control? When it looked like he started to be a real threat to Bush, the governor's backers in the Senate started trying to goad McCain on the floor of the Senate. At the end of 1999, in a vote over campaign finance reform, one senator after another from his own party baited him, hoping to bring out his temper.

"They tried to get him to explode on the floor," said McCain's ally, Democrat Russ Feingold. "They tried as hard as they could." McCain rocked in his shoes, as we described it in *Time.* He folded, and then unfolded his arms. He fidgeted with the papers on his lectern. But the man once called "Senator Hothead" did not blow. He later remembered, "I had to say to myself, 'Look, John. You're not going to get anything by displaying anger here.' "

Final Stretch in New Hampshire

Heading into the New Hampshire primary, Bush struggled to prove that, despite all of his support, he wasn't just a captive of the establishment. "My zip code. 78701. That's Austin, Texas," he told Bob Schieffer on *Face the Nation.* "It's not Washington, D.C. If you were to call me on the telephone it'd be area code 512. Not 202. I come from Texas. I've got a record as a governor. I've been setting agendas. I'm runnin' my campaign in Austin, Texas. But...and... and the reason I bring that up is I...I...I'm not of the Washington scene. I'm not a committee chairman. I'm not a chairman of a powerful committee, like the Commerce Committee. And so they can say what they wanna say, but the people of this party understand that I bring a fresh approach to politics. I come from outside Washington, D.C."

McCain had started out twenty points behind Bush, but then in January after nearly a hundred of those town halls, his pollster Bill McInturff got a call in the middle of the night from his assistant. "I literally could not breathe," he remembered. "Are you dying?" his assistant asked. He responded: "There are two people in the entire world that now know," said McInturff, "what could happen in New

Hampshire. How big this is. And it's you. And me. And it's two in the morning."[207]

Before Election Day, McCain returned to Peterborough, New Hampshire, the site of his first town hall in July 1999, for his very last town hall, forty-eight hours before the vote. "I will not get emotional," he told the crowd before launching into the same jokes—dogs chase trees, Mo Udall and the barber, visiting Dixville Notch, and how he wouldn't hype his new book (before telling them it would be on sale in the back of the room or on Amazon).

"What happened in Peterborough, New Hampshire, is a metaphor for this entire campaign," he said before pausing. "Again, I will not get emotional. I will not get emotional." He rescued himself with a joke. Noting his kids were there, he described taking them to school for the first day. "Oh, Senator McCain, so nice of you to come to opening day of school with your grandchildren," said a teacher.

He made his pitches about how he was "fully prepared to assume the office of commander in chief. I do not need training on day one." And how he wanted to take the lineage of his family—"Three Americans who found virtue in their country's cause"—and try to build that for a new generation. He summed up the campaign on the eve of the vote. "This has been the greatest political experience of my life," he said.

On Election Night, the McCain campaign team met on a top floor of the Nashua Crowne Plaza in a suite filled with McCain's family. His older children from his first marriage and his young sons and daughters from his second. McCain's daughter Sidney spun the youngest, Jimmy, as if they were doing the Lindy hop.

McCain wasn't smiling. The polls had him up, but he didn't believe them. Also there was the worry of, what if he won? His seat-of-the-pants strategy-making was going to face a whole new kind of challenge if he prevailed.

It was Mark Salter, the writer and McCain's chief of staff, who is nearly as close to McCain as are any of the senator's children, who delivered the good news to the Arizona senator that he might not just be winning, but that he might be winning huge, that men and women, old and young, "independents and libertarians and vegetarians," as he'd say on the stump, were coming over.

"This could have implications," McCain deadpanned.

"Yes," responded Salter. "Like you could be president."

When the returns finally came in, McCain had not just won, he had walloped George Bush by eighteen points. His wife Cindy's hands flew to her face. Her eyes filled with tears. McCain hugged his wife as tightly as his arms would let him. The aides let out a cheer.

A man few Republicans in Washington liked now suddenly stood a chance of grabbing the party's nomination from the well-liked, well-named governor of Texas. "Fine mess you've gotten me into, Weaver," McCain said to the forty-year-old political director John Weaver, who had gone to McCain in February 1997 to persuade him to run. As word of McCain's rout spread, his kids started chasing each other between the chairs and sofa, grazing the table, spilling a Shirley Temple.

The acceptance speech was ahead. "Slow. Slow. Slow," McCain said to himself as he paced the suite. It was as if he were preparing to deliver a eulogy rather than frame the meaning of this moment. This was not a time for whooping or wisecracks. Most Americans were now going to be seeing him as a possible president for the first time. "The only other speech that will be more important will be his acceptance speech at the convention," said his California coordinator, Ken Khachigian.

The goal was to take the reform message that had played so well in the small politics of New Hampshire and make it the basis of a national crusade. Reform had to mean more than McCain's campaign finance agenda. It had to mean something larger. "They said there wasn't room for reform in the Republican Party," said McCain in his victory speech. "Well, we've made room."

That night, McCain got on his plane and flew down to South Carolina, where he was met at 3:00 a.m. at an airport hangar by hundreds of college kids and the earsplitting techno sounds of Fatboy Slim. It was so loud it almost parted your hair. Signs were waving. Bodies were hopping on the concrete floor, all for the father of seven, who'd spent five and a half years in a dark box during a war that was over before many of the kids yelling and jumping up and down were even born.

"He's the last hero of American politics," Brandon Goeringer, twenty-two, told me. Goeringer had driven all the way from Greenville to get a good spot near the stage. "I don't agree with all of his policies on abortion and other stuff. But he tells the truth."

"There's something a little magical going on here," said McCain on the bus afterward, looking dazed by the crowd. "There's something happening out there."

In the end, after McCain's surprise, blistering victory in New Hampshire, the insurgency it launched was not to be. The empire struck back in South Carolina. The Bush campaign went fully negative, and its local operatives played dirty, their tricks reportedly included putting leaflets on cars that said McCain's adopted daughter from Bangladesh was a love child from an affair. McCain was defeated, and he got nasty in Michigan, claiming that Bush was an anti-Catholic bigot. It all came to an end on March 7, Super Tuesday. Bush won big states. California, Ohio, and New York. The establishment won.

John McCain's insurgent campaign wasn't supposed to have a chance. George W. Bush had the famous name, had locked up all the money and support of all the insiders. But John McCain made a run at the nomination anyway. He said the game George W. Bush was winning was fixed and voters didn't have to put up with it. If they were cynical that anyone could change things, his campaign was going to show people how it could be done. If he could win, maybe the larger system where the guys who ate at white tablecloth restaurants had more influence than entire states' worth of people could be broken up, too. His message and his candidacy were the same thing. He didn't just tell voters he was going to break up the cozy status quo. He was going to show them how he could do it. And he showed them in New Hampshire.

PART V

Too Close to Call

1976—Republicans Are People, Too

AP Photo

Reagan Comes Calling

On November 19, 1975, Ronald Reagan called President Gerald Ford to wish him a speedy retirement. "Well, Mr. President, I'm going to make an announcement tomorrow and I want to tell you about it ahead of time," Reagan said. The former California governor was announcing his challenge to the incumbent for their party's nomination. "I'm sorry you're getting into this," Ford responded. "I believe I've done a good job and that I can be elected. Regardless of your good intentions, your bid is bound to be divisive. It will take a lot of money, a lot of effort, and it will leave a lot of scars. It won't be helpful, no matter which of us wins the nomination." Reagan said, "I don't think it will harm the party." "I think it will," said Ford, hanging up. Ford wrote in his memoir: "How can you challenge an incumbent President of your own party and not be divisive?"[208]

The next day, Reagan flew across the country and spoke in Ford's backyard at the National Press Club.

"In Washington, D.C., our nation's capital has become the seat of a buddy system that functions for its own benefit," said Reagan, "increasingly insensitive to the needs of the American worker who supports it with his taxes." Reagan was a vision of midseventies fashion. He wore a purple plaid shirt, a pin-striped suit, and a polka-dotted tie. A white silk handkerchief plumed from his breast pocket. "Today, it is difficult to find leaders who are independent of the forces that have brought us our problems; the Congress, the bureaucracy, the lobbyist, big business, and big labor . . . I don't believe for one moment that four more years of business as usual in Washington is the answer to our problems. And I don't think the American people believe it, either."

He had come to Washington to denounce it.

Really, Gerald, the campaign won't be divisive at all.

It was a risky move. Not since 1884 had a political party refused to nominate its sitting president. That year, Republicans passed over Chester Arthur, another vice president who had moved out of the on-deck circle like Ford. But that wasn't the most dangerous thing that happened to Reagan on the first day of his campaign. After he spoke at the Press Club, he boarded a charter plane to Miami. Waiting for him was Michael L. Carvin, a college dropout, with a .45 revolver ready to aim at him.

The Secret Service agents who'd been assigned to Reagan seized Carvin, wrestled him to the ground, and whisked Reagan and his wife, Nancy, off to safety. The gun, it turned out, was a replica. Carvin, who had also telephoned threats against Ford, would be sentenced to ten years for the stunt, which he had performed in the hopes of springing Lynette "Squeaky" Fromme from jail. Fromme, a member of the Charles Manson family, had tried to assassinate President

Ford a month earlier. (After he got out, Carvin would make similar threats against radio show host Howard Stern).

It was a near-miss start to a near-miss candidacy. Ronald Reagan's failed 1976 campaign was just as divisive as Gerald Ford had predicted, and more of a threat than Ford anticipated. It was the last time during the twentieth century that a primary season ended without a presumptive nominee, and the battle and bitter convention fight crippled Ford for the general election against Jimmy Carter. Reagan was not shunned for doing this. He emerged stronger. It laid the foundation for his triumph in the 1980 campaign and helped resurrect the conservative movement that still thrives at the heart of the Republican Party today.

Republicans Are People, Too

Reagan had an opening because the Republican Party was wandering through an identity crisis. The Nixon hangover lasted long after the disgraced president lifted off the South Lawn for his last helicopter ride. At first Republicans had been cheerful. "Happy New Year," said GOP senator Mark Hatfield to a friend at Ford's first State Dinner for the King of Jordan in August 1974. But a month into Ford's tenure, he pardoned Nixon. The voters objected. Democratic lawmakers hinted there had been a secret deal: Nixon would step down after impeachment and give Ford the job if Ford pardoned him afterward. A handmade sign at a rally in Ann Arbor read: Ford, Nixon's Getaway Car. Ford had promised to turn the page after Nixon's lawlessness. By pardoning him, Ford looked like he was circumventing the law just as Nixon had. It led to big losses in the 1974 Congressional elections. Democrats took forty-nine seats from the Republicans in the House and four in the Senate.

To improve the Party's image, the Republican National Committee launched a public relations campaign. They printed buttons that read, "Republicans are people, too," which gave you some sense of just how deflated the beach ball had become. An ad asked, "When has it been easy to be a Republican?" They were one meeting short of printing bumper stickers that read: Hold Me.

Conservatives were deflated. Republicans looked like weak Democrats, chasing after some image of moderation. The party needed to stand up for the conservative principles of limited government, the free market, and a strong response to the Soviet Union. People could rally around that.

Moderates in the GOP thought this was lunacy. Barry Goldwater had nearly crippled the party in 1964, losing to LBJ 61.1 percent to 38.5 percent. Becoming more conservative would doom GOP prospects in the future.

Republicans reenacted this debate after the 2012 elections. After the GOP suffered its fifth popular vote loss out of six presidential elections, the RNC commissioned a report to explain what went wrong. Referred to as the "autopsy," its authors declared the party too old, white, and male. A Republican ad maker, unaware of his history, made a series of ads in which the tagline was (wait for it), "Republicans are people, too."

Conservatives in 2013 balked just as their predecessors had. The autopsy report promoted backing comprehensive immigration reform to attract the next generation of voters. True believers saw that as a capitulation of principles. That disconnect between the party elites and the grassroots fueled Donald Trump's anti-immigration candidacy, which won him the nomination.

Conservatives Look for an Exit

While Republican officials contemplated snappier buttons, conservatives looked for an exit from the party. "There's not the slightest chance, in my view, that the GOP can win in 1976, or, for that matter, ever again," said Ambassador Clare Boothe Luce. She demanded a new party because both parties, she said, were "dominated today by a small band of liberals whose domestic and foreign policies are bringing the nation to ruin." Paul Weyrich, who became an influential conservative activist, said, "The Republican Party is not built on principles. It's a tradition maintained by effete gentlemen of the northeastern Establishment who play games with other effete gentlemen who call themselves Democrats."

Some hoped to fashion a new party through electoral demolition. "If the Republican Party loses the White House, it will cease to be a party," said Howard Phillips, a leader in the New Right movement. "I'd just as soon let the Democrats take the White House and get Republicans out of the way and start building a new party."[209]

William Rusher, the publisher of *National Review*, tried to turn the complaints into action. He pushed for the formation of a third party committed to shrinking the size of government, which had grown under Republican Nixon; to holding traditional values amidst social liberalization and to confronting the Soviet Union and China after an era of detente in which Republicans Nixon and Ford had sought to manage the U.S. adversary rather than defeat it. The newly formed party would be a combination of the right of the right and the right of the left—the voters who had supported Alabama Governor George Wallace. Ronald Reagan would lead this new party.

Conservatives first started taping pictures of Reagan on the inside of their school lockers during the 1964 Goldwater campaign. The former actor delivered a televised address about the movement behind Goldwater, and the speech enthralled conservatives across the country. It would become known as the "A Time for Choosing" speech. It softened the hard face of Goldwater's pitch and suggested to voters that to love liberty and fear government was the natural state of things. They were normal for the beliefs they had. They weren't extremists. "You and I are told increasingly we have to choose between a left or right," said Reagan. "Well, I'd like to suggest there is no such thing as a left or right. There's only an up or down: man's old, old-aged dream, the ultimate in individual freedom consistent with law and order, or down to the ant heap of totalitarianism." (Forty years later Barack Obama would also try to tear up the left-right dynamic in a speech to the 2004 Democratic convention.) The Gipper's speech bulged with commonsense stories where liberals behaved like pointy-headed elites and conservatives' horse sense prevailed.

Afterward, Goldwater's staff called Reagan to tell him that the switchboard had been pressed to its limits from calls pledging money. "I then slept peacefully," wrote Reagan. "The speech raised $8 million and soon changed my entire life."

Reagan: A Nuisance More than a Threat

By the time Reagan challenged Ford, he'd served two terms as governor of California, fighting welfare cheats and campus radicals. In 1975, he'd entertained GOP dinners across the country. By July, boosters formed a Citizens for Reagan committee. Still, as late as September of that year, Ford and his aides discounted a Reagan run. They thought he was just the willing dupe of cranky conservatives. Or it was his ambitious wife. "I would bet money that Nancy Reagan was the one pushing him hardest to run," said Ford.

At times the Ford team seemed confused about the Reagan threat. Though they thought he wasn't going to run, they maneuvered to keep him from entering the race. Ford's political aides locked down endorsements from party elites and party officials across the country in order to make any challenge seem daunting by stacking up support from party regulars.

In retrospect Reagan looks like an immovable force, but at the time, launching a conservative insurgency was a gamble in a party that not only had a moderate middle but also a liberal wing. Stacking up endorsements could easily have scared away a more timid candidate.

Plus, Ford thought he was plenty conservative. After all, he'd beaten a Republican incumbent from the right when he first ran for Congress. The Democrats called him the most conservative president since Hoover. And they'd meant it as an insult!

Today, Republican lawmakers face threats from the right, but in the pre-Reagan era they faced pressure from the right and left. Ford aroused discontent from more moderate Republicans. Sen. Charles Percy of Illinois and Sen. Charles "Mac" Mathias from Maryland contemplated primary challenges from Ford's left. Conservatives weren't measuring Ford against those two, though. They were measuring him against Reagan.

Purity tests don't measure against a fixed standard. They measure where candidates stand relative to the other candidates. In 2008, conservatives loved Mitt Romney when John McCain was likely to be the Republican nominee. But then in 2012, conservatives didn't think Romney was conservative enough when measured against Rick Santorum or Newt Gingrich.

Even Reagan wasn't conservative enough for some members of the New Right trying to form a third party. "If he gets in, we're out," Paul Weyrich reportedly said of Reagan. "We'd have no input in that administration."[210]

By late summer of 1975, Ford tried again to preempt a Reagan candidacy. He telephoned him personally and offered to appoint him ambassador to the Court of St. James's. Later he offered him secretary of transportation. Reagan declined both. Finally, he offered Reagan the post as secretary of commerce. Again Reagan declined.

Unable to take Reagan out or dissuade him, Ford's men took the next step doomed campaigns often take: they minimized the threat they had just been trying to get rid of. They dismissed Reagan as an intellectual lightweight supported only by "a bunch of right-wing nuts." Dick Cheney, Ford's chief of staff, said: "Reagan slips every time he opens his mouth because he has no background."[211] Ford also got that advice from Nixon, who sent him regular guidance about possible challengers. (In today's news environment, if the public learned the impeached and disgraced former president was giving political advice to his successor, the entire apparatus would seize up in shock.)

Ford strategists wrote their boss: "Despite how well Ronald Reagan does or does not do in the early primaries, the simple political fact is that he cannot defeat any candidate the Democrats put up. Reagan's constituency is much too narrow, even within the Republican Party... While not unmindful of his ability, he does not have the critical national and international experience that President Ford has gained through 25 years of public service."

The press held this view, too. "There is one way, it seems to us, in which the Republicans could dig their own political grave for 1976, as surely as anything can be done in American politics," said the *New York Times*. "That is by capitulating to the far right wing of the party that forms the core support of Governor Reagan in his quest for the nomination. To put it in the crudest political terms, the far right of the GOP has no place to go; yet the nomination of Governor Reagan for the Presidency (or, for that matter, even the Vice Presidency on a Ford ticket) would surely alienate the most important centrist and liberal segments of the Republican Party, without whose support it could not conceivably achieve national success."

Was the *New York Times* right? Were there more liberal and centrist Republicans than there were conservatives? What if the elites were wrong and the right candidate could tap a sleeping conservative vote? If so, the gentle, compromising RNC strategy would doom Republicans. The big-government experiment launched with the New Deal would roll on and on. So why not form a new party? Rusher told Reagan the Republican Party would never accept him.

Reagan flirted with backing a new conservative party instead of trying to rehabilitate the GOP. "Do you restore the confidence or do you change the name?"[212]

You Will Hear Us

While Republican leaders looked for direction, the conservative grassroots found a work-around way to put pressure on lawmakers through direct mail advertising. Richard Viguerie mastered the new technique. On three thousand rolls of magnetic tape he encoded the names of fifteen million conservatives. Once he mailed them about a given topic, the offices in Congress could then be lit simply by the glow of the phones that conservatives were calling in anger.

Ford had supported enlarging the right of unions to picket at construction sites. Then, three-quarters of a million letters and postcards were sent to the White House demanding a veto of the picketing bill.[213] Ford vetoed it, going back on his promise. The bill had been drafted by his own secretary of labor, Harvard economist John Dunlop, who resigned in protest. The *New York Times* reported that Ford had developed the "fear that if he lost any more of his conservative Republican support, he might not get his party's Presidential nomination."

In 1952 Eisenhower, the moderate, circumvented conservatives who controlled the party machinery. He built a grassroots movement, Citizens for Eisenhower, against the more conservative Taft, using primaries to win delegates instead of caucuses, which were controlled by insiders. By the midseventies, conservatives were doing the same thing, using direct mail to go around the existing power structure. They would seek to elevate Reagan the same way.

Halloween Massacre

Ford had two problems. Voters thought he was a weak leader, and conservatives didn't see any of their ideological brethren in his cabinet. Ford tried to fix both of these problems in one blow. On November 4, 1975, three weeks before Reagan joined the race, Ford replaced a number of prominent members of his cabinet with conservatives in the posts of national security adviser, secretary of defense, and head of the CIA, in what was known as the Halloween Massacre.

Ford's pollster Robert Teeter had commissioned surveys that found the public viewed Ford as a "nice guy" who wasn't up to the job. "Therefore I should project an image of quiet competence and firm determination," wrote Ford. "The campaign poster we selected had me looking belligerent as hell."[214] The massacre could have supported this image upgrade, but then word leaked that Chief of Staff Donald Rumsfeld had come up with the idea. That conveyed the idea that Ford was his own man as long as his staff told him to be.

In a Gallup poll taken before the massacre, Ford led Reagan among Republicans, 58 percent to 36 percent. An NBC poll taken after the massacre had Reagan up by a point. The massacre had backfired.

Drop the Rock

There was one great firing yet to go. Ford could sack his vice president, Nelson Rockefeller. It's hard to overstate how much conservatives disliked the former governor of New York and one time presidential candidate. He was the avatar of a certain kind of thinking—the Eastern establishment moderate who believed in intervention overseas, modifying the New Deal rather than scrapping it, and faith in government stepping in when the private sector couldn't solve something.

The vice president didn't hide his contempt for conservatives who at that time formed the base of the party in the Midwest and West. No moment encapsulated this more than his speech to the 1964 Republican Convention, during which he called out the extremists in the GOP ranks.

Rockefeller was also a usurper. California conservatives had thought Reagan should have had his job. After Nixon's resignation in 1974, they launched a draft-Reagan effort to convince Ford to bring him in as the number two. California State Republican Party chairman Gordon Luce wired the forty-nine other state chairmen asking them to support Reagan for the appointment.

The pressure campaign didn't work, but the bigger offense to conservatives was that Ford went with their enemy Rockefeller. Ford thought him more competent, and his aides argued that Rockefeller would send the political signal that the president wasn't captive of his right wing. Implicit in the choice was that Ford ratified Rockefeller's view that the conservatives were "a minority of a minority."

"Ford's selection of Rockefeller...was regarded in Sacramento as a slap in the face," Reagan biographer Lou Cannon wrote. "To Republican conservatives who recalled the [California] primary battle of '64... the selection of their old enemy was an unbelievable insult." In fact, "more than any other single act of Ford's, or indeed all of them combined," the nomination of Rockefeller to be vice president "fueled national interest among conservatives in a Reagan candidacy." William Rusher claimed the Rockefeller choice "represented a nadir" and ended "the conservative movement's long love affair with the GOP."[215]

By the spring of 1975, as Reagan toured the "mashed potato" circuit, smiling as people tugged on his shirtsleeves and asked him to run, Ford was looking for a way to solve his Rockefeller problem. He didn't say it out loud, but Ford's campaign manager did. Howard "Bo" Callaway, a stalwart conservative, declared Rockefeller the "number one problem" and told reporters, "You and I know that if Rockefeller took himself out, it would help with the nomination."

The vice president had tried to repair his liability status with trips to the conservative South where he upped his rhetoric. After hearing him attack government at all levels, an aide to conservative Alabama governor George Wallace was asked if Wallace had written Rockefeller's remarks.

"No," was the reply, "but we lost a speech the other day..."[216]

Rockefeller bristled against efforts to marginalize him. When asked what he was allowed to do as vice president, he responded, "I go to funerals. I go to earthquakes." Paying for the redesign of the vice presidential seal, he said, was "the most important thing I've done all year."

Finally at the end of October, at their weekly meeting in the Oval Office, Ford asked Rockefeller to resign. Rockefeller agreed, but argued that Ford was misunderstanding the appetite in the nation for a conservative. "Mr. President, I am confident that you will win the nomination, but I agree that Reagan is a formidable threat. I believe you have this choice: history will treat you better if you lose the nomination to Reagan, for he will lose the election next year, rather than if you win the nomination by making compromises that will cost you the election."[217]

On Rockefeller's way out the door, Ford kicked him in the seat of the pants. The next day, Ford gave a speech denying federal aid to spare the City of New York from bankruptcy—aid Rockefeller had lobbied for. The decision—immortalized in the New York *Daily News* headline FORD TO CITY: DROP DEAD—was another sign of Rockefeller's lack of influence.

Rockefeller didn't hide his irritation in a press conference. "I eliminated myself and therefore I eliminated the issue which was the basis of a lot of the squabble."

One thing that's amazing, given the polarization of our Supreme Court politics today, is that Ronald Reagan didn't use Ford's Supreme Court pick to replace Justice William O. Douglas as a political weapon. Ford picked John Paul Stevens eight days after Reagan announced. He was unanimously confirmed a few weeks later. Stevens would become a liberal vote for the court, though at the time of his naming that was hard to know. Regardless, today, any GOP candidate running to the right of a sitting president would label his pick squishy, no matter what the actual record of the nominee. For example, Donald Trump attacked Jeb Bush for being the *brother* of the president who nominated John Roberts, even though Roberts is far more conservative than Stevens.

Reagan's Appeal

Whatever Reagan eventually did as president to help the Republican Party, he contributed to the health of the party by not leaving it. If, as a charismatic leader, he had abandoned the GOP to form a third party, it would almost certainly have led to electoral defeat in 1976 as Republicans and conservatives split the vote. Operating as a majority party requires cohesion of a diverse coalition. Once you break the seal, ambitious upstarts won't be constrained in the future. Reagan might have been damaging the party by running against its president, but he affirmed that the party was worth keeping together.

The wise men didn't give him a chance once he announced. James "Scotty" Reston, the famous *New York Times* columnist, wrote, "The astonishing thing is that this amusing but frivolous Reagan fantasy is taken so seriously by the news media, and particularly by the President. It makes a lot of news, but it doesn't make much sense."

This is the PowerBar that fuels every long-shot conservative candidate. It is the GOP version of the DEWEY DEFEATS TRUMAN headline: elites write off conservatives because they misunderstand the country. They joked about Reagan and snickered at his followers.

Reporter Jules Witcover saw something happening with real people. Reagan was "taking not only the person's hand in his, but his or her eyes with his own, holding the contact until the other person's glance fell away. Anyone who saw him at the Sheraton Wayfarer Hotel in Bedford, New Hampshire, that night had to be convinced that Jerry Ford was going to have his hands full with Reagan."[218]

Ford, on the other hand, was not very good at campaigning. Stu Spencer, his political adviser, who had once worked for Reagan, told him bluntly, "Mr. President, as a campaigner, you're no f——ing good." Ford's biggest problem was that he paused for a few seconds between words. This gave the impression that the words being called to join the world were not available when summoned—and might never be. LBJ had once cracked that Ford had played football in college without a helmet. A meaner crack was: "Jerry Ford can't walk and chew gum at the same time."

In mid-October, Ford had led Reagan among Republicans by 58 percent to 36. By December, a Gallup poll showed Ford down 32 to 40. A cartoon in the *Denver Post* showed Ford, an avid skier, going down the slope backward. A bystander explained: "I understand his ski instructor is also his campaign manager." Rockefeller, no longer a part of the ticket, was still causing problems, telling Southern Republican Party chairmen they should work harder for Ford. "You got me out, you sons of bitches. Now get off your ass."

Winning Outside of Grand Rapids

Reagan planned to wound Ford in the first primary in New Hampshire, where conservative publisher William Loeb, of the *Manchester Union Leader*, supported him, then win in conservative Florida, and finish off Ford in Reagan's home state of Illinois.

Reagan said Ford shouldn't be treated as an incumbent. He hadn't been elected to the office, after all. He fell into the job after Nixon's resignation, and he'd only been in a position to do that because he'd been appointed to the vice presidency after Spiro Agnew resigned due to bribery allegations. So Ford had never really been chosen by Republican voters to anything other than his seat in Congress.

Ford was in trouble in New Hampshire and making life harder for himself. Ford told newsman Lowell Thomas that he wouldn't be skiing in New Hampshire, because the conditions were too icy; the state didn't have nice powder like Vail. True, of course, but insulting to a key industry in the state. Ford's press secretary, Ron Nessen, passed on this view to the press—and there is now a Box #300 in the Ford presidential library labeled "New Hampshire Skiing Furor" full of letters that testify to the backlash.

Congressmen from New Hampshire wrote to excoriate Nessen. Editorial writers across the country wondered aloud how the campaign could be so dumb. "A serious national campaign simply could not have committed the blunder perpetrated by the Ford people recently. If you're running in Georgia, you don't come out for the Boll Weevil and if you're running in Southern California you don't celebrate the Great White Shark," wrote syndicated columnist Jeffrey Hart. Another editorial musing whether Nessen was a Reagan plant in the Ford administration replayed Nessen's crack from when Ford visited Elkins, West Virginia. "Yes," Nessen had said, describing the location of the presidential visit, "I think the phone has reached there. They even have indoor toilets."

Residents sent posters that read, "It's a wonderful year to ski in New Hampshire." The Mount Sunapee ski area offered to name a slope after Nessen. Five of the ski areas created a golden pass for Ford and invited the president to ski on any of their slopes any time he wished. He never took them up on the offer. A memo in the Ford archives tells us why: his political team was trying hard to elevate Ford's stature. "Stu agrees with us that skiing would not be helpful in establishing the President's leadership perception," wrote William Nicholson, one of Ford's aides.

It would have been all downhill from there, but Reagan had embedded a lifeline for Ford in a speech he gave in September in Chicago. Entitled "Let the People Rule," it called for slashing $90 billion from federal government and a shift of power to the states (about $400 billion in today's dollars). Standard conservative fare, but Ford and his allies did the math and pointed out that New Hampshire would have to raise taxes to handle that new burden. New Hampshire had no state income or sales tax.

By keeping the $90 billion proposal in the news, the Ford team kept Reagan pinned down defending his ideas and robbed him of a platform to attack Ford. The Ford team thought they had a template: hang Reagan by the simplicity of his solutions.

On the eve of the vote, Reagan left New Hampshire to campaign in Illinois. "By leaving the state on the eve of the election, I'd sent a message to the voters of New Hampshire that I was taking them for granted, that New Hampshire wasn't important to me," Reagan wrote in his autobiography. If you wonder where the conventional wisdom comes from that candidates need to show the voters that they aren't taking them for granted, this is one of those incidents that live on and determine the behavior of future campaigns.

Ford went to bed on the night of the New Hampshire primary thinking he'd lost, but at 5 a.m. Dick Cheney called. "Mr. President. I have some good news for you. You won by approximately 1,250 votes and you got every delegate but one." That was a squeaker, but expectations were working in Ford's favor. He wasn't supposed to win. "They can't say I've never won any place outside Grand Rapids," Ford said.[219]

North Carolina Resurrection

Ford then ran the table, winning the next four contests, including Florida and Illinois, totally swamping the Reagan strategy and smashing the idea that there was a conservative silent majority out there waiting for voting day so they could rush the polling places and finally take back the party from the capitulators and the sell-outs. By North Carolina, nine GOP governors called on Reagan to withdraw in the name of party unity. They whispered Reagan was being a sore loser. "I am not going to take my advice from the campaign organization of Mr. Ford," Reagan responded. The game was still in the first inning and "you don't take your bat and go home."[220] He predicted he would win North Carolina and run through the South and West. The state was a test of his last claim to viability.

Reagan increased his attacks on Ford. Though he liked to talk about the GOP's Eleventh Commandment commitment to not speak ill of a fellow Republican, that commitment had been shredded. Reagan, like every politician after him, said he was merely pointing out policy differences. "If he comes here with the same list of goodies as he did in Florida," Reagan said, "the band won't know whether to play 'Hail to the Chief' or 'Santa Claus Is Coming to Town.'"

On the one hand that was a policy critique: Ford was a big-government spender. On the other hand it was a character attack: Ford was trying to buy your vote. But it's not underhanded if it's true, which in this case it was. Ford was trying to buy votes. Before the Florida primary, he flew to Orlando to announce that it would be the site for the International Chamber of Commerce convention, pouring $1 million into the local economy. At several other stops, Ford mentioned the money coming to the area from general budget appropriations. (Ford writes about all of this freely in his autobiography, *A Time to Heal*, which gives you a sense of how much times have changed. No politician today would admit to using pork-barrel spending to get votes—particularly no Republican candidate would admit this.)

Reagan hit Ford and his national security adviser, Henry Kissinger, claiming they'd been soft on Communism. "Ladies and gentlemen, it's not easy for me to say the things I must say to you today. But I've decided that matters of national security defense are beyond politics... I'm deeply concerned about our defense posture. Despite the assurances of Dr. Kissinger and Mr. Ford, the United States is no longer the first military power." Ford believed in negotiation; Reagan, in confrontation. He felt that détente—the attempt at warming relations with the Soviets—was being used against the United States, that the Soviets were cheating on almost everything. "No words from Washington can hide the fact that we no longer deal from strength," said Reagan.[221]

A one-minute commercial paid for by Colorado brewer Joseph Coors featured a sinister-appearing Kissinger interspersed with pictures of schoolchildren, one of whom says, "How can he do that to me? It's my country, too."[222]

Reagan also charged that Ford was going to sell out America by handing over the Panama Canal, which he suggested put American security at risk. "We built it," he said. "We paid for it, and we're going to keep it."

The Ford team responded by stoking people's fears of a trigger happy ideologue playing cowboy in the Oval Office. Reagan would mash his fist on the nuclear button in haste. LBJ had used a similar attack against Goldwater. When Reagan was asked about a conflict in Rhodesia, the Ford team pounced. In Rhodesia, guerilla forces were fighting to win more participation in government. Reagan had said troops might be necessary to "see that there is no bloodshed." The Ford campaign dropped the "soft" advertisements it had planned to run and, replaced them with an ad in California that said, "Last Wednesday, Ronald Reagan said he would send American troops to Rhodesia. On Thursday he clarified that. He said they could be observers, or advisers. What does he think happened in Vietnam? When you vote Tuesday, remember Governor Ronald Reagan couldn't start a war; President Ronald Reagan could."

Lyn Nofziger, Reagan's Communications Director, fired off a telegram to Ford charging "a dirty political trick beneath the dignity of a President."[223] That wasn't the only dirty trickery. The Ford forces regularly whispered that Reagan's campaign had been taken over by his wife. Ford released his annual physical to raise other questions. "People had the right to know," he said. Reagan never disclosed his medical history.[224]

Ford also released his personal financial statement. "What I wanted to do of course," wrote Ford "was put pressure on Reagan to issue a complete financial statement of his own."[225] The Ford team thought they knew Reagan hadn't paid his fair share in taxes. Reagan released a vague accounting but not his tax returns.

On the ground in North Carolina, Reagan had the support of the state's conservative senior senator, Jesse Helms, who turned the primary into a referendum on his popularity. His team pulled out every stop, preparing a racist flyer that suggested Ford was going to name African-American senator Edward Brooke of Massachusetts to be vice president. (Accounts vary over whether the flyer was ever distributed.) Reagan also spent his last dime on a half hour of television speaking directly to the voters.

Ford boiled at Reagan's pat claims. Reagan knew how hard it was to govern. He'd made compromises as governor, raising taxes and not cutting spending. But when attacking Ford he made it seem like every governing compromise was a deep sellout. "There are no retakes in the Oval Office," boomed Ford at one event. "Glibness is not good enough. Superficiality is not good enough. Every serious candidate for the Presidency must be equal to the burdens and the responsibility of the Presidency."[226]

This irritation comes through in Ford's autobiography, written in 1979. He repeatedly refers to Reagan "peddling phony charges" and "inflammatory and irresponsible" claims. He felt Reagan was trying to fool voters. In 2015 when Republican Speaker John Boehner was pushed out by archconservatives he made the identical claim about their tactics, labeling them "false prophets."

Ford couldn't attack Reagan too hard, though. "My hardball tactics could so anger conservatives that they would sit on their hands during the fall campaign and the prize of the nomination wouldn't be worth a damn," wrote Ford.[227]

On the eve of the North Carolina vote, Ford's forces pulled back. They received signals Reagan might drop out. The situation looked so grim for Reagan that a *New York Times* headline read, REAGAN VIRTUALLY CONCEDES DEFEAT IN NORTH CAROLINA. Behind the scenes, Reagan's campaign manager, John Sears, hinted to the Ford camp the governor might drop out if they could help with Reagan's $1 million in campaign debt, which had just caused the campaign to give up its chartered United Airlines plane.

Ford spent his last day in North Carolina before high school girls attending a convention of the Future Homemakers of America. "I regret that some people in this country have disparaged and demeaned the role of the homemaker," said the president. "I say—and say it with emphasis and conviction—that homemaking is good for America. I say that homemaking is not out of date and I reject strongly such accusations." (This quote works best if you imagine Ford grasping both his lapels as he says it.)

Then the voters spoke and Reagan won. It was a huge surprise, only the third time in American history that an incumbent had lost a primary. Many credited the television infomercial. "It wasn't organization," said one of Ford's strategists in the state. "It was Sally Jones sitting at home watching Ronald Reagan on television and deciding that she didn't want to give away the Panama Canal."

Tammale and Tammale and Tammale

Texas was the site of Eisenhower's big insurgency in 1952, and it would serve the same purpose for Reagan. The establishment had backed Ford, including the only statewide officeholder, Sen. John Tower.

The contest was widely seen as a toss-up going into the vote. Reagan's campaign manager, John Sears, publicly conceded that if Reagan lost Texas, any hope for the nomination was gone.

Days before the primary, Gerald Ford enjoyed one of the most famous photo-op gaffes in campaign history. At an event at the Alamo he came upon a plate of tamales. Though the West was Reagan territory, the Michigander who liked to wear three-piece suits was trying to make the case that he was in sync with the people of the region. Perhaps to show this, or perhaps because he was simply hungry, Ford took the tamale, wrapped as it is in a husk, and made a run at biting it. You are supposed to unwrap the tamale first. A photographer captured Ford excavating the husk from his mouth, mingled as it was with the edible part of the tamale.

It became a symbol of the hapless candidate, and it took on legendary proportions when Reagan won Texas 2–1, taking every district in the state and claiming all ninety-six contested delegates.

Texas was also the first appearance of the Reagan Democrats, the crossover voters who would be so important to his general election victory in 1980. The open primary system allowed people to vote in whatever contest they wanted. "I've been a Democrat all my life," a roughly dressed man with a drawl declared in a Reagan commercial. "A conservative Democrat. As much as I hate to admit it, George Wallace can't be nominated. Ronald Reagan can. He's right on the issues. So for the first time in my life I'm going to vote in the Republican primary. I'm going to vote for Ronald Reagan." Analysts at the time suggested that the Wallace voters turned out for Reagan, because Kissinger had announced support for blacks seeking to oust the all-white government of Rhodesia.

In 1952, conservatives had argued Eisenhower's success in Texas was illegitimate because Democrats had supported him. In Reagan's case, conservative boosters argued that crossover Democrats proved his general election appeal. This was what Rusher had been selling when he argued a third party could form with conservative Wallace voters.

Reagan's Texas delegates gave him a big enough number to justify taking his fight all the way to the convention. The size of the victory also suggested that he was tapping into something large and hidden.

The win also suggested a shift in the Republican coalition. In 1948 and 1952 the more conservative candidate, Robert A. Taft, drew his support from the South and Midwest. Thomas Dewey and Dwight Eisenhower, the moderate-liberal candidates, were backed by Eastern and Western interests. By Reagan's time the conservatives had the South and West, and the moderates were doing better in the East and Midwest.

Reagan Iceberg

Texas was one of four straight wins for Reagan. The situation was so ugly that Rogers Morton, manager of the Ford campaign, ushered a new expression into the lexicon—at least according to *The Yale Book of Quotations*, which gives him credit for it. Musing about the recent losses, Morton said, "I'm not going to rearrange the furniture on the deck of the *Titanic*."

Reagan used the primary system to work around the party establishment the way conservatives used direct mail to assert power. Primary contests in which the delegates were bound to the winner helped the grassroots speak without the interference of the party bosses who controlled the caucus process. In the old days, if Reagan had won a primary, the unbound delegates might have been susceptible to party bosses encouraging the delegates to change their minds. In Ford's case, they could have used the power of the presidency to argue with those delegates to keep them in the Ford camp. But the number of pledged delegates (bound delegates) had increased, which meant that when the people spoke in the primaries, the delegates had to listen. In 1968, just 48 percent of the delegates were bound. In 1976, 85 percent of the delegates were bound.

Before Kansas City: The Fight for the 150

By the time the voting in the primaries and caucuses concluded, neither Reagan nor Ford had won the 1,130 delegates required to win the nomination. Ford was 170 short and Reagan needed 270. As they headed to the convention in Kansas City, both men were trying to woo the uncommitted delegates. One candidate was a sitting president, one candidate was a movie star, but as the *Chicago Tribune* put it, "There are some new Republican stars at this convention. They are the 'Not sayers.' They're not saying Ford and they're not saying Reagan."[228]

In the month before the national convention in Kansas City, both campaigns did whatever they could to pitch the uncommitted delegates.

James Baker, the future secretary of state, ran the Ford delegation stroking effort. In a memo entitled "Proposed Delegate Management Operation," he wrote, "The worst thing that can happen to a politician is not to have someone to talk to. The next worst thing is not to know what is going on."[229] So he commissioned a bath of communication that would keep delegates constantly marinating in attention from the Ford camp.

A dossier on each quarry included every piece of information about the delegate, what their interests were, what their hobbies were, what their professional goals were, what their interest in the party was, and their political history inside the Republican Party.

Records were kept of the wooing progress. This is the entry from June 18, 1976: "President sent him a thank you in response to letter of recommendation on behalf of [a candidate] for appointment to vacancy on the U.S. district court." "6/22—Per Jim Plummer: Will go for Ford on three conditions. If Ford does not veto the offshore oil revenue sharing bill; the vice presidential candidate is not unacceptable," and then in parentheses it has "Brooke" (Edward Brooke, the African American senator from Massachusetts) and Percy (Illinois senator Charles Percy, one of the more moderate in the party), "[and will not go for Ford if Ford challenges] Louisiana and Mississippi delegations [for not having] enough blacks, females, and young." Then two days later on June 24, it reads, "Baker: He needs lots of attention."[230]

A key person was assigned to each delegate—a "persuader"—and powers of the incumbency were used wherever they could be. Delegates were invited to State dinners—the chairman of the important Mississippi GOP, Clarke Reed, was invited to dine with Queen Elizabeth II. Others were invited to celebrate the bicentennial on board the USS *Forrestal* in New York Harbor as forty tall ships from around the world sailed past.

A delegate from Oakville, Missouri, named Marlene Zinzel sat in the beauty parlor having her hair set when the phone rang. Who was at the other end of the line? The President of the United States. Said Miss Zinzel, "I couldn't believe it. I can hardly remember it. He told me he could win over Carter. He asked me if I would consider him, and I said that I would."

Once the delegates knew that the bar was open, they asked for the drinks with the umbrellas. Baker was so disturbed by the out-of-bounds requests and so nervous that in the post-Nixon years it might come back to hurt the administration, he wrote a memo for his file outlining the seventeen different instances in which delegates got grabby, so there could be a record. One delegate from the Virgin

Islands wanted a federal building named after him in return for voting for Ford. A Missouri delegate offered to deliver uncommitted delegates if they were allowed to have a final say on patronage in the state. A Brooklyn delegate said basically he would go to the highest bidder.

In Kansas City, the parties and television networks coddled the undecideds or "not sayers." Overnight the Ford forces slipped the "Delegate Special" under each door. The Reagan team delivered "They'll Beat Carter News." Outside the delegates meeting, one could hear the high-pitched voices of "Schweik's Tykes," a group of children of delegates and staffers recruited to cheer. Named for Reagan's vice presidential pick, they sang "Dickie, Dickie Dickie Schweiker" to the tune of the "Battle Hymn of the Republic."[231]

The list of administration cabinet officials assigned to do television interviews was blank. Instead, news networks chased Eldon Ulmer, Eliza Sprinkle, and other delegates who couldn't make up their minds. "They're like a girl out at her first dance," said a delegate leaving the convention hall. "Until the clock strikes twelve, they're going to keep up the flirt."

When the convention kicked off there had been a bad omen of tensions to come. A 55-foot-tall inflatable elephant welcoming delegates ripped open. Down on the ground things were also coming apart.[232] The former governor of Illinois claimed Reagan supporters had tried to buy the votes of two Ford delegates.[233] Marie Goodlow, a Ford delegate from Chicago, said she had been offered $2,500 to pay for her travel expenses if she would vote for 16-C, a pivotal resolution being pushed by the Reagan team. She said, "I couldn't make no deal like that for the simple reason I believe in God...and I wouldn't sell my President out."[234]

The Reagan side charged it was the Ford campaign that had offered cash to one of the delegates to help with a congressional campaign that he was managing. It became such an issue that the FBI opened an investigation.

A man from Utah supporting Reagan charged that someone from

the New York delegation had taken a sign supporting Reagan and done something with it, so he ran over to the New York delegation and ripped the phone out. Phones mattered, because they connected the delegations on the floor to strategists from each campaign who were arrayed before a forest of phones, closely monitoring their delegate counts within the states to make sure they weren't losing any support.

At home, viewers were watching the chaos in real time. Walter Cronkite spoke to his correspondent who interviewed the man with the offended phone. "You know, some guy came chargin' over and tore out my phone... He also damaged my other phone... He was a Reagan man."

There was a lot of Reagan memorabilia. "They love to be identified, singled out from the rest of the crowd," wrote Sally Quinn of the *Washington Post*. "They wear knitted Reagan hats, Reagan ties, Reagan rhinestones... so nobody will mistake them for moderates." Buttons were the most pedestrian of the Reagan flair. Supporters blew two-foot-long plastic horns which the *New York Times* described as being "uncannily reminiscent of the ululations of Arab women."

One delegate draped in Reaganalia explained the difference between the two candidates: "Ford is for social change, and that Ms. [she drew out the *Mzzzzzzzzz* condescendingly] Betty, they're both promoting social change in America. And that," she added firmly, "is what we are against."

No competition seemed too small. Nancy Reagan visited the convention hall one night and danced to rousing applause. The next night Betty Ford did the same and appeared to receive more. The papers wrote about it. BETTY FORD BESTS NANCY REAGAN ON APPLAUSE SCALE was the headline in the *New York Times*.[235] In the lobby of the Crown Center Hotel, Ford and Reagan supporters shouted "We want Ford!" and "We want Reagan!" at each other for a protracted period. Every time "California, Here I Come," played somewhere, the Michigan fight song seemed to answer not far behind.

Reagan Goes Off Script

On July 26, Reagan and his strategists took a gamble that failed spectacularly. To balance out his conservative ticket, they picked moderate, maybe even liberal, Pennsylvania senator Richard Schweiker as Reagan's running mate.

"We just got the best news we've had in months," Dick Cheney told Ford. The president thought Cheney was playing a joke on him when he brought the news.

The move didn't pick up any new delegates for Reagan. In fact, he lost six uncommitted delegates in the Pennsylvania delegation. His base thought he was a sellout. Howard Phillips of the Conservative Caucus said Reagan had just "betrayed the trust of those who look to him for leadership." The person Reagan was trying to defeat had betrayed conservatives by picking Rockefeller. Why was Reagan copying him?

Rep. John Ashbrook of Ohio said it was "the dumbest thing I've ever heard of."[236] Illinois congressman Henry Hyde, another staunch conservative, said it was like "a farmer selling his last cow to buy a milking machine." Schweiker explained that he had been converted to Reagan's philosophical outlook, which convinced exactly no one.

Immediately dubbed the Schweiker "boo-boo" in the press, there was talk of dropping him from the ticket almost as soon as it was announced.[237] Schweiker had offered to withdraw. Reagan refused to accept his resignation, but his reasoning wasn't very impressive. "There was no way in this political world that it could be done without someone thinking I was pulling a McGovern-Eagleton deal," Reagan told reporters. Not exactly an endorsement of Schweiker to compare him to the most unsuccessful party vice presidential nominee in modern history.

Reagan said keeping Schweiker was a matter of principle. Reagan's Florida campaign chairman, Tommy Thomas said, "I told Governor Reagan that his principles are going to cost the Republican Party the election in November."

The Fight over 16-C

Having shot themselves in the foot, the Reagan forces tried to put the gun into Ford's hands in the hopes he would give it a go. They tried to force him to pick his vice president before the final delegate vote.

Like any good contested convention, the important action in Kansas City took place in the fight over the rules. The rules fights are proxy fights for the actual final vote on the nominee. They're tests of strength and prestige, used to show undecided delegates that one candidate or the other has a strong position, in the hopes of convincing those undecided delegates to get behind the clear winner.

Reagan wanted a rules fight, because while some delegates were committed to vote for the nominee on the first ballot, they could vote their consciences on procedural votes. If Reagan won a procedural vote, he could argue that this was a sign of what delegates really felt in their hearts. It was how delegates would vote on a second ballot, after they had become unbound. These Trojan Horse votes exposed the true sentiment of those delegates who were bound on the first ballot. What Reagan hoped is that unbound delegates would watch the behavior of their bound delegate brethren and vote for him. Then the bandwagon would roll to victory when everyone voted the way they wanted to in their hearts on the second ballot.

Reagan was right to think this. Ford's advisers were telling the president that some of his support was soft and that anywhere from fifty to a hundred delegates might jump to the other side.

The biggest rules fight was over rule 16-C. It required that all presidential candidates name their vice presidential candidates in advance. The Reagan folks wanted to force Ford to make the mistake that they had made by naming a pick and alienating either conservatives or moderates. The Ford forces called it the "misery loves company" rule.

The Mississippi delegation became Ground Zero for the 16-C fight. In Mississippi, they operated under the unit rule, which meant that all thirty delegates from Mississippi would be required to support either Ford or Reagan, whoever had a majority of the delegation. There were sixty people in the delegation, but only thirty actual delegate votes would go toward electing the president. If a candidate won 31 to 29, he would get all thirty delegate votes.

Clarke Reed, the head of the Mississippi delegation who had enjoyed meeting Queen Elizabeth II at Ford's invitation, was trending toward Reagan. But then Reagan picked Schweiker. "This kind of vice president is too big a price to pay for the nomination," he said. So Reed switched his vote, giving the majority of Mississippi delegates to Ford. Then the Mississippi delegation voted to give Ford his way on 16-C so he wouldn't have to announce who his vice presidential pick would be.

But, as if to snatch defeat from the jaws of victory, Ford was undone again by his campaign manager (or perhaps we mean mismanager) Rogers Morton. The Ford campaign chief told an Alabama newspaper that Ford would write off the "cotton South" against Carter in the general election. This infuriated Mississippi Republicans, because they wanted to play a role in the general election. They were so upset, they wanted to take back their vote on 16-C. They called an emergency meeting, huddling in the the CBS News trailer, which was the nearest spot available.

Mike Wallace gave the blow-by-blow to Walter Cronkite. "[Roger] Mudd, [Dan] Rather, [Morton] Dean, and I office inside there... And they've been in there for about ten or fifteen minutes. They are basically the Reagan people in the Mississippi delegation. What they wanna do is break that unit rule. As you know, earlier today, they voted 31 to 28 to go with President Ford and not with Ronald Reagan on 16-C."[238]

The Ford supporters in the delegation wouldn't cooperate, so the delegation couldn't take a revote. In the end, the Mississippi delegation went for Ford, and 16-C went down 1,180 to 1,069.

One Last Gambit

While the Reagan forces were trying to knock loose delegates by forcing Ford to name a vice president, other Reagan forces were trying to pressure Ford through the convention's policy platform. If they could force him to take the wrong position on an important policy issue, it might offend some delegates and send them to Reagan. Sen. Jesse Helms of North Carolina called the strategy "purposeful conflict on substantive issues."[239]

The big fight on the platform committee was over a constitutional amendment banning abortion. This was supposed to put Ford in a pinch. His wife was pro-choice and had made comments about how it was wonderful that abortion had been moved from the back alley to the doctor's office. (Most GOP candidates could not survive today if even a fourth cousin once removed said such a thing.)

There was one problem with Helms's strategy: Ford didn't fight. He said the constitutional amendment was just fine with him.[240] If it ever came to a general election fight over the matter, his out was that while the platform committee might call for a constitutional amendment, that wasn't the candidate's position. (Ford was anti–abortion rights but wasn't pushing an amendment.)

Somehow this was allowed, and the wiggle room between candidate and platform has been allowed ever since. The party nominee who represents the party nevertheless can claim distance from the party platform.

Still, once these items were written into the GOP platform, it became very hard to remove them. It's another legacy of Reagan's '76 race.

Ford Gets a Trophy But Reagan Wins

The night of the full convention vote on the nominee, Ford watched three television sets in his hotel room. As states were called, he marked the numbers down on a Xeroxed sheet, pulling occasionally on his pipe. A miniature elephant made of banana leaves concealed a microphone picking up the president's words for a campaign film being shot. Several times, Ford cheered delegation chairmen who arose to announce pro-Ford votes, saying, "Attaboy, attaboy." When the announcement came that he had won, he stood, shook the hands of his aides and announced, "I guess we don't have to change the acceptance speech."[241]

The president had a speech ready, but he didn't have a ready plan for the drama that would take place when he went to the hall to deliver it.

Immediately after winning, Ford visited Reagan in his hotel early in the morning to begin the unifying process. He'd promised Reagan aides that he would not ask Reagan to be his running mate; Ford would write later, though, that he heard afterward that Reagan had just been convinced to accept the offer if Ford were to make it. Ford, not knowing of Reagan's change of mind, talked to him only about other alternatives, including Sen. Bob Dole, whom Reagan liked and whom Ford ultimately picked.

The next day, when it came time for Ford to make his big speech to the convention the Reagan delegates were not cooperating. They chanted for Reagan to come down from his skybox to the podium. The governor said he would not. It was Ford's night. Still they chanted. Convention officials didn't know what to do. Ford's speech was being delayed. "Damn it!" Ford shouted to Cheney. "Tell him to get this thing under control," he said of the convention chairman. "I was angry," Ford wrote in his memoir, "and I used four-letter words I almost never use."

Finally Ford gave his speech. "The delegates applauded me an incredible sixty-five times," Ford recalled. Swept up in the feeling of triumph, Ford then waved to Reagan and motioned to him to come down. His primacy established, Ford hoped the moment would demonstrate party unity. The crowd roared.

Reagan stood up, and he put his fingers to his lips, and tried to kind of shush them. He smiled. He was hoping the madness would die down. It only got worse. People were yelling, "Speech, speech." Reagan didn't move. Ford upped the ante. "Ron, would you come down and bring Nancy?" he said over the public-address system.

Reagan disappeared, and no one knew what was going on. While everyone waited, Ford and his wife and the nominee Dole and the incumbent vice president Rockefeller all stood on stage smiling forcibly. It all started to look like a big group grimace. Everyone was wondering where Reagan was. The whole group "stretched their rictus muscles, too, until the stage, flashing with teeth, began to look like a tetanus ward," wrote Reagan biographer Edmund Morris of the moment.[242]

Reagan finally arrived and gave a speech without notes about a letter he'd written to put into a time capsule. He talked about the stakes for the convention and the country, asking Republicans to think of themselves as future generations would see them:

"Will they look back with appreciation and say, 'Thank God for those people in 1976 who headed off the loss of freedom? Who kept us now a hundred years later free? Who kept our world from nuclear destruction?' And if we fail, they probably won't get to read the letter at all, because it spoke of individual freedom and they won't be allowed to talk of that or read of it. This is our challenge and this is why here in this hall tonight, better than we've ever done before, we've got to quit talking to each other and about each other and go out and communicate to the world that we may be fewer in numbers than we've ever been, but we carry the message they're waiting for. We must go forth from here united, determined that what a great general said a few years ago is true: There is no substitute for victory."

Lou Cannon, the great Reagan biographer, said, "It was a speech formed around Reagan's very deep convictions. It gave a glimpse of what a visionary Reagan was. It was Reagan's heart that set him apart."[243]

There were reports that delegates wept. In the video of the convention it sure looks like they are weeping. If they're not, they are on the verge of it. Sam Donaldson, reporting for ABC said, this was "the first real emotion of the night," and it "wasn't for the ticket, but for the man who wasn't on it."[244] Kenny Klinge, a grassroots organizer for Reagan, stood in the aisle next to a Ford supporter from Florida who heard Reagan speak and then reportedly exclaimed, "Oh my God, we've nominated the wrong man."[245]

Ronald Reagan grabbed the heart of the Republican Party not so much by the conservative principles he espoused—it was not that kind of speech—but by making the audience feel good about America and itself. This was what no clever button could do. "In the time it took for Reagan to speak, the Republican Party escaped the clutches of its moderate establishment and fell into Reagan's lap," wrote Fred Barnes. "He lost the nomination, but won the party—and ultimately the Presidency, the country, and the world."[246]

Ford never recovered after the bloody fight with Reagan. The president and his advisers believe that Reagan doomed him. If he could barely win in his own party, how could he win the general election? He would go on to lose to Jimmy Carter.

Reagan, by staying in the Republican Party, proved there was an appetite in the GOP for his conservative ideas. That kept the most passionate voters inside the party and put a premium on cohesion, which would last for long after Reagan had served two terms and passed away. It would save conservatism from its most radical adherents.

In 1976, Reagan also gave hope to the legions of conservative candidates who would come after him, who would (despite loss after loss after loss in the primaries and caucuses) hold to the idea that there was a silent majority out there waiting to vote for them, if they just kept the faith a little bit longer.

The convention of 1976 was supposed to mark the end of one career and the start of another. It did, but just not in the order people had expected at the time.

1952—Thou Shalt Not Steal

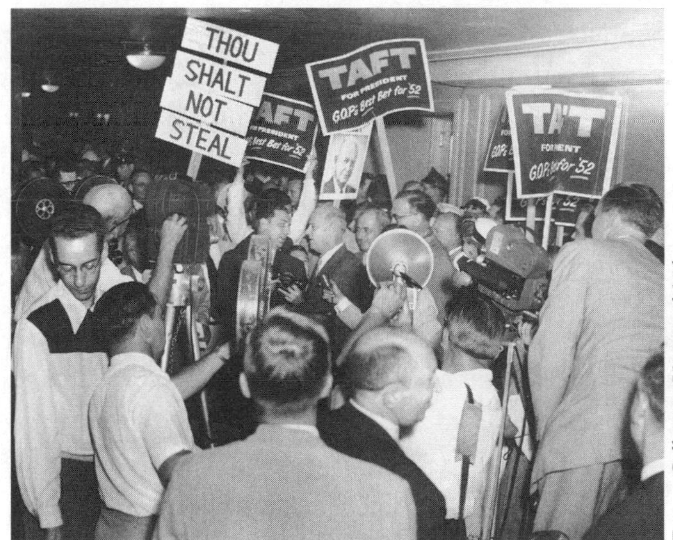

Everett Collection Historical / Alamy

A Battle in the Gold Room

At 10:17 a.m. on July 8, 1952, the presiding officer at the Republican National Committee's credentials committee meeting tried gaveling the group to order. No one listened. How could they even hear? A thousand people were gathered in the Gold Room of the Congress Hotel in Chicago. The room was only supposed to hold eight hundred, and they were all shouting at each other about how one half of the room was trying to steal the presidential nomination from the other half.

The Gold Room got its name from the gold leaf, rising up fifty feet to the ceiling. The room had been restored by Lido Lippi, a Florentine artist who also restored Michelangelo's Sistine Chapel.

Almost everybody in the room wore a boxy suit and carried a hat they'd stored under their chair. The party had to determine the simple question of who was a valid delegate and who was not. Then,

Republicans could figure out whether they wanted Dwight Eisenhower or Sen. Robert Taft to be president.

The two questions were closely linked. Who got seated as a delegate would determine who got the nomination.

Ninety-three delegates were in dispute. They came from the mostly Southern states of Mississippi, Georgia, Texas, Kansas, Louisiana, and Florida.[247] The states had two sets of delegates, one for each candidate. The Taft people said that Eisenhower's delegates were all Democrats who shouldn't have a say in determining the party leader. As one of the Taft people from Mississippi making his case said, "I don't know where these people came from. They just came from out of the ground."[248]

The Eisenhower team said the Taft forces were trying to "steamroll" their way to the nomination, using the Ohio senator's strength with the party apparatus to rig the game. The word *steamroll* was used so much, you would have thought they were all meeting for a construction trades convention. A giant sign hanging in the Eisenhower headquarters read, Thou Shalt Not Steal.

If the credentials committee said the Taft delegates were valid, he'd win. If Eisenhower's delegates were given the nod, he'd win. The only way a decision by the credentials committee could be overturned was if the larger GOP convention voted to overrule the smaller committee, but that had never happened and no one expected it to this time.

The crowd at the credentials meeting was so rowdy, officials considered bringing in security. Fights had broken out. Someone said a group of Eisenhower men pushed some Taft supporters down a stairwell. The two sides got so heated over where they could place posters in the convention hall that the GOP chairman had to make a ruling. In the hotel where they were staying, the Texas delegates for Taft broke into song, to the tune of "I'm Looking Over a Four-Leaf Clover," but they gave the tune their own spin "I'm getting sour on Eisenhower—he's losin' votes every day. He's a sure loser, he's a charmin' man. Charm will not win it—Taft is the man."[249]

Arthur Krock, the *New York Times* columnist, wrote, "There is a stratum of grim and possibly even lethal conflict here as the Republican Party delegates are about to meet."

A Battle for the Soul of the GOP

"There is more than a personal battle that is going on here," wrote the *New York Times*'s Scotty Reston. "The conservative wing of the party is fighting for its life."[250]

The Republican Party entered 1952 having lost every presidential contest for the previous twenty years. Inside the party there was an open debate over whether it would still continue to exist. Conservatives wanted to scrap the New Deal and Social Security, and were suspicious of foreign entanglements. They believed only by standing proud and bold behind Taft could they distinguish themselves from Democrats and give voters a clear choice. Moderates, led by Thomas Dewey, were more willing to work within a government reshaped by the New Deal and take a more internationalist posture. They believed that the party shouldn't be so doctrinaire as to turn off the wider group of voters. Sen. Margaret Chase Smith from Maine, a moderate, also spoke out against the tone of the conservative movement. She said she didn't want her party to ride to victory on "the Four Horsemen of Calumny: Fear, Ignorance, Bigotry, and Smear."

The most substantive debate at the heart of the politics was over the United States' role in Europe and NATO. Each man was the chief symbol of the respective sides. Eisenhower had been NATO supreme commander, and Taft had been the chief Senate opponent to a big U.S. role in Europe. "The Great Debate" over NATO was more nuanced than it was portrayed at the time, but it put Taft on the defensive against the charge that he was an isolationist. "Now this isolationist thing has come to be just a name-calling proposition," Taft said about the label, "something that's thrown against people who happen to disagree with the administration foreign policy in any respect. But it means nothing today."[251]

The old-guard conservatives said Eisenhower was too moderate and wanted to spread America too thin overseas. Eisenhower was "the candidate of those who would have American boys die as conscript cannon fodder thousands of miles across the oceans,"[252] said one of Taft's men. Clare Boothe Luce, an Eisenhower delegate and wife of the powerful *Time* magazine publisher, argued that because Taft was seen as an isolationist, Eisenhower's defeat "would be taken by European communists as a signal that America was going home. It would give Stalin the only real political victory."[253]

The *New York Times* ran a three-part editorial entitled, "Mr. Taft Can't Win," arguing that Taft was too conservative for a general election. Taft, of course, was arguing the opposite side of the case. If the Republican Party finally nominated a conservative, he maintained, they would win, and capture that huge silent majority out there.

Governor Thomas Dewey of New York had lost the last two presidential elections in 1944 and '48 as the party's nominee. As Alice Roosevelt Longworth said, "You can't make a soufflé rise twice." (Longworth had more than one line about him: "You have to know Dewey really well to dislike him thoroughly.") But Dewey didn't shrink away. Instead, he was working behind the scenes to promote Eisenhower. The Taft-Eisenhower fight was really a Taft-Dewey fight. A pamphlet being passed around at the Credentials Committee meeting said, "Tom Dewey is the most cold-blooded, ruthless, selfish political boss in the United States today. He stops at nothing to enforce his will. His promises are worthless. He is the greatest menace that the Republican Party has. Twice he has led us down the road to defeat, and now he is trying the same trick again, hidden behind the front of another man."[254]

The fight spilled out into the streets. A truck being driven by Eisenhower supporters had a mounted public address system blaring out the message "Thou shalt not steal." Another, competing truck had its own P.A. system that thundered, "Two-time loser Dewey wants to be president by proxy. Phooey on Dewey."And "Dewey is full of hooey."[255]

Reluctant Eisenhower

Dwight Eisenhower had planned to watch the Republican Convention from his Denver headquarters, but he changed his mind and decided to go early. He boarded a special train and headed for Chicago to "have a hand in the fight," picking up a ten-gallon hat along the way.[256] The General promised to "roar clear across the country for a clean, decent operation." He deplored the smoke-filled rooms, the "star-chamber methods," and chicanery.

Eisenhower was trying to appeal to a larger audience, to people other than the party insiders. Jack Porter, of the pro-Eisenhower delegation, declared, "This Texas steal is the rottenest thing in American politics. Hitler never did anything rottener." (This is proof that the reckless Hitler analogies aren't just the fault of the Internet.)

This was a pretty strenuous effort for a candidate who had entered the race only a month ago. The delegate fight was taking place in large measure because Eisenhower had loped into the race late and was trying an extraordinary tactical gambit to get around the existing party apparatus.

Eisenhower had been a White Knight candidate for both parties since the 1948 elections. Truman reportedly tried to get him to run, even though Truman was the incumbent president. Referring to the draft efforts, Eisenhower gave one of the great quotes about running for president. "I don't believe a man should ever try to pass his historical peak. I think I pretty well hit my peak in history when I accepted the German surrender in 1945. Now why should I want to get into a completely foreign field and try to top that? Why should I go out and deliberately risk that historical peak by trying to push a bit higher?"

As with all White Knight candidates, the response to this kind of blanket denial was: so you might run then? In 1950, a series of Republican wise men—Rep. Hugh Scott of Pennsylvania and Sen. Henry Cabot Lodge Jr. of Massachusetts, as well as Dewey—started to work on Eisenhower. They argued to him that the Republican Party was in danger of collapsing and leaving the country with just one party—the Democratic Party, which would drag everyone to socialism.

Hugh Scott had gotten Dewey nominated in 1948. He had been chairman of the GOP until he was removed from his post by the conservative Taft forces.

In 1950 Eisenhower told Scott, "I don't know about the future. But I will say this. I would not be interested in the sort of thing like a fight at the convention where X gets 385 votes and Y gets 455 votes, something like that."[257] Scott was encouraged.

Others started a Draft Eisenhower movement without talking to the general. He was asked about it wherever he went, even while in Europe with NATO, where he told reporters in 1948, "Ever since I have first heard my name connected with possible political office, I have consistently declined to consider such a contingency."

This posture by Eisenhower was maddening to the men working on his behalf. While Eisenhower was playing coy, Taft party men were locking up the organization and the party, making sure their supporters were working in the party apparatus throughout the country. Without a green light from Eisenhower, it was hard to get party people to commit to him. Without people inside the party organization, men like Scott thought, it would be almost impossible to go up against an opponent who was so wired on the inside he was known as "Mr. Republican."

Party people weren't even sure if Eisenhower was a Republican at all. And Eisenhower refused to say if he was a Republican. Hugh Scott flew over to Paris to lobby Eisenhower to say something about his connections to the Republican Party; then Scott could go back to the States and work Republicans, saying, "Hey, we've got this great candidate." But Eisenhower said, "Well, just look at my speeches. And you'll get an idea of what I believe."[258] Did he lick Hitler by being so coy?

Scott was irritated. "The unwillingness of the general to give his supporters an unmistakable green light was, of course, maddening. His reservations were honorable but crippling to a struggle to sway public opinion and to win delegates."[259]

By the beginning of 1952, though, the men working on Eisenhower's behalf were able to at least show something. Massachusetts senator Henry Cabot Lodge Jr., a leader of the moderate wing of the Republican Party in the Senate, told reporters that he'd gotten official word that Eisenhower would accept a draft movement. That allowed the Eisenhower men to move forward with putting his name on the ballot in various primary states.

It was a two-track process: get Eisenhower's name on the ballot and then convince Eisenhower to run. In February 1952, they arranged a late-night rally after a prizefight at Madison Square Garden. Eighteen thousand people attended the "Midnight Serenade to Eisenhower."[260] Humphrey Bogart and Lauren Becall, attended as did Clark Gable (making his first appearance on television), Ethel Merman, and the legendary songwriter Irving Berlin, who sang a new composition called "I Like Ike." Mary Martin, star of *South Pacific*, sang "I'm in Love with a Wonderful Guy."[261] The whole thing was put on film. And the film of the jamboree was flown to Paris to show Eisenhower that there was this groundswell for him.

New Hampshire Likes Ike

The New Hampshire primary was the first big test of whether there was an appetite for Eisenhower. Taft had the support of the *Manchester Union Leader* newspaper, but Eisenhower trounced him 50 percent to 39 percent. "Any American who would have that many Americans pay him that compliment would be proud or he would not be an American," said Eisenhower. He was an enigma machine.

What did this mean? No one knew what he thought of winning and whether he'd get into the fight.

Eyes turned toward the Minnesota primary. Voters had to write in Eisenhower's name if they wanted him. Here was how *Life* magazine reported what happened: "The one name penciled in again and again on the long scroll is sometimes spelled Eisenhaur, Isenhower, or Ike. But, however spelled, Eisenhower's name was scrawled 107,000 times on the ballots and voting machines in Minnesota's primary last week—a modern political miracle without precedent or parallel."

It became known as "the Minnesota Miracle." Eisenhower told reporters that he was astonished at "the mounting number of my fellow citizens who are voting to make me the Republican nominee." And then the cracks in the facade started to show. The result, said the general, was "forcing me to reexamine my personal position and past decision."

On June 4, 1952, Eisenhower made it official and jumped into the race. That was just one month before the meeting in the Gold Room that started this tale. From his hometown of Abilene, Kansas, Eisenhower made his first political speech. It was nearly as vague as his earlier pronouncements about his candidacy. B. Carroll Reece, who was supporting Taft, said after listening to Eisenhower's announcement speech, it "looks like he's pretty much for home, mother, and heaven."

This vagueness gave Taft an opportunity. Sure, Eisenhower was popular, but what did he really believe? Conservatives knew he was on the wrong side of the NATO debate. He was trying to win the nomination by appealing to independents and Democrats. That meant he was soft, and conservatives said that would lead the party down the Dewey road if they nominated a "me too" Republican. (Meaning not that different from the Democrats.)

This was the argument Ted Cruz made in 2016: if you run a truly principled conservative people will flock to him. There were Taft buttons at the Republican Convention that said, "No me-too in 1952." The *Chicago Tribune*, the conservative paper, said, "If the elephant remembers, he should be all thru with 'me too.'" Dave Ingalls, Taft's campaign manager, said, "Hero worship is no substitute for faith based on known performance, neither is glamour or sex appeal."

A moment of historical pause: imagine saying a general who had helped defeat the Axis powers had not shown "known performance." A person could say such a thing because back then the political skill was valued, and seen as different from other kinds of skills.

Meanwhile, the groundswell for Eisenhower was growing. In 1948, Walter Lippmann, the famous columnist, characterized him this way: "He is not a real figure in our public life, but a kind of dream boy embodying all the unsatisfied wishes of all the people who are discontented with things as they are." (This is a perfect description of the White Knight candidate elites search for nearly every campaign) But in '52, even Lippmann was feeling the love for Eisenhower, saying that he could "reunite the American people, to heal their divisions." And "Eisenhower is in the unique position of being the only available public man who has a reasonable prospect of bringing about a Republican victory which will unite the nation."[262]

The Texas Steal

Eisenhower, running as a unifier, had popular support, but he didn't have the GOP machine. The only way the Eisenhower folks could get around the Taft organization was to go down South and mount an insurgency there. Because the Republican party was so weak in the South, their organizations there were basically patronage dealerships. When a Republican eventually would get into the White House, the local GOP officials from the South would line up and get what they could from the head office.

Hugh Scott and other reform-minded Republicans wanted to build a vibrant party that people could join in the Southern states, not just maintain a shell of a party that was delivering feathers to the nests of a few. Eisenhower's candidacy would offer them that shot, and Texas would be the best proving ground.

The Eisenhower forces worked to get independents and Democrats to attend the precinct caucuses and county conventions. They put up posters that read, "You can vote Republican one day and Democratic the next."[263] When the Taft forces saw this happening, they insisted that anybody who voted in a caucus or precinct must sign a loyalty oath. Eisenhower's men told the crossover Democrats and Independents, go ahead and sign it, because it'll never hold up in court.

Outraged, the Taft forces charged that these were mere "Republicans for a day." In the caucus process Eisenhower won the day, but the Taft forces refused to acknowledge that Eisenhower's were the rightfully chosen delegates. They named their own slate of delegates.

The argument was to be settled at the Texas state Republican convention at Mineral Wells, where 12,000 Republicans showed up on May 28. Mineral Wells only had a population of 7,800 at the time.

It was not friendly turf for Eisenhower. Taft controlled the state committee. So, of the 519 contested delegates, the committee seated only 30 of them for Ike. It gave the rest to Taft. Later that day, the pro-Taft credentials committee gave Taft 21 more delegates. Eisenhower claimed, "Rustlers stole the Texas birthright instead of Texas steers."

At this point, it was the Eisenhower team's turn to pick up their marbles and go home. They created a rump convention across the street in the community center. They picked their own slate of delegates. And they raised placards reading, "Rob with Bob" and "Graft with Taft." They pledged that they were going to go to the GOP convention in Chicago to "wipe out the infamy of Mineral Wells so that we can go out before the American people with clean hands."

Chicago Showdown

When Republicans arrived in Chicago to the International Amphitheatre, the whole business stunk. Not because of the bitter political fight or the controversy over the stolen delegates. It smelled instead like bull manure. The amphitheatre had originally been built for livestock shows. Temperatures inside reached 110 degrees, particularly in the working press rooms below the stockyards.

In the convention hall a twelve-foot-high portrait of Lincoln hung from the rafters.[264] A live baby elephant was escorted by two girls in tights.[265] Outside, for the first time at a convention, buzzed little blimps with "Ike" written on the side of them. The delegates sat in folding chairs that were bolted together, offering, as one person described it, "little regard for the dignity or comfort of the individual delegate."[266] It was a sardine tin of humanity, and by the time it was all over, the delegates had listened to 150,000 words by one estimate, sometimes going until 1:00 or 2:00 in the morning.

Journalist William White set the stage for the candidates as they arrived:

"In July of 1952, the bitterness of the 25th Republican National Convention had not been matched for 40 years. In 1912, Bob Taft's father, President William Howard Taft, had gone to the same city of Chicago, determined to smash the pretensions of a more popular and more liberal but less Republican challenger called Theodore Roosevelt. Bob Taft went there in 1952, in determination to smash the pretensions of a more popular and relatively more liberal but less Republican challenger, Dwight Eisenhower. The father and his managers had held the party machinery in an iron grip. So did the son 40 years later. Like father, like son."[267]

Eisenhower had to find a way to build public momentum for the seating of his delegates. He pushed to have cameras show the proceedings of the credential committee. If not, the steal could be carried out without the public watching. "On TV we can portray in vivid terms and through visual exhibition the fraudulent character of the Taft group, said one of Eisenhower's lieutenants.[268]

At first, the party chairman, handpicked by Taft, said no to the cameras, so the networks focused just on the brass knobs of the doors for the viewers at home, behind which the credentials committee would meet.

Representative Hugh Scott, supporting Eisenhower, stood in front of those doors and clutched his breast for the cameras. "Those doors are locked," he recounts in his book *Come to the Party*. "And they are being kept locked. Why? Because inside are people who are trying to do in secret what they don't dare do in public. They do not want you to see them deny the rightful claims of delegates to sit in this convention and vote for Eisenhower. Those doors are not closed against the press. They are closed against you, the people." A few hours later, the chairman of the party announced that the cameras would indeed be allowed.[269]

For the first time in American history, between sixty and seventy million citizens were able to view firsthand the workings of a national convention. One hundred and six stations broadcast the spectacle over the nation's four networks, reaching nearly 40 percent of the population.[270] It was a symbolic victory for the Eisenhower underdogs who had proclaimed themselves the popular choice. "Another victory on behalf of the American people won by the Eisenhower forces," said one.

On July 6, as the party functionaries were still arriving, Taft walked into a press meeting, carrying a huge bundle of telegrams, 530 of them, from delegates who'd said they were going to back Taft. By Monday morning, Taft had 607 such assurances. That was more than he needed to win the final nominating vote.

This wasn't all Taft had going for him. He had the whole structure filled with his supporters; both the temporary and permanent committee were pledged to him. He had the platform committee, the Credentials Committee, and a majority on the national committee. All the speakers were his supporters, including General Douglas MacArthur. His aides had even picked the music that was to be played and the singers who would sing. There seemed no way he could be turned back.

Part of playing the inside game was the explicit promise of patronage jobs for those who played ball with Taft, who was known as "the

Republican of the United States." So it was Mr. Republican versus Mr. America which was the way Eisenhower was portraying himself.

As Eisenhower traveled to the convention, he stopped on July 4 in Ames, Iowa, to be a guest on an NBC program called *We the People*, celebrating Independence Day. By this time, Eisenhower had picked up his rhetoric, attacking Truman and promising "to lift off our backs the curse of inefficient and .22-caliber men in Washington."[271]

But if Mr. America was gonna beat Mr. Republican, the only way he was going to do it was by creating a moral case for Taft's theft of delegates in Texas and other Southern states. He had to convince party insiders through public pressure that they should drop their loyalty to the machine and to those jobs they might get under Taft.

"It [politics] is not a network of privilege, or of cynicism, or of iron party discipline that reaches out from Washington to the fringe of the last cheap little deal," said Eisenhower. "Whether politicians are to be loyal servants or arrogant masters is the issue at this very moment in Chicago."[272]

While Taft was brandishing those telegraph pledges from delegates, Eisenhower forces had mailed a broadside, twenty-four by thirty-six inches in size, to all 1,206 delegates. It contained letters of protest about the Texas steal through which Taft forces had assigned delegates to their man even though Eisenhower had more supporters at the Texas caucuses. "Not being able to secrure enough delegtes," said Taft, "they apparently are going to try to overwhelm the convention by unlimited use of propaganda."[273]

Round One in Chicago

There were four important rounds of battle at the 1952 GOP convention. Three of those rounds were over the contested Southern delegates: the Texas delegates and delegates from a few other Southern states, the fourth round was the actual vote on which candidate would be the nominee of the Republican Party.

The first round on the first day was a vote on what Eisenhower called the "fair play" amendment. Though the Southern delegates were in dispute, Taft's had already been seated temporarily, following rules written after the last big GOP fight in 1912.[274] That meant they could participate in the vote over whether they should be permanent delegates. Since they were Taft delegates, they were going to side with the Taft position which was that they should be seated for Taft. Delegates, validate thyself! That seems rigged, right? Eisenhower thought so, too. He said delegates in dispute shouldn't be allowed temporary status to vote on their own future. It was like allowing the accused to sit in the jury box.

The general and his troops were so effective in making this moral case—the signs saying, Thou Shalt Not Steal; trucks going through the streets with a P.A. system blaring, "Thou shalt not steal"—that it knocked Taft off course. He had so planned the normal way of doing things that this public fight, which required adaptation and quick tactical maneuvers, befuddled him. Here was the way William White wrote about it: "A kind of evangelistic fever swept Chicago. The Eisenhower men paraded about, shaking at the Taft people signs that read 'Thou shalt not steal.' Taft, working 20 hours a day at his headquarters in the Conrad Hilton Hotel blinked under this brandishing of the commandment. He was not stunned. He was simply and wholly uncomprehending. The whole Chicago proceeding had turned into one from which he instinctively fled. He was enormously uncomfortable in the face of any emotional displays. And in this regard, Chicago was at that time a great bath of emotion. He did not have the faintest realization of the movement that had gone like a brushfire through Texas, a movement not simply to select General Eisenhower over Senator Taft, but to elect Eisenhower to the presidency."

Under pressure, Taft said he would allow some of Eisenhower's Texas delegates to be seated. Senator Lodge, who was running the show for Eisenhower, said no. He didn't want the compromise. He had to keep this a moral fight about right and wrong. "It's never right to compromise with dishonesty," said Lodge. A compromise would let Taft off the hook, making it appear the matter was only a clerical dispute, not a titanic battle over the very foundation of honest dealing and sagacious constancy. Taft took out a newspaper ad in the *Chicago Tribune* claiming that the Eisenhower managers were trying to "divide and destroy the party."[275]

The newspapers saw a shift in power. Ike's men had been talking about the "immorality" of Taft's tactics, but, said one politico, "it wasn't the steamroller they objected to—it was the fact that Taft had one and they didn't. Now they're getting one of their own, they're ready to ride it roughshod over everybody and everything."[276]

Former president Herbert Hoover, a Taft man, weighed in with a suggestion that maybe an impartial committee could be appointed to look over this delegate matter. Lodge kept up the pressure: "No, that would be improper to have a backroom arrangement cheat the American people." For Lodge, only total and utter surrender by Taft would meet the test. Even that might not have worked, because the whole point of accepting no deal from Taft was to build a case for Eisenhower that would carry over into the larger vote. An early resolution of the procedural matter would not have allowed the negative impression to grow about Taft. Lodge was not just fighting for those Southern delegates. He was trying to build support among all the other delegates for the final vote on who the party nominee would be.

Ike got an assist from Republican governors meeting in Houston. Twenty-three of the twenty-five Republican governors wrote a letter saying that if the convention didn't accept the fair play amendment, "The Republican nominee will enter a vital and difficult campaign under a serious moral cloud." It was a sign that Taft was losing support in the party structure if the governors were abandoning him.

At the last moment before the vote on fair play was to be taken by the entire convention, the Taft forces tried to monkey with the language of the fair play amendment. But with the delegates smashed in together one on top of the other, they were barely able to hear what was being said from the podium. What they were saying was hard to decipher even in a quiet hotel room with the aid of a set of diagrams. A Taft man, took to the podium and said, "I move, Mr. Chairman, to amend the Langley substitute by changing the figure 68 as appears in line nine, striking out those figures, and substituting in place therefor the figure 61, and further to decide from the accompanying list of delegates the seven delegates from the district of Louisiana."

Got that? The Taft forces were trying to make a last-minute change in the fair play amendment. Nobody could understand what was going on. They knew the difference between right and wrong, however. The convention voted 658 to 548 in favor of Eisenhower's fair play amendment. The controversial delegates from the South would not be allowed to vote on their own status when the time came around to hold that vote.

This was only a vote about who would get to vote later. The convention hadn't yet voted on the actual disposition of those contested delegates. But it was a big psychological victory for Eisenhower over Taft. This was the first evidence that Eisenhower, through making a public case, could appeal to those 1,206 delegates and overcome all the careful planning and scheming of the party insiders.

Eisenhower watched the roll call from room 508 of the Blackstone Hotel wearing a maroon bathrobe, shorts and slippers. When the final tally was in, he collected a dollar from one of his aides, Sen. Frank Carlson of Kansas. Eisenhower had bet that his vote was going to be nearer to 650 than 600.[277] Eisenhower said that the vote "was proof that this convention belongs to the delegates and the people who elected them."[278]

Round Two in Chicago

Now back to the actual matter of how to deal with the permanent status of those contested delegates. The next round in the four-part battle between Eisenhower and Taft took place on turf that was more favorable to Taft. Instead of a contest for affections among the 1,206 delegates who voted on the fair play amendment, the candidates were about to fight it out for the votes of the smaller credentials committee. That takes us back to the action at the start of our narrative (convention stories about byzantine rules fights are really doing their job if they mirror the complexity they're describing).

The committee, meeting in the Gold Room at the Congress Hotel, was filled with party insiders, most of whom were for Taft. They were about to determine whether to seat Taft's or Eisenhower's Southern delegates. The candidate whose delegates were approved out of the credentials committee would be the one with the advantage on the final vote over who should be party nominee.

The debate in the credentials committee started in the morning and went until 1:45 a.m., each state delegation making the case for whether the Eisenhower or the Taft delegates should be seated.

Because Taft controlled the room, he won that second-round battle. His Southern delegates were seated, giving him the majority of delegates for the ultimate nomination vote. All that stood between Taft and the nomination was the vote of the whole convention okaying what the back room boys in the credentials committee had done.

Round Three in Chicago

It would normally be unheard-of for the entire convention to overturn the ruling of the Credentials Committee, but Eisenhower had captured the emotions of the crowd. He had also ensured—through the fair play vote—that the temporary Taft delegates would not be allowed to ratify the credentials committee decision.

The Taft men knew they had to take emergency action. They turned to the most mellifluous voice in the conservative ranks: Sen. Everett Dirksen of Illinois made the case to the convention for why those delegates selected by the credentials committee should be seated for Taft.

The senator reportedly gargled with Pond's Cold Cream, which was a very weird thing to do, but the maintenance regimen gives you some sense of his theatricality and attention to oratorical flair.

Dirksen was called the Wizard of Ooze because his voice, which was hard to characterize, sounded like a burbling brook and the sweet confidences of a Renaissance suitor all rolled into one. At least he thought so. Brooks Atkinson, the *New York Times* drama critic, said, "His voice is like the froth on a warm pail of milk just extracted from a Jersey cow."[279] Well into his oration about his commitment to the party and its previous nominees, the senator said: "Now I say from an earnest heart that I trust tonight we will not commit suicide and impair the chances of victory, that are like something bright and iridescent upon the horizon right now. I say it with earnestness because most of my mature life has been given to the Republican Party." (That last word he pronounced "paw-TEA.")

Dirksen argued if the whole convention overturned that vote in the credentials committee, it would send a horrible message to the country that the Republican party structure was corrupt, because it would mean the whole convention had overturned the party apparatus. That would taint whoever the nominee was.

At the emotional peak of his oration, Dirksen raised his finger and pointed at Dewey, the governor of New York, who sat with the New York delegation, holding the pole with the state name. He'd been the Republican nominee for the last two cycles. Dirksen argued that Dewey's two losses as a nominee foreshadowed what would happen if the entire convention supported Eisenhower, another squishy moderate. By rooting for the "minority report," delegates would overturn that vote in the credentials committee and give Eisenhower the delegates instead. That would ensure his nomination. "Reexamine your hearts before you take this action and support the minority report, because we followed you before. And you took us down the road to defeat. And don't do this to us," said Dirksen.

Pandemonium ensued when Dirksen called out Dewey. Things

got so out of hand that William Cloon, a member of the Michigan delegation, collapsed from nervous exhaustion. He had to be carried from the hall and given emergency medical treatment. An NBC commentator thought something else had happened. Seeing Cloon on the stretcher, he said, "Somebody threw an awfully good punch there."

After Dirksen made his case, the entire convention voted on whether what had happened in the Gold Room had been kosher. State by state they voted, and when the numbers were tallied, Taft lost! The entire convention had supported the minority report, the Eisenhower position, undoing what the credentials committee had decided.

As the vote moved against him, Taft tried to make another deal again with Eisenhower, offering to seat Eisenhower's delegates from Texas. He was trying to somehow salvage some shred of the moral high ground, or rob some thunder from Eisenhower's victory. Taft was essentially trying to run out in front of the parade, which was already well formed and on the march. It was a desperate play, but it was the only possible way he could regain standing so that delegates might somehow vote for him on the final vote on the actual party nominee.

It was too late. Things were so bad for Taft that the old-guard conservatives briefly thought about abandoning him to push General MacArthur to go up against Eisenhower in that final round of voting. No one followed through with the plan, though.

With the delegates seated for Eisenhower, his march was irreversible. Mrs. Doris Petitbon, of New Orleans, broke down in tears of happiness when her group of Eisenhower delegates were accredited to the convention.

Taft Leads to Nixon

When the convention voted on the nominee, General Eisenhower, his southern delegates seated and validated, won on the first ballot 845 to 280. Eisenhower immediately began the work of trying to repair the party. He called the vanquished Taft right away, and the two men met.

The General went to Taft's private office on the ninth floor of the Conrad Hilton Hotel. Women workers in Taft's headquarters were crying as the beaming general arrived. As Eisenhower appeared, the women dried their tears and began chanting somewhat feebly, "We want Taft."[280]

After enduring that, Eisenhower spoke to the cameras: "I have just completed a call on Senator Taft. I extended an invitation to cooperate with me from now on, and he agreed to do so in a very warm-hearted fashion, which pleased me very greatly."

The columnist Walter Lippmann wrote about Taft's defeat this way, making the case that this wasn't just a defeat for a man, but it was a defeat for an entire old way of doing business in the Republican Party. "By their handling of the contests and their use of television, the Eisenhower managers succeeded in demonstrating how much the control of the party organization depends on politicians from states and territories where the Republicans are not, in fact, a political party at all. There has been a devastating exposure of an old skeleton in the cupboard, namely that the party bureaucracy and management do not rest on a popular basis."

That's the way Lippmann saw it—it was a conclusion about the party's health that Dirksen had prophesied. The conservatives saw it an entirely different way. For them, this was the fourth time in a row the GOP had turned to the candidate with the best perceived chance of victory in the autumn instead of the politician who reflected the actual philosophy of people in the party. Of course, unlike the previous three times, Eisenhower would go on to win, and the GOP would take control of both houses of Congress.

That victory didn't calm conservatives. As *National Review* publisher William Rusher later reminisced, "Modern American conservatism largely organized itself during and in explicit opposition to the Eisenhower administration." There would be other repercussions as well from this battle. To appease the conservative wing, Eisenhower settled on a running mate quickly, who was an anticommunist darling of conservatives at the time: Richard M. Nixon.

There was a time when people weren't even sure that Eisenhower was a Republican. Now his picture hangs in the lobby of the Republican National Committee. He and his running mate would dominate Republican politics for roughly the next twenty years.

1824—The Corrupt Bargain

A FOOT-RACE

The People's Candidate

If there is a constant to the American campaign story, it is that elites can't predict the future very well. News is what surprises us, which is why the political press always has news: voters are always undoing our certainties. We had been certain that Truman was a gone goose in 1948, that a B-list actor with simple views could never get elected in 1980, and that Donald Trump would flame out after a week in 2016.

In 1824 insiders were certain that Andrew Jackson was not a serious contender for the presidency. (Unless the contest were to be decided by a fistfight.) He had a thin political résumé, and while he was a military hero with bullets still in his body and a road map of scars, the general was also a hothead—a frontier wild-man too ill-tempered for the job. Jackson agreed. "I can command a body of men in a rough way," he reportedly said in 1821, "but I am not fit to be President."[281]

Plus, Jackson was competing with a tough field. The campaign of 1824 was packed with veteran legislators and cabinet officials—secretaries of state, war, and treasury—the farm team from which all presidents but George Washington had been chosen. There had been nine elections in America. There was a pattern to how these things went.

Jackson was such a long shot, men in the know figured the first-term Tennessee senator was only in the race to cause mischief. One Pennsylvania paper saw him as the agent of the Federalist party that had all but died. "The artful Federalists," it said, "knowing the General's popularity, as a patriotic warrior, have started his name for the Presidency…for the purpose of sowing dissensions in the Democratic party."[282] Other wise men thought Jackson would split the vote with the other candidates. This would allow John Quincy Adams, the son of the former president, to step up from his post as secretary of state, which had been the anteroom to the presidency for Madison and Jefferson. "There are men behind the curtain who are pushing Jackson," said the *National Advocate*, "perfectly aware that he cannot be elected and supposing that his strength will ultimately go for Adams."[283]

They were all wrong. Jackson was not a stalking horse for John Quincy Adams. He would become Adams's fiercest challenger, propelled by voters demanding a bigger role in picking their president. A new era had begun, though the political class didn't quite know it. They had underestimated the force that always surprises us: the voters. The American system, which had operated as a republic run by elites, was moving toward a popular democracy where the people would have their say.

Jackson did so well in the 1824 campaign that by the end of the year, if there had been cable television pundits, they would have said it was certain he would win the presidency. When John Quincy Adams won instead, Jackson's supporters cried "Corrupt bargain!" and another American electoral phenomenon was born: a revenge movement led by voters who felt robbed. The conclusion to the 1824 campaign was the spark for Jackson's 1828 campaign of vindication and the two terms in the White House that followed.

Throwing His Hat Near the Ring

It was hard to see the fire in Jackson's belly for the presidency, because he did not start his race by charging up the hill. Local Tennessee politicians trying to build support for their faction of the party convinced him to enter the race in 1822. By nominating Jackson for the White House, they hoped to use his fame as a military hero to draw voters to their slate of candidates for governor and the legislature. Voters holding the Democratic-Republican ticket in their hands might be unfamiliar with the names listed on it, but they would be drawn to the likeness of their hero at the top of the paper.

Jackson's friends thought he was being used and took offense on his behalf. Sen. Hugh Lawson White complained that "scoundrels" were using Jackson's name "to effect their dishonest or dishonorable purposes... They have no more notion of trying to make him president than of making me."[284]

If the hero of the Battle of New Orleans had any design, it was thwarting his chief local rival in his run for the Senate. Jackson's motivations were a muddy stream to the public, though. He talked about wanting to retire and struck the pose required at the time, where candidates were not supposed to look like they were working to take office. "The office of chief magistrate," Jackson wrote, "is one of great responsibility. As it should not be sought... my political creed prompts me to leave the affair... to the free will of those who have alone the right to decide."

Candidates who really wanted to be president had to pretend they were anxious to stay home and tend their fields or bee houses and say they weren't interested, even when they were deeply driven. The founders designed the government to guard against ambition so the norms of the time dictated that the only men worthy of operating in that government hide their ambition. Given this tension—you needed ambition, but had to hide it—everyone in politics was obsessed with intrigues and misdirection.

Jackson appears to take this code to heart, in a letter to William Berkeley Lewis dated March 31, 1824, writes of presidential ambition in more human terms: "I have no doubt... if I was to travel to Boston where I have been invited that it would insure my election—But this I can not do—I would feel degraded the ballance of my life—If I ever fill that office it must be the free choice of the people—I can then say I am the President of the nation—and my acts shall comport with that charecter."

Candidates were not supposed to "to be out on an electionering pilgrimage," as Jackson put it, because it would tempt them to make promises in order to win.[285] That would keep them from doing the right thing once they were in office. Voters would also be tempted to demand goodies from their candidates.

Jackson didn't have to promise voters anything to get attention. They knew who he was: Old Hickory, a name given to him by his troops for being "as tough as old hickory on the battlefield." He stood over six feet tall, his eyes were said to resemble a "chafed lion" when excited, and history remembers him with a shock of gray hair at attention and waving free. He carried two bullets in his body from dueling, which was why people joked that he rattled "like a bag of marbles" when he walked. Jackson's body full of lead also meant he suffered regular hemorrhages that brought him low and often required him to administer a bleeding to himself before bedtime so that he could have the strength to get up in the morning. He did not have to battle the wimp factor.

In 1816, Jackson had fought the Seminole Indians and, before that, licked the British at the Battle of New Orleans in 1815. In that battle, Jackson and his forces were so successful despite being outnumbered, it's amazing the story hasn't been repeatedly adapted for a theater near you. Three hundred British soldiers were killed and another twelve hundred were wounded; only thirteen of Jackson's troops died and just fifty-nine were wounded.

Six years afterward, they were still throwing flowers at Jackson on the streets of New Orleans. "The attention and honors paid to the General far excel a recital by my pen," Jackson's wife, Rachel, wrote to a friend after a visit by the couple to New Orleans. "They conducted him to the Grand Theater; his box was decorated with elegant hangings. At his appearance, the theater rang with loud acclamations, 'Vive Jackson!' Songs of praise were sung by ladies, and in the midst they crowned him with a crown of laurel."[286]

In Tennessee, Jackson was even more acclaimed. "Among the people," one Tennessee newspaper noted, "his popularity is unbounded—old and young speak of him with rapture." [287] By the end of 1823 this acclaim led the state legislature to appoint him to the Senate. If he was headed to the White House, he was going to stop by the other end of Pennsylvania Avenue first.

Hero Worship

Eighteen twenty-four was a great year to be a military hero. The Marquis de Lafayette returned to the United States for a thirteen-month tour of parties and celebrations. When his ship docked in New York Harbor, upwards of fifty thousand people turned out to welcome the general who, as a twenty-year-old, had joined the Revolutionary cause. Women wore gloves printed with his likeness. (When greeting one so appareled he did not kiss her gloved hand, saying he did not wish to kiss himself.) A Connecticut newspaper wrote that Lafayette's pilgrimage kindled in Americans "a delirium of feeling, a tumult of the soul, from which one never wished to be awakened to the dull, sober realities of common life."[288]

The aging general marveled at all that had changed since he routed the redcoats. The country had grown to ten million from 2.5 million during colonial days. The thirteen colonies had grown into twenty-four states, including Ohio, Florida, and Missouri.

The republic had survived the first tests to its experimental system of shared powers arranged to protect individual liberty. The election of 1800 had been a bit bumpy—requiring thirty-six ballots in the House to resolve an Electoral College tie—but even then, power had transferred successfully. The partisan rancor of the early republic had fallen away with the Federalist Party's decline after the War of 1812.

America was in an "era of good feeling." James Monroe had been elected essentially unopposed.

While Lafayette marveled at the "immense improvements," since the visits of his younger days there was also a tension in America between change and tradition. The Westward expansion had brought about speculation. Banks had issued paper money that became worthless, leading to the Panic of 1819 that crippled the nation's economy.

The debate over Missouri's entrance into the union as a slave state surfaced bitter sectional feelings that would ultimately lead to the Civil War. Northerners condemned Congress's Missouri Compromise, because it allowed slavery to continue in the new territory. Americans in Southern states recoiled at the idea Congress would take upon itself the power to regulate slavery in any way.

Lafayette's return kindled a re-appreciation the heroism of the Revolutionary age and created a national celebration of the attributes of bravery and character. With the Revolutionary generation dying off, Americans were looking for a new crop of leaders with the same attributes. A number of people thought the roster was thin.

Jackson, who bore the scars of his participation in the Revolutionary war as a young scout, played on these desires. His biographer and close friend John Eaton promoted Jackson as a Founding Father of a new generation in *The Letters of Wyoming*, a series of eleven letters, attributed to the author "Wyoming," that railed against the political era of intrigue and misrule and promoted Jackson as a bridge to a virtuous age. Historians have concluded that while Jackson didn't write *The Letters of Wyoming* he played a role in their production, and the thinking certainly mapped his own.

Wyoming wrote that the era of good feeling had lulled the country into a trance. One party control of government had bred corruption and manipulation. Power passed so easily between members of the same clan, because the system was rigged. "Look to the city of Washington," wrote Wyoming, "and let the virtuous patriots of the country weep at the spectacle. There corruption is springing into existence, and fast flourishing."

In previous elections voters could trust the founders to protect their liberties against despotism. Since then, the founders had been replaced by mere politicians, men skilled at managing power, keeping office through patronage and cozy arrangements with the political class. It was time for the people to intercede and give power to someone who was not tainted by the political process.

Jackson's critics saw his lack of political polish as a flaw, but he was pitching it as a virtue. Only someone from the outside could clean out the stable. Today we recognize this posture as the classic outsider candidacy, but it was a revolutionary gambit at the time. It represented risk and a deviation from what was comfortable. That worried elites, but the larger public was in a mood for change. After the Panic of 1819 many shared Jackson's view that it was the comfortable, well-connected politicians—and what Jackson called the "moneyed aristocracy"—who had caused the recession by supporting the Second Bank of the United States. Voters wanted more say over the politicians who would be making decisions about policies that could affect them so directly.

Jackson was just the right leader, wrote Eaton, because he "is the last of those valiant establishers of the liberty of our Republic, who can succeed to the highest office known to our Constitution."[289] Like the "immortal Washington," Jackson was Revolution tested. He could take on the "dangerous trends of the modern age" and restore "the cherished values of old."[290]

Fear the Demagogue

Today we're familiar with candidates who present themselves as the people's champion. The founders had tried to create a system that was resistant to such men. America was not created as a democracy. The founders formed a republic expressly as a check on the popular will. The Electoral College, the election of senators by state legislatures, limited suffrage, and the nominating caucus were all designed to take the car keys from those inebriated by momentary enthusiasms. No one wanted to sit in the rubble after electing a demagogue and mumble "it seemed like a good idea at the time."

The roots of this fear traced all the way back to the philosophers who informed the founders. Plato quotes Socrates as saying, "Tyranny is probably established out of no other regime than democracy."

The danger of making one man the route to the protection of liberty, as Jackson's backers did, is that the focus on a single person invites personal hero worship. People will be tempted to hand over too much power to a single person based on affection rather than reason. Such a person, once elevated, may be driven by human pride, particularly if that person is a military hero. "Dazzled by military glory," wrote Albert Gallatin, running mate to Jackson's campaign rival, William Crawford, the people give up their "rights and liberties to the shrine of that glory."

Eaton's pitch that Jackson contained special virtues necessary to take the country back to its founding would have shocked the founders, whose values he was promising to revive. Thomas Jefferson was, indeed, unsettled by Jackson: "I feel much alarmed at the prospect of seeing General Jackson President," he told Daniel Webster. "He is one of the most unfit men I know of for such a place. He has had very little respect for laws and constitutions, and is, in fact, an able military chief. His passions are terrible. When I was President of the Senate, he was Senator; and he could never speak on account of the rashness of his feelings. I have seen him attempt it repeatedly, and as often choke with rage. His passions are, no doubt, cooler now; he has been much tried since I knew him, but he is a dangerous man."

Jackson, like Donald Trump, reveled in the criticism. In a letter on March 6, to his nephew Andrew Jackson Donelson, he wrote that the "abuse" in the papers from his opponents "will increase my standing with the nation more than any other course they can pursue; They will elect me, contrary to their wishes, by their *abuse*—I do assure you my young friend, that I would rather be abused by these hireling writers than receive their praise, for the praise of such men would be Viewed by all honest disinterested men, as a cause to suspect my honesty & integrity. When I review my course, my conscience tells me I have acted right—it was a course marked out with the sole View to the good of my country—an honest community View, & approve it as such, & I am at perfect peace with myself."

Jackson's critics had plenty of reason to think he might overreach. As a militia leader he had executed mutineers and broken the terms of treaties with the Indians. In New Orleans, Jackson imposed martial law on the city, defying a writ of habeas corpus and jailing the federal district judge who issued it.[291] While pursuing the Seminole Indians he overstepped his authority, and his execution of two British citizens created an international incident. "His entire career seemed to contradict the most basic democratic processes for which this country stood," wrote Jackson scholar Robert Remini.[292]

Jackson's campaign rivals, House Speaker Henry Clay and Treasury Secretary William Crawford, were more than just competitor-critics. They had pushed official inquiries into his treatment of the Spanish as governor of Florida. Clay denounced him for two hours on the floor of the House, comparing him with military tyrants like Alexander, Caesar, and Napoleon.[293] Several years later as a candidate competing against him, Clay wrote a friend, "I cannot believe that killing 2,500 Englishmen at [New] Orleans qualifies for the various, difficult, and complicated duties of the Chief Magistracy."

The *Raleigh Register and North-Carolina State Gazette* summed up Jackson's career as "a disgusting detail of squabbling and quarreling—of pistollings dirkings and brickbattings and other actions reconcilable neither to regulations nor morals." *The National Advocate* said, "As to General Jackson, his temper and talents are by no means suited to the office. There would be no safety under his administration." [294]

Jackson had plenty of supporters, however. Jackson's savage treatment of the Indians as a military commander and president has opened him to a historical reevaluation, but his ruthlessness was a considerable asset at the time that lived on long after he died. During an immense open-air picnic Sen. Stephen A. Douglas said, "I wish to

God we had an old Hickory now alive in order that he might hang Northern and Southern traitors on the same gallows." The applause was reported to be loud and sustained. When Lincoln suspended habeas corpus during the Civil War, he pointed to Jackson's precedent in New Orleans.

Well aware of this reputation, Jackson was wary when he first arrived in Washington as a senator. Radicals tried to bait him into "some act of violence" to destroy his candidacy, but "in this they have much mistaken my character."[295] He delighted in surprising Washington hostesses when he arrived as a senator. "When it becomes necessary to philosophise and be meek," he wrote, "no man can command his temper better than I."[296] He was pleased by what he described as the shocked reception to his bows and polite charms. "I am told the opinion of those whose minds were prepared to see me with a Tomahawk in one hand, and a scalping knife in the other has greatly changed and I am getting on very smoothly."[297]

Death of King Caucus

Readers of the *National Advocate* on April 10, 1824 would have come across an imagined conversation between a carpenter and a mason. "I am almost tired of reading every day about the next President," says the carpenter, testifying that campaign fatigue didn't start with cable news. "Is it of much consequence who we elect?" The mason responds quickly, "Certainly it is. Every true American should feel a deep interest in the choice of a Chief Magistrate of his country, because he is the man selected to see the laws faithfully executed, and upon a judicious choice depends our safety at home, and our respect abroad."

The carpenter wonders if it is possible "with all the checks imposed by our constitution and laws, and those greater checks of public opinion, that the President can do any injury to the country." Of course it's possible, responded the mason, who illustrates for his friend the ways a president can abuse the country without being checked. He "may elevate to power men of suspicious and doubtful characters; he may fill the high places with persons more devoted to his private views than the public good...in short, the office is a dangerous one in the hands of bad men."

The message of this dialogue was that if every person was not vigilant, the politicians would hoodwink them, serving themselves and their friends. The mason was no doubt thinking about that February's attempted hoodwinking with the Democratic-Republican nominating caucus.

"King Caucus," a meeting of the party's elected representatives to Congress, was the traditional route candidates took to the presidential nomination. Elected officials from a broad geographical region, accustomed to reasoned discourse with each other in legislative matters, turned their wattage toward the question of who might make the best servant of liberty and American traditions. That was the way advocates saw it, anyway, and it was the method used by the Democratic-Republicans to pick Jefferson, Madison, and Monroe, the previous three presidents.

The caucus was falling out of favor, though. State politicians and voters didn't want to have their choice handed to them by Washington politicians. They were demanding a greater say in a party's nominee through state legislatures and conventions. This election was particularly important, because the Washington politicians in their caucus would be picking more than just the nominee of the party. In this case, the small number of men would wind up picking the president, because no other party existed to challenge the candidacy of the Democratic-Republican nominee. That would rob the people of any say in the presidency. "This is a great national *crisis*," said the *Louisville Public Advertiser*, "involving the question, whether the PEOPLE are *sovereign in elections*, or whether their *servants* shall rule them!"[298]

Jackson wrote his friend John Coffee, "I intermix with none of those who are engaged in the intrigues of caucus, or president makers."[299] He didn't have to. Though Jackson wasn't bothering with King Caucus, his allies were working hard on regicide. So were the allies of Jackson's rivals, Secretary of State John Quincy Adams and House Speaker Henry Clay.

The three competitors had reasons other than principle for their joint efforts against the caucus. The process was almost certain to pick Treasury Secretary William Crawford of Georgia. He was the front-runner, which confirmed the underlying suspicions of caucus critics. Crawford had resisted challenging James Monroe in 1816 with the implicit understanding that he would receive the caucus nomination eight years later. It was his turn.

"It is said there is to be a *caucus*. This I cannot believe," wrote Jackson, "but it is the last hope of the friends of Mr. Crawford…such is the feelings of the nation that a recommendation by a congressional caucus would politically [damn] any name put forth by it."[300] The caucus managers, led by future president Martin Van Buren, were pushing Crawford even though he was still recovering from a stroke five months earlier that had left him nearly blind and feeble.

That party managers were pushing the ailing Crawford—particularly strategist Van Buren—underlined Jackson's point. They just wanted a warm body in the post to be agent of their their aims. Van Buren and his allies also needed the caucus system to continue. It was the only way to keep the party under some semblance of control. Anyone who was ambitious and wanted to rise needed to keep the caucus happy. This meant no party member could do anything too radical for fear of losing favor of party leaders.

State legislatures from across the country passed measures calling for a stop to the caucus. Just before the vote, the Washington *National Intelligencer* printed a notice signed by eleven congressmen calling on their colleagues to join with them to recommend a presidential candidate to the people. However, the same issue of the newspaper also carried an announcement signed by twenty-four members of Congress representing fifteen states opposing a caucus.[301]

The caucus went ahead anyway. Only sixty-eight members showed up; 193 were absent.[302] Forty-eight were from four states—New York,

Georgia, North Carolina, and Virginia. When the balloting was over and the results announced, Crawford won sixty-four votes. The gallery was packed with onlookers who groaned loudly.

"Everything is carried by intrigue and management," Jackson wrote to Coffee. "It is now a contest between a few demagogues and the people; and it is to be seen whether a minority less than one fourth of the whole members of Congress can coerce the people to follow them; or whether the people will assume their constitutional rights and put down these Demagogues."[303]

The crowd watching the caucus vote might not have been pleased, but plenty of people felt as though the system had worked. The system was designed to allow men who understood the attributes required for the job to pick someone they knew who had those attributes from long service in public office. It was the opposite of leadership by rabble. Crawford represented stability as it was defined by the authors of the American system.

Caucus supporters had their own reason to see intrigue in the motivations of their opponents. They charged that Jackson, Adams, and Clay wanted a messy national vote instead of a reasoned pick from the caucus because they wanted to split the vote and have no electoral vote majority. That would throw the election into the House of Representatives. In the House they could influence the final outcome. The *Washington City Gazette* concluded (through a certain kind of magical math) that if the election were sent to the House, it would be determined by thirty-two representatives from thirteen states. The pro-Crawford *National Advocate* embraced their calculations: "The Anti-Caucus writers and orators denounce the mere *nomination* of *candidates* by 64 Representatives, and are willing to give the *election* of President to these 32."

Another criticism of the caucus was that it meant lawmakers were violating the separation of powers. They were nominating a candidate they might have to face later if the election was sent to the House of Representatives. Crawford's supporters responded by saying they had merely voted in the caucus as private citizens, not representatives. Thus they drew a distinction between their nominating and electoral roles.

This fooled no one. More important, it was over-the-top spin that helped make the anticaucus case. It became an example of just how much pro caucus forces would bend reason to fit their prefered outcome. "The forlorn members of the caucus, seem to imagine that they have nothing more to do to reconcile the people to a shameful act, than to declare that they have done the deed, not as the representatives of the people, but as private individuals," said the *New Hampshire Statesman*. "Here is a practical illustration of the means and miserable subterfuges which men are compelled to resort to, when they leave the high road of faith and honor."[304]

Defending the caucus, the *Raleigh Register and North-Carolina State Gazette* offered one of the greatest arguments for the silent majority in political history:

> Because half a dozen Grasshoppers, under a hedge, make the field ring with their importunate chink, whilst the great Cattle repose beneath the shade, chew the cud and are *silent*—pray do not imagine that those who make the noise, are the only inhabitants of the field . . . let us not, brother editors, fancy that those who make the most "noise" are the only people interested in the great national questions now pending. No—many of the wisest and most intelligent men of our country are "chewing the cud in silence," anxiously awaiting the result.[305]

After the caucus vote the party had its nominee in Crawford, but the outcome was essentially meaningless. The states still wanted to vote to select their electors. Crawford still faced opposition from Andrew Jackson, John Calhoun the flinty secretary of war, Henry Clay, and John Quincy Adams. They were not going to automatically ratify the caucus's selection. As Jackson had predicted, the railroading of the process undermined it, marking the first tectonic shift in 1824. It would be the last time the party would choose its nominee that way. King Caucus was dead.

Old Hickory in Harrisburg

Not long after Crawford's Pyrrhic victory in King Caucus, Jackson notched a victory in Pennsylvania of a kind that would be much more important in the new order of things. It would mark the second big shift of 1824.

Jackson had to prove that he had support outside of the West and South. "It does not appear... that his qualifications for the Presidency are sufficiently obvious to induce any state, with the exception of Tennessee, and, perhaps, Alabama to give him the vote," wrote another shortly-to-be-proven-wrong pundit in the *Supporter and Scioto Gazette* from Chillicothe, Ohio.

All the candidates had to overcome this regional hurdle. Secretary of State John Quincy Adams of Massachusetts was strong in the Northeast. John Calhoun of South Carolina was strong in the South; House Speaker Henry Clay of Kentucky competed with Jackson for support in the West. William Crawford of Georgia didn't have to worry about regional balance as much, because he was placing his bets on the residual power of the inside caucus game.

Given that much of the map was already distributed, states like Pennsylvania were important, because they were essentially up for grabs. Except Pennsylvania, the second-largest state in the union behind New York, wasn't really up for grabs. Jackson had going for him what other candidates lacked. For two years, Jackson supporters, including men who had served under him in battle, had organized and worked the state. He had the early support of Stephen Simpson, editor of the *Columbian Observer*, who had fought at the Battle of New Orleans and was a fierce critic of the banks.

In the end, Jackson won the Harrisburg state convention 124 to 1. Though the victory was the result of careful behind-the-scenes planning, it was framed as a grassroots groundswell—"A cause where every tongue is eloquent in its favor"—by both supporters and opponents.[306]

"The public sentiment towards General Jackson, is, in fact, a spontaneous emotion among the people," said the *Aurora General Advertiser*. "[As] he has outstripped all his competitors in Pennsylvania, without the assistance of public journals...we may pronounce him as being in the most extensive sense of the term, the people's candidate."[307]

One Pennsylvania supporter claimed that Jackson was on his way to clean out "the Giant Augean Stable at Washington" of the corruption and scheming. (Hercules had been tasked to clean out in a single day the stables of King Augeas, who owned more cattle and horses than anyone in Greece. The phrase became so popular the election tickets in Jackson's 1828 race carried a picture of a broom with the slogan "To Sweep the Augean Stable.")

Jackson's victory surprised Secretary of War John Calhoun, his chief rival in the state, and knocked him from the race—though delegates at the Pennsylvania convention did back Calhoun as a vice presidential choice.

Calhoun supporters complained after the Pennsylvania convention about the "grog shop politicians of the villages and the rabble of Pittsburgh and Philadelphia."[308] Newspapers critical of Jackson were in fits. "That the less thinking part of the community should be captivated by the pomp of military fame, is not to be wondered at," said the *Raleigh Register and North-Carolina State Gazette*, "but that the State of Pennsylvania should not have made the proper distinction between the qualifications of a Soldier and a Statesman, is extraordinary."[309]

The Corrupt Bargain

With so many candidates running, no candidate in the election of 1824 won a majority of votes in the electoral college. The Twelfth Amendment, ratified after the deadlock in 1800 between Thomas Jefferson and Aaron Burr, dictated that an election with no majority of electoral votes should be decided by the House of Representatives. That meant insiders leapt into control. Candidates could promise patronage or sectional payoffs, once they became president, in exchange for votes. "The people have two great dangers to guard against," said the *Louisville Public Advertiser*. "First, the influence of King Caucus. Second, the failure of the electors to choose a president, and of the election thus devolving on Congress."[310]

This outcome had long been what concerned those fearful of intrigue in Washington. "Candidates have been encouraged to run who have no hopes of success," worried the *National Advocate*, "merely to bring the election into the House of Representatives, and they are thus encouraged by men from whom the nation has a right to look for better things."[311]

In the Electoral College, Jackson was the leader of the pack with the plurality of electoral votes and the most actual votes. Out of the majority 131 electors required, he was short 32. In the total vote count, Jackson out-polled Adams 152,901 votes to 114,023.

Newspapers printed tally sheets for all to see the numbers in black and white—For the pro-Jackson team, the conclusion was obvious: "A decided answer, ought, one would suppose, to be settled, by ascertaining *for whom the people have shown a decided preference*...Let facts speak in place of arguments or assertions...From the foregoing table it appears that Mr. Jackson has received *nearly double the number of votes from the people, received by Mr. Adams!*"

You didn't have to operate a pro-Jackson calculator to see that he had more electoral votes and popular votes, but as historian Donald Ratcliffe has persuasively argued, the totals were skewed. Adams had won many of his electors through legislative vote, where people had voted for their legislators with the clear understanding that those legislators would vote for certain presidential candidates. New York was one such state. It was the largest state, with one-seventh the total population. It was an Adams state. Jackson was a non-story there. If you took the legislative vote in New York, which was intended to support Adams and allocated those people to the popular vote total Adams came out ahead. "In no way was Jackson the clear choice of the people in 1824," concludes Ratcliffe.[312]

The Twelfth Amendment dictated that only the top three finishers in electoral votes moved to the next round, which eliminated House Speaker Henry Clay, who came in fourth. This made him very popular. He was Speaker of the House, which gave him one kind of leverage over the proceedings, and he had influence over the states of Kentucky, Ohio, and Missouri, which had voted for him.

Adams, Jackson, and Crawford supporters called on Clay regularly to induce him to help their man's cause. "I sometimes wish it was in my power to accommodate each of them," said Clay.[313]

Clay was able to see the lighter side of his burden. While the nation waited for the House vote, Jackson, Adams, and Crawford retained their social engagements. At one soiree, Adams and Jackson sat next to each other, separated only by an open chair. Clay moved across the room and sat between them. "Well, gentlemen, since you are both so near the chair, but neither can occupy it," he said, "I will step in between you, and take it myself." Everyone in the room thought it was very funny. Adams and Jackson were reported in all accounts to not have laughed along. The era of happy parties was in peril.

In advance of the House vote, conversations in Washington were full of tales of intrigue. There was vote buying going on, whispered Washington insiders. Adams was reportedly promising the vice presidency. "Conjectures wander about, like the birds from the Ark, finding as little rest for the soles of their feet, and catching at every straw and green leaf that float on the tide of rumor," wrote an apparently inebriated correspondent from the *Providence Patriot*.[314]

Rumors got so out of hand that one paper reported twenty thousand

"Whiskey boys" were headed to Washington on behalf of General Jackson to overthrow the selection of Adams to the presidency.[315]

In his private letters Jackson maintained the posture of rigid virtue. "I envy not the man who may climb into the presidential chair in any other way, but by the free suffrage of the people," he wrote. "The great whore of Babylon being prostrated, by the fall of the caucus, the liberty of our country is safe, and will be perpetuated, and I have the proud consolation to believe, that my name aided in its downfall."[316]

Had it been known ahead of the House vote that Clay and Adams met on the evening of January 9, the city would have erupted. Clay had told an associate in a letter that he planned to back Adams, so the meeting could very well have been to simply smooth over old differences in advance of Clay announcing his support. The two men were not completely in sync. They had battled over the Transcontinental Treaty, but Adams supported the national bank, a tariff, and internal improvements that were a part of Clay's economic program known as the "American System." The two also both disliked Jackson. Clay had said that electing Jackson would be "the greatest misfortune that could befall the country."[317]

As the vote approached, Jackson couldn't have authored his own intrigues even if he had wanted to. After meeting late one night with members of Congress who urged him to take some action to stop Adams and Clay, he fell on his on his way to his rooms, tearing his injured shoulder and initiating a incapacitating hemorrhage.

Clay arranged for his home state of Kentucky to vote for Adams—even though Adams had not won the popular vote there, and even though the state legislature had instructed its congressmen to vote for the second-place finisher, Jackson. It was the norm for members to follow the instruction of the state legislature. On the same day the Ohio delegation also announced that it would support Adams. Clay clearly had a strong influence. The move ensured that Adams would win. In the House Adams won 87 votes to Jackson's 71.

The outcome seemed such a surprise because the papers had been predicting a Jackson victory. "When Congress first assembled," wrote a correspondent for the *Louisville Public Advertiser*, "fresh from the people, there was an universal impression, that Gen. Jackson would certainly be elected…He was decidedly the strongest with the people of the whole Union; and if the question could have been decided by them, there was not the slightest doubt but that he would have been chosen."[318]

The union between Clay and Adams was immediately denounced. The West, which Clay represented, didn't want John Quincy Adams. It had voted nearly unanimously for Jackson. Clay's move confirmed every suspicion of intrigue. "Mr. Clay has sold himself and the west, to Mr. Adams, for a place in the cabinet, or for the promise of a foreign mission," wrote one paper."[319]

Outwardly Jackson maintained decorum. Inwardly he seethed. "So you see," he wrote a friend, "the Judas of the West has closed the contract and will receive the thirty pieces of silver—his end will be the same." Jackson proclaimed that the "rights of the people have been bartered for promises of office."

One Jacksonian newspaper cried: "Expired at Washington on the ninth of February, of poison administered by the assassin hands of John Quincy Adams, the usurper, and Henry Clay, the virtue, liberty and independence of the United States."[320]

Clay's defenders explained that he had saved the country from itself. "Shall we prefer a man whose sphere in life has, in some respects, been foreign to the office in question, to one who has become almost identified with, and part of that sphere?" asked the *Daily National Journal*. "If Mr. Clay has given his influence to Mr. Adams, it must be apparent to the world that he has been influenced by a deep sense of what he owes his country."[321]

Clay responded in the papers to the charges of a corrupt bargain with his reasoning:

> I have interrogated my conscience as to what I ought to do, and that faithful guide tells me that I ought to vote for Mr. Adams. I shall fulfill its injunction. Mr. Crawford's state of health, and the circumstances under which he presents himself to the

> House, appear to me to be conclusive against him. As a friend of liberty and to the permanence of our institutions, I cannot consent, in this early stage of their existence, by contributing to the election of a military chieftain, to give the strongest guaranty that this Republic will march in the fatal road which has conducted every other republic to ruin.

The idea that there was a "corrupt bargain" between Adams and Clay where Adams offered Clay the post of Secretary of State in return for his support in the election in the House was never proved. Clay was a perfectly reasonable person to name as secretary of state, and he had been a lifelong enemy of Andrew Jackson. Still, it could not have been scripted better to give evidence to those who thought the political system was a self-dealing game played by elites.

Philadelphia merchant John Pemberton wrote to Jackson shortly after the vote: "The Pride of Kentucky (Henry Clay) like Lucifer has fallen! and still hopes to involve you in the vortex of his ruin! He never can forgive you, for the noble services you have done your Country! nor for being in the way of his towering ambition! You will pardon my telling you we all feel an honest pride, in your dignified conduct, during the late contest for the Presidency; and your subsequent magnanimity has extorted praise, even from those, who would have sacrificed you, to promote their unhallowed ends! So powerful is the upright man, that the most depraved have to make obeisance to him—"

Jackson resigned from the Senate and returned to Tennessee, the Western frontier where freedom flourished untrammeled by the corruption of the East. But it wasn't really a retreat. It was the start of a new campaign. A campaign for vindication. In October 1825, the same month he resigned, the Tennessee legislature unanimously nominated Jackson to be president in 1828—the earliest such nomination by far in any presidential election. The battle for the presidency in 1828 started almost as quickly as the one in 1824 had come to a conclusion. Jackson's future victory would be born out of his defeat.

PART VI

Tar and Feather

1800—Keep Your Attack Dog Fed

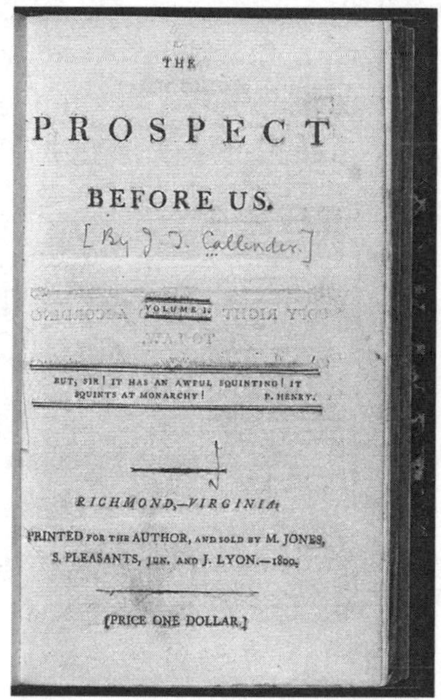

THE

PROSPECT

BEFORE US.

[By J. T. Callender.]

VOLUME I.

BUT, SIR! IT HAS AN AWFUL SQUINTING! IT SQUINTS AT MONARCHY! P. HENRY.

RICHMOND,—VIRGINIA:

PRINTED FOR THE AUTHOR, AND SOLD BY M. JONES, S. PLEASANTS, JUN. AND J. LYON.—1800.

(PRICE ONE DOLLAR.)

On July 13, 1798, a disheveled man walked the dusty road from Philadelphia on his way to an undetermined location below the Potomac River in Virginia. A widower who had just lost his wife to yellow fever, he was penniless, reportedly feeding himself and his children on "broken victuals" from a wealthy neighbor and relying on small donations from acquaintances to buy firewood and snuff. Unkempt, with a hunted look, he might have seemed a pitiable figure, but there was little to pity in the fellow, especially if you were a member of the Federalist Party, which controlled Congress and the White House.

His name was James Thomas Callender, a journalist working for the Republican cause and a drunkard. His enemies called him a scandalmonger. "He was a Scotchman of whom nothing good is known," wrote John D. Lawson in *American State Trials*, an account of Callender's celebrated prosecution under the Sedition Act in 1800, "He had the pen of a ready writer and the brazen forehead of a knave."

That summer, Callender was on the run from Federalist enemies who had threatened him for savaging their cause. Assassins had visited his house on two different occasions, he said, though given his reputation for befouling the truth, that could mean that none had visited at all. It was true, though, that assassins would have had a reason to visit. Callender had been responsible for ruining Alexander Hamilton by exposing the first public sex scandal in American politics.

Callender is one of history's discarded characters, so there are few unbiased accounts of what he looks like, but there are many characterizations of his look by those who did not like him. William Cobbett, a famous Federalist writer and Callender enemy, described him as a "little mangy Scotsman who has a remarkably shy and suspicious countenance; loves grog: wears a shabby dress, and has no hat on the crown of his head; I am not certain whether he has ears or not... [He] leans his head toward one side, as if his neck had a stretch, and goes along working his shoulders up and down with evident signs of anger against the fleas and lice."

The put-upon pilgrim had abandoned his four children to the care of a friend and seemed in a hurry to shed his widowerhood, telling a friend that after his trip south, he hoped to find a "hearty Virginia female" who could "fatten pigs, and boil hominy, and hold her tongue."

During his trek south, Callender learned he was still being hunted. He had to turn down an ally's offer of a carriage for fear that would make it easy for villains to spot him. So he walked—or, more accurately, he weaved. Outside of Leesburg, Virginia, he was arrested, drunk and loitering outside of a local distillery (perhaps trying to get a contact high). He was charged with vagrancy and in a report of the event was described as follows: "With shaved head and greasy jacket, nankeen pantaloons, and worsted stockings."

Callender did have one very good thing going for him, though.

His most influential patron was Thomas Jefferson, the Vice President of the United States. He would help Callender back on his feet and in turn, Callender would lend his pen to Jefferson's cause in the election of 1800. "His business was to gather all the political scandal, all the foul abuse, all the libels, all Congressional speeches, to misinterpret good acts, to attribute false motives, to digest the scurrility," wrote John D. Lawson who wrote a history of Callender's Sedition trial. He was Jefferson's attack dog, the most famous of the "gladiators of the quill," and the philosopher president's secret weapon, who would ultimately turn on his patron and reveal his most personal secret.

America's First Ugly Campaign

The election of 1800 is considered one of the ugliest campaigns in history. James Callender helped make it so, carrying out attacks on behalf of his patron Jefferson that were so severe the incumbent president, John Adams, threw Callender in jail for his writings. But Callender was more than just a fierce partisan; as a journalist he revealed that a system built on virtue was run by men who were privately not so virtuous.

When James Callender crossed the Atlantic and arrived in America on May 21, 1793, he was already on the run. He had attacked Samuel Johnson and the King of England, once referring to his government as a "mass of legislative putrefaction." Facing sedition charges he fled, landing in America where he was free to unbuckle his talents. "It was the happy privilege of an American that he may prattle and print in what way he pleases," Callender wrote, "and without anyone to make him afraid." His career would test that proposition.

Callender secured one of the four official stenographer posts in the new Congress when it moved to Philadelphia not long after he arrived in America. Newspapers paid stenographers, not the government, which meant scribes were constantly accused of embroidery, making their foes sound dumb and their allies brilliant.

The newspaper wars of the 1790s, in which Callender enlisted, were ferocious. "The golden age of America's founding was also the gutter age of American reporting," writes historian Eric Burns.[322] Papers were partisan, not impartial, and editors attacked each other in the street. Editors cursed each other with prolixity, and backward-running sentences. They seemed to have the typesetting equivalent of unlimited minutes when it came to using insulting synonyms found in the thesaurus. Their enemies were "depraved," "worthless," "vile," "intemperate," and "wicked." Accusations of drunkenness were frequent (and accurate) as were charges of corruption and debauchery.

Callender fit in nicely in this gritty world and quickly came to have a reputation for clattering among the empty bottles and carrying a foul odor. He was once ejected from Congress because he was "covered in lice and filth," according to a report that may even have been true. At Federalist gatherings he was lampooned along with Ben Bache, Republican editor: "Tom Callender's a nasty beast, / Ben Bache a dirty fellow; / They curse our country day and night, / And to the French would sell her."

Thomas Jefferson testified to the ugliness of the trade when he described what he looked for in a good editor. He lamented that such a person would have to:

> set his face against the demoralising practice of feeding the public mind habitually on slander, & the depravity of taste... Defamation is becoming a necessary of life; insomuch, that a dish of tea in the morning or evening cannot be digested without this stimulant. Even those who do not believe these abominations, still read them with complaisance... [and] betray a secret pleasure in the possibility that some may believe them, tho they do not themselves.

This sounds just as high-minded as we'd expect from the author of the Declaration of Independence, but it's blarney. Jefferson was fine with slander, feeding the public need for low entertainment and fact-free denunciations just as long as they were aimed at his rivals. He had no problem supporting or arranging to support newspapers that did just that.

Like today, in the age of our Founders one person's depravity and slander was another person's fact. What Jefferson would have roared about, his rival Alexander Hamilton would have applauded as plain truth. Each side in the debates of the early republic thought they were the hero in the morality play of the infant republic. This is why it got so hot so fast. They were righteous and saw themselves as setting the precedent for a new nation.

Unlike the righteous, infantile, and heated debates of social media that clog our modern age, the stakes in these verbal wars were high. These men thought they were determining the course of the nation and a free mankind—that gave them the excuse to employ any means to meet their ends. But there was a tension in this. If the presidency was to be run by virtuous statesmen, there was no greater test of that virtue than how those would-be presidents behaved in their private acts. By funding the scandalmongers and encouraging them, Jefferson and others failed at what they would have said was the the first test of character: doing the right thing when no one was looking. That they were doing so in order to make sure a man of virtue held the office doesn't erase the offense.

When George Washington left the White House, he warned against the "spirit of party" that would turn the disputes between men like Jefferson and Hamilton into a permanent state of combat. It was too late; the debate between the Hamiltonian Federalists and Jeffersonian Republicans over the best way to interpret the Constitution and the authority it gave to the federal government was well established. The argument formed the basis of America's two-party system.

Callender sided with the Jeffersonian Democratic-Republican Party, which believed in a limited federal government that would allow states to determine their own future. Republicans, as they were known until 1828 when they would become the Democratic Party, believed Congress had principal power in national affairs, since it was closer to the states and the people. A too-powerful executive, supported by a large army, would encourage monarchism. Republican distaste for the monarchy inspired their support for the freedom-loving revolutionaries in France over Great Britain's king.

Hamilton aligned his thinking with the interests of the major trading centers of the Atlantic. He supported a stronger central government, because he believed that only the federal government could inspire the confidence necessary for a strong national economy spread over an extended geographical space.

Jefferson and Hamilton were both members of Washington's cabinet, and they carried out their office disagreements through proxies. Hamilton supported the *Gazette* and Jefferson the Philadelphia *National Gazette*. "The *Gazette of the United States* and the *National Gazette* were conceived as weapons, not chronicles of daily events," writes historian Burns.[323]

Jefferson noticed Callender because he was on the hunt for allies in his battles against Hamilton and the Federalists in advance of the election of 1800. By the end of the Washington administration in 1796 there were scarcely thirty papers that could be classified as Republican, compared to about 120 that were Federalist.

Newspaper patrons like Jefferson built lists of subscribers, solicited donations, and provided anonymous tracts for publication. The secretary of State even leaked confidential documents to his favorite editor and begged his friend James Madison to attack Hamilton in print: "Nobody answers him, and his doctrines will therefore be taken for confessed. For god's sake, my dear sir, take up your pen, select the most striking heresies, and cut him to pieces in the face of the public."

Hamilton complained about Jefferson's back-stabbing in print. "Can he [Jefferson] reconcile it to his own personal dignity and the principles of probity to hold an office under [the government] and employ the means of official influence in opposition?" he wrote in the *Gazette of the United States*. He even complained to President Washington. Jefferson wrote the president a four-thousand-word defense in which he denied any involvement in newspaper writing so categorically he might as well have denied ever reading a paper. It was a lie, of course, wrapped in high-minded philosophical hand waving. As Si Sheppard details in his book on media bias, not only had Jefferson supported the opposition press, he'd written some of the articles himself.

Callender Undoes Hamilton

So it should not surprise us that the man with the sandy hair and thoughts of Palladian architecture in his head met with the disreputable Callender in the Philadelphia print shop of Snowden and McCorkle in the summer of 1797. It certainly would have surprised the public, though. Callender had built his reputation, in part, on savaging the president for whom Jefferson had just served as secretary of state.

"If ever a nation was debauched by a man, the American nation has been debauched by WASHINGTON," wrote Callender. "If ever a nation has suffered from the improper influence of a man, the American nation has been deceived by WASHINGTON. Let his conduct then be an example to future ages. Let it serve to be a warning that no man may be an idol, and that a people may confide in themselves rather than in an individual."

Attacking Washington was just a starter course for Callender. The summer of his meeting with Jefferson, he was the talk of drawing rooms for what he had uncovered about Alexander Hamilton's sex life. Callender was different than other writers. He literally named names, dropping the convention of only using the first and last letters of a person's name. According to Callender's biographer Michael Durey, he had a "complex and contradictory character. He was self-righteous, strongly puritanical with regard to personal morals, insufferably proud, with a deep and abiding mistrust of human nature." His view was that only virtuous leaders could ensure the continued vitality of the Republic, and only by incessantly watching them could their virtue be assured. His rival, Federalist writer William Cobbett, agreed, writing, "Once [a man] comes forward as a candidate for public admiration... every action of his life public or private becomes the fair subject of public discussion."

What Callender uncovered started before he had even come to America. In 1792, the thirty-six-year old treasury secretary Alexander Hamilton started an affair with the twenty-three-year old Maria Reynolds while his wife and children were away. Reynolds had claimed that her husband had abandoned her and her daughter, and she'd asked Hamilton for enough money to get to New York. "It required a harder heart than mine,' he wrote, "to refuse it to Beauty in distress." When he delivered the money in person, Maria offered a quick repayment. "I took the bill out of my pocket and gave it to her," Hamilton later wrote of the moment of his ruin. "Some conversation ensued from which it was quickly apparent that other than pecuniary consolation would be acceptable."

Reynolds's husband, James, soon learned about the affair and initiated an extortion scheme. Or, as some have suggested, he initiated a long-planned extortion scheme that had been mapped out long before Maria Reynolds ever knocked on Hamilton's door. Hamilton paid the notes and continued the affair through the end of the year. Ultimately Hamilton would pay nearly $1,000, about $24,000 in today's dollars.

On December 15, 1792, future president James Monroe, then a senator from Virginia, learned of Hamilton's payments to James Reynolds and confronted him. The information had come to Monroe from a Virginia prison cell, where Reynolds was serving time for another swindle involving unpaid wages to Revolutionary war veterans. Reynolds tried to limit his days on bread and water by trading information for a lighter sentence. He let it be known that he could "make disclosures injurious to the character of some head of a department."

Armed with the accusation, Senator Monroe, Speaker of the House

Frederick Muhlenberg, and another member of Congress began a short, secret investigation. They accused Hamilton of using his position to enrich himself through speculation, and they threatened to tell the president. Enraged, the treasury secretary invited the three men to his house to show them letters that proved he was innocent of malfeasance. He had simply been guilty of adultery.

After a sweaty and tense exchange, the three men were satisfied. There was a wall between public and private life, and as public men it was in their interest to keep that wall strong. Though Monroe was a Jefferson ally in the daily newspaper battles against Hamilton, he and Jefferson didn't use the material learned in the private investigation. Monroe and his two colleagues put all papers related to Hamilton—including some of his correspondence with James Reynolds—in a safe place.

Not safe enough. Monroe said he had entrusted the correspondence to "a respectable person in Virginia." Some historians believe it was Jefferson. He might have been responsible for ultimately leaking them four years later in 1796, but the consensus view is that the culprit was John Beckley, a Jefferson ally and clerk of the House. In 1796, Federalists had pushed Beckley from his post, and he wanted to get back at their leader Hamilton, so he leaked everything related to the affair to Callender.

The full story appeared in the *History of the United States 1796*, a dull name for a volume that like a brown wrapper obscured what was inside. "This great master of morality," Callender accused, "though himself the father of a family, confess[ed] that he had an illicit correspondence with another man's wife." Callender labeled James Reynolds a "procurer" (a pimp) and said that since that was the lowest of all human character traits, Hamilton's commerce with him, brought him lower than his mere adultery did.

Callender's bigger charge was corruption. He didn't buy Hamilton's private excuse. "So much correspondence could not refer exclusively to wenching," he wrote. "No man of common sense will believe that it did. Hence it must have implicated some connection still more dishonourable."

On July 5, 1797, Hamilton wrote to Monroe and the two members of Congress who had been with him, asking them to make public their original conclusion, that there was nothing amiss in his public conduct while secretary of the treasury. Two complied, but Monroe did not. Hamilton was enraged and accused Monroe of leaking to Callender, since Callender's report had included original documents from Monroe and Hamilton's meeting in December 1792.

Hamilton and Monroe nearly met in the field with loaded pistols, according to one account:

> Colo. Monroe rising first and saying do you say I represented falsely, you are a scoundrel. Colo. H. said I will meet you like a gentleman[.] Colo. M. said I am ready get your pistols, both said we shall[,] for it will not be settled in any other way.[324]

The fight was broken up by Aaron Burr, who would later kill Hamilton in a duel, which took place after Burr had represented Maria Reynolds in her divorce proceedings. Hamilton would also later defend a journalist accused of printing false statements about President Jefferson. (You get the feeling there were only a half-dozen men in America in the early days.)

Hamilton thought his public virtue on the question of financial corruption was all that mattered. So two months after Callender's article, unable to get Monroe to vouch for him, he defended himself against the corruption charge with a ninety-five-page pamphlet that foreshadowed its cumbersome argument with the winding-road title *Observations on Certain Documents Contained in No. V & VI of "The History of the United States for the Year 1796," in Which the Charge of Speculation Against Alexander Hamilton, Late Secretary of the Treasury, Is Fully Refuted. Written by Himself.*

Hamilton denied any improper speculation with James Reynolds, but confessed "my real crime . . . is an amorous connection with his wife."

The old codes of honor which had governed the private affairs of men were being undone by the new political system fed by the popular press. Hamilton would get caught between the two. He was exonerated by the small group of three lawmakers, but when his sins became public he was vilified. Hamilton warned if this trend continued, "the business of accusation would soon become in such a case, a regular trade, and men's reputations would be bought and sold like any marketable commodity."

Hamilton misread his audience. "You have widened the breach of dishonor by a confession of the fact," one New Yorker told him. Republican papers said he was trying to legitimize adultery, that he had "violated sacred promises." They railed against the injury he did to his wife by his admission, and concluded, as public moralists often do today, that to be dishonest in one sphere is necessarily to be dishonest in another. "If a man will rob his family of their peace, and enjoyment, if he will abandon himself to the vilest connections; if he will place daggers in the breast of a virtuous wife, and stab the reputation of his children, where are the bonds of honor to vouch for his fidelity in any other transaction?"

Doggerel soon followed: "Dear Col'nel did you never hear, / (If you did not, I think 'tis queer) / That only fools do 'kiss and tell,' / Ev'n tho' they tell their story well." An anonymous penman named "Virtus" caricatured Hamilton: "I have been grossly and injuriously charged with guilt. I have been charged with being a *speculator;* whereas I am only an *adulterer.* I have not broken the *eighth* commandment . . . It is only the *seventh* which I have violated."

The Federalists came after Callender with a hammer. "In the name of justice and honor, how long are we to tolerate this scum of party filth and beggarly corruption, worked into a form somewhat like a man, to go thus with impunity?" said the *Gazette of the United States.*

"Do not the times approach when it must and ought to be dangerous for this wretch, and any other, thus to vilify our country and government, thus to treat with indignity and contempt the whole American people, to teach our enemies to despise us and cast forth unremitting calumny and venom on our constitutional authorities?" The publication suggested that Callender's behavior had made him entitled "to the benefit of the gallows."

Savior Jefferson

The pressure from the Federalists drove Callender from Philadelphia and into Jefferson's Virginia. Callender was gleeful about what he had goaded Hamilton into. "If you have not seen it," he wrote Jefferson, "no anticipation can equal the infamy of this piece. It is worth all that fifty of the best pens in America could have said against him." This blow was about more than a simple presidential election. In an ideological battle for the direction of the new country Callender had struck mute the most articulate advocate for the other side.

If Jefferson had been as concerned about the press as he said, he should have been repulsed by Callender's behavior, even if it did undermine a rival. Instead, he was drawn to Callender, supporting him as he headed south.

Newly installed in Virginia, Callender complained to Jefferson that Republicans owed him. He also simpered that he was "belied and stared at, as if I was a Rhinoceros," escalating his bath of self-pity to exclamations that "I am in danger of being murdered without doors." Jefferson loaned him $50, which helped him get on his feet until he could secure a place at the *Richmond Examiner*, edited by Jefferson's close associate Meriwether Jones.

Jefferson continued to loan Callender money and asked his friends to do the same, arguing to Madison that it was "essentially just and necessary" that Callender should be aided. Jefferson also sent Callender encouraging letters elevating his sufferings. "The violence which was mediated against you lately has excited a very general indignation in this part of the country," Jefferson wrote about the arrest outside the distillery. Letters like this deepened Callender's fondness for the master of Monticello.

The Prospect Before Us

In the election of 1800, President Adams defended his tenure against Vice President Jefferson, who had won office in one of the last elections in which the vice presidency went to the runner-up.

It was a test of whether the new nation could hand over power peacefully between two factions. Or would the faction in charge use the tools of power for personal ends, corrupting the experiment so soon after it had started? Jefferson had said to Adams, "Were we both to die today, tomorrow two other names would be put in the place of ours, without any change in the motion of the machinery," which was how it was supposed to work. But that machinery hadn't been tested, and everything about the election of 1800 suggested that both sides were trying to tear down the leaders of the opposite party with the implicit view that were they allowed to succeed, they would destroy the machinery.

Neither Jefferson nor Adams campaigned for the job outright, but both urged friendly writers to support them in the papers. Jefferson and the Republicans set up a "correspondence committee" to write friendly articles for the papers. He helped to distribute the writings, including purchasing some papers in bulk and making sure they were put in the hands of influential gentlemen who could spread the information. "This summer is the season for systemic energies and sacrifices," wrote Jefferson to Madison. "The engine is the press. Every man must lay his purse and his pen under contribution."

Callender was crucial in this campaign, trading secret letters with Jefferson, who did not sign his: "You will know from whom this comes without a signature." Secrecy was crucial, as Callender's biographer

Durey points out, because "evidence that Jefferson was supporting from his own purse the notorious defamer of Washington, Adams, and Hamilton would have destroyed his carefully constructed image of being above base party intrigues."

Callender, a writer of such drive that he often talked about scrawling himself into headaches, wrote a 183-page pamphlet *The Prospect Before Us* in which he savaged the incumbent: "the reign of Mr. Adams has, hitherto, been one of continued Tempest of malignant passions." The author was kind enough to send a copy to the president. Future historians, he predicted, "will enquire by what species of madness America submitted to accept, as her president, a person without abilities, and without virtues: a being alike incapable of attracting either tenderness, or esteem." Callender didn't limit his attacks to the simply professional, calling Adams "a hideous hermaphroditical character which has neither the force and firmness of a man, nor the gentleness and sensibility of a woman."

The book encouraged the country to vote for Jefferson, who had paid to produce the volume. "Take your choice," Callender wrote, "between Adams, war, and beggary, and Jefferson, peace, and competency!"

The harangue pleased Jefferson, who wrote to Callender that the book "cannot fail to produce the best effect." Given that Adams and Jefferson had once been such friends, this was extraordinary. Jefferson had once written Adams "The departure of your family has left me in the dumps." Now he was helping orchestrate his downfall.

Callender was delighted at the pat on the head and wrote that he was not done. "I had once entertained the romantic hope of being able to overtake the Federal Government in its career of iniquity; but I am not satisfied that they can act much faster that I can write after them."

The Federalists returned fire, spreading rumors that Jefferson was an atheist from whom the God-fearing would have to hide their bibles. "Should the infidel Jefferson be elected to the Presidency," said the *Hudson Bee*, quoting another Federalist paper, the *New England Palladium*, "the seal of death is that moment set on our holy religion, our churches will be prostrated, and some infamous prostitute, under the title of the Goddess of Reason, will preside in the Sanctuaries now devoted to the Most High."

The *Gazette of the United States* asked:

> THE GRAND QUESTION STATED At the present solemn and momentous epoch, the only question to be asked by every American, laying his hand on his heart, is "shall I continue in allegiance to GOD—AND A RELIGIOUS PRESIDENT; Or impiously declare for JEFFERSON—AND NO GOD!!!"

Federalists charged that Jefferson had run from the redcoats while governor of Virginia during the Revolutionary War. They even printed an erroneous report that he'd died. Eric Burns, in his book *Infamous Scribblers*, quotes from a correspondent to the *Connecticut Courant* who explained why it was okay that they got it wrong. Jefferson was probably alive after all, the paper's correspondent decided, but the rumors had been offered by "some compassionate being," trying to cheer people up during the ugly presidential campaign and had "very humanely killed Mr. Jefferson."

Stop Callender Now

Callender's writings were so hot, President Adams came after him. In July 1798, Congress gave Adams a new weapon: the Sedition Act, which criminalized making false statements that were critical of the federal government. Federalists wrote the legislation in a desperate act to muzzle the Republican newspapers that had been beating them so thoroughly. Republicans howled, not only because it was an attack on their voices but also because it was a Constitutional overreach that smacked of monarchical control. Federalists were behaving in just the high-handed manner those Republican writers said they would, calling on wartime measures to quiet political criticism.

Jefferson railed against the Act as "an experiment on the American mind to see how far it will bear an avowed violation of the constitution." This was the corruption that Republicans had worried about. Those in power would overthrow the Constitution to keep themselves in power. This wasn't just a fight over personal ambition, it was a precedent-setting moment for the new nation, said Jefferson:

> If this goes down, we shall immediately see attempted another act of Congress, declaring that the President shall continue in office during life, reserving to another occasion the transfer of the succession to his heirs, and the establishment of the Senate for life.

The Sedition Act is considered one of the great mistakes of the early republic—Callender was the last person prosecuted under the law, and Congress would repudiate it publically many years later. It is possible to see how Federalists could get worked up enough to support such a law. The newspaper accounts weren't just full of mean philippics that hurt people's feelings. To some, they were a danger to the entire system. They elevated partisanship over truth, self-dealing over selfless virtue, which meant the central activity at the heart of the campaign—these newspaper attacks—were poison to the presidency the campaign was being fought to fill. Ugliness in politics may always have been with us, but as the country was taking its baby steps, the bile was considered a dangerous poison.

The Sedition Act seemed designed to capture Callender, and on May 21, 1800, it did. Exactly seven years after he arrived in America on the run from sedition charges and celebrating that he could say anything, Callender's pen sent him to the pen.

At the trial, the scribe faced notorious Adams partisan and Federalist circuit justice Samuel Chase, who brought his righteous fire to

Richmond in the hopes of locking Callender away. "Judge Chase," the *Aurora General Advertiser* taunted, "the pious and religious Judge Chase, is going to Virginia where, he says, if a virtuous jury can only be collected, he'll punish Callender with a vengeance."

Chase made sure the jury was packed with local Federalists. Jefferson and the Republicans rallied to Callender's cause. Jefferson made sure his three defense attorneys were some of the state's most prominent lawyers, including the state attorney general and assembly clerk. They all served without pay, which indicates how seriously the Republicans took the matter.

The indictment accused Callender of defaming the president: "Can any man of you say that the president is a detestable and criminal man," asked Chase, and "excuse yourself by saying it but mere opinion?" Callender claimed his opinions didn't need to be backed at every turn: "If it shall be insisted, that I aver what I have not proved, I answer, that for many averments regular proof is not required. Common report is sufficient." Chase had an easy time of it. The government did not have to prove that the seditious writings were false. Instead, the accused had to disprove the charges against him. This was a total reversal of the principles of justice upon which the American system was based.

When Republican senator John Taylor tried to argue that Adams had shown aristocratic behavior much like Callender claimed, Chase barred Taylor's testimony, because it did not precisely track Callender's assertions.

Callender's lawyers tried to challenge the constitutionality of the Sedition Act before the jury. Chase called their argument "irregular and inadmissible." The defense was not going to win, and in the end Chase convicted and sentenced Callender to nine months in jail and a fine of $200, asserting that Callender in attacking Adams had made "an attack up on the people themselves."

Behind bars, Callender taunted the judge by continuing to write. He entitled one new chapter "More Sedition" and attacked Adams as "insolent, inconsistent, and quarrelsome to an extreme... Every inch which is not full is rogue." Transcripts of his trial were also published, adding to his notoriety.

Republicans rallied to Callender's cause as a symbol of the egregious villainy of the Sedition Act and the Federalists who supported it. Jefferson wrote to his scribe in jail offering sympathy and consolation for the man whose "services to the public liberty" he had praised. This kind of correspondence, writes Callender's biographer, fed into the writer's need for a father figure. His emotional mentor and acolyte connection to Jefferson deepened.

Who Is This Callender You Speak Of?

The presidency and the new republic survived the test of the election of 1800. Despite the daily warfare between the two parties, power was transferred peacefully from the Federalists, who had been founded under Washington, to the Jeffersonian Democratic-Republicans.

But there was a wrinkle—not between the parties but between Republican rivals. Presidential electors were given two ballots to cast for two candidates for president. The greatest vote getter would become the president, and the number two finisher would be appointed to the vice presidency. Adams lost, but electors who voted for Jefferson also voted for Burr, which meant in the end the two men were tied.

Republicans had voted with the expectation that Jefferson would be the president. Burr had said if there were a tie, he would obviously step aside. "It is highly improbable that I shall have an equal number of votes with Mr. Jefferson, but if such should be the result, every man who knows me ought to know that I should utterly disclaim all competition." But when there was a tie, and the election was sent into the House of Representatives, Burr didn't step aside. House members voted repeatedly and neither man could win a majority. It took thirty-six ballots before Jefferson could win a majority and be declared the new president. Alexander Hamilton had helped break the deadlock, expressing his support for his old enemy Jefferson over his even greater rival Burr. He had particular sway, because the Congress that was voting to select the new president was the sitting one, controlled by Federalists, not the Republican one that would come in as a result of the 1800 election.

Hamilton told his friend Oliver Wolcott Jr. that Jefferson "is by far not so dangerous a man and he has pretensions to character." Those pretensions to character had not kept Jefferson from supporting the newspapers that ruined Hamilton and fought his cause at every turn, but never mind. Hamilton concluded that Burr was even worse, "far more cunning than wise, far more dexterous than able. In my opinion he is inferior in real ability to Jefferson."

No one was more delighted than Callender that Jefferson won the election of 1800. "Hurraw!" he yelped. "How shall I triumph over the miscreants! How, as Othello says, shall they be damned beyond all depth!" At toasts to Jefferson's victory, he was celebrated. "To James Callender," said Capt. Edward Moore, lifting a glass at Richard Price's tavern in Albemarle County, "who looks down on his persecutors with their merited contempt."

As president, Jefferson immediately distanced himself from Callender. He pardoned him along with all others convicted under the Sedition Act, but Callender wanted more in return for all he'd done. He needed that $200 fine back, and he wanted to be elevated to postmaster of Richmond. Jefferson who had been chatty, suddenly stopped responding to letters. Callender got antsy. "By the cause, I have lost five years of labor; gained five thousand enemies; got my name inserted in five hundred libels...I mention these particulars as this is probably the close of my correspondence with you, that you may not suppose that I, at least, have gained anything by the victories of Republicanism."

This letter also received no reply. By Sunday, April 12, 1801, Callender wrote Madison that he was "hurt" by the "disappointment" of not having his fine repaid. "I now begin to know what ingratitude is," he wrote, sounding more and more like a jilted lover. He further wrote that the president had spurned his many favors by acting "to discountenance me and sacrifice me, as a kind of scapegoat to political decorum [and] as a kind of compromise to federal feelings."

With no replies from Jefferson, Callender wrote Monroe and other Republicans. "I might as well have addressed a letter to Lot's wife," he complained of his unanswered notes. "Mr. Jefferson has not returned one shilling of my fine... I am not a man who is either to be oppressed or plundered with impunity."

It's not hard to understand why Callender was being put in the spam folder. Jefferson and his allies didn't want to associate with someone as unpredictable as Callender once they were in power. They certainly didn't want to give him a patronage job. "Callender was already too well known, and too much despised to be thought worthy of public trust: and Mr. Jefferson disdained employing any person who was unworthy," wrote Meriwether Jones.

According to Jefferson biographer Jon Meacham, Jefferson wrote off Callender because "rising men do not like to be reminded of the smell of the stables." Jefferson didn't want to be reminded that he'd used the low road to get to high office. Michael Durey expands the claim to the entire party. Republicans were happy enough to have the writer who could stir the common passions in an election, but they didn't want to embrace the implications of the common-man pitch by giving them jobs. They still wanted elites to be the ones who had the power when Republicans were in control.

Angry that he wasn't getting the responses he wanted, Callender traveled to Washington to meet with Madison. "The money was refused with cold disdain, which is quite as provoking as direct insolence," Callender wrote of his request for payment. "Little Madison... exerted a great deal of eloquence to show that it would be improper to repay the money at Washington." The secretary of state "seemed to think that he had become a sort of semi-divinity, and that poor Callender was not worthy to be his foot-stool."

Callender may also have been desperate for the postmaster job because he thought it might win him a wife. "Do you know that besides his other passions he is under the tyranny of that of love?" Madison asked Monroe in a letter. "The object of his flame is in Richmond. I did not ask her name; but presume her to be young and beautiful, in his eyes at least, and in a sphere above him. He has flattered himself into a persuasion that the emoluments and reputation of a post-office would obtain her in marriage. Of these recommendations, however, he is sent back in despair."

Madison briefed the president, who dispatched Meriwether Lewis on May 28, 1801, to give Callender $50 to tide him over until the fine could be repaid in full. Callender's attitude toward Lewis, who Jefferson would later send to explore the Northwest territory, suggested that Jefferson might well have a larger problem than he realized. "His language to Capt. Lewis was very high toned," Jefferson wrote Monroe in an account of the meeting. Callender threatened to release letters showing that he had colluded with Jefferson in attacking Adams. "He intimated that he was in possession of things which he could and would use of a certain case: that he received the [$50] not as charity but as a due, in fact as hush money."

Jefferson's African Queen

When it became clear that Jefferson was not going to name Callender to the postmaster job, Callender left Madison and headed to the Rhodes' Hotel in Washington where he got potted. "You wallowed in your own excrement, while you lavished execrations on those who would not dishonor themselves by employing you," wrote publisher and future treasury secretary William Duane in a letter to Callender.

Sen. John Taylor had warned Jefferson years before that Callender might turn on him. "Upon any disappointment of his expectations," he wrote, "there is no doubt in my mind, from the spirit his writings breathe, that he would yield to motives of resentment."

Callender had always been motivated by revenge, and it would sober him up this time, too. He raged back to Richmond and helped establish the Richmond *Recorder*, dedicated to attacking Jefferson and the hypocrites of the Virginia aristocracy. He took on the gamblers and duelers and slave owners who fathered children with their slaves who all pretended, as members of the Virginia gentry, that they did none of those things.

Callender started slowly at first on Jefferson. He pointed out that the president had praised him for his writings and supported him financially. He quoted liberally from Jefferson's lettters as proof. Hamilton's newspaper, the *New York Evening Post*, published Callender's articles and accused Jefferson of inciting Callender to expose Hamilton's affair with Maria Reynolds.

"I am really mortified at the base ingratitude of Callender," wrote Jefferson to Monroe. "It presents human nature in a hideous form. It gives me concern, because I perceive that relief, which was afforded him on mere motives of charity, may be viewed under the aspect of employing him as a writer."

The claim of simple charity is hard to support, given the letters that are now public. Jefferson explained himself to Abigail Adams, who had written him to claim a "personal injury" at the disclosure that he had supported this man who had attacked her husband so relentlessly. Jefferson pleaded that "nobody sooner disapproved of [Callender's] writing than I did," which is a bracing lie. There's not one word of censure in the Jefferson and Callender correspondence. There is however, encouragement and easy familiarity.

Republicans in Philadelphia attacked Callender to discredit anything he might write in the future. Duane wrote that Callender's wife had died from a sexually transmitted disease "on a loathsome bed, with a number of children, all in a state next to famishing...while Callender was having his usual pint of brandy at breakfast."

This was not wise. In retaliation, Callender went nuclear. After his disastrous meeting with Madison, Callender had written, "Black Sally was fluttering at my tongue's end; but with difficulty I kept it down."

That was a reference to Sally Hemings, Jefferson's slave and mistress. On September 1, 1802, Callender no longer held his tongue:

"It is well known that the man, whom it *delighteth the public to honor*, keeps, and for many years has kept, as his concubine, one of his slaves. Her name is SALLY. The name of her eldest son is TOM. His features are said to bear a striking although sable resemblance to the presdient himself.... By this wench, Sally, our president has had several children... THE AFRICAN VENUS is said to officiate, as housekeeper, at Monticello."

Callender argued that "the public have a right to be acquainted with the real characters of persons, who are the possessors or the candidates of office." It was hard for Republicans who had made such use of Callender's attacks on Hamilton to disagree. In signing off his piece, Callender let Jefferson know that he had done this to himself. "When Mr. Jefferson has read this article, he will find leisure to estimate how much has been lost or gained by so many unprovoked attacks upon J.T. Callender."

Callender's End Date

Unlike Alexander Hamilton, Jefferson did not answer the claims about Sally Hemings. Callender wrote about it repeatedly and subscriptions grew, but eventually he could not top his blockbuster story. An ongoing fight with the paper's publisher (which included charges that Callender had sodomized his brother), and constant threats to his safety by Republicans, put Callender more and more in a mood to drink. To be sober, said the *Recorder*'s publisher, was for him to be drunk only once a day and that his normal drink would fell two grown men. The stories of his antics while pickled mounted; according to one story, he stumbled into his host's bedchamber in the middle of the night to demand that a servant be whipped.

Jefferson's ally Meriwether Jones wrote in his diary, "Are you not afraid, Callender, that some avenging fire will consume your body as well as your soul? Stand aghast thou brute, thy deserts will yet o'ertake thee."

In the end, it wasn't fire, but water. Early in the morning of Sunday, July 17, Callender was observed wandering the town in a drunken stumble. Soon after, his body was found floating in the James River. He appeared to have drowned in a very shallow amount of water. A doctor "tried every method to restore him to life—but all his efforts proved ineffectual." After a brief coroner's inquest, which recorded accidental drowning while drunk, Callender was buried that same day in the local church yard. As Durey writes, "It was as if the citizens of Richmond could not wait to destroy all evidence of his existence."

A scoundrel and a drunk, James Callender has long been treated as a historical cur, but the chaos he unleashed in both parties uncovered the truth that the men of virtue who founded the country were not as virtuous as they pretended, either in their private lives or in the way they carried out their public debates. Thomas Jefferson, in particular, was willing to endorse, finance, and encourage the basest personal attacks on his rivals while bemoaning the coarse nature of the public press. It was a hypocrisy that swelled until Thomas Callender punctured it. A country moving toward popular sovereignty was destined to have more of these clashes, as the habits of the elites were brought to the public by the press. Callender also codified an important maxim of politics: If you're going to get an attack dog, keep him well fed.

1884—Ma, Ma, Where's My Pa?

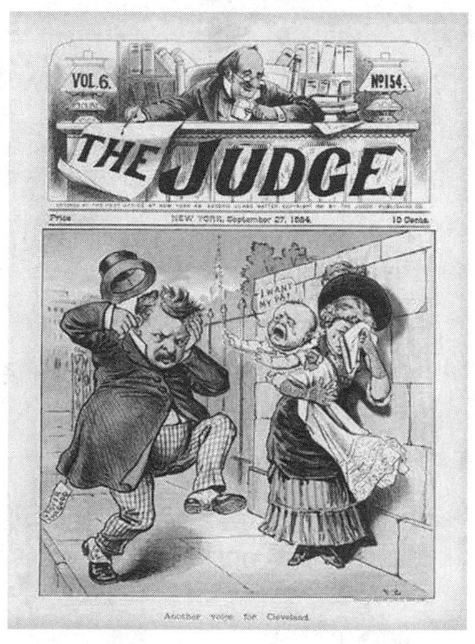

On the night of October 3, 1884, New York governor Grover Cleveland attended a dinner at the vast house of the widow Julia Cary in Buffalo, New York. The streetlamps illuminated the house's mansard roof with pointed arch dormers that seemed to stretch into the rain clouds. Inside, the doors were so ornate, it required three men to carry just one of them when they were installed. Beneath the widow Cary's eighteen-foot ceilings Cleveland, the Democratic presidential nominee, piloted his 280-pound frame through the conversational witticisms of some of the city's leading citizens.

The papers described Mrs. Cary as "a lady of the highest social station and of the most rigid code of social and moral ethics." This explains why Cleveland was dining at her house . If what the Republicans had been saying about Cleveland's debased moral character were true, a lady of Julia Cary's significance, stature, and fixed position would not besmirch her good name by allowing one whisker of his walrus mustache past her threshold.

Cleveland, forty-seven years old when he first ran for president, impregnated Maria Halpin in 1874. Or as the *Chicago Daily Tribune* put it, “When he was a man of 40 lusty summers sowing his wild oats.” He admitted as much, and when the news broke during the presidential campaign, he admitted also that he'd been supporting the child since its birth. His boosters said this was proof of Cleveland's good character. He did the honorable thing.

The preachers and the Republicans reacted to this news in escalating horror. *A Treasury of Great American Scandals* catalogs descriptions of Cleveland as a “rake,” “libertine,” “father of a bastard,” “a gross and licentious man,” a “moral leper,” “a man stained with disgusting infamy,” “worse in moral quality than a pickpocket, a sneak thief or a Cherry Street debauchee, a wretch unworthy of respect or confidence.” (Cherry Street was the address one went to in Buffalo to procure prostitutes.)

With all of that dumped on his head with just a month to go before the election, Cleveland returned to his home town, Buffalo, on a kind of redemption tour.

Cleveland hadn't campaigned much in the election of 1884. His Republican opponent, James G. Blaine, clocked four hundred appearances, but Cleveland was a bit of a stiff. He kept his head down behind his rolled desk, tending his duties. By this point, though, he was desperate. The questions about his moral character had mounted. New York was a crucial swing state. He needed to be seen in society to calm the stories and to bask in the glow of his hometown acclaim. The message he hoped to convey was that those who knew him best knew his character was strong.

Buffalo gave him what he needed. When he arrived, he was greeted by a procession stretching down Michigan Street and blocking the side streets. The *New York Times* described it as “a continuous ovation. The principal streets were jammed. Men and woman stood, many of them without protection from the pelting rain, waiting patiently for the procession to pass. There was little jostling and no disturbance. Democrats, Republicans, and men of every shade of political belief vied with each other in honoring their distinguished fellow citizen.[325] At his hotel, Cleveland was greeted with a huge banner that read: A Man of Destiny. No one in the crowd dared to yell the cry that had been haunting him and sung out at Republican rallies since the late summer: "Ma, Ma, where's my Pa?"

In the campaign of 1800, Thomas Jefferson was accused by scandalmonger James Callender of having fathered a child with his slave. In 1828 Andrew Jackson's opponents pointed out he married his wife before she was divorced from her previous husband. (Some even said the constant hounding caused the heart attack that killed her.) But the election of 1884 was the first time that the sex bomb really exploded in a presidential campaign. As a result, the election of 1884 is considered one of the nastiest in history. As Henry Adams, the author of the novel *Democracy*, wrote to a friend, "We are all swearing at each other like demons."

Grover the Good

In the election of 1884, Cleveland was up against history and a more charismatic opponent. Republicans had won every election since the disastrous James Buchanan was replaced by Abraham Lincoln in 1860. Sen. James G. Blaine seemed likely to keep that string going. At the Republican convention, his nomination was greeted with rousing cheers. One account said, "Whole delegations mounted their chairs to cheer."

But Cleveland and the Democrats had an opening—liberal Republicans—or "Mugwumps," as they were called. They thought Blaine was corrupt. One charged that he "wallowed in spoils like a rhinoceros in an African pool." An observer noted at the Republican convention, "These Republican liberals applauded with the tips of their fingers held immediately in front of their noses."

In the public adjudication of Cleveland's moral rectitude the Mugwumps were important character witnesses. If Republicans testified that Cleveland was not a moral debauch, then that might sway the public. They were also the crucial bloc Democrats needed in New York, which was a swing state in that election the way Ohio and Florida are in contemporary elections. That was what made Cleveland such an attractive candidate. Before news broke about his private lustings on the hustings, he was considered the kind of guy you'd want to bring home to mother—particularly if mother lived in New York, where he was a popular politician.

Cleveland had been sheriff of Erie County, governor of New York, and he earned his reputation for honesty. When the *New York World Herald* supported his nomination, it did so for four reasons: "1) He is an honest man, 2) he is an honest man, 3) he is an honest man, 4) he is an honest man." Cleveland's nickname was "Grover the Good."

The *New York Times*, a Republican paper, rattled the teacups a little when it endorsed Cleveland, saying that, "He was a courageous man whose absolute official integrity has never been questioned."

Birth of a Rumor

Cleveland was such a sterling, honest fellow in his public behavior that his own party machine didn't like him. To keep him from getting the nomination, the Tammany Hall bosses spread rumors throughout the Democratic convention in the summer of 1884. (Cleveland himself had mentioned his "woman scrape" to a prominent New York Democrat Alfred C. Chapin before the convention.)[326] "The hotels were filled with gossip," wrote the *Chicago Tribune*, "but that did not seem to disturb the Democrats much." One of the wags trying to stir up conversation about Cleveland's private affairs by saying "It's true that while Cleveland was sheriff in Buffalo, he had hanged people, but that in fact, he had brought more people into the world than he had taken out of it."

Cleveland was not married, and perhaps that was why the rumor never got the delegates fulminating. It might also be true that there was no other winning candidate with New York ties like Cleveland, and every politician knew that to win the election, the Democrats had to carry the entire South and New York. On July 11, 1884, Cleveland won the nomination.[327]

Ten days later, on July 21, the story broke, in "a poverty-stricken and obscure Buffalo newspaper," as one Democratic newspaper described it. The *Buffalo Evening Telegraph*, a tabloid of the day, ran the sensationalist story entitled A TERRIBLE TALE, outlining the details of Cleveland's love child with a single woman—a child referred to as a "nullius filius"—the son of a nobody. In this account, the woman at issue, Maria Halpin, had been seduced by Cleveland. When she became pregnant, he led her to believe he was going to marry her. Instead, he forced her to send the baby to an orphanage, and she was forced to leave town. The *Telegraph*'s account also charged that his behavior had not ceased. It reported that he frequently drank and went to brothels.

The story was born of agitations by the Reverend George H. Ball of the Hudson Street Baptist Church of Buffalo. Ball and other clergy pushed the tale to make a larger point about the licentiousness in the culture, presenting themselves as stalwarts against fornication and moral lapse. The local Democratic Party bosses, those Tammany folks, angry at Cleveland's do-goodism, saw the naughty tale as an opportunity to destroy him.

Republicans piled on. An account from the *St. Louis Globe Democrat*, a Republican paper, described the situation: "He [Cleveland] is charged with crafty, cruel lust in the case of Maria Halpin. He is circumstantially portrayed as a lecher, whose assaults upon chastity are only varied by shameful lewdness with the already polluted."

The *Chicago Daily Tribune* said, "If true, the story shows him to be unworthy of an honorable place in society. It shows him to be utterly wanting in moral sentiment and manly instinct....a villain, unfit to associate with honorable men or pure-minded women." It wasn't just that Cleveland had fathered a son. The papers charged that he had tried to hush up his mistress by having Halpin institutionalized and the son deposited in an orphanage.

Once the dam broke, stories about Cleveland appeared everywhere. One newspaper reported that, "Judge James Sheldon of the Superior Court reported that he had direct proof of Governor Cleveland's recent attempt to seduce a young lady of excellent character, but she becoming aware of his intent repelled him so spiritedly that he beat a hasty retreat." Another story emerged about Cleveland and a lawyer in a terrible fight over a lewd woman.

The *St. Louis Globe Democrat*, the conservative paper where Pat Buchanan would later launch his career, said, "The press of the country should not cease from agitating the arraignment of Governor Cleveland's moral character until he resigns or is withdrawn from the Democratic presidential nominee. It is the province of the Democratic press particularly to bring this scandal to a head. All Americans are disgraced so long as the vile story remains uncontradicted and Cleveland a presidential candidate. The virtue of our women is the basis of the family. And the family is the cornerstone of the state. We dare not present an inebriate as the mold of American reform, the example to our youth, and the candidate for the most exalted post within the gift of our galaxy of proud commonwealths."

Some Democratic papers were not on Cleveland's side. The *New York Sun*, then a Democratic paper, said, "We do not believe the American people will knowingly elect to the presidency a coarse debauchee who would bring his harlots with him to Washington and hire lodgings for them convenient to the White House." Had this news broke open before the Democratic convention, it might have prevented Cleveland from getting the nomination.

Partisan papers were on a romp, but not every paper knew what to do with such salacious material. The *Chicago Daily Tribune* noted,

"The details of the affair are unfit for publication in the columns of the paper that goes into the homes of respectable people."

Cartoonists, much like our late-night comedians today, had the most fun. The most famous depiction came from the *Judge*, a satirical magazine. It showed a weeping Maria Halpin holding a crying baby. And the baby was howling, "I want my Pa." Next to them was a vast and orotund Grover Cleveland, whose overcoat had a label sewn on like Paddington Bear that read, "Grover the Good." He appeared so undone by the crying baby that his top hat had flown off. The cartoon was entitled, "Another Voice for Cleveland." This was the cartoon that launched the song, "Ma, Ma, Where's My Pa?"

The Race to Confirm

Once the story broke, newspapers on both sides raced to validate or debunk the details. Democrats closing ranks rushed to the candidate looking for a battle plan. Reportedly Cleveland simply responded, "Tell the truth." That also made a good story for a virtuous and candid candidate. Democrats then reported that when Cleveland was shown material dug up on his rival Blaine, Cleveland took it, tore it into bits, and threw the pieces into the fire. And he said, "The other side can have a monopoly on all the dirt in this campaign."

That didn't stop the newspapers and Cleveland's friends from trying to undermine the Halpin story. There were at least three, maybe five, investigations by friends and foes. Buffalo was crawling with investigators.

In the end, the investigators hired by Democratic newspapers concluded, not surprisingly, that "there was no seduction, no adultery, no breach of promise, no obligation of marriage." The campaign issued one of these reports in a pamphlet called *The Facts and Evidence Concerning the Private Life of Grover Cleveland.*

Here's how the Democrats described the scandal in the *Milwaukee Journal Sentinel*: "It is admitted by Governor Cleveland's friends that 12 years ago, he formed an irregular connection with the widow with two children, the eldest 14 years old; that she was a person of intemperate habits and that the paternity of the child born subsequently was doubtful, but he [Cleveland] accepted it and made provision for the child; that after suffering much annoyance from her, one of the natural and common penalties of such errors, and after satisfying her brother-in-law who appeared on the scene as her protector, that he had behaved fairly towards her, he laid the whole matter before Mr. Burrows, a lawyer of high standing in Buffalo, [who] advised him to leave it to him and thereafter took charge of it." The story went on to say that the lawyer, now taking care of Ms. Halpin and the son went to look in on her or, in fact, sent in a detective to look in on her.

The report concluded: "He found the mother suffering from delirium tremens and threatening to kill the child which lay on the floor. He carried her off then to the Inebriate Asylum for treatment, and she stayed there until she was cured."

In the Democratic account, Halpin was described as a "person of intemperate habits"—a gentle way of calling her a harlot. Cleveland, on the other hand, was a hero. The investigation suggested that whatever his original sin, he more than made up for it by supporting the child and then rescuing him from his drunken mother, a move made possible only because Cleveland was monitoring the good lad's progress in the world. This version of the account also suggested that the boy might not even be his. Still, Grover the Good accepted responsibility for the baby to rescue the reputations of the other men sleeping with Halpin who were being blackmailed by her.

In this avenue of the narrative there was more intrigue. Some of Cleveland's defenders posited that Cleveland was covering for his former law partner, Oscar Folsom, for whom the baby was named.

Oscar Folsom was also the father of Cleveland's eventual wife, Frances Folsom, who was twenty-seven years younger. This opens up a lot of complicated possibilities for anyone trying to sketch the Cleveland/Halpin/Folsom family tree.

Democratic papers also cited character witnesses in support of Cleveland. Ms. Hathaway, an elderly resident of Buffalo, New York, wrote, "Our family have lived neighbors to Cleveland's family and have been intimately acquainted with Gov. Cleveland since before the time of his election as sheriff. A more honorable and pure man in his private life I have never seen."

The Republican papers didn't buy this account. The *Chicago Daily Tribune* said, "None of these facts were exonerating points...It is perhaps worthy of note that Grover Cleveland is the only authority cited...in the fascinating narrative." The paper notes that "Governor Cleveland is so choice in his associations that he and two dear friends at the same time held relations with a woman which left the paternity of her children doubtful."

No detail was too small for debate in the papers. When Cleveland dined at the widow Cary's house in October 1884, the Democratic papers published the news across the land. Cleveland's managers made sure the papers used it as evidence of his exoneration.

The *Milwaukee Sentinel*, which covered the dinner, said, "A lady gave him a dinner party during his visit with the purpose of placing his social standing beyond question." But since the *Milwaukee Sentinel* was a Republican paper, it wasn't taking the facts purely as presented. "It is reported on what seems to be unimpeachable authority that at the dinner party given by Mrs. Cary in Buffalo for Grover Cleveland, there were 14 invited guests, and 11 sent their regrets. Comment is unnecessary. Dinner invitations to meet the Governor of the State of New York and the candidate of a great party for the Presidency of the United States are not declined unless with good reason."

Blaine's Counter-Scandal

Despite what Cleveland said about not wanting to dig up dirt, Democrats also tried to fish around in James G. Blaine's private life. The *Indianapolis Sentinel* wrote that Blaine "betrayed the girl whom he had married"—which is to say he impregnated her—"and then only married her at the muzzle of a shotgun. If after despoiling her, he was too craven to refuse her legal redress giving legitimacy to her child until a loaded shotgun stimulated his conscience, then there is not a blot on his character more foul."

Republican papers rushed to defend Mrs. Blaine. "There is unanimity of opinion that Mrs. Blaine has lived since her marriage a blameless, Christian life and that she has been a true and noble wife and mother."

Blaine sued the paper that printed this story, but the suit went nowhere. It may even have backfired, giving ammunition to his enemies. A Lincoln, New Mexico paper the *Golden Era* wrote in an editorial: "Blaine did the only unmanly thing that could be done, attempt to make political capital out of the suit, create a temporary hurrah for Blaine and then have upon his hands a disgusting suit, the progress of which must keep the name of his wife in a most distressing manner before the whole country for an indefinite amount of time."

Cleveland Finds a Savior

More than an exonerating trip home to Buffalo, what Cleveland really needed was a high-toned, godly man to stand up for his character. General Horatio C. King, whom Cleveland had recently named judge advocate general in the New York State National Guard, was drafted to convince Henry Ward Beecher, pastor of Brooklyn's Plymouth Church and one of the most influential Protestant clergymen in the country, to publicly endorse Cleveland. Beecher sent King to investigate in Buffalo and relay his findings. After looking through the information, Beecher announced that he had come to a verdict. At a rally in Manhattan, he declared that he was going to support Cleveland despite all the terrible claims. "In all the history of politics, we don't believe that lies so cruel, so base, so malign have ever been set in motion. The air is murky with stories of Mr. Cleveland's private life," he said. "We find that they are circulated in many cases by rash and credulous clergyman. They could not go to Cleveland with honest inquiry, so they opened their ears to the harlot and the drunkard. I will not see a man followed by hounds, serpents, or venomous stinging insects and not, if I believe him innocent, stand with him and for him against all comers."

But then Beecher added a little too much to the soup. "If every man in New York State tonight who'd broken the seventh commandment voted for Cleveland, he'd be elected by a 200,000 majority." The Republican *New York Tribune* responded that this amounted to "a call to adulterers to vote Democratic." (Beecher had other reasons to hold this view. He had also gone through a widely publicized trial for adultery with one of his parishioners.)

The Republican *Chicago Tribune* responded to King's investigation: "This so-called 'vindication' of Gov. Cleveland will no doubt be read with astonishment especially by those who for years have been familiar with this case, and that it should have satisfied Mr. Beecher will not impress the public very forcibly with his knowledge of human nature or his lofty advocacy of morality."[328]

Mark Twain, watching the whole business, concluded, "The present campaign is too delicious for anything. To see grown men apparently in their right minds seriously arguing against a bachelor's fitness for president because he has had private intercourse with a consenting widow. These grown men know what the bachelor's other alternative was, and tacitly they seem to prefer that to the widow. Isn't human nature the most consummate sham and lie that was ever invented?"

Halpin Speaks

The one person investigators for both interests had not yet spoken to on the record was the wronged woman. It wasn't for a lack of trying. "Thursday afternoon, the town was full of strangers, politicians, detectives, and police officers and plain clothes," wrote one New Rochelle paper. The Republicans had sent people to find Halpin so they could get her to put her story on the record. Democrats were trying to find her, too. According to one account, they did find her, put her into a disguise, and set her on a train to New York. They were able to do this because a Democrat had been operating the telegraph machine and saw a wire come in from Republicans in New York to their friends in New Rochelle that said they had a fix on Halpin's location.

The Democrats stole the telegraph, found Halpin, dressed her up, and sent her into New York, where she was spirited away. But suddenly, in one of the first October surprises in political history, Halpin appeared in a Republican newspaper. "She feels like she has to break her silence because Henry Ward Beecher and others have said that she was a harlot, that Cleveland was the honorable man who had saved her, and that she couldn't let this stand. That her family was being undone and its reputation being undone by these stories," wrote the editor.

Halpin, in these accounts, was described as a "quiet, decorous, unobtrusive woman." She explained what happened. In her account, Cleveland didn't sound like a very good fellow at all. "I was employed at Flint and Kent," she wrote. It was a dry goods store, where she was the head of the cloak department—when Grover Cleveland persistently sought and finally made my acquaintance. I was not as stout as I look now, being tall and slender, and it is a wonder that I endured all I suffered in the years from 1874 to 1877. My child, Oscar Folsom Cleveland, was born September 14, 1874. Grover Cleveland is his father. And to say that any other man is responsible for his birth is infamous. It does not seem possible after all I've suffered for Grover Cleveland and my boy's sake that an attempt would be made to further blacken me in the eyes of the world. No one knows the extent of my sufferings. After my child was taken from me, I begged Cleveland on my knees to let me have a sight of my baby. He was immovable. I found where the boy was, and one day I rushed in upon his keeper, snatched him up and ran away before they could stop me. My sufferings subsequently, my fruitless efforts to have him [Cleveland] fulfill his promise of marriage, his neglect of myself and child, my abduction and violent treatment by his hired tools was truthfully but only partially told in the *Buffalo Telegraph* of July 21st. It would be impossible to cover events that made up these years of shame, suffering, and degradation forced upon me by Grover Cleveland."

Finally, Halpin was asked if she was going to offer a statement exonerating Cleveland, as the Democratic papers had claimed. "Make me make a statement exonerating Grover Cleveland? Never. I would rather put a bullet through my heart."

This account, which appeared in several newspapers, concluded, "Cleveland might enjoy honors and wealth, while on his account she was excluded from kindred and friends, and patiently waited for death to end her misery."

It didn't end there. Halpin issued a second description of the night in question and portrayed the encounter as rape. "On my way to call upon an acquaintance by the name of Mrs. Johnson at the Tifft House in the city of Buffalo, I met Grover Cleveland whose acquaintance I had formed months previous to that time. The said Cleveland asked me to go with him to take dinner, which invitation I declined because of my prior engagement. But by persistent requests and urging, he induced me to accompany him to the restaurant of the Ocean House where we dined. After dinner, he accompanied me to my rooms at Randall's boarding house on Swan Street, as he had quite frequently done previous to this time and where my son lived with me. While in my rooms, he accomplished my ruin by the use of force and violence and without my consent. After he had accomplished his purpose, he told me that, 'he was determined to ruin me if it cost him $10,000.'"

After this, there was still no mercy for Maria Halpin from Cleveland's supporters. The *Golden Era* from Lincoln, New Mexico, a paper that claimed to be independent but seems to be of Democratic leaning, said, "The woman in this case can claim no sympathy from the public, since in violation of all sense of decency, she has prowled herself about the affair with a looseness of tongue. This fully justifies the allegation that before she met Mr. Cleveland, she had been quite liberal with her favors."

It wasn't easy for a woman to be faced with such charges. As the Democratic *Indianapolis Sentinel* declared with a fine pretense of indignation, "The most scandalous feature of the present campaign is 'the dragging of Maria Halpin from her modest retirement.' A few months ago, 'her name was an unknown one to the American public and now she is being daily pulled into the streets and trampled into the mud.' "[329] Women's groups, including a leading suffragette newspaper, *Women's Journal*, also called it an "affront to decent women." Few shared the indignation of William Dean Howells who wrote to Mark Twain about the moral convolution in censuring Halpin to clear "Grover the Good": "As for Cleveland, his private life may be no worse than that of most men, but as an enemy of that contemptible, hypocritical, lop-sided morality which says a woman shall suffer all the shame of unchastity and man none, I want to see him destroyed politically by his past."[330]

Halpin wrote to Cleveland twice during his second term as president asking for money, but there is no record of a response. Halpin was married twice more, first to James Albert Seacord, who died in 1894, and then to New Rochelle stove, furnace, and hardware dealer Wallace Hunt. She died at her home in New Rochelle on February 6, 1902.

In the end, the truth of Cleveland's behavior was a muddle. He benefited from running against an opponent whose malfeasance in office is worthy of its own *Whistlestop* chapter. As Lord James Bryce wrote, the campaign became "a contest over the copulative habits of one and the prevaricative habits of the other." Another Mugwump explained his vote for Cleveland over Blaine by saying: "We are told that Mr. Blaine has been delinquent in office but blameless in private life, while Mr. Cleveland has been a model of official integrity but culpable in his personal relations. We should therefore elect Mr. Cleveland to the public office, which he is so well qualified to fill, and remand Mr. Blaine to the private station which he is admirably fitted to adorn."

This was what the country did. Grover Cleveland won in a squeaker—it took a couple of weeks to ratify the election results. After he was declared the winner, Democrats put forward an addendum to the chant that had been so often sung at Republican rallies. "Ma, Ma, where's my Pa?" Republicans chanted, to which Democrats now added, "Gone to the White House, ha, ha, ha."

1884—Burn This Letter!

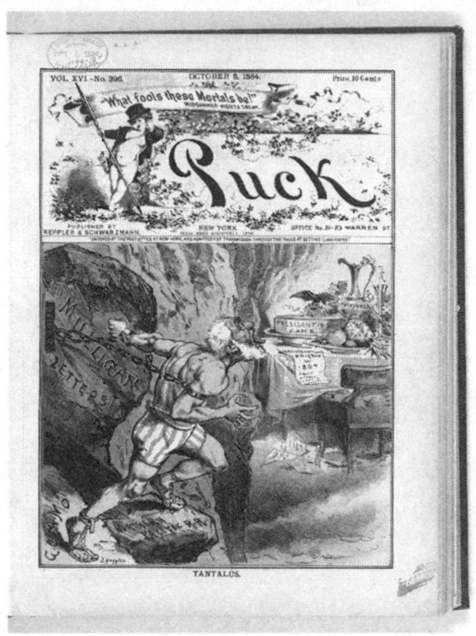

We're Blaine to a Man!

On September 27, 1884, Sen. James G. Blaine, the Republican presidential nominee, rode his campaign train through Elyria, Ohio. The former Speaker of the House from Maine with the pointed white beard and imposing form passed by the Lake Erie Company. The candidate walked out onto the train platform to a greet group of men in the yard. "When Blaine appeared," reported the *Milwaukee Sentinel*, "a large body of men came running out of the shops and rushed forward, shouting and cheering to shake hands with Mr. Blaine. They were evidently genuine working men, with bare breasts and arms, and sweating and begrimed faces."

Blaine leaned forward, held out his hand and yelled, "How are you boys?" The men shouted back: "We're Blaine to a man." The *Sentinel*, a Republican paper, found this remarkable. "Whatever be said," continued the paper, "and much must justly be said against Blaine as a public man, only the blindest and bitterest prejudice can deny that he possesses the quality of interesting the minds and making friends among the people. Curiosity alone does not bring working men from their shops and tradesmen from their stores, and farmers from their fields to welcome a public man. He has some secret quality which is very near to greatness. He has the quality of a popular leader, the power to stimulate the imagination and attract sympathies of masses of men. He is a splendid and imposing figure upon the public stage, exciting powerful friendship or hatred. He is both abused and praised to success, but nowhere does he meet with the indifference that falls to the lot of mediocrity."

This was why they called him the Magnetic Man. James G. Blaine was perhaps the most charismatic politician of the late nineteenth century. But when a partisan newspaper heralds its party's candidate as "exciting" and a cure to indifference, they're not telling you something. *Drunk driving may be dangerous, but no one reacts to it with indifference.* In this case, the paper was eliding that while Blaine made men run to his train, he was often running from accusations about trains. He was alleged to have been bribed by railroad barons as Speaker of the House. His malfeasance was discovered in a set of correspondence, which Blaine, who also served as secretary of state under President James Garfield, then tried to destroy. Known as The Mulligan Letters they became the focus of the 1884 campaign and helped undo Blaine, in much the same way that Republicans hoped Hillary Clinton's treatment of her correspondence on a private e-mail server as secretary of state would undo her in the 2016 campaign.

Crafty, Clever, and Conniving

James G. Blaine was one of the most exciting politicians to never become president of the United States. Speaker of the House from 1869 to 1875, a senator from 1876 to 1881, and twice secretary of state, he is credited with expanding American influence in Latin America and setting the precedent for a more active U.S. foreign policy. Republicans also put him up for nomination three times. He only secured the nomination in 1884, and unlike his rival in the 1884 campaign—Grover Cleveland, who was known for his diligent, head-down approach to his work—Blaine was a flamboyant public man. A silver-tongued speaker in an age of billowing, window-fogging oratory, the beaky, white-bearded Blaine reminds a modern reader of Bill Clinton, though his white beard makes him look more like the actor Donald Sutherland. He had die-hard fans, a talent for convincing men, but also had a string of controversies that followed him along like tin cans tied to his ankles. Despite his faults, even his enemies had trouble hating him. "Now there's Blaine, damn him!" said one Southern congressman to another, "but I do love him."[331]

The Mulligan Letters, Part I

In 1876, Blaine was the favorite in the Republican nominating contest. He had been popular as Speaker of the House and an ally to President Grant without being tainted by the scandals that rocked that administration. His star had risen particularly high in a fight over amnesty for Confederate soldiers. Blaine had been behind the amnesty for all except Confederate president Jefferson Davis. The public, which had little understanding of his previous fights for tariffs and currency, rallied around his denunciation of "the rebel chieftain" and his defense of the "boys in blue."[332]

As he climbed toward the nomination, his ascent was interrupted by a scandal over favors he allegedly performed for the railroad industry in exchange for bribes.

In 1869, as a newly installed Speaker of the House, Blaine helped the Little Rock and Fort Smith Railroad with a land grant. Emerging from the Civil War, the American railroads were laying track at a brisk rate. The first transcontinental railroad was finished on May 10, 1869, when the Central Pacific Company building from Sacramento met the Union Pacific Company building from Omaha at Promontory in Utah Territory. For a still largely rural country, this began the opening that would speed industrialization and connect the majority of the population to the West, an area that for most in America was as remote as the moon.

The amount of track in the United States grew from 35,000 miles in 1865 to 254,000 miles in 1916, the eve of America's entry into World War I.[333] To accommodate this expansion, the federal government provided land grants, one of the great national acts of infrastructure investment. Private bankers were nervous about gambling on railroads. They didn't want to loan out money that would take so long to repay. To fix this, Congress granted railroad companies millions of acres of public land, which they then sold to make money and build the railroads. Four out of the five transcontinental railroads were built with help from the federal government.

In addition to helping the Little Rock and Fort Smith Railroad obtain its land grant, Blaine also held bonds in the company. In 1876 word surfaced that in the intervening years those bonds had been bought back from Blaine at well above market value. On April 11, The *Indiana State Sentinel* published an editor's note that said, "A prominent banker of this city is in possession of a secret the exposure of which will forever blast the prospects of a certain candidate for the Presidency."

The rumor burbled. Blaine was expected to call for an investigation to clear his name. That was the usual route for exoneration, but he didn't want to call for an investigating committee. Even if it exonerated him, it would keep a cloud of suspicion alive during the nominating convention that was two months away.

So Blaine tried to seize the moment by explaining himself to the House of Representatives. As a torrential rain flooded the grounds around Congress, Blaine spoke to a damp, packed gallery about his innocence. He provided several letters from executives at the railroad and the banking company testifying that no money had been paid, no disbursements disbursed. After laying out the evidence, Blaine then went on at great length about the facts of the case and his own personal finances, winding it all up with flowery descriptions of innocence. "I have never done anything in my public career for which I could be put to the faintest blush in any presence, or for which I cannot answer to my constituents, my conscience, and the great searcher of hearts."

The speech was met by members of both parties as a smashing success. "As far as allegation can go, Mr. Blaine has vindicated himself," said the *Nation*, which claimed to speak for independent voters. Even one of his old Democratic opponents from Maine wrote to pat him on the back: "Allow me to congratulate you upon your complete vindication of yourself in the House yesterday," wrote A.P. Gould. "The charge was an improbable one; but in these days of general corruption almost any charge against a public man is credited by many. I trust that the attempt to defeat your nomination by such foul means, will advance your prospects, as it ought."[334] Remember, Blaine was the Magnetic Man.

Judiciary Committee Follies

Not everyone was convinced. Democrats, whose rise to power had taken Blaine's Speakership from him, started an investigation. At first the hearing went quite well for Blaine. Witness after witness testified that he had not been involved at all.

Then it all fell apart for Blaine. A new witness, James Mulligan, of Boston was sworn in and examined. He had been a clerk for Warren Fisher, the railroad's owner and manager, and he told a different story than Blaine had been telling. In Mulligan's version, the Union Pacific Railroad had purchased the worthless Little Rock bonds from Blaine in return for favors completed and favors yet to be asked for. His testimony bounced along until he was asked how he could back up these assertions. He said that he was in possession of several letters from Blainc to Fisher that laid out the whole business.

Blaine had thought the letters were destroyed when Fisher settled his accounts in 1872. When he heard that Mulligan had them he whispered to William Lawrence, a Republican member of the committee from Ohio, "Move an adjournment," upon which point Mr. Lawrence stood and, with an air of sobriety, announced, "Mr. Chairman, I am very sick and I hope the committee will adjourn." At this point the entire room erupted in laughter.

Despite the laughter, the hearing was adjourned, perhaps because people thought it was contagious.

What happened next is best told by the transcript of the House Investigating Committee, because any proceeding where a member can feign immediate sickness and get the whole thing stopped is worth checking directly. Plus, it provides a highly entertaining description of Blaine's drama following the committee's adjournment and members of Congress debating Blaine's fate.

Here's an introduction of the key players: Rep. Eppa Hunton of Virginia was the chief prosecutor. William Frye, was a Republican congressman from Maine with sympathies for Blaine. What follows is the excerpt of the conversation as it commences on the question of the illness that caused the previous day's adjournment:

> **Mr. Hunton.** The gentleman has stated the matter exactly as it occurred. He did come in, in the morning, sick.
>
> **Mr. Lawrence.** Yes, sir.
>
> **Mr. Hunton.** But he went to work in a most vigorous style for two hours.
>
> **Mr. Lawrence.** But I became exhausted.
>
> **Mr. Hunton.** When those letters were mentioned the gentleman became sick, and somebody else sicker. [Laughter] And the motion to adjourn was made at his suggestion.

After some more discussion of the sickness, Hunton explained what he learned during the interlude: Mr. Blaine had been in touch with Mulligan before the previous day's events even started, when Mulligan and his boss, Fisher, arrived in Washington.

Mr. Hunton. Upon the evening of his first arrival in the city of Washington, before I knew he was in the city, [Mr. Mulligan] and Warren Fisher were waited on by Mr. Blaine. They were invited to the house of Mr. Blaine. Mr. Mulligan said, "Mr. Blaine, I decline to go to your house; I do not want to talk about what I have been brought here for. I desire to take the stand tomorrow untrammeled by conversation of any kind with anybody." Warren Fisher [the railroad executive] went to the house of Mr. Blaine. Twice Mr. Blaine sent a messenger down to induce Mulligan to come to his house. Mr. Mulligan still declined, and presently Mr. Blaine and Warren Fisher came into the hotel where Mulligan stopped in the city of Washington.

So it turned out that Blaine had tried to accost Mulligan before he ever appeared before the committee.

Mr. Hunton [continued]. Mr. Mulligan was in the barber-shop, undergoing the pleasant operation of shaving, or about to undergo it, and Mr. Blaine followed him into the barber-shop and commenced to entreat and earnestly to request that Mulligan would give up those letters which Blaine had addressed to Warren Fisher. Mulligan declined to do it.

Mr. Frye. Mr. Speaker, if the gentleman—

A Member. I object to interruption.

Mr. Frye. I ask my colleague of the committee if I may interrupt him?

Mr. Hunton. Yes, you may.

Mr. Frye. The gentleman is now stating evidence, and I desire him to be very careful, because, as I remember it, there is no testimony whatever showing, or tending to show, that

Mr. Blaine, in a barber-shop, in the presence of the barber, entreated Mulligan for those letters.

Mr. Hunton. It matters not where he entreated him. I am under the impression it was there, but I am not certain.

Mr. Frye. The letters were not read in any barber-shop.

Mr. Hunton. I will take him out of the barber-shop. It does not matter in the least where the entreaty was made. Mr. Blaine entreated him. I give you now the substance of the language of the witness. He entreated him with tears in his eyes, going down on his knees, or almost on his knees—

Mr. Frye. In the barber-shop?

Mr. Hunton. I did not say in the barber-shop. I do not care where it was. It was in his room, I believe; but he made this entreaty. The witness said, "with tears in his eyes, almost, if not quite, on his knees;" " 'if you do not deliver those letters to me, I am ruined, and my family disgraced.' " Of course I mean to be understood here that the witness meant that Blaine's family would be disgraced through the ruin of Mr. Blaine. He also threatened to commit suicide. Mr. Mulligan refused to deliver the letters. He said: "Mr. Blaine, I see by the evening paper that my testimony given to the committee today is to be assailed,"—to use his own word, "impugned,"— "and in case my character and testimony are assailed, I want those letters to justify me in my testimony before the committee." Mr. Blaine asked: "Do you suppose I am going to assail you?" The witness said: "If you do not assail me, others may, and my character is too dear to me not to vindicate it if I can." Mr. Blaine then tried politics with him, and he asked the witness: "Are you content with your station?" To this Mulligan said he would like to improve it if he could. Mr. Blaine said: "Would you like a political office?" Mulligan replied he did not like politics, and did not care about it. Mr. Blaine then asked how he would like a foreign consulship. He said he would not like it; and, after that Blaine said: "Let me see the letters, to peruse them." The witness objected, but he said finally,

> upon a pledge of honor from Mr. Blaine that he would return the letters, they were given him to read. He read them over once or twice, and returned them to the witness. Again he made an effort to obtain those letters, and Mr. Mulligan left the company and went into his room. In a short time Mr. Blaine followed him into his room, and this scene occurred between the parties without any witnesses. Mr. Blaine again endeavored to get possession of the letters. The witness again declined to deliver them. The witness says that Mr. Blaine said: "I want to re-read those letters again, and I want to have them for that purpose...
>
> He asked the witness to let him see the letters again; and the witness said that on a like pledge of honor to return them to him, he delivered those letters over a second time to Mr. Blaine, to read and return them; and when Mr. Blaine had read them and kept them a short time, he refused to deliver them. The witness became excited, demanded his letters, and followed Mr. Blaine into the room of Mr. Atkins on the floor below, and there demanded his letters from Mr. Blaine; and he not only demanded his letters, but he demanded the private memorandum which the witness himself had made to use on his examination before the committee, to refresh his memory. This was taken by Mr. Blaine, and this also he refused to deliver.

At this point in the story, Mulligan was a man with no letters, and the committee work ground to a halt. A fight ensued over whether the letters actually belonged to Blaine, who had written them, or to the executive Fisher, who had been sent the letters. When you send a letter, is it still yours, even after somebody else receives it?

One of Blaine's pursuers asked, "If there was nothing in those letters, why would he have occasion to blush over them. Why should he be so determined to recover and retain them?"

On June 5, Blaine took to the House floor again. Word had gotten around that he was going to defend himself again, so the galleries were packed to suffocation. Unauthorized spectators rushed past the doorkeepers and crowded upon the very floor of the House itself. Blaine produced the letters from his pocket and gave a thundering oration holding the letters for all to see. Would any gentleman allow his private correspondence for the last eight or ten years to be scanned over and made public, he asked?

With that, Blaine slammed the letters down on the desk. He was not afraid, he said, and so he commenced to read from them. But of course just the innocuous bits. It was not unlike Nixon releasing edited transcripts of his own tapes during the Watergate investigation. More than that, Blaine attacked the committee, pointing out that his inquisitor in the matter was not one of the five Northern Democratic members of the Judiciary but the two "who were from the South and had been in the rebel army." Without making the direct charge, Blaine suggested that this was payback for his refusal to support amnesty for Jefferson Davis.

Finally, Blaine drew the crowd to their feet by challenging one of his prosecutors and asking if they had a telegram in their possession relating to him that they had not yet produced. Of course they did; the hearing was still going on. Not all evidence had been submitted. But Blaine made the mere possession of the telegram seem nefarious. When his pursuers admitted it existed, the crowd roared in approval of Blaine. He received "the award of innocence" and "the plaudits of righteousness," wrote his biographer (and cousin to his wife) Gail Hamilton.

1876 Republican Convention

Blaine emerged a hero from his trial to many in his party. In the second week of June 1876, the GOP met in Cincinnati, the "Queen City of the Ohio." Blaine's supporters were enthusiastic about his chances. Robert Green Ingersoll was particularly enthusiastic. The lawyer and staunch Republican was the first attorney general of Illinois, but his greatest achievement in life surely was conjuring perfumed clouds of purple rhetoric to fill the arena in praise of Blaine, who he proclaimed as having a reputation "spotless as a star." He continued:

> This is a grand year, a year in which we call for the man who has torn from the throat of treason the tongue of slander, a man that has snatched the mask of democracy from the hideous face of rebellion. A man who, like an intellectual athlete, stood in the arena of debate, challenged all comers and who, up to the present moment, is a total stranger to defeat. Like an armed warrior, like a plumed knight, James G. Blaine marched down the halls of the American Congress and threw his shining lances, full and fair, against the brazen foreheads of every defamer of his country and maligner of his honor.

Of course you know that "plumed knight" was going to stick and it did. The nomination, on the other hand, did not stick. The pro-Blaine camp was all frenzied adoration, but cooler-headed Republicans didn't trust him. The Mulligan letter investigation had left its mark. Even if Blaine hadn't done everything his Democratic opponents charged, he had categorically denied his connection to the Little Rock and Fort Smith Railroad on the House floor, which was not true, and the letters he had sequestered made that connection quite clear. The scandal is also credited with snuffing out his chances in 1880 as well.

Courting the Mugwumps

By 1884, the Mulligan Letters had faded as an issue. Blaine had served as secretary of state under James Garfield and then Chester Arthur, adding to his luster. He was once again considered a presidential contender.

He just had to get past the Mugwumps, the moderate Republicans bent on reforming the party and weakening party bosses. The word, an Algonquin Indian term meaning "chief," was meant to connote their high-minded above-it-all posture. More colloquially, they were described as having another posture: the aspect of a fence sitter, who has his mug on one side and his wump on the other. Die-hard party Republicans didn't like these independents. Sen. John Ingalls illustrated such disdain in likening the Mugwumps to eunuchs:

"Mr. President, the neuter gender is not popular either in nature or in society. Independents are effeminate without being masculine or feminine, unable either to beget or to bear, doomed to sterility, isolation, and extinction."

Blaine won the nomination, but he never convinced the Mugwumps who doubted his personal integrity. The *New York Times* said that his nomination would lead to a campaign of "prolonged explanation" and "a practical abdication of Republican character and purpose." When influential New York Republican Roscoe Conkling, with whom Blaine had often clashed, was asked to support him for the good of the party, he replied, "Gentlemen, I have given up criminal law."

A cartoon in the magazine *Puck* put it coarsely. In it, Blaine stands, clad in a loincloth, before an audience. A cloak that has just been removed from his shoulders reveals a body filled with tattoos that read "Mulligan letters," "Bribery," "Anti-Chinese Demagogism," "Jingoism," and "Bluster," each representing the various scandals that had stuck to him. With more than a million readers of *Puck* in the United States, the image of the tattooed man had a deep impact.[335]

Mulligan Letters, Part II

With doubts about his candidacy, Blaine threw himself into campaigning, making, by one count, more than four hundred different stops. Democratic papers accused him of vote begging. By contrast, said the *Nation*, Cleveland did not try "to snatch an office, which it was the people's privilege to bestow unasked."

Then another Mulligan bomb hit. On September 15, 1884, the *Boston Journal* published a letter from Blaine to Fisher that had not been in the batch he'd snatched back. The letter was a set of instructions for how Fisher could write a letter exonerating Blaine of the charges he was facing from the House Investigative Committee. Blaine not only suggested Fisher write the letter, he also gave him the actual text he should put in the letter, which Blaine could then show to his colleagues. In the letter, Blaine suggested Fisher should write:

"Concealment of the investment and everything connected with it would have been very easy, had concealment been desirable. But your action in the whole matter was as open and fair as the day. When the original enterprise failed, I knew with what severity the pecuniary loss fell upon you, and with what integrity and nerve you met it. Years having elapsed, it seems rather hard at this late day to be compelled to meet a slander in a matter where your conduct was, in the highest degree, honorable and straightforward. You may use this letter in any way that will be of service to you."

At the very end, Blaine wrote in his own hand, "Burn this letter." Instantly that phrase became the cry at every Democratic rally. Blaine was labeled "Slippery Jim" and "Old Mulligan Letters," and the most famous chant of all rang out: "Blaine, Blaine, James G. Blaine, the Continental liar from the state of Maine." The *New York Times* wrote that "Blaine was a prostitutor of public trusts, a scheming jobber and a reckless falsifier." Another *Puck* cartoon appeared on the cover of the magazine with Blaine as Tantalus, the Greek mythical figure made to stand in a pool of water beneath a fruit tree with the fruit ever eluding his grasp, and the water always receding before he could take a drink. Blaine appears chained to a gargantuan boulder labeled "Mulligan Letters," while just out of reach of his extended tongue was a table stocked with food, including a large cake with frosting that spelled "Presidential Cake" and a menu that read "Presidential Bill of Fare 1884."

As the election neared, the papers competed to shake their heads about the disappointing choice the voters faced between Grover Cleveland's private dalliances with Maria Halpin and Blaine's public scandals. The *Milwaukee Daily Journal* won the prize for the purplest prose: "The stinking meat, the moldy bread, rancid butter and drugged coffee will fill out the bill of fare which offers The Mulligan Letters and Maria Halpin for dessert. But it will not attract the people."

The final blow for Blaine came near the very end of the campaign. One of his strengths was his support among Irish Americans in New York, the most crucial battleground state in the nation. On October 29, Blaine appeared with a number of clergymen at a rally. One of them was a fellow named Samuel D. Burchard. Blaine was a little tired, so he wasn't paying attention, as most politicians don't, when the blowhards who introduce you go on and on and on and on. But candidates always have to be a little careful, because sometimes the blowhards have gained that reputation by saying things that are outrageous or outlandish, or in their one little moment in the sun they try to say something that will get them remembered.

Burchard was successful in getting remembered. He denounced the Democrats as the party "whose antecedents have been rum, Romanism, and rebellion." Blaine was so tired he didn't hear the remark, or if he did hear it, he didn't think to rise and refute it. But at the event was a Democratic operative who was transcribing all the remarks, much as these days each party sends an operative to the events with a video camera.

Democrats blasted the story to all their papers, hoping to offend the Irish Catholics who would see the remark as an attack on the Pope in Rome. Blaine was chased by the remark at all his future stops. As the game of telephone continued, the story grew and evolved. Soon it was passed around that Blaine himself had said it.

As Gil Troy writes in *See How They Ran*, the remark did more than sink Blaine in New York. It put a chill on campaigning for years after. People blamed Blaine for being on the stump too much, which put him in the position to be tarred by the crazy remarks of somebody else campaigning on the same platform. So for several elections afterward, candidates worried about being "Burchardized."

In the end, Blaine lost to Cleveland in New York by only a little over 1,000 votes and lost the whole election by only 23,000 votes. Cleveland won New York's thirty-six electoral votes, which put him over the top.

After Election Day, Blaine was happy to blame the whole thing on Burchard and not his own stack of ethical problems. "I should have carried New York by ten thousand, if the weather had been clear on Election Day," he said, "and Doctor Burchard had been doing missionary work in Asia Minor."

1840—The Birth of Umbrage

For presidential candidates, sometimes the best offense is to take offense. If your opponent does anything that can be interpreted as a slight, clutch your breast. Defend your honor. No matter how small the infraction, at least look aghast on cable news.

Taking umbrage generates sympathy for you and puts your opponent on the defensive. Play the victim on behalf of an entire voting bloc and you gain even more.

It can also help you raise money. *I need your help, Mrs. Smith of Sycamore Lane, to combat this calumny—which is really an offense against all right-thinking people, including you, Mrs. Smith!*

The tactic feels modern, but candidates have been collapsing on the fainting couch since the first genuine campaign. In 1840, William Henry Harrison's "log cabin and hard cider" crusade was founded on a protracted regimen of umbrage taking. It helped the Whig party defeat incumbent Martin Van Buren and end forty years of Democratic control of the presidency.

The Harrison Slur

If you know anything about William Henry Harrison it's probably that he didn't serve as president long enough to give a State of the Union address. He barely cleared a month in office. Maybe that's what makes the president with the raccoon eyes and prominent nose look most like an undertaker in the lineup of presidential portraits. Though it may have been the style of the times: his running mate and successor, John Tyler, also looks like he's very sorry for your loss and might be on the cusp of making a suggestion about a high-quality casket.

At sixty-eight, Harrison was the oldest president before Ronald Reagan, and in 1839 it was a dig at his advanced age that gave him and his party their umbrage opening. John de Ziska, writing in the Democratic *Baltimore Republican*, wrote dismissively of Harrison's presidential ambitions: "Give him a barrel of hard cider, and settle a pension of two thousand a year on him, and my word for it, he will sit the remainder of his days in his log cabin by the side of a 'sea coal' fire and study moral philosophy."

How dare the Democrats sniff at those who might enjoy hard cider or live in modest dwellings. "This slur filled the hearts of hearty frontiersmen and of the laboring man in the west and south, who lived in humble log cabins, with indignation," wrote one Whig newspaper.[336] (The rage that kindled in the hearts of moral philosophers went unrecorded, perhaps because a moral philosopher's first reaction is to have a good think about things.)

In the 2008 campaign, Sen. Barack Obama kicked up a similar reaction. At a fund-raiser, he tried to explain the mind-set of people in small towns who had been promised economic recovery but hadn't seen it. Given the repeated disappointment, the senator said, "It's not surprising then that they get bitter and they cling to guns or religion or antipathy toward people who aren't like them." Republican National Committee scientists put down their beakers. They couldn't confect a more potent spur to their base voters. Remember when your mother tried to tell you why you were upset about something? You were just tired or you had low blood sugar. That was what this liberal city fellow Obama was doing. It showed such contempt! He was defining two conservative passions as mindless salves of the weak. Eight years later, in 2016, I regularly hear this line repeated by Republican candidates and local officials trying to warm up a crowd. It works every time.

Ohio Whig Convention

Barack Obama was a leading candidate of the opposition party, so you can see why people might get upset. Plus, in the modern era, social media delivers this kind of news intravenously to partisans. John de Ziska wasn't a party representative. He was the equivalent of a blogger. Still, the Whigs took umbrage anyway and weaponized it. They used it to march men down the street in a frenzy.

On February 22, 1840, the Ohio Whigs held their convention in Columbus. To get a full view of the proceedings, a spectator would have had to climb onto the roof of the local public house at the corner of High and Broad Streets. You'd have had company. Whig party supporters lined the rooftops waving handkerchiefs embroidered with log cabins. Some wore black pins with a white log cabin and cider barrel. Others wore white portrait ribbons with General Harrison in his military uniform, his hand in his breast pocket, sword by his side, above a log cabin and cider barrel. The crowd ate cornbread and sang songs in unison with the throng filling the streets below. "All is one dense, enthusiastic mass of human bodies. On either hand, so far as the eye can extend, the streets are filled with flags, pictures and all sorts of signs and symbols," wrote one Ohio newspaper.

A life-size log cabin pitched and bobbed as a team of men pushed and pulled it through the crowd. On its walls hung coonskins, a Whig Party symbol. "Hard Cider" was scrawled on one side.

In 1840, political rallies were great public entertainments at a time when there weren't many other distractions from a life of hard labors. So the farmers, the blacksmiths, and the stable masters came that day even in the pouring rain. "Everywhere, there is mud," wrote A. B. Norton in *The Great Revolution of 1840*. "The roads were all mud, deep mud, nothing but interminable, unmitigated mud." No one seemed to mind the water or the muck. If nothing else, you could get a good meal. A 3,275-pound ox was barbecuing in the public square.[337]

There were wagons and carriages and drummers. A man held aloft a pole with a live bald eagle tied to the top of it. Veterans of the Revolutionary War marched under a banner reading, Last of the Life Guards of General Washington. A team of horses dragged a canoe that read on its side, Old Tippecanoe Forever, a reference to Harrison, who thirty years earlier had fought Tecumseh's Shawnee Indians at the Battle of Tippecanoe. Another float was a replica of Fort Meigs, a fort from a famous battle Harrison had fought in Perrysburg, Ohio, in the spring of 1813. It had a cannon that fired.

"The tide rolled in, and the multitude accumulated," wrote the *Fayetteville Weekly Observer* paper. "On they came, rending the blue welkin with their shouts."[338] (I saw Blue Welkin on their acoustic tour. If you're looking to name your new band, the election of 1840 offers many opportunities.)

The entire political enterprise seemed to be fueled by a ready supply of hard cider—fermented apple juice. Anyone who wanted a belt could have one. All you had to do was visit the platform rolling down the lane, and Whig men would dispense the amber liquid from huge barrels.[339]

Helping in the effort was E. C. Booz, a Pennsylvania distiller, who capitalized on the log cabin theme by selling whiskey in bottles shaped like log cabins. The bottles—emblazoned with his name—

became so popular, many believe it gave a boozt to using booze as a colloquial term for alcohol.

The Rise of the Popular Vote

Even if John de Ziska had writer's block, the Whigs would have found something else to rally around. The election of 1840 represented an expansion of white male suffrage. Since 1800, states had been gradually dropping the property requirement for voting, and only Virginia and Rhode Island still had one. Naturally that meant the competition for public opinion would come to dominate politics.

What better way to appeal to all those men than through their favorite pastimes? This is why candidates today are seen in bowling alleys and in duck blinds. The appeal of the booze was easy enough to understand—it had been a part of the American political tradition since Washington's time in the Virginia House of Burgesses—but the association with the log cabin was something more powerful. The log cabin represented self-sufficient, hardworking pioneer families who could make something of themselves from scratch.

The log cabin was the essential dwelling Americans built as the nation moved West. To be born in a log cabin was a sign of the rugged, independent-thinking American. It was an offshoot of Jefferson's noble farmer, whose toil on the land was proof of his good character. "The Western yeoman," wrote Henry Nash Smith in *Virgin Land*, "was a different creature altogether because he had become the hero of a myth, of the myth of mid-nineteenth-century America."

It became so fashionable to be born in a log cabin that Daniel Webster, who was a very accomplished fellow, nevertheless was a little sheepish about not having been born in one, though he proudly announced that members of his family had been born in a log cabin. (And he'd seen a log cabin. And one time, he got a splinter from walking near a log cabin.) "A man who, by his capacity and industry, has raised himself from a log cabin to eminent station in the country is of more than ordinary merit," said Webster.[340]

So Harrison's campaign was a campaign of the people. The People Are Coming! read one banner at a Whig march. Another said, The People Must Do Their Own Voting. Harrison was called "the poor man's friend," and "the people's choice." His biography was wrapped in humble clothes. The Farmer of North Bend, read the sail of a ship carrying scores of men that rolled through that Ohio Whig parade; it referred to Harrison's time in North Bend, Indiana, where he had been governor of the Indiana Territory for a period.

At several of the Ohio Whig rallies, the Buckeye Blacksmith entertained the crowd. He wore his weathered work apron and used his blacksmith tongs to shred copies of Democratic newspapers. He promised that he was not some broke-down lawyer. In the 2008 presidential campaign, Joe "the Plumber" Wurzelbacher played a similar role. He confronted Senator Obama at a rally, claiming that Obama's tax plan would raise his taxes. When Obama explained the benefits of his tax plan and used the term "spread the wealth around," it became a conservative rallying cry. Wurzelbacher, who had worked as a plumber, achieved notoriety among some conservatives for his commonsense, regular-guy wisdom.

Golden Spoon Oration

A successful class-based campaign has two elements: elevating your candidate as a man of the people and defining the opponent as a gold-dipped, effete aristocrat. In American politics, if you can put a crown on his head and call him a monarch, you're working at the expert level. That was what the Whigs did to Martin Van Buren.

To fix the incumbent Martin Van Buren in your mind, focus not on his height, for which he was given the nickname Little Van, but on his sideburns. Imagine two driver-side airbags fully deploying on either side of a man's face. This was what Van Buren—or Sweet Sandy

Whiskers, as they called him—looked like. You could probably have taken his sideburns in each fist and turned his head like a steering wheel. There is no figure in the presidential coloring book who looks more like the Wizard of Oz than Martin Van Buren.

On April 14, 1840, the House of Representatives met to consider the Civil and Diplomatic Appropriations Bill. A portion of the bill concerned appropriations "for alterations and repairs of the President's house and furniture, for purchasing trees, shrubs, and compost, and for superintendence of the grounds."

Charles Ogle, a Whig congressman from Pennsylvania, rose to speak against the provision. It was as if speech had been dammed up within him for some time. The appropriation brought forth the geyser. "Mr. Chairman, I consider this a very important item in the bill—not as to the amount, but as to the principles involved in it. I doubt much the policy of this Government in granting the Chief Magistrate emoluments or revenues of any kind, over and above the fixed salary paid to that officer out of the Treasury of the United States . . . No former Chief Magistrate ever acted upon the principle notoriously adopted by the present incumbent, of spending the money of the People with a lavish hand, and at the same time saving his own with sordid parsimony."

At this point, everyone in the gallery was pretty sure that the Whig congressman Ogle was going to go on a bit, slagging the incumbent for his gaudy ways. "Mr. Chairman I object to this appropriation on higher grounds. I resist the principle on which it is demanded as anti-democratic—as running counter in its tendency to the plain, simple, and frugal notions of our republican People. And I put it to you, sir, and to the free citizens of this country, whose servant the President is, to say whether, in addition to the large sum of *one hundred thousand dollars* which he is entitled to receive for a single term of four years, they are disposed to maintain—for his private accommodation—*a royal establishment* at the cost of the nation? Will they longer feel inclined to support their chief servant in a *palace* as splendid as that of the Caesars, and as richly adorned as the proudest Asiatic mansion?"

This is but the start of the oration. It would go on for almost three days and is one of the most baroque and powerful negative attacks on an incumbent in campaign history. The title of the speech was "The Regal Splendor of the President's Palace," but it would come to be known as the Gold Spoon Oration. It won that name from a widely circulated story about the Whig congressman Landaff Watson Andrews of Kentucky. A dinner guest at the White House, he was said to have picked up a "golden spoon" and held it up to the Democratic President, saying, "Mr. Van Buren, if you will let me take this spoon to Kentucky and show it to my constituents, I will promise not to make use of any other argument against you—this will be enough."

Ogle accused Van Buren of being "a democratic peacock, in full court costume, strutting by the hour before golden-framed mirrors, nine feet high and four feet and a half wide... The soul of Martin Van Buren is so very, very, very diminutive, that it might find abundant space within the barrel of a milliner's thimble to perform all the evolutions of the whirling pirouette avec chasse au suivant, according to the liberal gesticulations practiced by the most celebrated danseurs... Mere meadows are too common to gratify the refined taste of an exquisite with sweet sandy whiskers. He must have undulations, beautiful mounds, and other contrivances, to ravish his exalted and ethereal soul. Hence, the reformers have constructed a number of clever sized hills, every pair of which, it is said, was designed to resemble and assume the form of an Amazon's bosom, with a miniature knoll or hillock on its apex, to denote the nipple."

The Panic of 1837

Ogle's speech was reprinted in newspapers from April to August 1840 and turned into pamphlets to be spread about the country. The Gold Spoon Oration was so effective because in 1837 the United States had a full-blown financial panic. In May 1837, during the first year of Van Buren's presidency, all the banks in New York City suspended payments, and over three hundred firms failed. By January the next year, 618 banks had collapsed. In New York City, mobs broke into food warehouses. Churches gave food to the needy.[341]

Faced with hard times, the Van Buren administration did little to ease the suffering. It was not thought that the federal government would provide assistance as a means of combating the depression. Van Buren spoke to Congress of those "who were prone to expect too much of the Government." The banking legislation Van Buren did promote passed, and partisans gathered to cheer it in the streets, but after a brief recovery, the country was headed downhill again by 1839. "Down with Martin Van Ruin," shouted Whigs at their rallies. The nickname stuck.

Average Americans blamed the New York banks and Eastern industrialists for the economic contagion that spread throughout the country. That was why log cabins took on a greater resonance. It was the dwelling of the regular people who had been swamped by the far-off forces of those who lived in city town houses. As historian William Nisbet Chambers wrote, Little Van was to become "the first victim of an aroused electorate in a presidential contest that followed an economic collapse."[342]

This is what helped goose turnout. In the previous three elections—including the election of 1828, which brought Andrew Jackson to power and is considered the first great popular election—turnout averaged only about 57 percent. It was in 1840 that Americans who had the franchise exercised it fully. "We have many recruits in our ranks from the pressure of the times," said Harrison.[343] Almost 40 percent of the ballots in 1840 were cast by first-time voters. In the end, 80 percent of those who could vote cast a ballot.

"Let Van from his coolers of silver drink wine," the Whig crowds sang, "And lounge on his cushioned settee; / Our man on a buckeye bench can recline, / Content with hard cider is he." It wasn't just that Van Buren was a fancy dandy. His friends were, too. "The fact is worth noticing," wrote the *Philadelphia Gazette*, "that among the defenders of the Administration and Mr. Van Buren are numbered a few of the richest bloods and most effeminate dandies in the town."[344] (Effeminate Dandies played in the Village in the '70s).

A campaign "metamorphic" card showed a picture of Van Buren smiling with a glass of champagne from a "beautiful goblet of White House champagne." When you pulled the tab at the bottom, the wine was replaced by hard cider, and Van Buren's eyes rolled back in his head. As Henry Clay told a Whig audience, this was a "contest between the log cabin and the palace, between hard cider and champagne."[345]

Assigning voters by alcoholic preference would continue well into the modern era, where Republicans made fun of Chablis-swilling elites and the Democratic Party split between blue and white collar was often described as a split between the beer track and wine track. When I asked Bernie Sanders to explain the gun culture to liberals, he immediately compared it to drink: "While some people in New York like to sip wine on the weekends, others like to hunt."

The Panic of 1837 was about more than simply the failings of a single president. A Whig cartoon showed a destitute family gathered around their moping patriarch who cannot find a job; on the wall are pictures of Van Buren and his predecessor, Jackson. This was the failing of a party and an economic philosophy. "We now begin to see, and shall FEEL and feel it keenly too, the effects of Jeffersonian Economy, of which the Democrats have so long boasted," said the *Vermont Patriot*.[346]

The rise of distinct political parties created an atmosphere of permanent electoral combat. This was just what the founders had worried about. Parties would engage in constant conflict, making their candidates into simple vehicles for their aims. A president would lose all agency if he was just a puppet of party string pullers. Parties also made it easier for the electorate to stop thinking. Their feelings about events and leaders were predetermined by the political team they belonged to and rooted for. It was one challenge to have the rush of white men overwhelm the careful democratic republic; it was a greater one to have that pulse of new voters sorted into permanent parties engaged in destructive combat.

Whigs Steal the Democrats' Playbook

This onslaught from the Whigs burned Democrats so thoroughly, because it was proof that the minority party had completely adopted the Democratic playbook. "They have at last learned from defeat the art of victory," said the *Democratic Review* of the Whig Party in June 1840. "We have taught them how to conquer us!"

Andrew Jackson's victory in 1828 was a crusade for the people against the East Coast elites who sought to keep control in the hands of the moneyed interests. (And who Jackson believed had swiped the election from him in 1824.) Though General Jackson didn't openly campaign, he did offer policy positions, which was new in presidential politics and moved the candidate closer to the people. After being elected in 1828, Jackson declared the president "the direct representative of the people." The founders had worried about the influence of the mob, but by 1835 Alexis de Tocqueville wrote that "the people reign over the American political world as God rules over the universe."

The Whig party, which had come to power to fight Jacksonianism, had resisted this movement. Henry Clay, Jackson's nemesis, disliked "appealing to the feelings and passions of our countrymen rather than to their reasons and judgments."[347] Those who decry Donald Trump and his appeals to the common passions and his theatrical displays—including flying over a football stadium in Alabama in his plane with his name on the side—are reprising the Whig argument: if you make campaigns a circus, you might elect a showman and not a statesman.

But by 1840, the Whigs had given up their concerns about the mob and started to adopt the techniques of the Democratic Party. They had learned to "make the hurrah appeal." That was what was going on in the streets of Columbus on that day. As Robert Gray Gunderson wrote in *The Log-Cabin Campaign*, "It was a new departure for sedate and aristocratic Whigs who heretofore had preferred attempts to limit the suffrage rather than to degrade themselves by taking their case to the rabble... no longer could genteel aristocrats regulate the course of political events merely by caucusing in paneled drawing rooms. An appeal must be made to his Majesty, the Voter."[348] Said one Whig strategist proving this point: "Passion and prejudice, properly aroused and directed, would do about as well as reason in a party contest."[349]

Not every Whig was pleased about the party's shift in tactics. "The whole country is in a state of agitation upon the approaching Presidential election such as was never before witnessed," wrote John Quincy Adams in his diary. "Not a week has passed within the last few months without a convocation of thousands of people to hear inflammatory harangues against Martin Van Buren and his Administration! Here is a revolution in the habits and manners of the people. Where will it end? These are party movements, and must in the natural progress of things become antagonistical... Their manifest tendency is to civil war."

Democratic editorial writers found themselves in the unusual position of noting the ruin that was likely to come from turning an election into a spectacle. "Truly we arrived at a strange pass in President-making. To see intelligent and high-minded men—claiming a share of common sense, parading about the country in 'an immense log cabin,' splendidly adorned with mock flags, skunk skins, cider barrels, old mops, brooms, swill pails, and all the et cetera of fol-derrol, hurrahing their daylights out as the spirit of 'old Burgundy' (apple juice) stirs through the 'cobwebs' of their upper story." [350]

The Whigs weren't just beating Democrats at their own game; they were beating one of the great political practitioners of the time. Van Buren was the nation's first professional national politician.[351] He wrote in his diary in 1831, "For more than a quarter of a century..."

there had scarcely been one [day] during which I had been wholly exempted from the disturbing effects of partisan agitation...whether as a subordinate and doubtless, at times, over-zealous member of the political party in which I had almost literally been reared from childhood or as its leader...[Politics] had always absorbed my time and faculties."[352]

Van Buren helped elect Andrew Jackson in 1828 and built the Democratic Party. His skills as a strategist were so well known, Whigs had repeatedly tried to make them a liability, calling him "the Little Magician" and a mere wire puller, a phrase derived from the wires that control a marionette. He put "party above country," charged Daniel Webster.[353] One Whig newspaper called Van Buren "a man of many offices without any deeds of public usefulness." He was such a slippery character, Davy Crockett wrote, that he could "take a piece of meat on one side of his mouth, a piece of bread on the other, and cabbage in the middle, and chew and swallow each in its severalty, never mixing them together."[354]

Log Cabin Fact-Check

Portraying Van Buren as a simpering bureaucrat surrounded by perfumed pillows and gold leaf is an even greater political achievement when we measure how little truth there was to the claim. Of the two candidates, it was Van Buren who grew up without meat on the table every night. His father was a tavern owner, and his family of a half dozen crowded into a single room upstairs. Harrison had not been born in a log cabin, but in a Virginia manor, to one of the First Families of Virginia. His father was a signer of the Declaration of Independence and he'd been governor in Virginia. As an adult, Harrison lived in a seventeen-room house that had taken two years to build. The glass in the house was imported from Europe. It had a circular staircase and a name: Grouseland.

Van Buren was also not the dandy of the White House. As a

widower he liked to go out, and there were women who hoped to help him bring an end to his bachelorhood. That gave him an elevated flair, but his Pennsylvania Avenue home was nothing close to Ogle's description. James Silk Buckingham, a member of the British Parliament who visited in 1838, said the White House was "greatly inferior in size and splendor to the country residences of most of our [British] nobility," and the furniture was "far from elegant or costly." He described the whole air of the mansion as "unostentatious... without parade or displays... well adapted to the simplicity and economy which is characteristic of the republican institutions of the country."

The story of the Gold Spoon that had kicked off Ogle's oration was also apocryphal. Rep. Andrews rose at the start of the oration to say it never happened, but Ogle was undaunted. "You might as well turn the current of the Niagara with a ladies' fan as to prevent scheming and intrigue at Washington," complained Van Buren.

Harrison Hits the Trail

Van Buren couldn't defend himself the way an incumbent might today. (Donald Trump would have produced a gigabyte of tweets responding to Ogle.) Candidates didn't campaign for themselves, and a president certainly would never think to do such a thing. The founders had prized virtue as a bulwark against ambition and despotism. Anyone who campaigned showed a deficit of virtue, because it showed they were seeking to elevate their station, putting their personal desires above the good of the country. To grab for the job hinted at the very ambition that demonstrated you were unfit for it. Anyone who wanted to be president was simply supposed to act as a man of virtue in a glass case unsullied by the process and allow the white propertied men who selected him to be moved by this virtue.

The presidency was an office that should be neither sought nor denied. George Washington was the model, as he was in so much else. After his war victories, Washington returned to Mount Vernon. He didn't seek elevation. It sought him. He didn't want to be president, but when news was delivered to him that he had won the job, he sublimated his desires and took the post for the good of the country.

To seek the good opinion of voters was to put yourself in a competition where you would be tempted to change your views to make them happy so that they might vote for you. And the people would come to expect that they could influence you, so they'd gradually expect even greater acts of hoop jumping. It would create a system where popular will, not reason and virtue, directed the affairs of men.

This isn't to say that Van Buren didn't try to campaign. In the summer of 1839 he took a trip to the North, like his predecessors Thomas Jefferson, James Madison, and Andrew Jackson. But unlike those previous presidents, Van Buren combined his state visits with political speeches. Instead of simply responding in his ceremonial role when local reception committees welcomed him, Van Buren responded by talking about his policies. He wasn't seeking the vote, Van Buren said, he was merely responding to questions, a necessary part of the commerce "indispensable to the maintenance of a republican government."

The Whigs pounced. They charged him with degrading the office with "self-justificatory effusions."[355] "Mr. Van Buren appears to run among the States of the Union like a little whale among 26 well-armed Nantucket whale-boats. Each one, as he passes, buries a harpoon to the handle in the blubber of the monster."[356] A Whig paper mocked the "Electioneering Cabinet" of the Democratic administration by printing quotations from the party's hero, Thomas Jefferson: "It is expected that [any officer of the government] will not attempt to influence the votes of others, nor take any part in the business of electioneering, that being deemed inconsistent with the spirit of the Constitution and his duties to it." In another quotation, Jefferson suggested that electioneering was grounds for removal from office because "the enormous patronage of the General Government" would interfere with fair elections.

Whigs wrapped the incumbent in the pomp of the presidential receptions he received on this tour, calling him "His Majesty, King Martin the First." Some consider this the first campaign swing of an incumbent president, but the abuse was so heavy that Van Buren had to cancel a trip to visit Jackson in Tennessee for fear of being accused of electioneering again.[357]

The political parties, on the other hand, could campaign openly. They rallied for the presidential candidates at local party dinners, barbecues, and picnics. Surrogates spoke on behalf of the candidate. The most robust speakers were known as slangwhangers (probably the second half of a heavy-metal double bill). Davy Crockett writes in his diary of one of them, "He talked loud, which is the way with all politicians educated in the Jackson school: and by his slang-whanging drew a considerable crowd around us."[358]

If you were looking to chart the evolution of the campaign tradition of criticizing your opponent for the very thing that you are engaged in, the election of 1840 offers a good starting point. The Whigs were against party politics while being furiously partisan. They complained about Van Buren campaigning and then launched Harrison out on the trail. He had campaigned a little in 1836, but in 1840 he gave about two dozen speeches in what is considered by many to be the birth of campaigning.

So how did Harrison get away with this hypocrisy? Umbrage. "He confessed that he had suffered deep mortification since he had been placed before the people as a candidate for the highest office in their gift—nay, the most exalted station in the world," wrote one correspondent covering a Harrison campaign stop, "that any portion of his countrymen should think it necessary or expedient to abuse, slander, or vilify him. His sorrow arose not so much from personal—dear as was to him the humble reputation he had earned—as from public considerations."[359] (Backwards ran the sentences written by writers of that day.)

So you see, Harrison was compelled to campaign, not to defend himself against the calumnies being everywhere stacked against him, but because he couldn't let the democratic process be sullied by these kinds of attacks on any candidate.

The first charge that Harrison had to answer was that he was too old. His opponents called him "granny." At nearly seventy he had outrun life expectancy at the time, which for a man was about the midforties. By campaigning, Harrison showed that he was vigorous. Partisan papers dutifully attested to his "excellent health" and that he spoke "with a fervor and animation belonging rather to youth than to age... The fire of his eye is not dimmed by age, nor has the strength of his manly intellect suffered in the least."[360]

The next charge Harrison had to fight was that he hadn't really won the military honors he claimed. He was a "petticoat general," whose exploits at Tippecanoe and Fort Meigs were overblown. THE CELEBRATION AT FORT MEIGS A POLITICAL FARCE! read the headline of the *Ohio Statesman*. "The old Granny let loose to amuse the children with Spook Stories and recount the wonderful adventures of her life!"[361] One Democratic senator rose to speak about it on the floor of the Senate and suggested Harrison was trying to steal the glory from others who had fought more bravely in the same battles. "Mr. Chairman, I can discover no high attributes about his character, civil or military. I shall only say, that the Senate, that august body of Americans, refused him the compliment of a sword. This speaks volumes against him. Besides, he must have been deficient in glory, for we see him plucking the laurels from the brave young Croghan, in order to build up his own fame. The people will no doubt consign such a man to his log cabin."[362]

In the 2004 election this would become known as swiftboating, when Republicans questioned John Kerry's Vietnam heroism as a swiftboat captain, which won him three purple hearts, the bronze star, and the silver star. In defending his record, Harrison was given an excuse to boast about it on the campaign trail. Soldiers joined him onstage. Tears were reportedly shed. At one rally, a British soldier who'd been fighting against him in the War of 1812 told the story of shooting at Harrison twenty times. But he couldn't hit him, because Harrison was such a brave man.

The most important thing about Harrison's exploits at Tippecanoe is that they took place in proximity of a location suitable for rhyming. No one was going to successfully rhyme anything useful with Fort Meigs, but when your running mate is John Tyler, it leads to one of the most famous rhymes in political history: "Tippecanoe and Tyler too."

The rhymes kept the crowds engaged.[363] Who doesn't like a good song when you're pickled in hard cider? Those songs were available to everybody, because printing had become much cheaper. For pennies you could buy *The Harrison and Log Cabin Song Book* and sheet music and a broadside of "Log Cabin Anecdotes." The Whigs put a press—an actual printing press—on a horse-drawn cart and wheeled it down the street printing off song sheets for people as the procession marched, so that everyone could join in and sing the same lyrics.

"Harrison was sung into the presidency," wrote one New York Whig. And the songs were incredibly goofy. "What has caused the great commotion, motion, motion / Our country through? / It's the ball a rolling on, on, / For Tippecanoe and Tyler too." We owe the campaign of 1840 for many things, including the phrase "keep the ball rolling." At rallies, Harrison supporters would roll an enormous canvas ball through the streets. Slogans were written in strips along the ball as the crowd shouted "Keep the ball rolling!" The election of 1840 has often been called the "Campaign of Tomfoolery." New York diarist Philip Hone concluded the ticket had "rhyme, but no reason, in it."

Another song said, "They said he lived in a cabin / And lived on old hard cider too. / Well, what if he did? I'm certain / He's the hero of Tippecanoe. / He's the hero of Tippecanoe." The Democrats had their own songs. "Hush-a-bye baby," the Democrats sang, "Daddy's a Whig. / Before he comes home, / Hard cider he'll swig. / Then he'll be tipsy, and over he'll fall. / Down will come Daddy, Tip, Tyler, and all."

While we're totaling up the things for which we can credit the 1840 election, the Democrats made their own contribution to the lexicon. In the spring of 1839 the phrase "OK" began to circulate in Boston as shorthand for "oll korrect," a slangy way of saying "all right." Early in 1840, Van Buren's supporters began to use the trendy expression as a way to identify their candidate, whom they called "Old Kinderhook"—the name of his hometown—in an attempt to link him to the glory of his old boss, Andrew "Old Hickory" Jackson.

Democrats also charged that Harrison was a puppet of strategists and "wire pullers." He refused to tell the country what he believed because he believed nothing. He was the "dupe of designing knaves" (Maybe not a band name, but a surefire eighties sitcom hit.)

The last charge was a feature, not a bug. Harrison didn't want to express any views, because it would distract from the failures of the incumbent. The Democratic newspapers howled. "General Harrison being a candidate for the presidency is questioned by the American people who desire to vote understandingly on the exciting and important subjects now agitated before the country. But the policy of the general and his friends is to keep dark. They think they can get the most votes. And that is all they seem to think of by cheating the people by false representations to suit different latitudes."[364]

Mitt Romney pursued a similar strategy in 2012. Like Romney, Harrison's lack of positions helped paper over differences in a coalition that was formed not because they believed in a common ideology but simply because they all knew what they didn't like. It was "a party only in name, for its only bond of union was opposition to the administration of the day."[365]

But this strategy wasn't only political. There was a high-minded reason a candidate should not offer his views. It put the president above Congress, and that, said Harrison, "more than almost anything else, would tend to consolidate the whole substantial power of the government in the hands of a single man, a tendency which, whether in or out of office, I feel it my most solemn duty to resist."

Nicholas Biddle, the last president of the Second Bank of the United States, who supported the Whigs, put the strategy most entertainingly: "Let him say not one single word about his principles or his creed. Let him say nothing, promise nothing. Let no committee, no convention, no town meeting ever extract from him a single word about what he thinks now or what he will do hereafter. Let the use of pen and ink be wholly forbidden, as if he were a mad poet in Bedlam."[366]

The Papers Have Your Back

When Harrison rose to his defense to prove that his mind could produce its own material and not simply the packaged goods of his advisers, he had an army of newspapermen ready to believe him. "The story goes," said Harrison at one stop, "that I have not only a committee of conscience-keepers, but that they put me in a cage, fastened with iron bars, and kept me in that."

A correspondent without a byline wrote, "To one who looked at his bright and speaking eye, the light which beamed in its rich expression, the smile which played upon his countenance, blending the lineaments of benevolence and firmness, who remembered also that he was listening to the voice of a son of old Governor Harrison, one of 'the signers,' the pupil of old 'Mad Anthony,' the hero of Tippecanoe, the defender of Fort Meigs, the conqueror of Proctor—the idea of William Henry Harrison in a cage was irresistibly ludicrous!"[367]

Democratic papers covered these speeches quite differently. They reported brawls and drunkenness. Women were abused. "We were not prepared and did not expect," said one paper, "to see every principle of morality and common decency prostrated so low."[368] There is one long account of a preacher who was threatened.

In addition, Democratic papers fought back against this idea of

Harrison being the people's candidate, describing him as "dressed in the finest kind of imported broadcloth from top to toe and very delicate kid gloves on his hands, looking more like some sprig of aristocracy emerging from a banking house or a ballroom than a farmer."[369] Another paper took note of those gloves and snickered, "This then is the hard working log cabin candidate, with hands so soft that the skin wears off by a little shaking. No one ever saw Mr. Van Buren with gloves on shaking hands with his fellow-citizens."

There was also opposition research. "General Harrison, when Governor of Indiana, approved a law prohibiting free men from voting unless they owned fifty acres of land! And yet Harrison and Tyler are the candidates of the Whigs—those dear lovers of the People!!"[370]

Partisan newspapers made these events sound so attractive because they hoped to make partisanship seem essential to men's identities.[371] That was about building party membership but also guaranteeing future readers.

Writing for a partisan newspaper also gave you a shot at a patronage job once your candidate won, so the writers really went for it. An example: "So deeply enthused were all that they lost sight of their ailments and became oblivious to ague, rheumatism, gout, neuralgia and other ills in their zeal for Harrison."[372]

Audiences were ravenous. Newspapers were chronicling what was perhaps the most popular spectator sport in America at the time: politics, a diversion with color and drama in which men could participate to give energy to their drab lives. Literacy rates for whites were nearly 90 percent, and advances in technology made cheap printing easy. In 1790 there were 92 newspapers in America, by 1828 there were 861 newspapers, and by 1840 there were 1,577, of which 209 were dailies. This was the era of the penny press, and New York City saw the birth of the *New York Herald* and *New York Sun*; the *Sun*'s publisher promised to provide "the public with the news of the day at so cheap a rate as to lie within the means of all."

With the political press working for the Democrats, said Martin

Van Buren, "we can endure a thousand convulsions... without them, we might as well hang our harps on willows." In Psalm 137:2, the Jews hang their harps as useless things when persecuted. Essentially, Van Buren is saying, without the press we might as well hang it up.

October Surprise

The growth of newspapers and the blossoming of two parties in constant opposition created a sense of permanent conflict. It was not man against man, but party against party, pushing and pulling the republic in a contest that increasingly seemed separate from the issues of the day but simply one long continuous conflict based on greed, power, and ambition.

An example of this is an article published in the *Whig* from Jonesborough, Tennessee, on Wednesday, October 21, 1840:

"We have been telling our friends to look but for some desperate charge against the Whigs on the eve of the approaching contest for the Presidency, that it was coming; and we are now prepared to state what that charge is. The cat is now out of the wallet! Hear it and guard against it!! It is that great card that the party intended to play!!!"[373]

Obviously, the exclamation point is not a modern burden of the e-mail age. They were warning against what we'd call an October Surprise these days—a late-breaking campaign development that can change the course of the race.

The paper continued to outline a scheme where Democratic governors were faking umbrage in letters to Whig papers. The letters are "purporting to be indignant replies to a Mr. Gates of New York, a Whig Abolition member of Congress, as they charge, who has sent them, under his official frank, the proceedings of what is styled, the *World's Convention of Abolitionists*."

The charge here was that the Democratic governors were taking offense under false pretenses. There was no such World's Convention, and the Whig congressman Mr. Gates was not using his official frank—the privilege of sending free mail for government business—to advocate for the freeing of all slaves. But by sending the letters to the papers and pretending to be outraged, the Democrats—so the charge goes—were trying to make it seem as if the Whigs were closet abolitionists, which would have hurt the party in the South and West, where the voters wanted to keep their slaves.

The paper tried to call out the Democrats for this phony scheme. "Suddenly the Governors of three slave States, publish in the newspapers letters of the same date, containing the same matter!... The thing carries its own condemnation—its own refutation, upon its very face."

Do as I Say, Not as I Do

In the end, Harrison's umbrage campaign was crushingly successful. He won 234 electoral votes to 60 for Van Buren, though the popular vote was closer. Harrison won by 145,000 votes of the 2.4 million cast. The Whigs then went on to win the House and the Senate. Van Buren, the political wizard, was left to mope: "Why the deuce is it that they have such an itch for abusing me? I tried to be harmless, and positively good natured, and a most decided friend of peace."[374]

Despite being the walking symbol of one of the most successful party campaigns in history, Harrison the president did what future presidents would do: He pretended the campaign that had preceded had never happened.[375] Though as president he wore white gloves with log cabins stitched on them—the symbol of his party—in his inaugural address, he warned against parties: "Fellow citizens, I must say something to you on the subject of the parties at this time existing in our country. To me, it appears perfectly clear that the interest of that country requires that the violence of the spirit by which those parties are, at this time, governed must be greatly mitigated, if not entirely extinguished, or consequences will ensue which are appalling to be thought of."

Umbrage had been replaced by chutzpah.

For a long time, observers blamed his nearly two-hour inaugural speech for Harrison's death. He'd gone on so long to prove to doubters that he wasn't too old and infirm (at 8,445 words, the speech is the longest inaugural address in history). He wore no hat, overcoat, or gloves. (John Kennedy would do the same thing to send similar signals of vigor in 1961.) Harrison was exposed to the weather for so long, doctors thought he had caught pneumonia. It's actually more likely that he died from enteric fever from bacteria in a marsh near the White House that was full of local sewage. After a brutal regimen of cures that almost certainly made his condition worse, Harrison expired.

John Tyler was the first vice president in American history to have to step into the office. Despite the catchy campaign slogan, many people didn't know him. Wags at the time changed the campaign jingle to "Tippecanoe and Tyler who?" It was a characterization to which he, no doubt, took umbrage.

PART VII

Crashing the Party

1980—A Cure for Malaise

AP Photo/Bob Daugherty

On July 6, 1979, Jimmy Carter sat on the floor of the Aspen Lodge of the presidential retreat of Camp David in the leafy Catoctin Mountain Park. Wearing blue jeans and a polo shirt, he propped himself against a pillow and pressed his pen with purpose on the curling pages of a yellow legal pad.

He'd been taking notes for the last three days from a string of visitors he'd called into give him advice on the desperate state of his presidency. "I feel I lost control of the government and the leadership of the people," he told each group.[376] Governors, preachers, teachers, and politicians gave him their thoughts about how he could take control of his presidency and maybe elevate his approval rating from 28 percent.

He should have been splashing around in the Hawaiian surf. That had been his plan, but he had shelved the trip. Returning from Japan, he spoke to his pollster, Pat Caddell, who had told him, "You People have got to come home now. You have no idea how bad it is here." Carter cancelled the vacation and began a ten-day secluded hiatus of introspection and presidential reclamation.

Carter's days at Camp David giving the legal pad the heavy treatment and the unsuccessful remedies he employed to right his presidency drew Ted Kennedy forward to challenge Carter for the Democratic nomination. In 1976, Ronald Reagan tried to encourage Republicans to be the first party to toss an incumbent for the first time in nearly a hundred years. It had weakened Ford and helped Carter to the White House. Democrats, seeing the damage that had been done by the intraparty fracas, decided they'd put the car keys in the electrical socket too. In the election of 1980 Sen. Edward Kennedy tried to unseat Jimmy Carter, leading to an identical, debilitating fight that left Carter mortally wounded for the fall election.

Malaise

In March 1979 Jimmy Carter had celebrated a breakthrough agreement between the Israelis and Egyptians, the end to more than thirty years of fighting. It meant stability for a key U.S. ally in a volatile region. Americans didn't much care, because they were suffering at home. Inflation was up past 10 percent. The unemployment rate was about 6 percent. GDP growth was negative. The country was in a recession.

It was also the summer of gas lines. Every night on the evening news, it seemed, there was a different angry man with long hair pushing his mammoth vehicle toward some exhausted pump, his wide lapels waving.

Carter had gone to Camp David to work on the fifth energy speech of his presidency, but he realized that everyone had stopped listening to him. "Jimmy had made several speeches on energy, and it just seemed to be going nowhere with the public," remembered his wife, Rosalynn. "So he just said, 'I'm not going to make the speech.'"

Instead, he came up with the idea for the interviews. It would keep with his promise during the 1976 campaign to stay in touch with the country. "I felt a remarkable sense of relief and renewed confidence," wrote Carter in his diary, "after I canceled the speech and began to shape the thoughts I would put into the next week's work."

Thus commenced one of the great acts of presidential naval gazing in modern memory. Over a period of eight days, nearly 150 different people came through Camp David. He brought in historians, policy experts, preachers, teachers, newsmen and newswomen, and wise men of Washington like Clark Clifford, who had helped rescue Truman's reelection in 1948.

The sessions were brutal. The president sat there dutifully taking notes as visitor after visitor told him how poorly he was doing and how he had disappointed the country. The press didn't know what to make of the daily pilgrimages to the mountaintop resort, but the papers were filled with speculation about all the ways Carter was flailing. "The entire exercise had begun to work against itself as soon as the White House staff decided to turn it into a public event," wrote Clifford. "It worsened the very problem it was designed to solve, conveying the sense that the President was confused and had lost confidence in both himself and the American people."[377]

After Carter's seminar of self-reflection, he delivered an Oval Office address on the third anniversary of his nomination. "It's clear that the true problems of our nation are much deeper, deeper than gasoline lines or energy shortages, deeper even than inflation or recession. And I realize more than ever that, as president, I need your help," he said. Carter told the nation it was experiencing a crisis of confidence and he asked people for a renewal of faith in the future of this nation. The "Crisis of Confidence" speech would later become known as Carter's "malaise" speech. Though that word had not been used in the address, it was the word that had appeared repeatedly in the articles characterizing the Camp David meetings. When Kennedy later launched his campaign, his staff named his campaign plane Air Malaise.

Carter quoted from then Arkansas governor Bill Clinton, though he didn't refer to him by name.: "This from a southern governor: 'Mr. President, you're not leading this nation. You're just managing the government. You don't see the people enough anymore. Some of your cabinet members don't seem loyal. There is not enough discipline among your disciples. Don't talk to us about politics or the mechanics of government but about an understanding of our common good. Mr. President, we are in trouble. Talk to us about blood and sweat and tears.'"

Carter started the speech promising to be the president "who feels your pain," a phrase that has since come to be more associated with Clinton's presidential career. The advice was vintage Clinton—show empathy for regular people and show you were working hard—a fact we know only because a dozen years later he used it to rescue himself during the New Hampshire primary and win the White House.

The speech was considered a success at the time. Snap polls showed that people liked it. But the "malaise" speech would come to be considered a disaster because of what happened soon afterward. Several days after the speech, Carter announced that he had asked for the resignations of all his Cabinet-level officials and senior White House staff, thirty-four people in all.

The president had talked about not panicking. There was no reason to touch that red button. The message this sent though, was: PANIC! Carter didn't get this at the time. "The news reports, predictably, made a crisis of the cabinet offering their resignation," he wrote in his diary, "ignoring that the cabinet resigned in support of me, to give me a clear hand in handling replacements." Afterward, someone quipped that Carter was going to be the first president whose approval rating would slip below inflation.

Save Us, Ted!

At this point Democrats turned to Senator Kennedy. His numbers sure looked good. A Gallup poll from August 1979 showed that Kennedy was ahead of Carter among Democrats by two-to-one.

Kennedy's standard response was the obvious dodge: he expected Carter to be re-nominated, he expected him to be reelected, and he intended to support him.

It wasn't just that there seemed to be a law that Ted Kennedy had to be asked about running in every presidential election since his brother Bobby's assassination in 1968. He had also been positioning himself as the Democratic opposition to the administration since the Democratic Party meeting in Memphis, Tennessee, in December 1978. Democrats were unhappy with the lack of boldness from the president. Carter had been trapped from doing anything bold by inflation and a weak economy. He didn't want big spending programs, and he'd been trying to hold the deficit in check.

When Carter spoke in Memphis, he didn't tell people what they wanted to hear. He gave a kind of temporizing, moderate Democratic pitch. On the question of health care, Carter had been concerned about the level of federal spending, and so he said, basically, he wasn't going to do anything big on health care. Perhaps he would propose and support a catastrophic health-care plan that would help people in dire need, but it would not cover everyone.

Kennedy, meanwhile, wanted universal coverage. He delivered a stemwinder of a speech, calling health care "the great unfinished business on the agenda of the Democratic Party." He also took issue with Carter's tentative leadership, saying, "Sometimes a party must sail against the wind. We cannot afford to drift or lie at anchor. We cannot heed the call of those who say it is time to furl the sail." (This was, it must be mentioned, the greatest record for the number of extended sailing metaphors used in politics in a single speech at the time.)

When Hamilton Jordan, Carter's political brain, heard the speech, he reportedly turned to Carter's pollster, Pat Caddell, and said, "The son of a bitch is gonna run." When a group of congressmen visited the White House, Carter told them bluntly about Kennedy: "I'll whip his ass."

Why Do You Want to be President?

Sen. Gary Hart put the contest between Carter and Kennedy into perspective this way: "The American people are looking for a politician of stature, perhaps as a substitute for solutions."

Kennedy had stature but it was a heavy coat. There was the Kennedy myth, filled with all the romanticism that came with his famous name, and then there was Kennedy the politician, who was an uneven performer. All White Knight candidates have to suffer with the inevitable disconnect between the mythical qualities that people grant them and their reality. That's why political hacks say that the best day for a candidate is the day before they announce. That's the day when they are still the vessel for voters' hopes and dreams and not yet the sum of the long, brutal trail of disappointments that is the modern campaign.

In the book *Watershed* John Stacks tells the story of the Florida State comptroller leading the "Draft Ted Kennedy" movement: "He began a nearly euphoric account of Ted Kennedy's qualities. Soon, however, it was clear he was not talking about just Ted Kennedy. Rather, he was talking about John Kennedy and Bob Kennedy."

The gulf between Kennedy the heroic mashup of the brothers and Kennedy the man was exacerbated by his uneven speaking style. He could give a stemwinder, like the health-care speech in Memphis, but then he could also produce a mushy pile of sonorous sounds that mimicked speech but, in their totality, added up to cloud of fog.

Edward Fouhy, who covered Kennedy for a number of different networks, said, "He couldn't articulate an English sentence. He was hopeless on the stump." How bad was it really? "The standards at NBC"—where Fouhy worked at the time—"required that someone take down, word for word, what the speaker says in any sound bite we're going to use on the evening news. The guy who did that took down something Kennedy said and then brought me what he'd written. You couldn't make any sense of this." It could be very, very bad.

This problem came into focus (or showed its lack of focus, as the case may be) in a famous interview Kennedy did with Roger Mudd of CBS, which came weeks before Kennedy was supposed to make his formal announcement in November 1979. Mudd was working on an hour-long special on Kennedy. He'd asked him several probing questions about the accident at Chappaquiddick, where Mary Jo Kopechne had died after Kennedy had driven off the bridge.

Then Mudd asked Kennedy the simplest question of all: "Why do you want to be president?" It should have been a layup. Kennedy was running as a bold leader eyes bright with promise and clarity about the future. Instead, Kennedy's answer ambled over hill and dale, past the glade with the stream and into the deep forest where it was lost forever:

> Well, I'm...were I to...to make the...the announcement, and...to run, the reasons that I would run is because I have a great belief in this country, that it is...there's more natural resources than any nation of the world. There's the greatest educated population in the world, the greatest technology of any country in the world. The greatest capacity for innovation in the world. And the greatest political system in the world. And yet...I see, at...the current time, that...most of the industrial nations of the world are exceeding us in terms of productivity, are doing better than us in terms of meeting the problems of inflation. That they're dealing with their problems of energy and their problems of unemployment.
>
> And it just seems to me that...this nation can cope and deal with its problems in a way that it has in the past. We're facing complex issues and problems in this nation at this time. But we have faced similar challenges at other times. And

> the . . . energies and the resourcefulness of this nation, I think, should be focused on these problems in a way that . . . brings a sense of . . . restoration . . . in this country, by its people, to . . . in dealing with the problems that we face, primarily the issues on the economy, the problems of inflation, and the problems of . . . energy. And . . . I would . . . basically . . . feel that . . . that it's imperative for this country to either move forward, that it can't stand still, or otherwise, it moves backward.

The interview aired on the same night as the horror movie *Jaws*, where a number of people meet their violent end. Republican senator Bob Dole quipped, "Seventy-five percent of the country watched *Jaws*, twenty-five percent watched Roger Mudd, and half of them couldn't tell the difference." In his diary, Carter wrote: "We watched a CBS special Sunday night about Kennedy, which I thought was devastating to him. It showed him not able to answer a simple question about what he would do if president."

Bob Shrum, the political brain behind Kennedy, called it a "train wreck of an interview" that previewed the weakness of a Kennedy strategy based on playing it safe. Since he was far ahead in the polls, went the theory, "he should measure his words carefully to avoid sounding too 'liberal' or taking sharp issue positions," according to Shrum. "This strategy didn't fit the candidate. It made someone with strong convictions awkwardly self-conscious about what he could and couldn't say. Edward Kennedy is the worst politician I've ever seen at saying nothing."

Shrum sets up a competition between liberal ideas and campaign competence. Was Kennedy a bad candidate with good ideas? Or did Kennedy lose because New Deal liberalism didn't have a big enough audience even in the Democratic Party?

In the summer of 1979 the Carter campaign team held a retreat on the Eastern Shore of Maryland. Several at the meeting wanted to know how to handle the Kennedy challenge. Hamilton Jordan, Carter's strategist, shut down the talk, according to Tom Donilon, then a young campaign aide who would go on to be President Obama's national security adviser. "Hamilton shut down the discussion in a way I'd not seen before, saying that Kennedy had been running against Carter since 1978, and that the only discussion he wanted to have was about how to beat Kennedy," remembered Donilon.

Jordan's view was that Kennedy was a vulnerable opponent, despite all the hype and the family name. Jordan wanted to take on Kennedy, because when Carter won, it would make him a giant-slayer, doing more for his image than any presidential event could.

It was a risk. Kennedy sure didn't look weak. The polls had him soaring high into the white clouds above Carter. The *New York Times* reported that Kennedy's lead over Carter in the fall of '79 was 61 to 33 percent. They also reported that he was preferred as the candidate, even in the South, where Carter was from, by 44 to 40 percent. Thirty-six percent of registered Democrats and 41 percent of self-described independent voters said they wouldn't consider voting for Carter in 1980.

The Kennedy enthusiasm was driven not only by antipathy for Carter, but also the idea that perhaps Kennedy would be—if he could win the nomination—the strongest candidate against Ronald Reagan. In August 1979, a Yankelovich report had Kennedy over Reagan at 54 to 34 percent, which was perhaps why it also showed Kennedy as the preferred candidate over Carter among Democrats by 58 to 25.

According to Peter Canellos in his book *Last Lion: The Fall and Rise of Ted Kennedy*, Carter's pollster, Pat Caddell, did an in-depth set of interviews with people across the country in November and December 1979. As Caddell recalled, "We asked people, 'Okay, the election is over. Teddy is now president, how would he do?' A lot of people said he'd be fantastic." Caddell brought these results to the president, who locked them in his safe and said, "No one is ever to see this."

You're No Jack Kennedy

The first salvo in the competition between Kennedy and Carter took place at the inauguration of the Kennedy Library in October 1979, a month before Kennedy would declare his candidacy. Carter knew that Ted Kennedy was likely to run, so in his speech he tried to use his brother JFK's legacy against him. Carter argued that the world of 1980 was as different from the world of 1960 as 1960 was different from 1940. When Jack Kennedy ran in 1960, he said he was representing a new generation for a new world, but his brother Ted was offering a more nostalgic approach. "The carved desk in the Oval Office, which I use, is the same as when John F. Kennedy sat behind it," said Carter. "But the problems that land on that desk are quite different … We have a keener appreciation of the limits now, the limits of government, the limits on the use of military power abroad."

Carter was saying that the limitless, liberal, big government that Kennedy believed in was no longer applicable in a world of limits. Of course, this lack of vision and incremental approach was just what irritated liberals about Carter and why they compared him to Herbert Hoover.

House Speaker Tip O'Neill believed that a lot of representatives in the Democratic Party simply feared that if Carter was renominated, they'd lose their seats. Dozens of congressional Democrats were moving toward urging Carter to step aside in 1980, because they thought that so many Democratic voters would stay at home that Democrats in the House would suffer as badly as Republicans did after Watergate.

It was so bad that the Congressional Black Caucus, representing a constituency thought to be loyal to Carter, endorsed Kennedy. One of the architects of Carter's victory in 1976 in Pennsylvania came out for Kennedy. Sen. Dick Clark quit his job as the administration coordinator for Refugee Affairs to work full-time for Kennedy.

The sole good news came from Sen. Joe Biden, who called to say he'd polled fourteen senators who were up for reelection in 1980, and only one of them wanted Kennedy to run.

Rose Garden Offense

Four days before Kennedy was to announce his candidacy, fifty-two American hostages were seized at the American embassy in Tehran. Though the hostage crisis would drag on for 444 days and be seen as a sign of Carter's weakness, the American public rallied around the president at first.

Kennedy was in a box. He had to carry on with his campaign, especially after the negative reviews of his interview with Roger Mudd, but he couldn't attack Carter too much. He didn't want to look unpatriotic by criticizing the president during a crisis. Still, the show had to go on, so Kennedy and his enormous press entourage arrived at Boston's Logan Airport in two different planes.

He arrived with Secret Service protection. Carter had extended the offer of protection to Kennedy a month before he actually declared on the theory that news of Kennedy's coming candidacy would make him a political target. There had been shootings in the '68, '72, and '76 presidential races.

Kennedy's brothers had announced their presidential campaigns in the Russell Senate Office Building. He made his pitch at Faneuil Hall, in a Massachusetts accent that would have made it feel like Boston even if he'd been in the Senate. Without mentioning Carter, he made it clear that he was attacking his leadership:

> For many months, we have been sinking into crisis. Yet, we hear no clear summons from the center of power. Aims are not set; the means of realizing them are neglected. Conflicts in directions confuse our purpose. Government falters. Fears spread that our leaders have resigned themselves to retreat. This

> country is not prepared to sound retreat. It is ready to advance. It is willing to make a stand, and so am I.

While Kennedy was hitting the trail, Carter was retreating from it. The hostage crisis allowed Carter to initiate what became known as the "Rose Garden strategy." He announced that he was dropping out of the campaign, saying he wouldn't concern himself with national politics while the crisis continued: "Abraham Lincoln said, 'I have but one task, and that is to save the Union.' Now, I must devote my concerted efforts to resolving the Iranian crisis," said Carter. Then, as if to further scramble the international situation and block Kennedy's advance, the Soviet Union invaded Afghanistan on Christmas Eve.

Every day the president delivered sober, thoughtful messages about the world and what troubles America faced, with the backdrop of the White House. Kennedy, meanwhile, had only the backdrop of the diners and overheated high school gymnasiums where he was spending his days in early primary and caucus states.

On December 28, Carter announced he would not participate in the debate scheduled for January 7 among the Democratic candidates. That was a huge blow to Kennedy, who had counted on the opportunity to confront Carter face-to-face. Carter said he was too busy dealing with international affairs, but privately told his diary the real reason he was ducking the debate. "It's inconceivable to me," he wrote, "that they"—meaning his political advisers—"would pursue the matter of the debate because it's obviously counterproductive politically. When we decided to do the debate, it was just me and Kennedy. Kennedy was two to one ahead of me in the polls and we didn't have the Iranian crisis on my shoulders. Now, all those factors have changed. Rosalynn thinks I'm right."

The country had rallied to Carter after the hostage crisis. In a December poll, he was ahead of Kennedy 48 to 40 percent among Democrats, and far ahead in a general election match-up against Reagan. A January 1 poll had Carter leading Kennedy by twenty points, a forty-point swing in the polls. Eighty percent of the country, according to the Roper Center, was confident in Carter's ability to handle the crisis.

Carter wrote in his diary: "The evening news reported that the ayatollah had come out against me for president, which will give another boost to our campaign." The mayor in one Iowa town publicly switched his support from Kennedy to Carter, saying he was impressed with Carter's handling of Iran. And a Rep. James Howard of New Jersey did the same.

Kennedy, on the other hand, was not having a very good crisis. In early December, he criticized the U.S. support for the Shah, saying that the Shah "ran one of the most violent regimes in the history of mankind in the form of terrorism and the basic and fundamental violations of human rights in the most cruel circumstances to his own people." Everyone, including Republican George Bush, said Kennedy was giving aid and comfort to the Iranian hostage takers.

With the electorate focused on the dangers a president might face, Carter and his team wanted to focus voters on what Kennedy would be like as president. The crisis had helped change the debate from one of ideas and values to the practical business of handling crises as president. "We're going to go all out to win in Iowa and New Hampshire and convince the American people that a vote for Kennedy in the primaries is the equivalent of a vote for him for president," wrote Carter. "According to polls, Kennedy has the qualifications of an exciting candidate, but very negative image as an actual president. The more we change towards a general election attitude, the better off we would be."

Kennedy's strategy was to put his chips on Iowa, too. A win in the state that had launched Carter would be a tremendous blow. The problem was that Kennedy wasn't a very good campaigner. According to *Newsweek*, "He sometimes sounded like Dwight Eisenhower delivering Franklin Delano Roosevelt speeches, dropping malapropisms like 'fam farmilies' when he was trying to say, 'farm families.' Or he would say, 'Roll up your sleeves and your mothers and your fathers.' "

Kennedy also wasn't saying much when his words did more or less make sense. Bob Shrum, Kennedy's adviser, argued for a traditional, liberal campaign, while others in the Kennedy camp pushed Kennedy to simply speak of the idea of leadership. Kennedy was told he had to frame himself as presidential material and that he should present himself as a candidate of control, whereas Carter was a candidate who lacked control. That didn't lend itself to stirring the electorate.

One Iowan recognized this cautious switch. "When he came out here in 1978, it was like a shot of adrenaline to your heart. You had to be for him. But now, it's all gone." Kennedy lost the Iowa caucuses by a whopping 59 to 31 percent. Carter had not campaigned a day in the state. Kennedy's sister Eunice tried to comfort Kennedy as the results came in. "You still have me," she said. He responded: "I'd rather have Iowa."

Carter was convinced at this point that his strategists were right. Fighting Kennedy was making him stronger. He wrote in his diary about a conversation that he had with Clark Clifford: "Clifford said it would be a great achievement for me to defeat Kennedy, with momentum going into the general election. An opponent like Kennedy kept us on our toes." Clifford told the story of a fisherman who caught a delicious fish called turbot, but found that once in their vessel's tank the turbot got fat and lost its flavor. "Putting one small barracuda in the tank kept thousands of fish lean and tasty. And the barracuda ate only three or four fish."

Kennedy Shakes His Head Clear

After the Iowa caucus loss, the Kennedy forces gathered in his Senate office to figure out whether he should end his campaign. They took a vote: four said he should stay in, and four said he should drop out. The senator himself broke the tie by saying he was going to stay in. And he said, "Let's get ready and go."

Great. He was in the race, but he still didn't have a strategy. He didn't know why he was running, and voters responded in kind. He had to change tactics. After playing it safe, he would now run as a proud liberal. They decided to reset the campaign in a speech at Georgetown University. He'd stop temporizing and tiptoeing around and take on Carter on the issues and announce the guts of what he was really running for.

This is a familiar turn in a campaign, where the true believers call for the candidate to just be himself. Let Reagan be Reagan, they said after he lost in Iowa in 1980. Kennedy's loyalists were saying the same thing. He needed to stop being safe in order to win the general election for fear of being so safe that he would lose the primary.

In the Georgetown speech, Kennedy took on Carter's foreign policy stewardship. He noted that Hitler's conquest in France had not stopped public or presidential debate in 1940 and said, "If the Vietnam War taught us anything, it is precisely that when we do not debate our foreign policy, we may drift into deeper trouble." Kennedy said Carter had misread early warning signs about Afghanistan and had been caught by surprise when the Soviets invaded. "It is less than a year since the Vienna Summit, when President Carter kissed President [Leonid] Brezhnev on the cheek," said Kennedy. "We cannot afford a foreign policy based on the pangs of unrequited love." Kennedy also broke with mainstream public opinion by arguing that U.S. support for the Shah of Iran had invited the Iranian Revolution.

Kennedy also put forward a platform for the liberal wing of the Democratic Party based on its bedrock belief in promoting social progress and equality. He promoted controls on wages and prices, a six-month freeze on inflation, legislation for equality for women and gays, a bill that would bail out farmers and support for a public health system.

"Voters rally to more specific messages," his political director, Bill Carrick said. "They identify with 'em, with their hopes and aspirations." Kennedy was sending a message not just about the specifics but about the strength of his fight. He ended with the refrain, "I have only just begun to fight." He may have lost Iowa but he was not going away.

The speech won praise from unexpected quarters. "What a pleasure it is to see," the conservative columnist William Safire wrote, "the chastened man shake his head clear, get up off the floor, and by dint of the emotional and intellectual efforts of a powerful speech, give his presidential campaign life and give his political life meaning."

Carter responded to Kennedy by throwing the penalty flag. "The thrust of what Senator Kennedy has said throughout the last few weeks is very damaging to our country and to the establishment of our principles and the maintenance of them and to the achievement of our goals to keep the peace and get our hostages released."

Then Kennedy lost and kept losing. He lost Maine, New Hampshire, and Vermont.

Then came Illinois, where Kennedy had aligned himself with Chicago's mayor, Jane Byrne. The endorsement for Kennedy from Byrne, when it came in October 1979, was a bit of a coup. And it irritated Carter, who wrote in his journal, "Jane Byrne announced that she would support Kennedy, violating a direct, unequivocal commitment to Jack Watson, to Rosalynn and to me personally. This is a rare event in politics when somebody deliberately lies."

But by the time the primary rolled around, though, Byrne had proved unpredictable and irritated the local Democratic machine. Kennedy, who had promised to walk with her in the St. Patrick's Day Parade, literally distanced himself from her as they marched. As one account put it, He spent time "darting to one side and then the other, like a hummingbird." When you're losing, no one is nice. Along the parade route hecklers wouldn't let him forget the Chappaquiddick incident, shouting "Where's Mary Jo?"

Carter gloated after winning the primary in Illinois. "It's difficult for us to maintain the posture of an underdog."

Carter Does a Little Too Well

In New York, Carter, the national security president, had a stumble. The UN Security Council voted to reprimand Israel for building settlements on the occupied West Bank of the Jordan River, concluding that those settlements had no legal standing. Instead of abstaining, as the United States had in the past, Carter's UN ambassador voted yes. It was the principled thing to do, but it was very unpopular in New York. The outrage among New York's large Jewish community was immediate and painful. A number of Jewish leaders started to campaign against Carter.

Kennedy also ran an effective ad using the star of the popular sitcom *Archie Bunker's Place*. In the show, the main character was a Wallace voter, or what we might call a Tea Party voter today. But the actor, Carroll O'Connor, was an old-fashioned liberal. "Herbert Hoover hid out in the White House too," he said, looking directly at the camera. "Jimmy's depression is going to be worse than Herbert's." The spot ended with a tagline: "Kennedy for president. We gotta fight back."

The notion started to bounce around in political circles that maybe Carter had won those early primaries and caucuses because people were rallying around the office of the presidency, but that in truth, absent the false propping up of foreign crises, he was a flawed candidate. Kennedy's political man, Bill Carrick, said, "Carter looked like he was winning and then people woke up and said, 'Oh my God, he's winning.' "

Kennedy followed up with a win in Connecticut, which meant New York wasn't just a fluke. This put a little blood in his mouth. "You've gotta come out and face the American people sometime," Kennedy said to Carter, who was still running that Rose Garden strategy.

Carter Goes There

Heading into the Pennsylvania primary, Carter and his team were jittery. Pat Caddell, his pollster, remembers it this way, "That's when I pulled the trigger on the character issue. Yes, it would do irreparable damage if we talk about Chappaquiddick. He'll never forgive us. But we'd have lost Pennsylvania by twenty points or more. Even with the delegate lead, what happens if we lose all the remaining primaries?"

Carter had been poking at the character issue, emphasizing in ads that he was a husband, father, and president, three jobs he'd done with distinction. Talking about fatherhood and monogamy was an implicit criticism of Kennedy. In Pennsylvania the criticism got explicit. In a series of spots, average people looked into the camera and said about Kennedy, "I don't trust him" and "I don't believe him."

Kennedy beat Carter by only a whisker (45.68 to 45.40 percent), but the incumbent's comeback helped rescue him from free fall. The two traded the remaining primaries, Carter winning even after an April hostage rescue mission in Iran failed miserably, when helicopters failed and crashed in the desert, killing U.S. servicemen.

In the end, Carter won enough delegates to be renominated. Kennedy didn't concede. He'd had those bursts at the end, and if it was true that Carter had been artificially shielded by patriotism during those moments of crisis, perhaps Kennedy could make a case to the delegates.

Taking It to New York

On June 5, 1980, Kennedy visited Carter in the White House. "I met with Kennedy, who came in apparently completely obsessed," wrote Carter. "It took him about an hour to fumble around and say we still had issues dividing us and we needed to have a personal debate in front of the TV cameras in order to resolve those differences." Other accounts of the meeting say it was much more acrimonious, with

Carter accusing Kennedy of essentially helping Ronald Reagan by tearing down Carter during the primaries.

At the end of the meeting, Kennedy refused to endorse Carter if Carter was nominated at the convention. And he said that unless Carter debated him, he would not throw his support behind Carter and he would fight him all the way to the convention. In his diary, Carter said that it was the first time the electorate had ever rebuffed a Kennedy, and he realized the senator couldn't get over it.

Carter considered Kennedy's idea of having a debate, because he wanted to be done with him. Plus, if he had a debate, he could use the free airtime to turn toward the general election competition with Ronald Reagan. His cabinet agreed it was a good idea. Then Carter talked to Vice President Walter Mondale, who hated the idea. A debate would elevate Kennedy. Once elevated, he would withdraw his promise to drop out and go to the convention.

Carter changed his mind and called Tom Donilon, telling him that Kennedy was going to contest the convention. It was Donilon's job to make sure the delegates who had been pledged to Carter would stay with Carter. Those were the people Kennedy was going to try to flip with every argument and inducement he could think of. Donilon said later that after he put down the phone, he went down the hall to the bathroom and threw up.

When delegates arrived in New York City, some were furious that at the convention Kennedy would try and destroy the chief executive of his own party. Others, though, were susceptible to Kennedy's argument that the late primaries had uncovered that Carter was weak and would lose to Reagan.

Democrats were concerned about unity. Mo Udall, the wry Arizona congressman, spoke at the opening of the convention and said, "Let me recommend Dr. Udall's patented unity medicine. Take one tablespoon, close your eyes and repeat, 'President Ronald Reagan.'"

Kennedy's strategy to flip the Carter delegates was to get rid of the "robot rule," which pledged delegates to the candidate they were assigned to by their state's primary or caucus. Kennedy had several powerful senators on his side including Daniel Patrick Moynihan, Scoop Jackson, and Robert Byrd.

Delegates were not bound by the robot rule on rules votes. So if Kennedy could persuade the delegates to overturn the robot rule, that would be a proxy vote for the ultimate nominating vote.

Donilon had to win the rules fight. Because the Carter team controlled the rules process and controlled the schedule, they wanted to make sure to have the rules fight before Kennedy had a chance to speak to the convention. If Kennedy gave a big, rousing speech, whipping up the troops—as he had in Memphis and at Georgetown—then Carter could face a revolt, lose the vote on the robot rule, unbinding those delegates, and then those delegates would vote for Kennedy.

To block Kennedy, the Carter team deployed the "gerbils," as they called their young campaign team. They were outfitted with the latest computer and radio technology to manage the floor, checking in on those delegates, making sure they weren't going to slip away somehow and vote for Kennedy on the robot rule. When the vote came, the work had paid off. Some delegates abandoned Carter, but he won by well over six hundred votes. "As Donilon walked through the crowd of people in our command headquarters," Carter wrote. "I could hear them shouting, 'Donilon for president.' "

Kennedy watched from his hotel room and decided that he would withdraw. He spoke to Carter. Carter asked Kennedy if he would join him in the famous show of unity on the platform, and Kennedy didn't answer.

The Dream Will Never Die

Though Kennedy was out of the race, he was still scheduled to speak. It turned out to be perhaps his most famous speech, validating the Carter strategists who had made sure he didn't give it before the vote on the robot rule.

"The commitment I seek is not to outworn ideas, but to values that will never wear out. Programs may sometimes become obsolete. But the ideal of fairness always endures. Circumstances may change, but the work of compassion must continue. It is surely correct that we cannot solve problems by throwing money at them. But it is also correct that we dare not throw out our national problems onto a scrap heap of inattention and indifference. The poor may be out of political fashion. But they are not without human needs. The middle class may be angry. But they have not lost the dream that all Americans can advance together."

Kennedy was answering Carter's argument from back at the Kennedy Library in October of the previous year. The Kennedy flame had not died out. There were values and fights that would never die, the enduring stuff of the Democratic party. It was Kennedy's concluding words that became so famous. "For me, a few hours ago, this campaign came to an end. For all those whose cares have been our concern, the work goes on. The cause endures. The hope still lives. And the dream shall never die."

The auditorium erupted. The applause and cheers went on, according to one account, for half an hour. Delegates repeatedly chanted, "We want Ted, we want Ted!" The band, which was under control of the Carter forces, kicked up "Happy Days Are Here Again" to try to drown out the calls for Ted. "Carter's hour of triumph was shadowed by a rush of nostalgia for his defeated rival and by the plain unenthusiasm of his party for him or his prospects," said *Newsweek*.

Unlike Reagan, who received the same kind of adulation in loss in 1976, Kennedy could not rise to the presidential ranks afterward. The Reagan era capped that stage of liberalism and gave the final blow to the old New Deal coalition. But the Kennedy message was energetic and popular enough to challenge a sitting president. The Reagan era ushered in a conservative period in America, but Kennedy identified a core liberal constituency that was alive inside it. The idea that a liberal economic message could have attracted the blue-collar voters who left the Democratic Party for Reagan would remain a liberal dream unfulfilled.

Disunity Moment

Kennedy had one more bitter pill: the unity moment that Carter had talked about on the call. Both men would stand on the platform and raise their hands. Kennedy practiced this bit of theater with Bob Shrum in his hotel room at the Waldorf Astoria.[378] Shrum forced Kennedy to do it over and over again. As they arrived at Madison Square Garden for Carter's acceptance speech, Shrum said, "Don't forget" to Senator Kennedy.

Carter's speech didn't rival Kennedy's. How could it? When he tried to praise Hubert Horatio Humphrey, stalwart of liberal causes from Minnesota, he praised Hubert Horatio Hornblower.

When Kennedy finally did come to the stage, as he'd promised, the two shook hands. To many, it looked perfunctory. And that hand raising—that hand clasping and raising the hands up in the air—that never happened. Carter wrote in his diary, Kennedy "seemed to have had a few drinks, which I probably would have done myself. He was fairly cool and reserved. I thought it was adequate. But the press made a big deal of it." Indeed, the press did make a big deal of it, because it didn't look like this was a unified party at all.

It had obviously in the end been a disaster to not try to head off Ted Kennedy before he launched his campaign. Hamilton Jordan, so cocky at that Eastern Shore meeting, came to recognize this. On June 25, 1980, he wrote an eyes-only memo for Carter addressing the problems facing the campaign. "The Kennedy challenge hurt us very badly, not only within the Democratic party, but with the electorate as a whole. Because the process had been going on for a year the American people today are sick of the process and tired of the candidates. Kennedy's sustained and exaggerated attacks on your record and his unrealistic promises have alienated key groups in the Democratic party by obscuring the solid record we have. The Kennedy attacks reinforced by the media's natural tendency to see everything in the context of the campaign, have made you seem like the manipulative politician bent on reelection at all costs, and not the man—and the president—that you are. For all of the reasons presented here, we have come out of this primary year and the unsuccessful Kennedy challenge not enhanced or strengthened by the contest, but damaged severely."

Nineteen eighty was a bad year for the party. Conservative Republican Ronald Reagan was elected 51 to 41 percent, a landslide. And the GOP gained the majority in the Senate. It was the first time since 1954, the Republican Party controlled either house of Congress. Many years later, Jordan was asked to assess the damage the Kennedy challenge had caused, and despite the economy, the hostages and Reagan's skills as a campaigner he replied, "It was the single critical factor in his defeat."

1968—What Kind of a Nut Is George Wallace?

"We'll Let The Overcoat Out All The Way, And The Robe Will Hardly Show At All"

The Herblock Foundation

Nuts and Kooks for Wallace

On November 3, 1967, aides for Alabama governor George Wallace hauled his 1,500-pound bulletproof lectern onto the stage at the Orange County Fairgrounds Pavilion. For ten days in California he'd been railing from behind that barricade in what analysts deemed a fruitless effort to get on the ballot as an independent candidate in all fifty states.

The segregationist rallied the crowd of three thousand to his message of states' rights and his promises to get tough on crime. "If you're molested when you leave here tonight, the molester will be free before you are out of the hospital."

For forty-five minutes he fulminated. He was a balled-up fist of a man with deep set eyes, black, caterpillar eyebrows applied to a face that looked at times like an angry parsnip. At five foot seven he stood erect as if trying to argue out every last inch of height he might get. When not fulminating, he made preparations to fulminate—husbanding grievances. He had the best grievance garden of any modern politician. He tended it in quiet, while other men slept, and then used cuttings to feed his entertaining sessions on the stump. "They've never paid any attention to anything that the people of your state and my state did or said in the past," Wallace told audiences. "They ignored us and looked down their nose at us and called us everything under the sun. And I am sick and tired of it and I resent it."

Wallace really only had one riff, but he chopped it up in different ways—a master at just-in-time packaging. He fed bite-size versions to reporters on his campaign plane and at press conferences. He railed rat-tat-tat against the "asinine" Supreme Court and "pointy-headed intellectuals" in Washington who made decisions for communities they knew nothing about. He abused, foreign aid (money "down a rat hole"), open housing, pseudointellectual professors, rioters, anarchists, communists, "the left-wing press," and the world generally, all arrayed against the average workingman.[379] He said he was "sick and tired of big government telling us when to get up and when to go to sleep."

Wallace pointed to the anti-war and civil rights protests and called on the attorney general of the United States to recognize the difference "between dissent and overt acts of treason"; Those who supported a Viet Cong victory "ought to be grabbed by the beard, taken before the grand jury and indicted."[380]

When you bristle that much, you're going to need an army, and at the Orange County rally, it looked like Wallace had recruits. A number of the local police wore Wallace buttons. Some signed up to join his new party. The candidate also traveled with sixteen buzz-cut members of the Alabama state police, who were carrying .38-caliber pistols and looking over every passerby like they were assessing just what kind of sleeper hold they'd like to put them in. One bruiser visited San Francisco's Haight-Ashbury district to look at the hippies and visit a couple of topless clubs. "I've read in the Bible about Sodom and Gomorrah," he concluded. "And I'd say that San Francisco is about to have another earthquake."[381]

Wallace's audiences prized his candor and his lack of political correctness. "You don't have to worry about figuring out where he stands," said one voter. "He tells it like it is."[382]

Some in the Orange County audience pushed to stop him. "Sieg Heil," shouted someone. The crowd responded, "We want Wallace!" Outside a placard read that Wallace is "99 44/100 per cent pure... Bigot." Another proclaimed him "Imperial Wizard." After a long while, security walked the protesters out as the crowd sang a chorus of "America." This call and response of the nation's cultural argument interrupted many of the governor's speeches.

To register voters for the American Independent Party, the Wallace caravan started at 8:00 a.m. and rolled until 11:00 p.m. Each stop kicked off with a country music band; then Chill Wills, a gravelly voiced Western movie actor, took the stage to promote the candidate—but not for too long, because while Wills's occasionally tearful exhortations in favor of the candidate were moving, they were also a sign that he was in the bag, up to his earlobes in drink and very likely to wheel around on those cowboy boots and tumble over. Asked to sign an autograph by a mother for her son, he asked, "So what's the little bastard's name?"

"Day after day Wallace harangues and tours, harangues and tours," wrote Drew Pearson and Jack Anderson in the *Washington Post*.[383] The governor believed the riots in America's cities and the peace demonstrations had created an appetite for his tough medicine. "Someday I'll be President of that," Wallace said flying to California, his rickety DC-6 wobbling over the snow-peaked Cascade Mountains in Oregon. As the plane hit turbulence, he danced in and out of the cockpit, telling the pilots, "Now you be careful, you may have the next president on board." (On the next leg, the cockpit doors were locked.)[384]

"Stand Up for America" Wallace preached—and who could disagree with that?—but elbowing his way on to the California ballot required getting 66,059 signatures, a big task. It required finding voters who were registered to one of the two parties and getting them to switch their registrations. Every registration form had to be executed in the presence of a person designated by county election officials as a deputy registrar of voters. Wallace recruited two hundred registrars for the Orange County rally alone, signing people to the rolls from 6:30 p.m. till midnight.

California had the earliest legal deadline for ballot qualification. If Wallace made it there, it would help his efforts in the other forty-nine states. But he wasn't doing so well, in part because the state election officials dragged their feet and didn't help with the complex process. They belonged to one of the two existing parties. They didn't like the competition.

Working to meet the January 2, 1968 registration deadline in California was a transplanted team of fifty Alabama irregulars, so called because it is irregular to have members of a state legislature working to get a person on the ballot in a different state.

Wallace's floor leader in the Alabama State Senate led his registration drive in Orange County. The Alabama superintendent of banks ran the Sacramento-area effort. Dave Benton, the thick-armed director of Alabama's Healing Arts Board (the regulatory agency for chiropractors) helped coordinate each campaign stop.

Wallace's wife, Lurleen, served as the sitting governor of Alabama. She had been elected after her husband served the maximum two terms. Lurleen Wallace, let everyone know that it was okay for state officials to work for her husband. "I know that what we are trying to accomplish in California would be pleasing to the people of Alabama," she said.

The California corps included Alabama businessmen in shirtsleeves and black glasses whose ventures were regulated by Lurleen's administration.

Anyone who signed on with Wallace was aligning him- or herself with a party that had no national or local status, no elected or selected leaders, and no actual platform. That was just fine with many of the new Wallace fans. They were outsiders. His campaign relied on the help of the John Birchers, conspiracists, and generally extravagant people whom even the candidate described as "nuts and kooks." For them, Ronald Reagan wasn't conservative enough. They complained that he signed a bill "plotted by the Communist Party," providing for bilingual instruction for Mexican-American children. Reporter Carl Greenberg quoted one saying that "if you do not sneer at patriotism" you'll back Wallace because "Reagan is taking the country down the road to slavery.[385]

At one of Wallace's stops, a VFW post commander hung around reporters to make sure they noted that he and twenty-four of his men had carried arms to the meeting place that night but had kept them in their cars after the police advised them their help wasn't needed. "But there'll be a day," he promised.[386] Reporters were not sure if it was wishful thinking or prudence that made him say that.

Dan Carter, in his Wallace history *The Politics of Rage,* tells a story of a California Wallace volunteer who reported he would be unavailable to work for the Wallace campaign on the weekend. He would be tied up with "maneuvers." Asked if he was in the National Guard, he said no. "We've got our own group," he said lifting the tarp in the back of his truck to expose a cache of weaponry. Are you worried about the communist takeover? he was asked. "Hell no, the Rockefeller interests—you know, the Trilateral Commission—that's what we're worried about."

On December 28, the *Los Angeles Times* banner front-page headline announced, WALLACE DOES IT—PARTY REGISTRATION MAY HIT 75,000. The actual registration total exceeded 100,000. A California poll of his supporters revealed that "his appeal is closely proportionate among presently registered California Democrats and Republicans."

The California victory inspired Wallace supporters throughout the country, and in 1968, building on the California foundation, Wallace was able to put the American Independent Party on the ballot in every state in the nation.[387]

He would go on to shock the political sages, winning ten million votes, 23 percent of the total, adding up to 46 electoral votes from five southern states.

In 1968 George Wallace was a nationalist outsider promising a restoration of real America. He was suspicious of both parties and handy with quick and easy solutions to intractable problems. If only the clueless people in charge had a little common sense.

The governor appealed to voter anger and frustration in all parts of the country—not just in the South—anger about the pace of cultural change, the urban riots, the muddle in Vietnam, and the feeling that the federal government didn't have a handle on things; if it did have a handle, it was on the spoon they were using to force their dumb, blunt medicine on the American people. "Wallace almost single-handedly alerted the national custodians to a massive, unsuspected, unanswered constituency, a great submerged continent of discontent," wrote Marshall Frady who covered Wallace for Newsweek.

But Wallace did more than capture anger.

Wallace perfected the use of the racial dog whistle, though in his case he played something more like the pan flute. He was a virtuoso. He keyed on white fears of blacks in the South and the North with his jeremiads against crime and unelected limousine liberal" judges. Other national politicians would follow that path explicitly and implicitly for the next forty years.

Standing Athwart History and Keeping Negroes Out

In 1963, when Wallace gave his inaugural address as governor, he delivered his most notorious public line: "In the name of the greatest people that have ever trod this earth, I draw the line in the dust and toss the gauntlet before the feet of tyranny, and I say segregation now, segregation tomorrow, segregation forever." The stand grew out of his failed 1958 campaign for governor. After losing, he declared "I was out-niggered, and I will never be out-niggered again."

By the time Wallace was collecting signatures in 1968, he was nearly ten years into his ascent as the nation's most prominent opponent to forced integration. In 1959 Wallace refused to cooperate with the U.S. Civil Rights Commission, designed to investigate voting rights abuses. William F. Buckley Jr. defined conservatives as those who stand athwart history yelling stop; Wallace literally did so. On June 11, 1963, at the University of Alabama, Wallace stood in the schoolhouse door, temporarily blocking the admission of two black students who had legally enrolled at the university. Although Wallace soon backed down, footage of the event was broadcast on national television

On March 7, 1965, "Bloody Sunday," voting rights advocates attempted to march from Selma to the state capital, Montgomery. Wallace had tried to prevent the march by calling on the highway patrol. State troopers used tear gas and violence, including clubs, to hold back the marchers.

Wallace was enough of a national figure by 1964 that when he entered three Democratic primaries, he did surprisingly well, garnering 34 percent of the vote in Wisconsin, 30 percent in Indiana, and 45 percent in Maryland.

Riots Become Wallace Rallies

In 1965, the riots in the Watts section of Los Angeles initiated a period of civil unrest over poverty, inequality, and racial discrimination that lasted the rest of the decade. Sparked by a police incident, the outbreak of violence in Watts led to thirty-four deaths. The conditions that had led to the outburst were exacerbated by passage in November 1964 of Proposition 14 on the California ballot, overturning the Rumford Fair Housing Act, which had established equality of opportunity for black home buyers. Leaders of the effort to overthrow the housing bill became the backbone of the Wallace effort in California.

In 1967, riots flared in Detroit and Newark, New Jersey. In Newark, twenty-six people were killed in five days; in Detroit, forty-three died. George Romney, the governor of Michigan, had to call out the National Guard. The image of a city block wrapped in smoke became a regular feature on the news programs Americans watched at dinnertime.

Wallace was convinced this would create a constituency for his candidacy. "No one doubts that Wallace had more than a mere notion of running," wrote NAACP leader Roy Wilkins in the *Los Angeles Times* on August 14, 1967, "but his little helpers, the rioters and the looters, in Madison Avenue language, have 'finalized' his decision."

Wallace came to power with the help of people who were committed, adamant racists. The Klan, the White Citizens' Councils, the Liberty Lobby, and other groups founded around segregation and racial hatred all worked for his election. In some cases Wallace attended their rallies. He never attended a Klan rally, although at an Alabama Wallace rally in 1968, the governor was filmed shaking hands with a wizard of the KKK. His security man took the film from ABC correspondent Sam Donaldson and refused to give it back. The candidate said he regretted the incident—by which he meant the theft of the film, not the communing with the KKK.

The leader of his California effort, William Shearer, was the secretary-treasurer of the California Association of Citizens' Councils, a white supremacist organization. He said segregation was "necessary—the same as the American Revolution was necessary."[388]

Still, Wallace insisted that he wasn't a racist. He was standing up for America, quoting the founders, and appealing to voters' proper and deeply ingrained skepticism about a big federal government.

Wallace presented the electorate, the press, and politicians with a dilemma: while he may have been a racist, did that make his supporters racists? If you agreed with what he was saying on Vietnam or about communists or even if he spoke to your fears about riots in the streets, did that mean you were signing up for his view that people with black skin should be separate in America because they were of inferior makeup and character?

Wallace voters didn't believe everything Wallace did. The fact that he was supported by the most loathsome bigots who ever wriggled out of the ooze didn't condemn those voters who simply thought the federal government should not make decisions for them. But he created a link between those voters, which meant that any other politician who wanted to appeal to the less objectionable group was in danger of playing footsie with the one that had white sheets in the coat closet and not just in the linen drawer. Wallace spoke in a coded language that let voters know he understood their race-based fears. His appeal was like the code contained in the tiny Confederate flags that waved at his rallies.

"Wallace constantly talked about defending the integrity of neighborhoods and neighborhood schools," said his biographer Dan Carter, "[knowing] that everyone was aware he was talking about white neighborhoods, or defending white schools."

He was not the first to do this, but he was very good at it. Race was his subtext in an appealing message around the issues of busing, education, federal overreach, antielitism, and anticommunism.

A Wallace campaign advertisement opens with the shot of the back of a school bus, white children looking out the window, pressed against the glass like they might be trying to get out. "Why are more and more millions of Americans turning to Governor Wallace?" the ad asks. "Follow as your children are bussed across town." Then the ad cuts to a picture of Wallace talking about local control. He seems like a reasonable fellow behind that podium in a suit and tie. Then the narrator returns with bad news: "Why are more and more millions of Americans turning to Governor Wallace? Open a small business and find out." At that point in the ad, the plate glass window of a small TV repair shop is broken and a conflagration ensues.

Wallace found support for his message outside the South. William S. White wrote in the *Washington Post* on July 19, 1967: "Wallace was in a fair way to cut deeply into traditional Democratic low-income white wards in the North, because it is these whites who are more intimately touched by integrated housing and who are in job competition with the Negroes. The Newarks are now immensely sharpening these Negro-poor white abrasions and it is obvious that many angry white laborers are turning from their old association with the Democrats toward Wallace in fear and frustration."

Samuel Lubell pointed out that Wallace's support among northern voters was strongest in white neighborhoods that abutted heavily black districts.[389]

While Wallace did not make overt racial appeals, he drew bright lines with his rhetoric so it was clear which side the blacks were on and which side the whites were on.

A former Alabama senator told Wallace biographer Marshall Frady, "It's conceivable that he could win a state like Illinois or even California when he puts the hay down where the goats can get at it. He can use all the other issues—law and order, running your own schools, protecting property rights—and never mention race. But people will know he's telling them, 'A nigger's trying to get your job, trying to move into your neighborhood.' What Wallace is doing is talking to them in a kind of shorthand, a kind of code."

He was very hard to pin down when he started to send the subliminal signals. On CBS's *Face the Nation*, reporters were nearly sputtering as he dodged and weaved:

Wallace: I don't know why Negro citizens attack and assault one another—

Reporter: Are you saying it's only Negro citizens, Governor? I mean, is that your point?

Wallace: Am I saying what?

Reporter: That it's only Negro citizens. You keep telling me—

Wallace: I'm saying that the high crime rate [in Alabama] comes about because of the high predominance among Negro citizens against each other. And that is an absolute fact. I was a judge for six years in Alabama and I know...

Reporter: Governor, aren't you really saying that you can make safe...the streets for white people but you don't know why you can't make them safe for Negroes?

Wallace: I'm not saying that.

Round and round it went with Wallace. Reporters couldn't pin him down. But they drew conclusions anyway. Historian Dan Carter quotes NBC's Douglas Kiker, a native Southerner: "George Wallace had seemingly looked out upon those white Americans north of Alabama and suddenly been awakened by a blinding vision: 'They all hate black people, all of them. They're all afraid, all of them. Great God! That's it! They're all Southern! The Whole United States is Southern!'"

The cartoonists and television comedy shows had a field day with Wallace. On NBC's *Rowan & Martin's Laugh-In* there was the line, "George Wallace your sheets are ready."[390] In a Herblock cartoon a tailor hems the long coat of a man wearing a Ku Klux Klan hood. On the coat is written "law and order talk," but the hem doesn't go all the way down to cover the bottom of the white sheet he wears beneath the coat. On the sheet is written "racism." On the man's top hat read the words "states' rights."[391] The hat covers his KKK hood.

Wallace's states' rights argument rested first on constitutional grounds. Like Barry Goldwater and others who opposed the Civil Rights Act of 1964 or the Voting Rights Act of 1965, Wallace did so on the theory that it was not within the proper power of the central government to compel states to run their domestic institutions a certain way.

The *Los Angeles Times* editorialized: "Wallace denies that he is a racist, or that he would run as a racist candidate. His talking points for the last four years have been opposition to 'big government.' But while he has tried to embrace several issues... there is no doubt that Wallace's primary targets are those federal laws, actions and court decisions which have worked against segregation in the South. Wallace's forte, however disguised in high rhetoric, is to play upon the fears, frustrations and bigotry of the discontented and the ignorant."

What gave Wallace cover was that he had plenty of targets in his "law and order" campaign other than African-Americans protesting in the big cities: the hippies, anarchists, and communists. "A group of anarchists lay down in front of [Lyndon Johnson's] automobile and threatened his personal safety," he told crowds. "The president of the United States! Well I want you to tell you if you're to make me the president and I go to California and some of them lie down in front of my automobile, it'll be the last automobile they ever lie down in front of."

Wallace supporters were additionally irritated by the mobs of smelly hippies because they forced Americans raised on World War II victory stories to confront the brutal fact that America could no longer assert its will across the world.

Wallace complained about the criminals who were released too easily and the permissive culture that made excuses for them instead of treating them like the savages they were. If "policemen could run this country for about two years," he said, "they'd straighten it out."[392]

Theodore White recorded the signs for Wallace in Chicago that spoke to the emotions he aroused: "I worked to buy my house, George, protect our home." "News media unfair." "Law and Wallace." "Wallace—friend of the working man." "Voters ring the bell of liberty with Wallace." "Give America back to the people, vote Wallace."

Pointy Head Versus the Common Man

Wallace loved locking arms with regular people. The two parties had ignored their worries. Wallace elevated them, by identifying with their resentment. "They've never paid any attention to the aspiration of the average man on the street, to the oil worker, to the shipyard worker, the autoworker, the communications worker, the businessman, the white-collar worker. They've said no, we're going to bus your children. We're going to tell you who to sell your property to." He told an audience at the Virginia Polytechnic Institute that he had more faith in taxi drivers to know what was right for the country than he did in the "elite cult" of "ivory tower folks with pointy heads who couldn't park their bicycle straight."

On foreign policy, he said, even the "rednecks" had enough sense "to know Castro and Mao Tse-tung were communists when the theoreticians were praising them as agrarian reformers."

To bolster his point that he was in touch with the common man, Wallace very often referred to polls that showed support for him. "He never seems to forget the results of a favorable primary or poll," wrote Gene Roberts of the *New York Times*. "Even the most obscure. 'This TV station in Sacramento took a poll, 5,000 people called in and 68 percent were for me. They really like me in Sacramento. We're going good all over. And let me tell you about the poll two weeks ago in Houston...'"

Heaven help the pollster Wallace didn't like. In June 1967, Gallup showed that Wallace had a 58 percent unfavorable rating and only 24 percent favorable.[393] "They lie when they poll," he said. "They are trying to forge public opinion in the country, and professional polls are owned by eastern monied interests, and they lie. They're trying to rig an election."[394]

Noisy protesters showed up at nearly every Wallace rally to make sure he knew there was genuine anger behind those unfavorable poll numbers. A long-haired student in faded dungarees and sandals held up a sign: "Support Mental Illness—Wallace for President."[395] In Ohio, a thousand protesters greeted him. At some rallies, anyone with long hair or casual dress was kept out.[396] Placards read, "If you liked Hitler, you'll love Wallace" and "Wallace is Rosemary's baby." Protesters held their arms straight out, forming a Nazi salute. Chairs were thrown. Punches, too. One woman reportedly went to greet the candidate and put a lit cigarette in his hand. African-Americans held up signs that read "Black power" and "The world is watching." People wore sheets and paper bags over their heads.

Wallace often delighted in these confrontations. He promised to sign the sandals of the hippie protesters. He said they looked lovely and then mock-corrected himself, "Oh, I see that you're a he and not a she." The only four letter words they didn't know were W-O-R-K and S-O-A-P, he said. Wallace welcomed protesters, wrote the *Chicago Tribune*, "believing their presence will bring him voters from fed-up Americans." Sometimes he even blew kisses toward hecklers and cried: "They got me a million votes!"[397] Aides joked that if the protesters didn't show up, Wallace would have to hire them.

"Let me say this much," Wallace would warn. "Have your fun now, because after November fifth you are *through* in this country."

He's Not Just a Noisy Gong

Wallace said there wasn't "a dime's worth of difference" between Republicans and Democrats on major issues. He called the Republicans and Democrats "Tweedle Dee and Tweedle Dum."

The governor never had a real shot at the presidency. He did, however, have a shot at chaos. If he kept Humphrey or Nixon from getting a majority of the electoral votes required to win, the vote would move into the House of Representatives for the first time in 144 years. He wouldn't be president, under such a scenario, but he would be kingmaker. He'd give his endorsement in return for support on his key issues, like stopping forced school integration and housing reforms.

Wallace threatened Nixon the most. He was such a threat, columnists regularly speculated that Lyndon Johnson had quietly encouraged Wallace to run to undermine Republicans. Without Wallace, Nixon could be confident that Democrats in the South were still angry enough at Johnson and Democrats for the Civil Rights Act that they would never vote for him or his party. With Wallace in the race, those voters had another person they could follow other than Nixon.

If voters were going to leave Nixon, it would be over two issues: integration and law and order. Wallace denounced the Supreme Court's 1954 decision in *Brown v. Board of Education,* which outlawed racial segregation in the nation's public schools. Nixon accepted the decision but objected to measures taken by the Johnson administration to encourage integration. On law and order, the differences were hard to see, but Wallace claimed Nixon was just weak tea compared to the Wallace authentic brew.

Nixon wanted to sap Wallace's strength without actually directly antagonizing the Wallace voters, so he argued that a vote for Wallace was a wasted vote. Worse, a vote for him might help elect Humphrey by denying Nixon electoral majority. That meant more busing. More federal meddling. More drift in Vietnam.

Conservatives also criticized Wallace as a big spender. He supported, among other things, an expansion of Social Security payments, and allowing older people to deduct drugs and other medical expenses. A poll of conservatives by *Human Events* magazine found almost unanimous opposition to Wallace.

Democrats "at first were inclined to view the Wallace bid with some complacency and even smugness," wrote David Broder in June 1967.[398] But as the former governor rose, they realized a lot of the cars parked at his rallies had Democratic bumper stickers on them. Wallace was making inroads among white lunchpail voters in Northern industrial cities who saw an emerging African-American working class as a threat to their livelihoods. They bristled as well at rising taxes and the squeeze of inflation of the Johnson-Humphrey years. Though Wallace didn't address those issues as much, his promotion of simple commonsense solutions gave voters hope that he could lick those problems, too.

Wallace soon enjoyed the imitation that comes with success. Nixon and Humphrey were trying so hard to copy Wallace on the law-and-order issue, San Francisco mayor Joseph Alioto finally concluded: "None of the candidates is running for president. They're all running for sheriff."

Nixon and his running mate, Spiro Agnew, also started to sound like Wallace on the stump. The trick for Nixon and all future candidates who hoped to benefit from the "Wallace factor" was to exploit the grievances he stoked while not straying into the racism at the heart of his message. On the other hand, they didn't want to miss people's legitimate fears about law and order.

Richard Nixon spoke this language at the Republican National Convention in 1968, in Miami, where he beat out Ronald Reagan for the affection of the Southern delegates. His ally was 1948 Dixiecrat candidate Strom Thurmond of South Carolina, who had the credentials with the Wallace base. In return for giving Thurmond vetting power over his vice presidential pick and promising to protect South Carolina textile workers, Nixon got a trusted stamp or approval in the South.

In one meeting with the Southern delegation orchestrated by Thurmond, Nixon showed how he could do the Wallace wink. Without ever explicitly renouncing his own past support for desegregation, Nixon got it across to his listeners that in the White House he would do as little as possible to execute federal court mandates. We know this because the *Miami Herald* asked a member of the Florida delegation to carry a concealed tape recorder. Nixon said that as president he would not "satisfy some professional civil rights group, or something like that."

George Wallace's successful manipulation of racial and social issues gave birth to imitation and suspicion in future campaigns. In Ronald Reagan's 1980 campaign kick-off tour, he visited the Neshoba County Fair in Mississippi and spoke about state's rights. The fairgrounds were just a few miles from Philadelphia, Mississippi, a town associated with the 1964 murders of three civil rights workers from the North. Liberals heard a deliberate eco of Wallace's appeal to white voters.

The president's men defended the reference as libertarian, merely a nod to the country's founding principle of local control. Critics couldn't get past the symbolism and coded language. The Reagan team manipulated symbol better than anyone. How could they not know what they were flirting with? "Reagan took the Republican Party from virtual irrelevance to the ascendancy it now enjoys," wrote William Raspberry. "The essence of that transformation, we shouldn't forget, is the party's successful wooing of the race-exploiting Southern Democrats formerly known as Dixiecrats. And Reagan's Philadelphia appearance was an important bouquet in that courtship."[399]

Bill Clinton defended his 1994 crime against charges that he had emphasized law and order issues to appeal to white voters worried about the black inner city. When Donald Trump campaigned in 2016 by talking about crime committed by illegal immigrants critics said he was making a Wallace-like appeal to the portion of the electorate that doesn't like people with skin of a different color. He also re-Tweeted messages from white supremacists. When he was slow to condemn groups aligned with the Klan, Republicans in Washington blanched. It looked like he was playing dumb, so as not to lose the bigot vote.

What had changed since Wallace's time was that political leaders were quicker to call out coded behavior than they had been in 1964."If a person wants to be the nominee of the Republican Party, there can be no evasion and no games," Speaker Ryan said, criticizing Trump. "They must reject any group or cause that is built on bigotry. This party does not prey on people's prejudices. We appeal to their highest ideals. This is the party of Lincoln. We believe all people are equal in the eyes of God and our government. This is fundamental, and if someone wants to be our nominee, they must understand this."

The Wallace Collapse

The violence of 1968 pushed Wallace higher in the polls. In April, Rev. Martin Luther King Jr. was assassinated in Memphis, which uncorked chaos in a hundred American cities. At that point Wallace was polling at 9 percent. Within days after the assassination of Robert F. Kennedy in early June, he polled at 16 percent. After the violence of the Democratic National Convention later in the summer in Chicago, his numbers jumped again. By mid-September, Wallace garnered 21 percent. On that kind of climb, he'd get to 30 percent by voting day. That would probably throw the election into the House.

Wallace was doing well enough to make Nixon worry that since the Democrats controlled the House, it was almost certain that Humphrey would make a deal with Wallace if the election wound up there. Toward the end of the campaign Nixon challenged Humphrey to agree that the winner of the popular vote should get the support of the loser, but Humphrey never responded; he was no dummy.[400]

Pundits didn't think Wallace could be stopped by the normal political roadblocks. "It is not an issues movement," wrote Max Lerner in the *Los Angeles Times*, "except for the one overarching 'law-and-order' issue. Instead it is a mood movement. Its mood is one of overwhelming protest and rage, curiously vigilantist despite its law-and-order rhetoric. That is why it cannot be fought as trade-union leaders are trying to fight it, by focusing on bread-and-butter arguments. Since it is an irrational movement, of recoil and fears, it cannot be met by appeals to reason."[401]

This sounds very modern. Liberals complain that Republicans have tricked white working-class voters by getting them to vote on cultural issues like abortion and opposition to same-sex marriage and based on their economic self-interest.

The pundits were wrong about Wallace though. Bread-and-butter appeals did work. As Wallace rose, unions sent out sixteen million fliers in states like Michigan, Pennsylvania, Ohio, Indiana, Illinois, and California.[402] "George Wallace could cost you $1,000 a year," said one, arguing that the average income in Alabama was $1,000 below the national average. The fliers also pointed out that Alabama's unemployment rate was higher than the nation's as a whole.

The union fliers made emotional appeals, too. One included graphic pictures of riots in the South and asked, "Do you want police dog, billy club and fire bomb law and order?" Another said Wallace had "no program other than racism."

"Let's lay it on the line," Hubert Humphrey told a Detroit audience. "George Wallace's pitch is racism. If you want to feel damn mean and ornery, find some other way to do it, but don't sacrifice your country. George Wallace has been engaged in union-busting whenever he's had the chance... and any union man who votes for him is not a good union man."[403]

Humphrey also helped draw Northern audiences away from Wallace by changing his position on the Vietnam War. On September 30, 1968, the Vice President came out against president Johnson's handling of the war. His numbers improved. Then Johnson called a halt to bombing, and Humphrey's numbers went up further.

Toward the end of the 1968 campaign, violence flared nearly everywhere Wallace went, much of it triggered by the candidate himself as he taunted hecklers at already tense rallies. At New York's Madison Square Garden, 3,500 police were required to keep the peace at a Wallace rally.[404] His gatherings devolved into shouting matches, which suggested chaos and hinted that his presidency might be one long string of disturbances.

The final thing that pulled Wallace back to earth was his selection of Curtis LeMay as his running mate. LeMay had been the U.S. Air Force chief of staff and head of the Strategic Command. He shared Wallace's ability to tell it like is, but he did not share his talent for knowing when to put a cork on the effluent.

The choice blew up on the launchpad at a Pittsburgh press conference where the jowly LeMay was introduced to reporters. They already knew him as cigar-chomping, tough-talking "Old Iron Pants," who had introduced colorful descriptions of nuclear holocaust into the popular conversation. He had mused about bombing "the North Vietnamese back to the stone age" and destroying "every work of man in North Viet Nam if that is what it takes."

LeMay had orchestrated the Pacific bombing campaign in World War II, planned the successful Berlin Airlift, one of the most extraordinary feats of modern logistics, and reorganized American defenses.

He was also a hothead whose fondness for metallic solutions made him the model for the deranged general Ripper in Stanley Kubrick's film *Dr. Strangelove,* distrustful of civilian authorities and quick to use bombs to solve problems. "If you have to go," John Kennedy once said of him, "you want LeMay in the lead bomber. But you never want LeMay deciding whether or not you have to go."[405]

LeMay mused, "The country had to use unorthodox methods to get out of the hole, and I think we're in that situation now."

At the joint press conference in Pittsburgh he seemed quite comfortable with the kind of warfare children practiced for by diving under their desks in regular air raid drills. "We seem to have a phobia about nuclear weapons," he said. "I think to most military men that a nuclear weapon is just another weapon in our arsenal. I think there are many occasions when it would be most efficient to use nuclear weapons. However, the public opinion in this country and throughout the world throw up their hands in horror when you mention nuclear weapons, just because of the propaganda that's been fed to them. If I found it necessary, I would use anything that we could dream up—including nuclear weapons."

Wallace repeatedly interrupted LeMay as he lumbered on about using nukes in Vietnam and elsewhere. In footage of the event, Wallace's eyes, which normally locked pointing straight ahead, darted from side to side as if he were desperate for an alarm to pull that might allow them all to escape. "Within the space of a minute," wrote *Time,* "LeMay had made even Wallace appear, by contrast, the image of the statesmanlike candidate."[406]

Upon reflection, LeMay was mostly saying that the deterrent value of nuclear weapons is lost if a nation declares that it will never use them, but even Wallace's men weren't sympathetic. Afterward, a

Wallace staffer told LeMay: "Keep yo' bowels open, and yo' mouth shut." Because of LeMay's exciting performance, the ticket was soon referred to as the "bombsy twins."

Marshall Frady refers to "the ponderous debacle of [Wallace] selecting General Curtis LeMay as his running mate—the general being about as politically graceful as an irate rhino in a game of ice hockey." Barry Goldwater, who faced some of the same accusations four years earlier about his nuclear instincts, fretted that perhaps LeMay shouldn't have interrupted retirement to join the campaign trail. "I hope he hasn't made a mistake, but I think he has."

By late October, Wallace's poll numbers had dropped, to 15 percent of the presidential vote.[407] "From the first week in October and the choice of Curtis LeMay, every poll, every sampling, even the very spirit of the Wallace campaign appeared to change," wrote Teddy White. "Down he went, gurgling, first in the Harris poll, then in the Gallup poll, followed by every other index, until finally, on Election Day."

In the end, George Wallace's message was simple, short, and clear. He was telling the people that their government had sold them out. They felt alienated. The old faith that America was a community and that government served the community had been destroyed. The government no longer served the interests of the people and so had to be ignored, then seized from the incompetent and compelled to work.

This idea did not die for Wallace with the loss in the 1968 campaign. In February 1968, David Broder reported on the prescient analysis of Lyndon Johnson's former Census Bureau chief, Richard E. Scammon. "Whatever else Wallace accomplishes, he seems sure to emerge from his 1968 campaign with an established personal organization in virtually every state. Scammon sees this as the second step in a three-stage effort by Wallace to establish a base for seeking the 1972 Democratic presidential nomination."

That was just what happened. In 1972 Wallace, running as a Democrat, won every single county in the Florida primary and was poised to become a force for the nomination. Then, campaigning in Maryland, he came out from behind his protective podium to mingle with the crowd. An assassin shot him five times. He survived, but his presidential star never rose so high again.

Acknowledgments

First, my wife, Anne. She has not only read this book many times over and made it better, but she also makes me better and has for the last twenty-seven years of putting up with my writing until late in the night and early in the morning. Next, Brice and Nan. You two can't imagine yet what a joy it is to come out from behind the desk and join your world. Your questions are my favorite thing in the world.

This book wouldn't exist without the virtuous direction of Andy Bowers of the *Slate* Panoply network. More than ten years ago, Andy came up with the idea of the *Slate Gabfest*, a podcast among friends trying to figure out what they think about things. That sense of adventure and experimentation led to an ongoing collaboration that created a platform for my first stabs at telling the stories in this book. From there Andy created *Whistlestop* with the help of Mike Vuolo and Steve Lickteig and Joel Meyer. Thank you also to *Slate* editor Julia Turner, who is a dream to work for and with.

I'll sneak my *Gabfest* colleagues Emily Bazelon and David Plotz in here. They are great friends and occasional combatants. The spirit of the voice in this book was born from conversations with them. Not only does their enthusiasm and inquisitiveness make them great company, but I also learn from them every week. I am also immensely grateful for the *Gabfest* and *Whistlestop* audiences. You are kind, patient with mistakes, and tolerant of our thinking out loud as we try to figure out complex issues—a rare thing these days. You make all the hard work worth it. One regular listener deserves special thanks. Stephen Colbert suggested I write this book. I'm glad he did, and I'm grateful for his example as an enthusiast in the world and for all the joy his work has given me.

I am deeply grateful to *Whistlestop* crackerjack researcher Brian Rosenwald. He is an actual historian whose sense of context and nuance is amazing, his range is vast, and his work ethic a marvel. The mountains of newspaper clippings, scholarly readings, and book passages were daunting each time he sent them, but they were always perfect, and his firm but precise guidance steered me away from many glib mistakes.

Izzy Rode, Carah Ong Whaley, and Elliania Bisgaard-Church formed a virtual research team operating in shared folders covering more than 200 years of history. They guided me to what I'd not accounted for in the reading and helped straighten me out when my thinking got sloppy. They tolerated confusing e-mails when I was way down some rabbit hole of history. Rick Ball combed through the manuscript and rescued me from a host of errors and made the facts sharper—and all in record time. I am grateful, too, for the opportunity to work once again with Lisa Null, who helped me with my first book. Her spirit, enthusiasm, and wisdom are a bright light in the world.

I started this project during my first year at *Face the Nation*, which was a bit insane and wouldn't have been possible without my tolerant and talented CBS colleagues. I am lucky to work at CBS, for which I have CBS president David Rhodes and Washington bureau chief Chris Isham to thank. At *Face* they integrated the new guy in such a way that I could keep covering the story the way I always have and I've always wanted to. I am particularly grateful to executive producer Mary Hager and my assistant, Cara Korte, for helping me keep this project going.

Working with history in such an intense way, I marvel at and am grateful for the historians who have done so much great work chronicling the American story. One in particular kicked this all off: Gil Troy's *See How They Ran* was a spark many years ago. To my fellow campaign reporters, current and past, I was told by my mother that there are no more amusing people to be with than members of the press. Mom was right. And after a year of reading bylines of my heroes and mentors and colleagues from campaigns of the past, I'm reminded how much hard work you've done, too.

Finally, thanks to the patient and clever Sean Desmond of Twelve. This was a breakneck project, and he managed the words and the deadlines with a marvelous deftness. He was a dream to work with. Thank you also to Libby Burton at Twelve for all her hard work.

This book wouldn't have come to life without my fabulous agent, Tina Bennett. I am thankful for her friendship, her sharp eye, her standards, drinks at sundown, and her constant faith that there is a book in there somewhere. Seems we found one.

Notes

1. Meacham, *Destiny and Power*, p. 228.
2. Annis, J. Lee, *Howard Baker: Conciliator in an Age of Crisis*, p. 173.
3. Francis X. Clines, "A Reporter's Notebook: Grand Old Pandemonium; Voices in the Chaos," *New York Times*, February 25, 1980.
4. Ibid.
5. Shirley, Craig *Rendezvous with Destiny*, p. 154.
6. Meecham, *Destiny and Power*, p. 232.
7. Ibid., p. 233.
8. Broder, David, and Lou Cannon. "A Polite Republican Race Takes Turn for the Bitter" *The Washington Post*, Feb 24, 1980.
9. Stacks, John, *Watershed*, p. 121).
10. Broder, David. "Dramatic Reversal of Fortune in New Hampshire" *The Washington Post,* Feb 28, 1980.
11. Stacks, *Watershed*, p. 119.
12. Brady Carlson, "Meet the Microphone Ronald Reagan Paid For at the Famous Debate in Nashua," New Hampshire Public Radio, December 5, 2015, http://nhpr.org/post/meet-microphone-ronald-reagan-paid-famous-debate-nashua.
13. Reeves, Richard. *President Kennedy:Profile of Power* (Simon & Schuster 1994), 16.
14. Kallina Jr., Edmund F. *Kennedy v. Nixon: The Presidential Election of 1960* (University Press of Florida), 56.
15. Humphrey, *The Education of a Public Man*, p. 152.
16. "John E. Amos Oral History Interview, JFK #1, 8/6/1965," John F. Kennedy Presidential Library and Museum, http://www.jfklibrary.org/Asset-Viewer/Archives/JFKOH-JEA-01.aspx.
17. Carroll Kilpatrick, "Kennedy Risks Prestige in W. Va.," *Washington Post / Times Herald*, April 22, 1960.
18. Lippmann, Walter, "Stevenson and Kennedy," *St. Louis Post-Dispatch*, April 15, 1960.
19. White, Theodore. *The Making of the President 1960* (Harper Collins), 101.

20. "West Virginia: Trips: 25 April 1960, JFK," John F. Kennedy Presidential Library and Museum, http://www.jfklibrary.org/Asset-Viewer/Archives/JFK CAMP1960-0969-031.aspx.
21. White, *The Making of the President 1960*, p. 125.
22. Alan L. Otten, "Candidates' Religion Will Mean Much Less in Future," *Wall Street Journal*, May 9, 1960.
23. Kilpatrick,Carroll. "Rural Vote Seen Defeating Kennedy Humphrey Victory Forecast in W. Va." *The Washington Post, Times Herald*, May 5, 1960.
24. Lawrence, W. H. "West Virginia Ad Asks Who's 'Bigot,'" *New York Times*, April 30, 1960.
25. Lawrence, W.H. "Humphrey Given Edge by Editors," *New York Times*, April 24, 1960.
26. Lippmann, "Stevenson and Kennedy." [4]
27. Roberts, Chalmers M. "New Hampshire Encourage Kennedy," *The Washington Post, Times Herald*, March 11, 1960.
28. White, *The Making of the President 1960*, p. 125.
29. Barnes, *John F. Kennedy on Leadership*, p. 30.
30. "John E. Amos Oral History Interview, JFK #1, 8/6/1965," John F. Kennedy Presidential Library and Museum.
31. Sabato, Larry *The Kennedy Half Century*, p. 50.
32. "West Virginia: Trips: 25 April 1960, JFK." John F. Kennedy Presidential Library and Museum.
33. "Not Running as Catholic, Kennedy Says," *Chicago Daily Tribune*, Apr 21, 1960.
34. Johnston, Richard J. H. "Kennedy Hailed in Mining Region," *New York Times*, Apr 27, 1960.
35. "Humphrey and Kennedy Keep Up Cross-Fire," *Chicago Daily Tribune*, Apr 26, 1960.
36. "The Kennedy Boys Return to Stump," *New York Times*, May 1, 1960.
37. Kallina Jr., Edmund F. *Kennedy v. Nixon: The Presidential Election of 1960* (University Press of Florida), 67.
38. Kilpatrick, Carroll. "Humphrey Angered by Big Outlays," *The Washington Post*, May 8, 1960.
39. "Kennedy-Humphrey Struggle Waxes Hotter," *Los Angeles Times*, May 1, 1960.
40. Carroll Kilpatrick, "Rural Vote Seen Defeating Kennedy, Humphrey Victory Forecast in W. Va.," *Washington Post / Times Herald*, May 5, 1960.
41. Loftus, Joseph A. "Kennedy Works to Last Minute," *New York Times*, May 10, 1960
42. Reeves, *President Kennedy*, p. 16.

43. W. H. Lawrence, "Kennedy Nominated on the First Ballot; Overwhelms Johnson by 806 Votes to 409," *New York Times*, July 14, 1960, https://partners.nytimes.com/library/politics/camp/600714convention-dem-ra.html.
44. "Winning West Virginia: JFK's Primary Campaign," *New Frontiers*, spring 2010, http://www.jfklibrary.org/Education/Teachers/~/media/07DE30D1FF68420E97B763781A874D2F.pdf.
45. "Oral History Interview with Oscar R. Ewing," Harry S. Truman Library & Museum, http://www.trumanlibrary.org/oralhist/ewing4.htm.
46. Shannon, William V. and Robert S. Allen *The Truman Merry Go-Round*, p 3.
47. Goldzwig, *Truman's Whistle-Stop Campaign*, pp. 11–12.
48. Ibid., p. 6.
49. Manchester, *The Glory and the Dream*. P. 547
50. Donaldson, *Truman Defeats Dewey*.
51. Walter Trohan, "Oratory Leaves Leaders of Both Parties Cold," *Chicago Daily Tribune*, September 27, 1948.
52. Folliard, Edward T. "Truman Feels He Made'em Mad Enough to Vote," *The Washington Post*, October 3, 1948.
53. Ibid.
54. Donaldson, *Truman Defeats Dewey*.
55. Goldzwig, *Truman's Whistle-Stop Campaign*, p. 39
56. Strout, Richard L. "Truman Belittles Plea for 'National Unity' Made by Republicans," *The Christian Science Monitor*, September 28, 1948.
57. Clark, John L. "Truman Helped Chances But Dewey Seen Winner," *The Pittsburgh Courier*, October 9, 1948.
58. Walter Trohan, "Oratory Leaves Leaders of Both Parties Cold," *Chicago Daily Tribune*, September 27, 1948.
59. "Truman Is Hailed by Jersey Crowds," *New York Times*, October 8, 1948.
60. Albright, Robert C. "Truman's Mostly Making Neighbors" *The Washington Post*, October, 17 1948.
61. Folliard, Edward T. "Truman Liked By Crowds in Offhand Role," *The Washington Post*, September 20, 1948.
62. Folliard, Edward T. "Truman Liked By Crowds in Offhand Role," *The Washington Post*, September 20, 1948.
63. The Associated Press. "Man Fined $50 for Move to Shake Truman's Hand," *New York Times*, October 11, 1948.
64. Goldzwig, *Truman's Whistle-Stop Campaign*, p. 32.
65. Trohan, Walter. "Oratory Leaves Leaders of Both Parties Cold," *Chicago Daily Tribune*, September 27, 1948.
66. Stokes, Thomas L. "Mood of America, Election Time, 1948," *New York Times*, October 17, 1948.

67. Donaldson, *Truman Defeats Dewey*, p. 173, quoting the *Louisville Courier-Journal*, November 18, 1948.
68. "President and Dewey Meet at 10 Paces in Ohio," *New York Times*, October 27, 1948
69. Albright, Robert C. "Truman's Mostly Making Neighbors," *The Washington Post*, October 17, 1948.
70. David Bauder, "Networks Try to Explain Blown Call," *Washington Post*, November 8, 2000, http://www.washingtonpost.com/wp-srv/aponline/20001108/aponline183922_000.htm.
71. Busch, Andrew, *Truman's Triumphs: The 1948 Election and the Making of Postwar America*, p. 159
72. Manchester,William. *The Glory and the Dream* p. 494
73. Reston, James. "Truman's Strategy Centered On Racial and Religious Plea," *New York Times*, October 26, 1948.
74. Michael R. Kagay, "History Suggests Bush's Popularity Will Ebb," *New York Times*, May 22, 1991, http://www.nytimes.com/1991/05/22/us/history-suggests-bush-s-popularity-will-ebb.html.
75. "Clinton Rebounds As People Seem To Accept Denial," *Reuters*, January 28, 1992.
76. Bill Lambrecht, "Clinton Shores Up Campaign; $500,000 Is Shifted to New Hampshire," *St. Louis Post-Dispatch*, February 18, 1992.
77. Cramer, Richard Ben (2011-08-02). *What It Takes: The Way to the White House* (p. 994). Open Road Media. Kindle Edition.
78. Cramer, Richard Ben (2011-08-02). *What It Takes: The Way to the White House* (p. 991). Open Road Media. Kindle Edition.
79. Meacham, *Destiny and Power*, p. 314.
80. Safire, William, "On Language; Calling Dr. Spin," *New York Times*, August 31, 1986.
81. Runkel, David R. *Campaign for President*, p67.
82. Meacham, *Destiney and Power*, p. 301.
83. Cramer, Richard Ben (2011-08-02). *What It Takes: The Way to the White House* (p. 886). Open Road Media. Kindle Edition.
84. Germond, Jack W. and Jules Witcover, *Whose Broad Stripes and Bright Stars*, 142.
85. Koch, Doro Bush (2006-10-06). *My Father, My President: A Personal Account of the Life of George H. W. Bush* (p. 252). Grand Central Publishing. Kindle Edition.
86. Germond, Jack W. and Jules Witcover, *Whose Broad Stripes and Bright Stars*, 144.
87. Clifford, Frank "GOP Throws Script Away for Frenzied N.H. Finale" *Los Angeles Times* February 14, 1988.
88. Baker, James, *Work Hard Study Hard and Keep out of Politics*, 255.
89. Meacham, *Destiney and Power*, p. 332

90. Ibid. p. 335
91. Johnson, Dennis W., *No Place for Amateurs*, p. 72.
92. http://iop.harvard.edu/sites/default/files_new/Proceedings/1988-1989.pdf
93. Roberts, Steven, "Bush Intensified Debate on Pledge, Asking Why It So Upsets Dukakis," *The New York Times*, August 25, 1988. http://www.nytimes.com/1988/08/25/us/bush-intensifies-debate-on-pledge-asking-why-it-so-upsets-dukakis.html
94. "Dukakis, Accusing Bush of 'Neglect,' Proposes Outline for Health Coverage" *New York Times* September 21, 1988
95. King, Josh, "Dukakis and the Tank," *Politico*, November 17, 2013
96. Weinraub, Bernard,"Campaign Trail; Loaded for Bear and Then Some" *New York Times*, September 14, 1988.
97. https://www.bostonglobe.com/news/politics/2014/08/07/capitalsource/VIJRlO5IVbNQ9306f3ZsdL/story.html
98. Bad Boy, p. 177.
99. "No Kick from Campaign," *Newsweek*, October 4, 1990.
100. Russell Baker, "Some Fun in the Chilblain Belt," *New York Times*, March 7, 1972.
101. Russell Baker, "Some Fun in the Chilblain Belt," *New York Times*, March 7, 1972.
102. Broder, David S. "Muskie's Self-Discipline," *The Washington Post, Times Herald*, February 29, 1972.
103. Belman and Pride, eds., *The New Hampshire Century*, p. 12.
104. Duart Farquharson, "Muskie, in Tears, Denies Insult to Franco-Americans," *Montreal Gazette*, February 28, 1972.
105. Richard T. Stout', "Jane Muskie: Campaigning," *Boca Raton News*, April 13, 1972.
106. Thomas W. Ottenad, "Muskie's Tearful Tirade May Hurt His Campaign," *St. Louis Post-Dispatch*, February 29, 1972.
107. Broder, David S. "Muskie's Self-Discipline," *The Washington Post, Times Herald*, February 29, 1972.
108. White, *The Making of the President 1972*, p. 85.
109. Donald Nicoll's interview with Tony Podesta in Shea and Harward, *Presidential Campaigns*, pp. 91–92.
110. Apple Jr., R.W. "Ohio Governor Dismayed at Muskie's Flagging Race," *New York Times*, April 12, 1972.
111. *Chicago Tribune*, March 5, 1972
112. "Interview with George J. Mitchell by Don Nicoll," September 19, 2002, Bates College Digital Library, http://digilib.bates.edu/collect/muskieor/index/assoc/HASH014f/14a4b1e5.dir/doc.pdf.
113. *Portland Press Herald*, March 9, 1972.
114. Associated Press "Democratic Race Tight", *Spokane Daily Chronicle*, March 8, 1972.

115. Alan Otten, "Muskie's Front-Runner Status Jeopardized and McGovern Takes Big Stride in Primary," *Wall Street Journal*, March 9, 1972.
116. Associated Press "Democrats Hunt Votes For Florida Primary," *Tennessean* (Nashville, TN), March 12, 1972.
117. Chalmers M. Roberts, "Rage and Tears—A Boon to Voters in the Long Run," *St. Petersburg Times*, March 8, 1972.
118. "And Now Florida," *Bridgeport (CT) Post*, March 13, 1972.
119. Sperling Jr., Godfrey. "It's not a 'new' Muskie," *The Christian Science Monitor*, March 22, 1972.
120. Thompson, Hunter S. *Fear and Loathing*, p. 127.
121. David S. Broder, "The Story That Still Nags Me," *Washington Monthly*, February 1987; also Broder, *Behind the Front Page*, p. 39.
122. Hart, *Right from the Start*, p. 243.
123. Nelson, Bryce. "McGovenr First Got Full Details Tuesday on Eagleton Health," *Los Angeles Times*, July 27, 1972.
124. Mankiewicz and Swerdlow, *So As I Was Saying…: My Somewhat Eventful Life*, p. 200.
125. Giglio, *Call Me Tom: The Life of Thomas F. Eagleton*, Kindle Location 2361.
126. Starr, Frank. "Psychiatric Care Told: Eagleton's Health Report," *Chicago Tribune*, July 26, 1972.
127. "Problem 'a Closed Chapter'; Eagleton Candid: McGovern," *Chicago Tribune*, July 26, 1972.
128. "Eagleton: Fifth Choice for Spot," *Chicago Tribune*, July 26, 1972.
129. Fuller, Jack. "Editorials Are Mixed on Eagleton," *The Washington Post, Times Herald*, July 28, 1972.
130. Roberts, Steven V. "Messages of Support Sent to Eagleton," *New York Times*, August 1, 1972.
131. Ibid.
132. Robert S. Boyd, "McGovern Backs Eagleton Despite Demands for Ouster," *Detroit Free Press*, July 27, 1972.
133. Garcia-Barcena, Rafael, Jr. "More on the Eagleton Case," *Washington Post*, Times Herald, August 1, 1972.
134. Giglio, *Call Me Tom: The Life of Thomas F. Eagleton*, Kindle edition location 2515.
135. Stern, Laurence. "Eagleton Race Assumes Aura Of Surrealism," *Washington Post*, Times Herald, July 30, 1972.
136. Apple Jr., R.W. "Eagleton is Firm Despite Pressure by 2 Party Chiefs," *New York Times*, July 31, 1972.
137. Ibid.
138. Giglio, *Call Me Tom*, Kindle edition location 2467.

139. Evans, Rowland and Robert Novak. "After the Eagleton Crisis," *Washington Post*, Times Herald, July 30, 1972.
140. Giglio, James N. (2011-09-16). *Call Me Tom: The Life of Thomas F. Eagleton* (MISSOURI BIOGRAPHY SERIES) (Kindle Location 2479). University of Missouri Press. Kindle Edition.
141. Jesse Jackson, "Eagleton Should Not Run," *Pittsburgh Courier*, August 5, 1972.
142. Lardner Jr., George. "McGovern Talked With 2 Eagleton Doctors," *Washington Post*, Times Herald, August 4, 1972.
143. Miroff, Bruce. *The Liberals' Moment* p. 96
144. "Eagleton's Withdrawl Sets Off Button Boom," *New York Times*, August 2, 1972.
145. Rogers, Warren. "Countdown: Eagleton's gone but Many Fear the Election is Lost," *Chicago Tribune*, August 3, 1972.
146. Miroff, Bruce. *The Liberals' Moment*, p. 96.
147. Shapiro, Walter. *One-Car Caravan*, p. 71.
148. Jodi Wilgoren, "In a Long Presidential Race, Dean Sprints," *New York Times*, August 27, 2003, http://www.nytimes.com/2003/08/27/politics/campaigns/27DEAN.html?pagewanted=all.
149. Kreiss, Daniel *Taking Our Country Back: The Crafting of Networked Politics from Howard Dean to Barack Obama*, p. 61.
150. Ibid., p. 52.
151. Maslin, Paul, "The Front-Runner's Fall," *The Atlantic* May 2004. http://www.theatlantic.com/magazine/archive/2004/05/the-front-runner-s-fall/302944/
152. Associated Press, "Dean: America Not Safer after Saddam's Capture," *Fox News*, December 16, 2003, http://www.foxnews.com/story/2003/12/16/dean-america-not-safer-after-saddam-capture.html.
153. "What Howard Dean Can Teach Us About 2016," FiveThirtyEight, February 4, 2016, http://fivethirtyeight.com/features/what-howard-dean-can-teach-us-about-2016/.
154. "The Dean Scream: What Really Happened," FiveThirtyEight, February 4, 2016, http://fivethirtyeight.com/features/the-dean-scream-what-really-happened/.
155. Kornblut, Anne E. "Candidates Jockey for Momentum," *Boston Globe*, January 18, 2004.
156. "What Howard Dean Can Teach Us About 2016." http://fivethirtyeight.com/features/what-howard-dean-can-teach-us-about-2016/
157. Pickler, Nedra. "Dean Looks to Revitalize His Campaign," *Associated Press*, January 20, 2004.
158. Kornblut, Anne E. "Kerry Wins in Iowa; Edwards is Close Second, Dean a Distant Third," *The Boston Globe*, January 20, 2004.

159. "The Dean Scream: What Really Happened." http://fivethirtyeight.com/features/the-dean-scream-what-really-happened/
160. Fitzgerald, Thomas. "A Dean roar is echoing far; Monday's manic speech could give voters pause, analysts said, likening it to a "Muskie moment." *The Philadelphia Inquirer*, January 22, 2004.
161. Johnson, Glen. "Dean Works to Assuage Doubts on Temperament," *The Boston Globe*, January 23, 2004.
162. Siegel, Robert. "Interview: William Powers Discusses Howard Dean's 'scream,'" NPR, January 21, 2004. Transcript.
163. Dowd, Maureen. "Riding the Crazy Train," *New York Times,* January 22, 2004.
164. Winebrenner, Hugh and Dennis J. Goldford, *The Iowa Precinct Caucuses: The Making of a Media Event*, p. 9.
165. "Was Howard Dean's presidential campaign really sunk by his infamous campaign speech scream; or were other factors to blame?" https://www.quora.com/Was-Howard-Deans-presidential-campaign-really-sunk-by-his-infamous-campaign-speech-scream-or-were-other-factors-to-blame
166. Jack Holmes, "The Dean Scream: An Oral History," *Esquire*, January 29, 2016, http://www.esquire.com/news-politics/a41615/the-dean-scream-oral-history/.
167. Ibid., p. 360.
168. "25,000 Protest Goldwater in S.F.," *Los Angeles Times*, July 13, 1964.
169. Theodore H. White, *The Making of the President 1964*, Kindle ed. (New York: HarperCollins, 2010), p. 211.
170. Ibid.
171. David Reinhard, *The Republican Right Since 1945* (Lexington: University Press of Kentucky, 1983), p. 155.
172. "Eisenhower Hit as Youths Toss Placard," July 12, 1964.
173. Lewis L. Gould, *Grand Old Party* (New York: Random House, 2003), p. 359.
174. *Goldwater Candidacy Revisited*, p. 667.
175. "2 in GOP Say Barry Perils 30 House Seats," *Washington Post*, June 7, 1964.
176. Perlstein, *Before the Storm*, p. 356.
177. "Nation: The Bitter Battle." *Time* magazine. Vol. LXXX, No. 16. (10/19/1962). http://content.time.com/time/subscriber/article/0,33009,827850-1,00.html
178. George D. Wolf, *William Warren Scranton: Pennsylvania Statesman* (University Park: Pennsylvania State University Press, 1981), p. 107.
179. Reinhard, *The Republican Right*, p. 187; *New York Times*, May 26, 1964.
180. Wolf, *William Warren Scranton*, p. 106.
181. http://content.time.com/time/subscriber/article/0,33009,827850-2,00.html.
182. White, *The Making of the President 1964*, p. 157.
183. Wolf, *William Warren Scranton*, p. 150.

184. Loftuss, Joseph A. "Scranton's Decision to Run: The Events Leading Up to His Change of Mind," *New York Times*, June 21, 1964.
185. *Chicago Tribune*, June 26, 1964.
186. Perlstein, *Before the Storm*, p. 360.
187. *Washington Post*, June 16, 1964.
188. Perlstein, *Before the Storm*, p. 363.
189. "Ohio Is Cool to Scranton; Romney Warm," *Chicago Tribune* June 26, 1964.
190. "Scranton Finds Ohio, Michigan Bit Cool: Questioned about Dirksen" *Washington Post*, June 26, 1964.
191. J. William Middendorf II, *A Glorious Disaster: Barry Goldwater's Presidential Campaign and the Origins of the Conservative Movement,* Kindle ed. (New York: Basic Books, 2008), p. 109.
192. "Aimed at Delegates: Battle of Billboards Precedes Convention," *Los Angeles Times* July 9, 1964.
193. Middendorf, *A Glorious Disaster*, p. 110.
194. Ibid., p. 109.
195. "Atmosphere in San Francisco" Drew Pearson, *Los Angeles Times* July 16, 1964.
196. White, *The Making of the President 1964*, p. 205.
197. Middendorf, *A Glorious Disaster*, p. 120.
198. "25,000 Protest Goldwater in S.F.," *Los Angeles Times*, July 13, 1964.
199. Telephone Conversation between LBJ and John Connally, July 23, 1964, 5:31 p.m., Citation #4322, Recordings of Telephone Conversations—White House Series, LBJ Library.
200. *The Magic Lantern*, p. 37.
201. Richard Norton Smith, *On His Own Terms: A Life of Nelson Rockefeller*, Kindle ed. (New York: Random House, 2014), locs. 82–85.
202. "GOP Buries Hatchet, Rallies to Goldwater," *Los Angeles Times*, July 16, 1964.
203. Wolf, *William Warren Scranton*, p. 86.
204. Scott, Hugh *Come to the Party*, p. 217.
205. "McCain Scores Because of the Grown-up Factor," *Time* 2/2/2000.
206. "McCain's history of hot temper raises concerns, McClatchyDC, September 7, 2008. http:// www.mcclatchydc.com/news/politics-government/article24498646. html#storylink=cpy
207. "John McCain's Pollster Recounts 2000 New Hampshire Win, And It's Amazing" by Sam Stein and Christine Conetta, Huffington Post, 10/13/15. http://www.huffingtonpost.com/entry/drinking-andtalking-john-mccain-bill-mcinturff_us_561c7d49e4b0c5a1ce6058d0
208. Ford, Gerald *A Time to Heal*, p. 333.
209. Harry Kelly, "Conservatives Seek New Party If Reagan Loses," *Chicago Tribune*, August 18, 1976.

210. Kalman, *Right Star Rising: A New Politics, 1974–1980*, p. 164.
211. "Memorandum of Conversation, February 5, 1976—Ford, Kissinger, Rumsfeld" (transcript), Gerald R. Ford Presidential Library and Museum, https://fordlibrarymuseum.gov/library/document/0314/1553357.pdf.
212. Frisk, David B., *If Not Us, Who?* p. 311.
213. Kalman, *Right Star Rising: A New Politics, 1974–1980*, p. 162.
214. Ford, *A Time to Heal*, p. 348.
215. Hayward, Stephen. *The Age of Reagan*, p. 398
216. Peter Lisagor, "Rocky, Wallace Themes Similar," *Lincoln (NE) Evening Journal*, August 27, 1975.
217. Cannon, James *Gerald R. Ford: An Honorable Life*, p. 399.
218. Perlstein, *The Invisible Bridge: The Fall of Nixon and the Rise of Reagan*, p. 546.
219. Kalman, *Right Star Rising: A New Politics, 1974–1980*, p. 166.
220. United Press International. "Governors Urge Reagan to quit" *Willmington Morning Star* March 20, 1976.
221. "Unemployment (2)," Gerald R. Ford Presidential Library and Museum, Ron Nessen Papers, Box 30, https://fordlibrarymuseum.gov/library/document/0204/7423910.pdf.
222. Cannon, Lou, "GOP Race Is Heated in Texas, *Washington Post*, Date April 30, 1976.
223. Witcover, Jules. *Marathon*, p. 431.
224. Ford, *A Time to Heal*, p. 362.
225. Ibid., p. 363.
226. *Public Papers of the Presidents of the United States, Gerald Ford 1976–1977*, p. 1254.
227. Ford, *A Time to Heal*, p. 389.
228. Anne Keegan, "New 'Stars' Stealing GOP Show," *Chicago Tribune*, August 18, 1976.
229. Baker, James A. *Work Hard, Study*, p. 40.
230. Ibid.
231. Hornblower, Margot. "Reagan: A Day of Delegation-Hopping" *The Washington Post*, Aug 17, 1976.
232. Wren, Adam, "It Was Riotous: An Oral History of the GOP's Last Open Convention" *Politico*. http://www.politico.com/magazine/ story/2016/04/1976-convention-oral-history-213793
233. Perlstein, *The Invisible Bridge*, pp. 773–74.
234. United Press International, "Angry Reagan Denies Vote Buying Charge," *Beaver County Times*, August 16, 1976.
235. Maurice Carroll, "Betty Ford Bests Nancy Reagan on Applause Scale," Week in Review, *New York Times*, August 18, 1976, p. 77.

236. "Republicans Surprised, Irked by Reagan Move," *Milwaukee Sentinel*, July 27, 1976; United Press International, "Reagan's VP Choice Startles Party," *York Daily Record*, July 27, 1976.
237. *Tuscaloosa News*, August 1, 1976.
238. CBS News Convention Coverage, August 17, 1976.
239. Perlstein, *The Invisible Brigde* p. 758.
240. "Dodging a Fight over Abortion," *Washington Post*, August 13, 1976.
241. Associated Press, "Ford Flashes Wide Smile as He Hears Victory Report," *Arizona Republic*, August 19, 1976.
242. Morris, *Dutch*, p. 402.
243. Shirley, *Reagan's Revolution*, p. xxiii.
244. Sam Donaldson, ABC Evening News, ABC, Videotape, August 19, 1976.
245. Shirley, Craig (2010-02-22). Reagan's Revolution: The Untold Story of the Campaign That Started It All (p. 355). Thomas Nelson. Kindle Edition.
246. Shirley, *Reagan's Revolution: The Untold Story of the Campaign That Started It All*, Kindle edition location 184.
247. W. H. Lawrence, "Committee Backs Taft Georgia Bloc; Floor Fight on Credentials Up Today; Hoover Says Democrats Curb Liberty," *New York Times*, July 10, 1952, https://partners.nytimes.com/library/politics/camp/520710convention-gop-ra.html.
248. "Bitter Committee Fight Described," *Los Angeles Times*, July 10, 1952.
249. "Texans Chant I'm Getting Sour on Eisenhower," *Chicago Daily Tribune* , Jul 7, 1952.
250. Reinhard', *The Republican Right Since 1945*.
251. *Meet the Press*, January 20, 1952.
252. Nashorn, Jerome, "Choosing the Candidates 1952," PhD diss., Harvard University, 1988.
253. "Sees Victory for Taft as Stalin's Too," *Des Moines Register* July 2, 1952.
254. Parmet, *Eisenhower and the American Crusades*, p. 96.
255. Marlow, James "Dirksen's Blast at Dewey Was Climax of GOP Factional Fight" July 11, 1952; Reinhard, *The Republican Right*, p. 85.
256. Porter, Russell. "Eisenhower Says He'll Take Delegate Fight to Floor," *New York Times*, July 4, 1952.
257. Scott, *Come to the Party*, p. 71.
258. Ibid., p. 78.
259. Ibid., p. 78.
260. "Ike Rally Held in New York," *Stanford Daily*, February 12, 1952, http://stanforddailyarchive.com/cgi-bin/stanford?a=d&d=stanford19520212-01.2.52.
261. Thomas, *Ike's Bluff.*

262. Walter Lippmann, "Ike Should Make No Effort to Win Delegates by Deals," *Pittsburgh Post-Gazette*, June 2, 1952.
263. Belair Jr., Felix. "Taft Aides Yield Louisiana Votes," *New York Times*, July 10, 1952.
264. Friedman, "Judge Wisdom and the 1952 Republican National Convention." He gives his source as Rita Fitzpatrick, "A Woman's Hand Brightens Hall for G.O.P. Convention," *Chicago Tribune*, July 5, 1952.
265. Clark, Albert. "Taft Tide Runs Strong As Roaring Convention Officially Opens Today," *Wall Street Journal*, July 7, 1952.
266. White, William S., *The Taft Story*, (Harper & Brothers), p. 171.
267. Ibid, p. 172.
268. Lawrence, W. H. "Taft Leader Backs Televised Hearing," *New York Times*, June 29, 1952.
269. Scott, *Come to the Party*, p. 98.
270. Joel William Friedman, "Judge Wisdom and the 1952 Republican National Convention: Ensuring Victory for Eisenhower and a Two-Party System for Louisiana," *Washington and Lee Law Review* 53, no. 1 (1996).
271. Gowran, Clay. "Ike Picks On Truman and Taft in Iowa," *Chicago Daily Tribune*, July 5, 1952.
272. Ibid.
273. Albright, Robert C. "Dixie Steal 'Shocks' Ike; Foe Claims He's Libeled," *The Washington Post*, July 6, 1952.
274. Lautier, Louis. "Howard in Spot to Seat GOP Delegates," *The Chicago Defender*, July 5, 1952.
275. *Chicago Tribune*, July 8, 1952, http://archives.chicagotribune.com/1952/07/08/page/27/article/display-ad-24-no-title.
276. Bryant, W.C. "General Dewey: New York's Governor Commands Ike's Men In Convention Battle," *Wall Street Journal*, July 9, 1952.
277. Reston, James. "Eisenhower Find Vote 'Heartening'," *New York Times*, July 8, 1952.
278. Ibid.
279. Brooks Atkinson, "A Suspension of Belief," *New York Times*, July 15, 1964.
280. Trohan, Walter. "Unite to Win: Ike and Nixon," *Chicago Daily Tribune*, July 12, 1952.
281. Ratcliffe, Donald (2015-11-16). *The One-Party Presidential Contest: Adams, Jackson, and 1824's Five-Horse Race* (American Presidential Elections) (Kindle locations 2164–2165). University Press of Kansas. Kindle Edition.
282. Ratcliffe, Donald (2015-11-16). *The One-Party Presidential Contest: Adams, Jackson, and 1824's Five-Horse Race* (American Presidential Elections) (Kindle locations 2318–2320). University Press of Kansas. Kindle Edition.
283. *The National Advocate* (London, England), Tuesday, April 06, 1824. (669 words)

284. Ratcliffe, Donald (2015-11-16). *The One-Party Presidential Contest: Adams, Jackson, and 1824's Five-Horse Race* (American Presidential Elections) (Kindle locations 2202–2203). University Press of Kansas. Kindle Edition.
285. From a letter to a friend in Pittsburgh declining to visit on his way back to Tennessee on May 20, 1824
286. Meacham, Jon (2008-11-04). *American Lion: Andrew Jackson in the White House* (Kindle locations 849–852). Random House Publishing Group. Kindle Edition.
287. Wilenz. Sean, *Andrew Jackson*, (New York: Harper Collins, 2008), p. 40.
288. Vowell, Sarah. *Lafayette in the Somewhat United States* (Kindle locations 126–127). Penguin Publishing Group. Kindle Edition.
289. Remini, Robert V. *Andrew Jackson and the Course of American Freedom, 1822–1832, Volume II.* (New York: Harper & Row Publishers, 1981), p. 76.
290. Remini, *Andrew Jackson and the Course of American Freedom, 1822–1832, Volume II*, p. 77.
291. Meacham, Jon (2008-11-04). American Lion: Andrew Jackson in the White House (Kindle locations 822–823). Random House Publishing Group. Kindle Edition.
292. Remini, *Andrew Jackson and the Course of American Freedom, 1822–1832, Volume II*, p. 79.
293. Cole, Donald B., *Vindicating Andrew Jackso* , (University Press of Kansas) p. 26.
294. "Political Conversations," *The National Advocate*, April 10, 1824.
295. Remini, *Andrew Jackson and the Course of American Freedom, 1822–1832, Volume II*, p. 73.
296. Jackson, Andrew and Sam B. Smith, Harriet Fason Chappell Owsley and Harold D. Moser, *The Papers of Andrew Jackson*, p. 378.
297. Remini, *Andrew Jackson and the Course of American Freedom, 1822–1832, Volume II*, p. 60.
298. *Louisville Public Advertiser* Wednesday, April 14, 1824.
299. Remini, *Andrew Jackson and the Course of American Freedom, 1822–1832, Volume II*, p. 62.
300. Wilenz. Sean, *Andrew Jackson*, (New York: Harper Collins, 2008), p. 63.
301. Remini, p. 64.
302. Parsons, Lynn Hudson (2009-05-01). *The Birth of Modern Politics: Andrew Jackson, John Quincy Adams, and the Election of 1828 (Pivotal Moments in American History)* (p. 83). Oxford University Press. Kindle edition.
303. Remini p. 65.
304. *New-Hampshire Statesman* (Concord, New Hampshire, Monday, March 29, 1824; Issue 13. (544 words).
305. "Caucus," *Raleigh Register*, and *North-Carolina Gazette*, February 20, 1824.

306. "Genl. Jackson," *Aurora General Advertiser*, February 9, 1824.
307. "Genl. Jackson," *Aurora General Advertiser*, February 9, 1824.
308. Wilenz. Sean, *Andrew Jackson*, (New York: Harper Collins, 2008), p. 45.
309. "General Jackson," *Raleigh Register*, and *North-Carolina State Gazette*, March 23, 1824.
310. Louisville Public Advertiser (Louisville, Kentucky, Wednesday, April 14, 1824; Issue 576. (1158 words).
311. *The National Advocate* (London, England), Tuesday, April 06, 1824. (669 words).
312. Ratcliffe, Donald (2015-11-16). *The One-Party Presidential Contest: Adams, Jackson, and 1824's Five-Horse Race (American Presidential Elections)* (Kindle locations 185–186). University Press of Kansas. Kindle edition.
313. Remini p. 86.
314. *Providence Patriot, Columbian Phenix* Saturday, February 05, 1825.
315. "Congressional," *The Supporter and Scioto Gazette*, February 24, 1825.
316. Remini p. 87.
317. Wilenz. Sean, *Andrew Jackson*, (New York: Harper Collins, 2008), p. 47.
318. *Louisville Public Advertiser* Wednesday, February 02, 1825.
319. *Providence Patriot, Columbian Phenix* February 16, 1825; Issue 14.
320. Dangerfield, George. *The Era of Good Feeling* (Chicago; Elephant Paperbacks 1989), p. 345.
321. *Daily National Journal*, Wednesday, February 09, 1825; Issue 156.
322. "The Journey from Albany: Governor Cleveland Enthusiastically Received" *New York Times,* October 3,1884
323. Brodsky, Alyn, *Grover Cleveland: A Study in Character*, p. 88.
324. "Not a Soldier on It," *National Tribune*, July 17, 1884.
325. Burns, Eric (2007-02-13). Infamous Scribblers: The Founding Fathers and the Rowdy Beginnings of American Journalism (p. 3). PublicAffairs. Kindle Edition.
326. Burns, Eric (2007-02-13). Infamous Scribblers: The Founding Fathers and the Rowdy Beginnings of American Journalism (p. 308). PublicAffairs. Kindle Edition.
327. "The Cleveland Scandal: Gen. King's Remarkable Explanation of the Affair," *Chicago Daily Tribune*, August 8, 1884.
328. *St. Louis Globe-Democrat*, October 11, 1884.
329. *Mark Twain's Letters, 1876–1885*, p. 81, Mark Twain Classic Literature Library, http://mark-twain.classic-literature.co.uk/mark-twains-letters-1876-1885/ebook-page-81.asp.
330. Muzzey, *James G. Blaine*, p. 83.
331. Ibid., p. 82.

332. "The Golden Age of American Railroading," University of Iowa Libraries, https://www.lib.uiowa.edu/exhibits/previous/railroad/.
333. Muzzey, *James G. Blaine*, p. 87.
334. Ibid., p. 276.
335. Norton, *The Great Revolution of 1840*, p. 10.
336. Ibid., p. 53.
337. *Fayetteville (NC) Weekly Observer*, March 4, 1840.
338. Norton, *The Great Revolution of 1840*, p. 50.
339. Norton p. 11.
340. Roberts, *America's First Great Depression*, p. 168.
341. Troy, Gil and Schlesinger, Arthur M., Israel, Fred L., *American Presidential Elections*, p. 295.
342. Alasdair Roberts, *America's First Great Depression: Economic Crisis and Political Disorder After the Panic of 1837*, p. 93.
343. *Philadelphia Gazette.*
344. Silbey, Joel H., *Martin Van Buren and the Emergence of American Popular Politics* p. 146.
345. Vermont Patriot, Montpelier, Vermont, Monday May, 25, 1840.
346. Troy, Gil (2012-09-18). *See How They Ran: The Changing Role of the Presidential Candidate* (Kindle locations 639–640). Free Press. Kindle edition.)
347. Gunderson, Robert Gray *The Log-Cabin Campaign* (Praeger, March 9, 1977), p. 7.
348. Widmer, Ted, *Martin Van Buren*, p. 10.
349. "Hard Times versus Hard Cider," Vermont Patriot, July 6, 1840.
350. Baker, Jean, *Affairs of Party* (Fordham University Press, June 1, 1998), p. 126.
351. Martin Van Buren, *The Autobiography of Martin Van Buren*, Vol. 2, 445.
352. Silbey, Joel H., *Martin Van Buren and the Emergence of American Popular Politics*, p. 103.
353. Norton p. 9.
354. Troy, Gil. *See How They Ran*, p. 28.
355. *Cleveland Daily Herald*, October 7, 1840.
356. Niven,John *Martin Van Buren: The Romantic Age of American Politics*, p. 453.
357. Ostler, Rosemarie, *Slinging Mud*, p. 14.
358. *Vermont Phoenix*, June 20, 1840.
359. *Boon's Lick Times* (Fayette, MO), October 3, 1840.
360. *The Ohio Statesman* Wednesday, June 24, 1840.
361. "An Address to the Democratic Association at Jackson," *The Mississippian*, October 23, 1840.
362. Collins, Gail. *William Henry Harrison: The American Presidents Series: The 9th President, 1841*, Henry Holt and Co., p 88.

363. Hone, *The Diary of Philip Hone*, p. 85.
364. *Edward Stanwood*, p. 123.
365. McGrane, ed., *The Correspondence of Nicholas Biddle*, p. 256.
366. *Jeffersonian Republican* (Stroudsburg, PA), June 27, 1840.
367. "The Street Brawls of General Harrison." The Ohio Statesman (Columbus, Ohio, Wednesday, July 15, 1840; Issue 3.)
368. "Gen. Harrison in Wilmington on the 14th Inst.—His Speech, &c." The Ohio Statesman (Columbus, Ohio, Wednesday, October 14, 1840; Issue 16.)
369. "*Dover Gazette* & *Strafford Advertiser*, October 13, 1840.
370. Varon, Elizabeth R. "Tippecanoe and the Ladies, Too: White Women and Party Politics in Antebellum Virginia," *The Journal of American History*, Vol. 82, No. 2, September 1995, pp. 494–521.
371. Norton, *The Great Revolution of 1840*, p. 52.
372. *Newbern Spectator* (New Bern, NC), October 31, 1840.
373. *Widmer*, p. 132.
374. *The President's House*, p. 233.
375. Clifford, *Counsel to the President*, p. 634.
376. Ibid., p. 635.
377. Shrum, Robert (2007-06-05). No Excuses: Concessions of a Serial Campaigner (p. 127). Simon & Schuster. Kindle Edition.
378. *New York Times*, November 26, 1967.
379. "Wallace Gets Cheers, Jeers in Costa Mesa," Independent Press-Telegram, Saturday November, 4 1967.
380. "On the Hustings with Wallace in California," December 17, 1967
381. *New York Times*, March 10, 1968.
382. "Wallace Steps Up Pace in Calif." Drew Pearson and Jack Anderson December 30,1967 *Daytona Beach Herald.*
383. "Someday I'll Be President of That," *Long Beach Independent,* November 3, 1967.
384. Ibid.
385. *Los Angeles Times,* December 26, 1967.
386. http://ucdata.berkeley.edu/pubs/CalPolls/580.pdf.
387. "Wallace Presidential Party Drive Launched," *Los Angeles Times,* June 21, 1967.
388. *Carter*, p. 349
389. Manchester, *The Glory and the Dream*, page 1376.
390. *History of American Presidential Elections*, p. 1332.
391. Manchester, *The Glory and the Dream*, p. 1399.
392. "George Wallace's Public Image," *Los Angeles Times*, June 7, 1967.
393. *Chicago Tribune*, October 27, 1968.
394. *New York Times*, May 1, 1967.

395. *Philadelphia Tribune*, November 28, 1967.
396. Paul F. Boller Jr., *Presidential Campaigns: From George Washington to George W. Bush,* Kindle ed. (New York: Oxford University Press, 2004), locs. 4479–80.
397. "Wallace Nightmare Haunting Political Bedfellows in Capital," *Washington Post*, June 7, 1967.
398. "Reagan's Race Legacy," *Washington Post,* June 14, 2004.
399. Richard Nixon, *RN: The Memoirs of Richard Nixon*, Kindle ed. (New York: Simon & Schuster, 1990), locs. 6116–18.
400. *Los Angeles Times*, September 25, 1968.
401. *Chicago Daily Defender*, November 4, 1968.
402. Theodore H. White, *The Making of the President 1968* (New York: Harper-Collins, 2014), p. 424.
403. *Chicago Tribune*, October 27, 1968.
404. "Nation: Bomber on the Square." *Time* magazine Vol. 92, No. 16 (10/18/1968). http://content.time.com/time/subscriber/article/0,33009,902426,00.html.
405. "The Campaign: George's General," *Time* magazine. (10/11/1968). http://content.time.com/time/subscriber/article/0,33009,902367,00.html.
406. *Chicago Tribune*, October 27, 1968.

Bibliography

Allen, Robert S. and Shannon, William V. *The Truman Merry-Go-Round*. New York: The Vanguard Press, Inc., 1950.

Baker, James A. *"Work Hard, Study... and Keep Out of Politics!"* Illinois: Northwestern University Press, 2008. Kindle edition.

Baker, Jean H. *Affairs of Party: The Political Culture of Northern Democrats in the Mid-Nineteenth Century*. Ithaca, Cornell University Press, 1998.

Barone, Michael, McCutcheon, Chuck, Trende, Sean and Kraushaar, Josh. *The Almanac of American Politics, 2014*. Chicago: The University of Chicago, 2013.

Barrett, Grant. *The Oxford American Dictionary of Political Slang*. New York: Oxford University Press, 2004. Kindle edition.

Berkeley, Edmund and Dorothy Smith Berkeley, "John Beckley: The First Librarian of Congress." *The Quarterly Journal of the Library of Congress* 32 (April 1975): 83–117.

Beran, Michael KnoBerkeley, Edmund and Dorothy Smith Berkeley, "John Beckley: The First Librarian of Congress," The Quarterly Journal of the Library of Congress 32 (April 1975): 83–117

Jefferson's Demons: Portrait of a Restless Mind. New York: Free Press, 2003. Kindle edition.

Berg, A. Scott. *Wilson*. New York: Simon & Schuster, 2013.

Bernstein, Irving. *Promises Kept: John F. Kennedy's New Frontier*. New York: Oxford University Press, 1991. Kindle edition.

Boller Jr., Paul F. *Presidential Campaigns: From George Washington to George W. Bush*. New York: Oxford University Press, 1996.

Bowen, Michael. *The Roots of Modern Conservatism: Dewey, Taft, and the Battle for the Soul of the American Party*. Chapel Hill: The University of North Carolina, 2011.

Buchanan, Patrick J. *Conservative Votes, Liberal Victories: Why the Right Has Failed*. New York: Quadrangle/New York Times Book Co, 1974.

Burns, Eric. *Infamous Scribblers: The Founding Fathers and the Rowdy Beginnings of American Journalism*. U.S.: Public Affairs, 2006.

Busch, Andrew E. *Truman's Triumphs: The 1948 Election and the Making of Postwar America*. Kansas: University Press of Kansas, 2012.

Callender, James. *The Prospect before Us*. Volume 7, Issue 2. Virginia: 1800.

Callender, James Thomas. *The History of the United States for 1796; Including a Variety of Interesting Particulars Relative to the Federal Government Previous to that Period*. Philadelphia: Snowden & McCorkle, 1797.

Canellos, Peter S., ed. *Last Lion: The Fall and Rise of Ted Kennedy*. New York: Simon & Schuster, 2009. Kindle edition.

Cannon, James. *Gerald R. Ford: An Honorable Life*. Michigan, University of Michigan Press, 2013.

Cannon, Lou. *President Reagan: The Role of a Lifetime*. New York: Public Affairs, 2000.

Cannon, James. *Time and Chance: Gerald Ford's Appointment with History*. Michigan: University of Michigan Press, 1998.

Caro, Robert A. *The Years of Lyndon Johnson: The Passage of Power*. New York: Alfred A. Knopf, 2012. Kindle edition.

Carter, Dan T. *The Politics of Rage: George Wallace, the Origins of the New Conservatism and the Transformation of American Politics*. Baton Rouge: Louisiana University Press, 2000.

Carter, Jimmy. *Why Not the Best?* New York: Bantam Books, 1976.

Chernow, Ron. *Alexander Hamilton*. New York: Penguin Books, 2005. Kindle edition.

Chester, Lewis, Hodgson, Godfrey and Page, Bruce. *An American*

Melodrama: The Presidential Campaign of 1968. New York: The Viking Press, 1969.

Clarke, Thurston. *JFK's Last Hundred Days: The Transformation of a Man and the Emergence of a Great President*. New York: Penguin Books, 2013.

Cobbett, William. *Life of Andrew Jackson: President of the United States of America*. New York: Harper and Brothers, 1834.

Cogan, Jacob Katz. "The Reynolds Affair and the Politics of Character." *Journal of the Early Republic*. Vol. 16, No. 3 (autumn, 1996), 389–417

Collins, Gail. *William Henry Harrison: The American Presidents Series: The 9th President, 1841*. New York: Macmillan, 2012.

Clinton, Bill. *My Life*. New York: Alfred A. Knopff, 2004. Kindle edition.

Clifford, Clark and Holbrooke, Richard C. *Counsel to the President: A Memoir*. New York: Random House, 1991.

Cohen, Michael A. *American Maelstrom: The 1968 Election and the Politics of Division*. USA: Oxford University Press, 2016.

Cole, Donald B. *Vindicating Andrew Jackson: The 1818 Election and the Rise of the Two-Party System*. Kansas: University Press of Kansas, 2009.

Collins, Gail. *William Henry Harrison: The American Presidents Series: The 9th President, 1841*. New York: Times Books, Henry Holt and Co., LLC, 2012. Kindle edition.

Conwell, Russell H. *The Life and Public Services of James G. Blaine*. Maine: E.C. & Allen Co, 1884.

Cramer, Richard Ben. *What It Takes: The Way to the White House*. New York: Open Road Media, 2011.

Clymer, Adam. *Edward M. Kennedy: A Biography*. New York: HarperCollins Publishers. 2015. Kindle edition.

Cohen, Michael A. *Live From the Campaign Trail: The Greatest Presidential Campaign Speeches of the Twentieth Century and How They Shaped Modern America*. New York: Walker & Company, 2008.

Crain, Andrew Downer. *The Ford Presidency: A History*. North Carolina: McFarland & Company, Inc., Publishers, 2014.

Cronin, Thomas E. and Genovese, Michael A. *The Paradoxes of the American Presidency*. New York: Oxford University Press, 2009.

Cummins, Joseph. *Anything for a Vote: Dirty Tricks, Cheap Shots, and October Surprises in U.S. Presidential Campaigns*. Philadelphia, Quirk Books, 2012.

Daniel, Marcus. *Scandal and Civility: Journalism and the Birth of American Democracy*. New York, Oxford University Press, 2009. Kindle edition.

Davies, Gareth and Zelizer, Julian E. Eds. *American and the Ballot Box: Elections and Political History*. Philadelphia: University of Pennsylvania Press, 2015.

Deaver, Michael K. and Herskowitz, Mickey. *Behind the Scenes: In Which the Author Talks About Ronald and Nancy Reagan and Himself.* New York: William Morrow and Company, Inc., 1987.

DeFrank, Thomas M. *Write It When I'm Gone: Remarkable Off-the-Record Conversations with Gerald R. Ford*. New York: G. P. Putnam's Sons, 2007.

Divine, Robert A., Breen, T.H., Williams, R. Hal, Gross, Ariela J. and Brands, H.W. *America: Past and Present, Volume 1.*

Divine, Robert A., Breen, T.H., Williams, R. Hal, Gross, Ariela J. and Brands, H.W. *America: Past and Present, Volume 2*. 10th Edition. New York: Pearson Education, 2012.

Donaldson, Gary A. *Truman Defeats Dewey*. Kentucky: The University Press of Kentucky, 1999. Kindle edition.

Durey, Michael."*With the Hammer of Truth: James Thomas Callender and America's Early National Heroes*. Charlottesville: University Press of Virginia, 1990.

Durey, Michael. *Transatlantic Radicals and the Early American Republic*. Kansas: University Press of Kansas, 1997.

Dutton, Frederick G. *Changing Sources of Power: American Politics in the 1970s*. New York: McGraw Hill Book Company, 1972.

Drew, Elizabeth. *Portrait of an Election: The 1980 Presidential Campaign*. New York: Simon & Schuster, 1981.

Edwards III, George C. *The Strategic President: Persuasion & Opportunity in Presidential Leadership*. Princeton: Princeton University Press, 2009. Kindle edition.

Ellis, Joseph J. *His Excellency: George Washington*. New York: Alfred A. Knopf, 2004. Kindle edition.

Ellis, Richard J. *Speaking to the People: The Rhetorical Presidency in Historical Perspective*. Amherst: University of Massachusetts Press, 1998.

Evans, M. Stanton. *The Future of Conservatism: From Taft to Reagan and Beyond*. New York: Holt, Rinehart and Winston, 1968.

Farquhar, Michael *A Treasury of Great American Scandals: Tantalizing True Tales of Historic Misbehavior by the Founding Fathers and Others Who Let Freedom Swing New York*: Penguin Books.

Ferling, John. *Adams vs. Jefferson: The Tumultuous Election of 1800*. New York: Oxford University Press, 2004.

Fick, Nathaniel. *One Bullet Away: The Making of a Marine Officer*. Boston: Houghton Mifflin Company, 2006.

Foster Wallace, David. *McCain's Promise: Aboard the Straight Talk Express with John McCain and a Whole Bunch*. New York: Little, Brown and Company, 2008. Kindle edition.

Ford, Gerald R. *A Time to Heal: The Autobiography of Gerald R. Ford*. California: Berkeley Publishing Group, 1980.

Ford, Gerald R. *Public Papers of the Presidents of the United States: Gerald R. Ford: Containing the Public Messages, Speeches, and Statements of the President. Gerald R. Ford, 1974–1977*. U.S.: U.S. Government Printing Office, 1980.

Frady, Marshall. *Wallace: The Classic Portrait of Alabama Governor George Wallace*. New York: Random House, 1968. Kindle edition.

Freeman, Joanne B. *Affairs of Honor: National Politics in the New Republic*. U.S.A.: Yale University Press, 2001.

Frisk, David B. *If Not Us, Who? William Rusher, National Review and the Conservative Movement*. Wilmington: ISI Books, 2012.

Garcia, Gilbert. *Reagan's Comeback: Four Weeks in Texas That Changed American Politics Forever.* San Antonio: Trinity University Press. Kindle edition.

Galvin, Daniel J. *Presidential Party Building: Dwight D. Eisenhower to George W. Bush.* Princeton & Oxford, Princeton University Press, 2010.

Germond, Jack W. and Witcover, Jules. *Blue Smoke and Mirrors: How Reagan Won and Why Carter Lost the Election of 1980.* New York: Viking Press, 1981.

Germond, Jack W. and Witcover, Jules. *Whose Broad Stripes and Bright Stars? The Trivial Pursuit of the Presidency 1988.* New York: Time-Warner, 1989.

Giglio, James N. *Call Me Tom: The Life of Tom Eagleton.* Missouri: University of Missouri, 2011.

Glasser, Joshua M. *The Eighteen-Day Running Mate: McGovern, Eagleton, and a Campaign in Crisis.* New Haven: Yale University Press, 2012.

Goldman, Peter, DeFrank, Thomas M., Miller, Mark, Murr, Andrew and Matthews, Tom. *Quest for the Presidency 1992.* College Station: Texas A&M University Press, 1994.

Goldzwig, Steven R. *Truman's Whistle-Stop Campaign.* College Station: Texas A&M University Press, 2008.

Goodwin, Doris Kearns. *Team of Rivals.* New York: Simon & Schuster, 2005.

Gould, Lewis L. *1968: The Election That Changed America.* Chicago: Ivan R. Dee, 2010.

Gould, Lewis L. *Grand Old Party: A History of the Republicans.* New York: Random House, 2003.

Gullan, Harold I. *The Upset that Wasn't: Harry S. Truman and the Crucial Election of 1948.* Chicago: Ivan R. Dee, 1998.

Gutmann, Amy and Dennis Thompson. *The Spirit of Compromise: Why Governing Demands It and Campaigning Undermines It.* Princeton: Princeton University Press, 2012. Kindle edition.

Graff, Henry F. *Grover Cleveland: The American Presidents*. New York: Times Books, Henry Holt and Company, LLC, 2002.

Greer, John G. *In Defense of Negativity: Attack Ads in Presidential Campaigns*. Chicago and London: The University of Chicago, 2009. Kindle edition.

Hamilton, Gail. *James G. Blaine*. Norwich: The Henry Bill Publishing Company, 1895.

Hayward, Steven F. *The Age of Reagan: The Fall of the Old Liberal Order: 1964–1980*. California: Prima Publishing, 2001. Kindle edition.

Hofstadter, Richard. *The Age of Reform: From Bryan to F.D.R.*: New York: Vintage eBooks, 2011.

Horn, Jonathan. *The Man Who Would Not Be Washington: Robert E. Lee's Civil War and His Decision That Changed American History*. Scribner eBook.

Howell, William G. *Thinking About the Presidency: The Primacy of Power*. Princeton: Princeton University Press, 2013. Kindle edition.

Jeffers, H. Paul. *The Bully Pulpit: A Teddy Roosevelt Book of Quotations*. Maryland: Taylor Trade Publications, 2002.

Kabaservice, Geoffrey. *Rule and Ruin: The Downfall of Moderation and the Destruction of the Republican Party, From Eisenhower to the Tea Party*. New York: Oxford University Press, 2012.

Hartmann, Robert T. *Palace Politics: An Inside Account of the Ford Years*. New York: McGraw-Hill Book Company, 1980.

Hamilton, Gail. *James Blaine*.

Jamieson, Kathleen Hall and Waldman, Paul, eds. *Electing the President, 2000*. Philadelphia, University of Pennsylvania Press, 2004.

Issenberg, Sasha. *The Victory Lab*. New York: Crown Publishers by Random House, 2012. Kindle edition.

Kalman, Laura. *Right Star Rising: A New Politics, 1974–1980*. New York: W. W. North & Company, LLC, 2010. Kindle edition.

Karabell, Zachary. *The Last Campaign: How Harry Truman Won the 1948 Election*. New York: Borzoi Book by Alfred A. Knopf, 2000.

Kaufmann, Karen M. Petrocik, John R. and Shaw, Daron R. *Unconventional Wisdom: Facts And Myths About American Politics*. New York Oxford University Press, 2008. Kindle edition.

King, Josh. *Off Script: An Advance Man's Guide to White House Stagecraft, Campaign Spectacle, And Political Suicide*. New York: St. Martin's Press, 2016. Kindle edition.

Knudson, Jerry W. *Jefferson and the Press: Crucible of Liberty*. South Carolina: University of South Carolina Press, 2006.

Lachman, Charles. *A Secret Life: The Sex, Lies, and Scandals of President Grover Cleveland*. New York: Skyhorse Publishing, 2011.

Larson, Edward J. *A Magnificent Catastrophe: The Tumultuous Election of 1800, America's First Presidential Campaign*. New York: Free Press, 2008.

Lawson, John D, ed. *State Trials: A Collection of the Important and Interesting Criminal Trials which have Taken Place in the United States From the Beginning of our Government to the Present Day, Volume 10*. St. Louis, P.H. Thomas Law Book Co., 1918.

Lim, Elvin T. *The Anti-Intellectual Presidency: The Decline of Rhetoric from George Washington to George W. Bush*. New York: Oxford University Press, 2008.

Manchester, William. *The Glory and the Dream: A Narrative History of America, 1932–1972*. Kindle edition. New York: Rosetta Books LLC, 2013.

Mankiewicz, Frank and Swerdlow, Joel L. *So As I Was Saying...: My Somewhat Eventful Life*. New York: St. Martin's Press, 2016. Kindle edition.

McCullough, David. *John Adams*. New York: Simon & Schuster eBook.

McCullough, David. *Truman*. New York: Simon & Schuster, 1996

McGinniss, Joe. *The Selling of the President 1968*. New York: Trident Press, 1969.

McMurry, Rebecca L. and McMurry Jr., James F. *Jefferson, Callender and the Sally Story: The Scandalmonger and the Newspaper War of 1802*.

Meacham, Jon. *American Lion: Andrew Jackson in the White House.* New York: Random House, 2008. Kindle edition.

Meacham, Jon. *Thomas Jefferson: The Art of Power.* New York: Random House Publishing Group, 2012. Kindle edition.

Meacham, Jon. *American Lion: Andrew Jackson in the White House.* Random House Publishing Group, 2008. Kindle Edition.

Mieczkowski, Yanek. *The Routledge Historical Atlas of Presidential Elections.* New York and London: Routledge, 2001.

Middendorf II, J. Williams. *A Glorious Disaster: Barry Goldwater's Presidential Campaign and the Origins of the Conservative Movement.* New York: Basic Books, 2006.

Moe, Richard. *Roosevelt's Second Act: The Election of 1940 and the Politics of War.* New York: Oxford University Press, 2013. Kindle edition.

Morris, Edmund. *Dutch: A Memoir of Ronald Reagan.* New York: Random House Publishing Group, 2011.

Mr. Blaine and the "Mulligan" letters: The whole story as told in the house of representatives, June 5, 1876. Reprinted verbatim from the "Congressional record." University of Michigan Library, 1884.

Muzzey, David Saville. *James Blaine: A Political Idol of Other Days.* Port Washington: Kennikat Press, Inc., 1934.

Nessen, Ron. *It Sure Looks Different from the Inside.* Playboy Press, 1978.

Niven, John. *Martin Van Buren: The Romantic Age of American Politics.* Newton: American Political Biography Press, 2000.

Nixon, Richard. *RN: The Memoirs of Richard Nixon.* Simon & Schuster eBook.

Nofziger, Lyn. *Nofziger.* District of Columbia: Regnery Gateway, 1992.

Norton, Mary Beth, Sheriff, Carol, Katzman, David M., Chudacoff, Howard P., Logevall, Fredrik, and Bailey, Beth. *A People & A Nation: A History of the United States: Volume One: To 1877.* Eighth Edition. New York: Houghton Mifflin Company, 2007.

Novak, Robert D. *The Prince of Darkness: 50 Years of Reporting in Washington*. New York: Crown Forum, 2007.

Parsons, Lynn Hudson. *The Birth of Modern Politics: Andrew Jackson, John Quincy Adams, and the Election of 1828*. New York: Oxford University Press, 2009. Kindle edition.

Parmet, Herbert S. *Eisenhower and the American Crusades*. New Jersey: Transaction Publishers, 1972.

Pearson, Drew. *Diaries: 1949–1959*. New York: Holt Rinehart and Winston, 1974

Perlstein, Rick. *Before the Storm: Barry Goldwater and the Unmaking of the American Consensus*. New York: Nation Books, 2009. Kindle edition.

Perlstein, Rick. *Nixonland: The Rise of a President and the Fracturing of America*. New York: Scribner, 2010. Kindle edition.

Perlstein, Rick. *The Invisible Bridge: The Fall of Nixon and the Rise of Reagan*. New York: Simon and Schuster Paperbacks, 2015.

Peterson, Merrill D. *Thomas Jefferson and the New Nation: A Biography*. New York: Oxford University Press, 1975.

Phillips, Cabell. *The Truman Presidency: The History of a Triumphant Succession*. New York: Macmillan Co., 1996.

Popkin, Samuel L. *The Candidate: What it Takes to Win—and Hold—the White House*. New York: Oxford University Press, 2012. Kindle edition.

Purdum, Todd S. *An Idea Whose Time Has Come: Two Presidents, Two Parties and the Battle for the Civil Rights Act of 1964*. New York: Henry Holt and Company, 2014. Kindle edition.

Randall, William Sterne. *Thomas Jefferson: A Life*. New York: Henry Holt and Company, 1993.

Ratcliffe, Donald. *The One-Party Presidential Contest: Adams, Jackson, and 1824's Five-Horse Race (American Presidential Elections)*. University Press of Kansas, 2015. Kindle Edition.

Reinhard, David W. *The Republican Right Since 1945*. Kentucky: The University of Kentucky, 1938.

Remini, Robert V. *Andrew Jackson and the Course of American Freedom, 1822–1832, Volume II*. New York: Harper & Row Publishers, 1981.

Roberts, Alasdair. *America's First Great Depression: Economic Crisis and Political Disorder after the Panic of 1837*. Ithaca: Cornell University Press, 2013.

Rolde, Neil. *Continental Liar: From the State of Maine*. Maine: Tilbery House, 2007.

Ross, Irwin. *The Loneliest Campaign: The Truman Victory of 1948*. The New American Library. New York: New American Library, 1968.

Rumsfeld, Donald. *Known and Unknown: A Memoir*. New York: Sentinel, 2012.

Rusher, William A. *The Making of the New Majority Party*. Illinois: Green Hill Publishers, 1975.

Samuel, Lawrence R. *The American Dream: A Cultural History*. Syracuse: Syracuse University Press, 2012. Kindle edition.

Scarborough, Joe. *The Right Path: From Ike to Reagan, How Republicans Once Mastered Politics—and Can Again."* New York: Random House, 2013.

Schlesinger Jr., Arthur M. *The Age of Jackson*. New York: Book Find Club, 1945.

Schurz, Carl. *Why James G. Blaine Should Not Be President*. Leeaf.com Books

Scott, Hugh. *Come to the Party*. New Jersey: Prentice-Hall, 1968.

Sharp, James Roger. *The Deadlocked Election of 1800: Jefferson, Burr, and the Union in the Balance*. Kansas: University of Kansas Press, 2010.

Shaw, Daron R. *The Race to 270: The Electoral College and the Campaign Strategies of 2000 and 2004*. Chicago: University of Chicago Press, 2006. Kindle edition.

Shea, David M. and Harward, Brian M. *Presidential Campaigns: Documents Decoded*. Santa Barbara: ABC-CLIO, 2013.

Shepard, Edward M. *Martin Van Buren*. Cambridge: The Riverside Press, 1899.

Sheppard, Si. *The Partisan Press: A History of Media Bias in the United States*. North Carolina: McFarland & Company, Inc., Publishers, 2007.

Shirley, Craig. *Reagan's Revolution: The Untold Story of the Campaign That Started It All*. Tennessee: Nelson Current, 2010. Kindle edition.

Shrum, Robert. *No Excuses: Concessions of a Serial Campaigner*. Simon & Schuster, June 5, 2007. Kindle edition, p. 127.

Sidey, Hugh. *John F. Kennedy, President*. New York: Atheneum, 1963.

Silbey, Joel H. *Martin Van Buren and the Emergence of American Popular Politics*. Rowman & Lanham: Littlefield Publishers, Inc., 2002.

Smick, Hedrick. *Who Stole the American Dream?* New York: Random House Publishing Group, 2013. Kindle edition.

Smith, Richard Norton. *On His Own Terms: A Life of Nelson Rockefeller*. New York: Random House Publishing Group, 2014. Kindle edition.

Stanwood, Edward. *A History of Presidential Elections—Primary Source Edition*. Massachusetts: The Riverside Press, 1892.

Strahan, Randall. *Leading Representatives: Interpreting American Politics*. Baltimore: The John Hopkins University Press, 2007. Kindle edition.

Summers, Wahlgren Mark. *Rum, Romanism, and Rebellion: The Making of a President 1884*. Chapel Hill & London: The University of North Carolina, 2000. Kindle edition.

Swint, Kerwin C. *Mudslingers: The 25 Negative Political Campaigns of All Time*. Praeger: Westpoint, 2005.

Tanenhaus, Sam. *The Death of Conservatism: A Movement and Its Consequences*. New York: Random House, 2010. Kindle edition.

Thomas, Evan. *Ike's Bluff: President Eisenhower's Secret Battle to Save the World*. New York: Little, Brown, and Co., 2012.

Troy, Gil. *See How They Ran: The Changing Role of the Presidential Candidate*. New York: The Free Press, 2012. Kindle edition.

Troy, Gil, Schlesinger Jr., Arthur and Israel, Fred L., eds. *History of American Presidential Elections, 1789–2008, Volume 1. Edition 4*. New York: Chelsea House Publishers, 2002.

Truman, Harry S. *1945: Year of Decision. Memoirs: Volume 1.* New World City, LLC, 2014. Kindle edition.

Truman, Harry S. *1946–52: Years of Trial and Hope. Memoirs Vol. 2.* New World City, LLC, 2014.

Vowell, Sarah. *Lafayette in the Somewhat United States* (Kindle Locations 126–127). New York: Penguin Publishing Group. Kindle Edition.

Wallace, George C. *"Hear Me Out."* New York: Droke House, 1968.

Witcover, Jules. *Party of the People: A History of the Democrats.* Random House, 2003.

Witcover, Jules. *The Year The Dream Died: Revisiting 1968 in America.* New York: Warner Books, 1997.

Wolf, George D. *William Warren Scranton: Pennsylvania Statesman.* Pennsylvania: Pennsylvania State University Press, 1982.

White, Theodore. *The Making of the President 1964.* New York: Harper Collins, 2010. Kindle edition.

White, Theodore. *The Making of the President 1968.* New York: Harper Collins, 2010. Kindle edition.

White, Theodore. *The Making of the President 1972.* New York: Harper Collins, 2010. Kindle edition.

White, Philip. *Whistle Stop: How 31,000 Miles of Train Travel, 352 Speeches, and a Little Midwest Gumption Saved the Presidency of Harry Truman.* New Hampshire: ForeEdge from University Press of New England, 2014.

White, William S. *The Taft Story.* New York: Harper & Brothers, 1954.

Widmer, Ted. *Martin Van Buren: The American Presidents Series: The 8th President, 1837–1841.* New York: Times Books, 2004.

Wilentz, Sean. *The Age of Reagan: A History 1974–2008.* New York: Harper Collins, 2008.

Wright, Jordan M. *Campaigning for President.* U.S.: Smithsonian Books, 2008.

Index

About the Author

John Dickerson is moderator of *Face the Nation*, political director of CBS News, and a columnist for *Slate* magazine. In the 2016 election cycle he has interviewed every major candidate multiple times and moderated both the Democratic and Republican debates.

Dickerson has been a reporter in Washington for almost twenty years, covering the White House, Congress, and political campaigns. Before joining *Slate*, Dickerson was with *Time* magazine for almost fifteen years. He is a regular guest on PBS's *Washington Week*, NPR's *The Diane Rehm Show*, and the *Charlie Rose* show.

ABOUT TWELVE

TWELVE was established in August 2005 with the objective of publishing no more than twelve books each year. We strive to publish the singular book, by authors who have a unique perspective and compelling authority. Works that explain our culture; that illuminate, inspire, provoke, and entertain. We seek to establish communities of conversation surrounding our books. Talented authors deserve attention not only from publishers, but from readers as well. To sell the book is only the beginning of our mission. To build avid audiences of readers who are enriched by these works—that is our ultimate purpose.